Peer-to-Peer Computing

Quang Hieu Vu · Mihai Lupu · Beng Chin Ooi

Peer-to-Peer Computing

Principles and Applications

 Springer

Quang Hieu Vu
Institute for Infocomm Research (I²R)
1 Fusionopolis Way
#21-01 Connexis, South Tower
Singapore 138632
Singapore
qhvu@i2r.a-star.edu.sg

Mihai Lupu
Information Retrieval Facility (IRF)
Operngasse 20b
1040 Wien
Austria
mihailupu@gmail.com

Beng Chin Ooi
Department Computer Science
School of Computing
National University of Singapore
Computing Drive
Computing 1
Singapore 117590
Singapore
ooibc@comp.nus.edu.sg

ISBN 978-3-642-42537-0   ISBN 978-3-642-03514-2 (eBook)
DOI 10.1007/978-3-642-03514-2
Springer Heidelberg Dordrecht London New York

ACM Computing Classification (1998) C.2, D.4, H.3, K.6

Cover design: KuenkelLopka, GmbH

Printed on acid-free paper

Springer is part of Springer Science+Business Media (www.springer.com)

Preface

Peer-to-peer (P2P) technology, or peer computing, is an emerging paradigm that is now viewed as a potential technology to redesign distributed architectures (e.g., the Internet) and, consequently, distributed processing. In a classical P2P network, all participating computers (or nodes) have equivalent capabilities and responsibilities. The nodes can directly exchange resources and services between each other without the need for centralized servers. They can collaborate to perform tasks by aggregating the pool of resources (e.g., storage, CPU cycles) available in the P2P network. The distributed nature of such a design provides exciting opportunities for new killer applications to be developed.

P2P computing distinguishes itself from traditional distributed computing in three main aspects. First, the scalability of P2P systems goes far beyond that of traditional distributed systems. In particular, since P2P systems are able to scale to thousands of nodes, they can harness the power of computers over the Internet. Second, P2P, in its most uncompromising definition, requires everything to be completely decentralized. Ideally, no centralized structures should exist in P2P systems. Finally, and also the most important one, P2P applications often work in highly dynamic environments. Specifically, in terms of network topology, since P2P nodes can join and leave the system anytime, P2P systems do not have a fixed topology. Instead, their topology changes according to nodes in the system. Furthermore, the system's content and load are distributed in real time according to the actual demand and resource capability of nodes. For example, if a sharing file becomes "hot", i.e., it is repeatedly requested by several users, the file can be duplicated and deployed in many parts of the system.

The scale and dynamism that characterize P2P systems require traditional distributed technologies to be reexamined. A paradigm shift that includes self-reorganization, adaptation and resilience is called for. In recent years, there has been a proliferation of research efforts to design P2P systems and applications. This book attempts to present the *technical* challenges offered by P2P systems, and the efforts that have been proposed to address them. The purpose of this book is to provide a thorough and comprehensive review of recent advances on routing and discovery methods; load balancing and replication techniques; security, accountability and anonymity, as well as trust and reputation schemes; programming models and P2P systems and projects. Besides surveying existing methods and systems, the book also compares and evaluates some of the more promising schemes.

The need for such a book is evident. It provides a single source for practitioners, researchers and newcomers on the state-of-the-art in the field. For practitioners, this book explains best practice, guiding selection of appropriate techniques for each application. For researchers, this book provides a foundation for development of new and more effective methods. For newcomers, this book is an overview of the wide range of advanced techniques for realizing effective P2P systems. This book can also be used as a text for an advanced course on Peer-to-Peer Computing and Technologies, or as a companion text for a variety of courses, including courses on distributed systems, grid, and cluster computing.

Organization of the Book

This book consists of ten chapters. Besides the first chapter that sets up the context and the last chapter that concludes with directions on the future of P2P, each of the other eight chapters is essentially self-contained and focuses on one aspect of P2P computing. These eight chapters can thus be read and used on their own, independently of the others.

- In Chap. 1, we provide background on P2P computing in general. We discuss the characteristics of P2P systems that distinguish them from other distributed systems. This chapter also looks at the benefits and promises of P2P, and some of the applications that will benefit from P2P computing. It examines the issues in designing P2P systems and sets the stage for subsequent chapters.
- Chapter 2 presents the various architectures of P2P systems. At one extreme, we have P2P systems that are supported by centralized servers. At the other extreme, pure P2P systems are completely decentralized. Between these two extremes are hybrid systems where nodes are organized into two layers: the upper tier "super" nodes act as servers for lower tier nodes. We compare these different architectures. In parallel to the static architectural considerations, we also look at how peers are defined—statically or dynamically. Support for dynamic reorganization of peers allows communities to be formed based on some common interests among nodes. For hybrid systems, we examine how nodes that are more powerful can be exploited to shoulder more responsibilities. Issues on incentives and fairness are also addressed.
- In Chap. 3, we focus on the issue of searching. There are several modes in which searching can be performed. First, a query node can broadcast queries to all nodes. Second, the query can be directed to nodes that are more likely to contain useful information first. This requires nodes to organize their peers based on some optimization criterion. Third, hashing techniques can be applied. We also look at how load-balancing can be realized in the hash-based category. Each of these techniques call for different metadata to be maintained.

- Chapter 4 presents techniques to perform complex queries. Besides simple keyword search, there is an increasing need to support more semantic-based queries for database and multimedia applications. These include partial match queries, range and join queries, and queries involving high-dimension vectors. We also look at how distributed queries are optimized and processed in the P2P context.
- Replication and caching are very effective mechanisms that can bring the data/results closer to the users to improve performance. However, in the P2P environment, it becomes much harder to control the optimal degree of replication, as well as to maintain the consistency between replicas. Chapter 5 presents the issues that need to be addressed and examines some of the existing solutions. In particular, we look at techniques that manage replicas/cache dynamically.
- Before P2P can be widely accepted by users, there are several other issues that need to be addressed: trust, privacy, anonymity, accountability, reliability, and security. These issues are discussed in Chaps. 6 and 7. In Chap. 6, we focus on security, privacy, and anonymity issues. We begin by discussing techniques designed to secure data as well as the overall P2P environment from different types of attacks. Then we present methods that prevent users from taking advantage of the system by freeloading off the resources contributed by a few. Finally, we look at techniques that are designed to support anonymity and privacy, to protect both the users that disseminate the data, as well as nodes that store the data. Techniques that authenticate third-party data publication are also examined in this chapter.
- Chapter 7 focuses on accountability, trust, and reputation. Here, we look at techniques that automate the collection and processing of information from previous queries to help users assess whether they can trust a server with a new query.
- In Chap. 8, we look at programming tools that are suitable for P2P environments. After having presented in the previous chapters the theoretical aspects of P2P systems, in this chapter we will identify tools to develop P2P systems, ranging from low level network programming tools, like sockets, to specific programming languages designed to be used for P2P applications.
- Chapter 9 describes some representative P2P systems and applications that have been deployed. We look at how different application environments and requirements drive the design and architecture of the systems. We discuss popular techniques employed in each type of applications. In particular, we present systems that support file sharing, data backup, structured data management, and data caching. Additionally, we also introduce mobile systems employing P2P technologies.

Finally, in Chap. 10, we make a conclusion of the book and suggest promising research topics that deserve further attention. Additionally, we also discuss a potential use of P2P in industry by analyzing a case of supply chain management system.

Acknowledgements

This book cannot be finished without the help of several people. The authors of this book would like to thank Dr. Kian-Lee Tan, Dr. Panos Kalnis, and Dr. Bei Yu at National University of Singapore, Dr. Aoying Zhou at East China Normal University, and Dr. Linhao Xu at the IBM China Research Laboratory for their contributions in the initial phase of the book.

Contents

Chapter 1
Introduction

Peer-to-peer (P2P) computing has been reincarnated as a promising paradigm for distributed computing. This thirty-year-old technology was deployed in USENET in 1979 and FiDoNet in 1984. At that time, the number of computer users was relatively small and P2P applications were less user-friendly. Moreover, users failed to recognize the benefits of the technology. However, recently, several trends have refocused the attention of researchers on this technology. First, the Internet has allowed a large number of computers to be connected. Second, the Internet has also provided an avenue for users to share and disseminate their data in a user-friendly manner. Third, "killer" P2P and social network based applications have surfaced. For example, the Napster [226] MP3 music file sharing applications served over 20 million users by mid-2000. As another example, by 2006, the SETI@home [288] program had accumulated over 2.5 million years of CPU time through more than 5 million users.

In this chapter, we provide background on P2P computing in general. We discuss the characteristics of P2P systems that distinguish them from traditional distributed systems. Next, we discuss the benefits and promises of P2P, and some of the applications that will benefit from P2P computing. We also examine the issues that need to be considered in designing P2P systems.

1.1 Peer-to-Peer Computing

Peer-to-peer (P2P) computing is essentially a model of how we (people) interact in real life. We deal directly with one another whenever we wish to. Very often, when we need something, we ask our peers (friends) who may in turn refer us to their peers. P2P technologies enable us, through our computers, to carry our interactions into cyberspace and to continue to deal with one another as we do in the real world.

The main interpretation of peer-to-peer is that nodes are able to directly exchange resources and services between themselves without the need for centralized servers. However, a more encompassing definition has been suggested in [292]: *"P2P is a class of applications that takes advantage of resources—storage, cycles, content,*

Q.H. Vu et al., *Peer-to-Peer Computing*,
DOI 10.1007/978-3-642-03514-2_1, © Springer-Verlag Berlin Heidelberg 2010

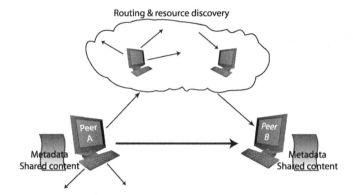

Fig. 1.1 Peer-to-peer computing. Peer A requests for some data that Peer B has. However, Peer A has to first locate Peer B through other peers in the P2P network. Once Peer B is located, Peer A deals directly with Peer B

human presence—available at the edges of the Internet." Overall, the system should be capable to aggregate resources and data from nodes to accomplish a task. Figure 1.1 illustrates how P2P computing operates for data sharing applications. Each node typically maintains some metadata that facilitates searching. For instance, this metadata might contain information about the types of data that the current peer will share with the community, as well as information about the data of other peers. A query involves a resource discovery process that, using such metadata, routes the query around the network to nodes that store the requested piece of information. This information may be stored on a single peer, divided amongst a set of peers, each having a part of it, or shared amongst a set of peers, each storing a copy. Upon identifying the storing peer(s), the query node can then directly communicate with it (them) to acquire the data.

P2P computing is one form of distributed computing. It shares the set of issues that distributed computing researchers have been addressing over the years (e.g., security, trust, anonymity, fault tolerance, scalability, distributed query processing, and coordination). However, P2P computing distinguishes itself from traditional distributed computing in several aspects. Some of the most important ones are:

1. *Symmetric role.* Each participating node in a P2P system typically acts both as a server and as a client. In fact, each node installs a single package that encompasses both client and server code. As such, a node can issue queries (like a client) and serve requests (like a server).
2. *Scalability.* Different from traditional distributed systems, P2P systems can scale to thousands of nodes. As a result, they can harness the power of computers over the Internet. To achieve this property, the P2P protocols do not require "all-to-all" communication or coordination.
3. *Heterogeneity.* A P2P system can be heterogeneous in terms of the hardware capacity of the nodes—a node may be a very slow machine and another may be a high-end super computer.

4. *Distributed control.* In its strictest definition, P2P requires everything to be completely decentralized. Ideally, no centralized structures should exist in P2P systems.
5. *Dynamism.* P2P applications often work in highly dynamic environments. The topology of P2P systems may change very fast due to joining of new nodes or leaving of existing nodes. The content and load of P2P systems typically change according to the actual demand and resource capability of nodes.

The scale and dynamism that characterize P2P systems invalidate many foundations that conventional distributed technologies have been built upon. A paradigm shift in the aspect of self-organization, adaptation, and resilience is part of the required changes, and this, to a great extent, resonates with the advocation for autonomicity in systems.

1.2 Potential, Benefits, and Applications

P2P computing has tremendous potential to meet many organizational and personal needs. It not only leverages on computing resources without incurring excessive cost, but it also allows information to be disseminated effectively. Furthermore, exercise full control over their data, either by making sure that the data is only stored on their machine, or, conversely, by P2P computing is very flexible in terms of content management. The content owners may opt to always store their data on their own machine, never allowing it to be copied and thus protecting their intellectual property. Conversely, they may decide to publish the data anonymously and have all traces that link them to that content erased by immersing themselves in a pool of nodes that collectively share the responsibility.

In recent years, there has been a proliferation of research efforts to design P2P systems and applications. These applications can be broadly divided into two categories: *resource sharing* and *data sharing*. In resource sharing, applications allow enterprises or individuals to leverage on available (idle or otherwise) CPU cycles, disk storage, and bandwidth capacity within the P2P network. P2P computing enables harnessing of underused resources to perform tasks that would otherwise require a much more expensive machine such as a super computer. Similarly, data storage devices are exploited to create a wide area storage network, and to push the data closer to the users.

In data sharing, applications allow users to access, modify or exchange data in a flexible manner. The distinction between *data sharing* and *data storage resource sharing* should be emphasized here. While the latter one simply assumes a scenario where one user is able to store his or her own content on another machine, the former implies much more. Data sharing could involve storage, but also access privileges, automatic notification systems, or multicast and broadcast techniques.

The remaining of this section makes a survey of existing and future applications, where P2P technology brings, or could bring, a significant advantage. They are listed

Fig. 1.2 P2P applications

chronologically according to their occurrence in the P2P context. Figure 1.2 summarizes them, indicating the environment for which they are most appropriate (i.e., personal vs. enterprise environments).

- *Digital content sharing.* The Internet is essentially an asymmetric repository of shared content, where there are a small number of content providers (servers) but a large number of content consumers (end users). This paradigm is rendered inviable by the new reality, where every user has the possibility to generate huge amounts of data. P2P technology overcomes this asymmetry by enabling users to act as a producer, as well as a consumer. Essentially, a request for some digital content is passed from peer to peer, and as each peer is traversed it transmits back the requested content, if any, either directly to the querying node, or through the peer that forwarded the request. At the same time, the peer forwards the request to other nodes. In this way, a peer contributes his/her content to the P2P network. Such content sharing not only allows owners to have control over their content, but also removes any single point of failure. Examples of P2P platforms that support content sharing are Gnutella [133, 172], Freenet [3, 189], Free Haven [108], and Publis [326].
- *Scientific computation.* Many scientific research projects involve extensive computation that typically require massive supercomputers. However, with P2P technology, we can now exploit the large number of computers (e.g., PCs) participating in the P2P network to perform the task. This not only saves cost, but also makes more effective use of the large number of idling computers sitting around. The most notable project is the Search for Extraterrestrial Intelligence (SETI) at Home (SETI@home) project [288].[1] We should note that in this particular case, of SETI@home or similar projects, the more general definition of P2P applies (that of Shirky [292]): even though they essentially rely on a server to provide the data tasks, the system uses resources at the edges of the Internet: to make use of less powerful computers, SETI splits each computational task into manageable *work units*. Each home PC operates on a work unit, and when it has completed

---

[1]Now part of the BOINC project at University of California at Berkeley.

its assignment, it picks up another work unit. In this way, SETI is able to develop the "world's most powerful computer". For example, as reported by Anderson [28], SETI@home is faster than ASCI White, at less than 1% of the cost. Moreover, in a typical day, SETI@home clients (i.e., the PCs) process about 700,000 work units, which works out to over 20 TeraFLOPS (TFLOPS). The success of SETI prompted more compute intensive projects (whose tasks can be split into subtasks with little or no interdependence and the ratio of communication overhead to computation is low) to exploit PCs within or outside an organization, e.g., the Folding@Home project that studies protein folding, misfolding, aggregation, and related diseases [2].

— *Gaming.* The recognition and attention given to P2P technology as a disruptive technology was mainly due to entertainment. This is due essentially to file sharing applications, but P2P also fits well for interactive gaming over the Internet. Such applications have been developed in several games and (e.g., Net-Z [230] and Star Craft [14]), more recently, in gaming consoles (e.g., PlayStation Portable and PlayStation 3). Each peer can store, manipulate, and process complex models involving 3D graphics. The communication overhead between gaming peers can be minimal, e.g., a few message exchanges may involve significant local computation and refreshing of the screen display (e.g., on how troops in a battle may be deployed).

— *Instant messaging.* People communicate and exchange information to acquire and share knowledge in real life. However, exchange of information can take place within the Internet through conversation or gossiping. This includes "meetings" organized among friends and associates in the Internet. Instant messaging (IM) is one such technology that enables users to locate their peers, provides a P2P communication path, and even offers an informal status of a peer's availability. Through IM platforms, users can compose messages and transmit files to one or more peers that are online. Typically, peers are connected to mediating servers who are responsible for negotiating the delivery and receipt of their clients' messages with other servers. The message is routed from node to node until the server closest to the recipient is reached, who will then deliver the message. Once connected to their servers, computers at the network's edge can establish real-time conversations with any other peers. Jabber [164, 222] is such a P2P Instant Messaging application, where users can either act as simple clients, or run their own Jabber server that communicates with other similar servers in a completely decentralized fashion. Similarly, Skype [140] uses a 2-level hierarchical architecture to allow users to exchange not only written messages but also voice streams.

— *Collaborative work environments.* Today's work environments involve people who may be geographically dispersed. As such, it is critical for net-based collaboration tools to be developed to facilitate cooperation. P2P technology lends itself well for cooperative collaboration environments. Here, a *collaboration* or *virtual space* will be created for the team members to interact and work together on project in real time. Shared content (e.g., documents and software) may be modified by any user, and automatically synchronized for consistency.

Groove [139] and Magi [11] are examples of two P2P collaboration platforms. Grove has been recently acquired by Microsoft and incorporated into its latest version of Office application suite.

- *Collaborative caching and storage.* Computers in a P2P system can contribute storage to enable content to be replicated and cached in different parts of the network. Such an environment offers many advantages. First, content can be brought nearer to users who need them. For example, in e-learning applications, an education center can minimize remote accesses to course content (and hence minimize bandwidth consumption) by caching materials that are frequently needed on local nodes. Similarly, internet accesses within an enterprise can exploit the local cache within each computer to share content that are common to most users [330].

  P2PTV has also gained its popularity in recent years. In such an application, P2P acts as a platform for redistributing video streams, and this is being exploited even by commercial entities to reduce the caching cost at the service providers near the edge devices. In such a setup, instead of downloading a video from the nearest server, a peer downloads segments of video from various peers that cache these segments. Since the quality of service and efficiency of transmission improve with the increase on the number of peers, P2P platform is amenable to scalability and cost saving. Joost [168] is one such application that distributes free content based on a hierarchical platform similar to the one used in Skype. In the enterprise context, the Kontiki Delivery Management System [322], recently acquired by VeriSign, Inc., provides a trust-aware environment for data distribution. Data warehouse is yet another practical application where caching is beneficial especially since the content of a warehouse is only updated periodically [169]. Here, P2P techniques enhance availability and security.

- *Distributed databases.* Content sharing can be taken a step further by allowing local databases stored in a database server to be shared. For example, in the health care domain, hospital specialists typically have a group of patients who are solely under their care. While some patient data are stored in a centralized server of the hospital (e.g., name, address, etc.), other data (e.g., X-rays, prescription, allergy to drugs, history, reaction to drugs, etc.) are typically managed by the specialists on their workstations. Similarly, in life sciences, when a new protein is discovered, a complex analysis needs to be done to determine the function and classification of the protein. This analysis process often involves a search of existing protein databases (e.g., GenBank, SWISS-PROT, and EMBL), which are maintained by different laboratories all over the world, to find similarities between known proteins and the newly discovered unknown protein. In both examples, it is cumbersome and costly for any single entity to manage the large amounts of newly generated data and therefore P2P becomes a good platform for such data sharing.

1.3 Challenges and Design Issues

P2P is not a panacea yet. While it offers great potential and promises, there are still many challenges that have to be addressed before its full potential could be realized. Some of these are:

— *Availability*. In a P2P environment, nodes are autonomous and can therefore join and leave the network as and when they like. This renders the system unpredictable: a resource (data or service) may be available at some time but not at others. As such, critical data or services may not be available when they are needed. Therefore, for a given query, the answer may be incomplete, and may also be different at different times. Mechanisms that replicate data or services can, to some extent, alleviate this problem.
— *Performance*. The same query, posed at different times, may be answered not only with different answers, but also with different costs, largely depending on node connectivity and the network topology at time of querying. Here, again, replication and caching may be useful in the sense that the data resides closer to the query nodes. Mechanisms that load-balance the system are very useful. For instance, nodes that are more powerful may be exploited to perform a heavier load. Still, sizing up the capacity of a node is not always straightforward.
— *Integrity*. The two problems above take replication as a possible solution. This, in turn, raises the problem of replica integrity. In a P2P environment, data may be replicated and cached in many nodes. It is hard to maintain the integrity and consistency of all the copies. There is a need to remove outdated copies or to refresh them. Techniques to validate or certify copies are also important, especially since it is easy to tamper with the content and further spread the modified copies.
— *Routing and resource discovery*. The main requirement from a P2P environment is to be able to locate data or resources. At one extreme, we can employ a Gnutella-like mechanism [133] that broadcasts a query from a query node to its peers, who in turn will relay the message to their peers and so forth. Such a method is simple, does not require any metadata to be retained and can potentially reach to a large number of peers in the network. However, flooding the network with queries is inefficient because it generates a huge amount of traffic. Moreover, a large amount of resources are expended to evaluate the query - even peers that do not contain the results. At the other extreme, each peer can store some metadata that can direct the search for data/resource to the peers that contain the data/resource. The challenge, however, is to determine the type of metadata necessary for effective searching. Moreover, the need to maintain the metadata can be complicated by peers' frequent connection and disconnection from the network. As such, there is a need to design effective and efficient data/resource discovery mechanisms.
— *Complex query processing*. Most of the existing P2P systems support simple queries such as keyword search. However, to support more advanced applications such as P2P-based database management systems or semantic information

retrieval systems, there is a need to design techniques for complex query processing. For the former, database-specific information needs to be indexed by the P2P system: columns, tables, local, and foreign keys must be searchable across the network. For semantic information retrieval, high-dimensional data might be needed, like in the case of Latent Semantic Indexing [102] or an ontology system could be reused [285]. Either way, new forms of querying need to be developed.

- *Security.* P2P systems present interesting security problems. Like any other applications, P2P applications could have security holes. The P2P ideology of openness and sharing just makes these security issues more acute. By allowing other nodes to access a node's content/service, the node is more vulnerable to attack in the situation where it acts only as a client. Similarly, because many nodes are used to transfer messages, the network could be vulnerable to denial-of-service (DoS) attacks. In unstructured networks in particular, it is relatively easy for a malicious node to flood the network with queries. Such attacks are much harder to detect since these are at the application level.

- *Trust and accountability vs. anonymity.* Since P2P computing has its core motivation based on the interaction between humans, one of the traits that characterize human interaction, *trust*, must somehow be implemented in P2P systems as well. Trust can be determined by reputation, which, in turn, requires accountability. At the same time, anonymity is required in some applications that wish to bypass censorship systems. How can one establish trust, while maintaining the openness and anonymity of the network, is an interesting and challenging research topic.

- *Incentives and fairness.* For P2P system to be successful, there must be incentives for nodes to participate and contribute to the community. For example, a node may find itself being swamped by requests for some data that it has cached; without incentives, it may decide to leave the network. On the other hand, there may be nodes that are exploiting the system resource while contributing very little in return. Some mechanisms should be developed to ensure fairness in the system.

- *Programming model.* Most of the existing P2P systems lack an adequate parallel programming model. Moreover, unlike parallel programming systems, the unique features of P2P environment such as dynamic resource discovery and fault-tolerance and availability should be considered to develop an integrated environment optimized for parallel computing. New programming models must be developed to fully exploit the potential of P2P computing.

From the above discussions, it is clear that P2P computing offers tremendous amounts of opportunity for research and development. This book is devoted to dealing with most of these issues and to reviewing the various approaches that have been adopted in the literature.

1.4 P2P vs. Grid Computing

Before leaving this chapter, we need to compare P2P with Grid computing [121, 122]. Grid computing has emerged recently with the intent of scaling the system performance and availability by sharing resources. Like P2P computing, Grid computing has been popularized by the need for resource sharing and consequently, it rides on existing underlying organizational structure. However, there are differences that distinguish the two.

- The grid network involves higher-end resources as compared to edge level devices in the P2P network. While the former requires large sums of money to be invested, the latter can tap into existing idle resources and hence requires less upfront cost commitment.
- The participants in the Grid network are organizations that agree in good faith to share resources with a good degree of trust, accountability, and common understanding. Membership can be rather exclusive and hence the number of participants is usually not large. The common platform for sharing is usually clusters that have been demonstrated to be cost effective to super-computing, and together they provide an enormous amount of aggregated computing resources. In contrast, the participants of the P2P network are mainly end-users and the platform of sharing is mainly individual Personal Computer (PC). However, due to the mass appeal, the network grows in a much faster rate and may scale up to thousands of nodes. Because of the loose integration, it is more difficult and critical to manage trust, accountability, and security.
- The Grid network is well structured and generally stable. As a result, resource discovery is less of an issue. On the contrary, P2P network is unstable—nodes can join and leave the network anytime. This complicates the design of resource discovery mechanisms. Nodes that leave the network may mean some directories may be temporarily "unavailable".
- Grid computing is more amenable to exploitation of traditional distributed query processing techniques and is able to ensure the completeness of answers. In contrast, nodes in the P2P network containing data may not be connected at the time of query, and hence answers are likely to be incomplete.
- Computational grids are largely set up in anticipation of resource intensive applications, e.g., BioGrid for bioinformatics. On the other hand, "killer" applications have surfaced in P2P naturally as exemplified by file sharing applications, telecommunication, P2P video streaming, and Web 2.0 applications.

In summary, the Grid structure may be considered a special case of P2P computing, where each participating node has a larger capacity and collaboration is more constrained and organized, and the nodes are generally closer in distance than in the general case of a P2P network. We believe that Grid computing will continue to play an important role in specialized applications. Notwithstanding, we also believe that P2P technology is more "user friendly" in the sense that it allows users (particularly those at the edges of the Internet) to share their resources and information easily and freely. P2P also offers more research challenges in view of the scale, free-and-easy membership, and instability of the network.

1.5 Summary

A "P2P system" can be broadly understood as a system where resources are pulled together from the edges of the Internet to achieve a desired goal. In some cases, this may involve a central server for coordination, in other cases there might be a set of coordinating peers, or in the purest of P2P systems—the coordination will be embedded in each peer. For all these variants, advantages and disadvantages compete and different applications, with different needs and different goals, may prefer one variant over another. However, what we should remember is that a P2P system, different from a Grid or other distributed systems, must take into account a much larger extent the dynamism of the participants. Either it must not rely on the presence of all or some subset of the peers at any particular time, or, it must take proactive measures to eliminate the adverse effects of a peer's temporary or definitive absence.

Chapter 2
Architecture of Peer-to-Peer Systems

Peer-to-peer (P2P) computing has been hailed as a promising technology that will reconstruct the architecture of distributed computing (or even that of the Internet). This is because it can harness various resources (including computation, storage and bandwidth) at the edge of the Internet, with lower cost of ownership, and at the same time enjoy many desirable features (e.g., scalability, autonomy, etc.). Since mid-2000, P2P computing technology has spurred increasing interests in both industrial and academic communities. As such, there are increasingly more applications being developed based on this paradigm. For example, digital content sharing (e.g., Naspter [226], Gnutella [133], and Shareaza [289]), scientific computation (e.g., BOINC [63] and Folding@home [2]), collaborative groupware (e.g., Groove [139]), instant messages (e.g., ICQ [9]) and so on. Furthermore, many research topics related to P2P computing have also been studied extensively—overlay network, routing strategies, resource location and allocation, query processing, replication, and caching. However, there has not been much effort to study the architecture of P2P systems. As the architecture of a system is the cornerstone of high-level applications that are implemented upon it, an understanding of P2P architecture is crucial to realizing its full potential. Such a study is important because: (a) It helps researchers, developers, and users to better appreciate the relationships and differences between P2P and other distributed computing paradigms (e.g., client-server and grid computing). (b) It allows us to be conscious of the potential merits of P2P computing for newly emerging application demands, and to determine the most suitable architecture for them. (c) It enables us to determine the architectural factors that are critical to a P2P system's performance, scalability, reliability, and other features. Therefore, we dedicate this chapter to summarize and examine the architecture of P2P systems and some related issues.

We first present a taxonomy of P2P architectures based on existing systems that have been developed. On one extreme, some P2P systems are supported by centralized servers. On the other extreme, pure P2P systems are completely decentralized. Between these two extremes are hybrid systems where nodes are organized into two layers: the upper tier servers and the lower tier common nodes. Second, we will conduct an extensive comparison among these three types of architectures. Third, we

Q.H. Vu et al., *Peer-to-Peer Computing*,
DOI 10.1007/978-3-642-03514-2_2, © Springer-Verlag Berlin Heidelberg 2010

will check how peers in different architectures define their neighbors (those that are directly connected)—statically or dynamically, and figure out the supporting techniques for dynamic reorganization of peers that allow communities to be formed based on some common interests among the nodes. We will also examine how nodes that are relatively powerful can be exploited to shoulder more responsibilities.

2.1 A Taxonomy

We begin by looking at a taxonomy of P2P systems. This taxonomy is derived from examining existing P2P systems. Figure 2.1 shows the taxonomy. In general, we can categorize the systems into two broad categories, *centralized* vs. *decentralized*, based on the availability of one or more servers, and to what extent the peers depend on the services provided by those servers. As expected, most of the research focuses on decentralized systems. There are essentially two main design issues to consider in decentralized systems: (a) the structure—flat (single tier) vs. hierarchical (multi-tier); and (b) the overlay topology—unstructured vs. structured. Besides these two main categories, there are also *hybrid* P2P systems that combine both centralized and decentralized architectures to leverage the advantages of both architectures. We shall examine each of these issues here.

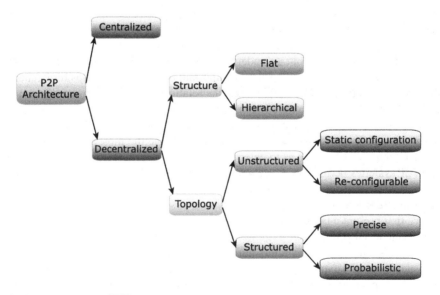

Fig. 2.1 A taxonomy of P2P systems

2.1.1 Centralized P2P Systems

Centralized P2P systems beautifully mix the features of both centralized (e.g., client-server) and decentralized architectures. Like a client-server system, there are one or more central servers, which help peers to locate their desired resources or act as task scheduler to coordinate actions among them. To locate resources, a peer sends messages to the central server to determine the addresses of peers that contain the desired resources (e.g., Napster [226]), or to fetch *work units* from the central server directly (e.g., BOINC [63]). However, like a decentralized system, once a peer has its information/data, it can communicate directly with other peers (without going through the server anymore). As in all centralized systems, this category of P2P systems are susceptible to malicious attacks and single point of failure. Moreover, the centralized server will become a bottleneck for a large number of peers, potentially degrading performance dramatically. Finally, this type of system lacks scalability and robustness. Some examples of this architecture include Napster [226] and BOINC [63].

2.1.2 Decentralized P2P Systems

In a *decentralized P2P system*, peers have equal rights and responsibilities. Each peer has only a partial view of the P2P network and offers data/services that may be relevant to only some queries/peers. As such, locating peers offering services/data quickly is a critical and challenging issue. The advantages of these systems are obvious: (a) they are immune to single point of failure, and (b) possibly enjoy high performance, scalability, robustness, and other desirable features.

As shown in Fig. 2.1, there are two dimensions in the design of decentralized P2P systems. First, the network structure can be *flat* (single-tier) or *hierarchical* (multi-tier). In a flat structure, the functionality and load are uniformly distributed among the participating nodes. It turns out that most of the existing decentralized systems are nonhierarchical. On the other hand, as noted in [126], hierarchical design naturally offers certain advantages including fault isolation and security, effective caching and bandwidth utilization, hierarchical storage and so on. In a hierarchical structure, there are essentially multiple layers of routing structures. For example, at a national level, there may be a routing structure to interconnect states; within each state, there may be another routing structure for universities within the state; and within each university, there may be yet another level that connects departments, and so on. Representatives of this category are the super-peer architecture [341] and the Crescendo system [126].

The second dimension concerns the logical network topology (the overlay network), whether it is structured or unstructured. The difference between these two designs lies in how queries are being forwarded to other nodes. In an unstructured P2P system, each peer is responsible for its own data, and keeps track of a set of neighbors that it may forward queries to. There is no strict mapping between the identifiers of objects and those of peers. This means (a) locating data in such a system is challenging since it is difficult to precisely predict which peers maintain the queried data; (b) there is no guarantee on the completeness of answers (unless the entire network is searched), and (c) there is no guarantee on response time (except for the worst case where the entire network is searched). The famous forerunners of unstructured P2P systems are FreeNet [3] and the original Guntella [133]. The former applies unicast-based lookup mechanisms to locate expected resources, which is inefficient in terms of response time, but efficient with respect to the bandwidth consumption and the number of messages used; the latter adopts flooding-based routing strategy, which is efficient in terms of response time but inefficient in bandwidth consumption and the number of messages used (since the network is flooded with exponential number of messages). A key issue in unstructured P2P systems is the determination of the neighbors. These neighbors can be (pre-)determined statically and fixed. However, more often, neighbors are determined based on a peer's (or rather the user's) interests. Thus, as the user interests (reflected by the queries) change, the set of neighbors may change. This is based on the inherent assumption that a peer is likely to be issuing similar queries during a period of time, and nodes that have previously provided answers are likely to be contributing answers as well. Thus, keeping these nodes as neighbors can reduce the querying time (in the immediate future). We refer to the latter approach as *reconfigurable* systems, and one such system is the BestPeer system [234].

On the contrary, in a structured P2P system, data placement is under the control of certain predefined strategies (generally a distributed hash table, or simply DHT). In other words, there is a mapping between data and peers. (Very often, for security/privacy reasons, the owners have full control over their own data. Instead, it is the metadata that is being "inserted" into the P2P network, e.g., (id, ptr) pairs that indicate that object with identifier id is located at peer pointed to by ptr. However, we shall use the term *data* in our discussion to refer to both.) More importantly, these systems provide a guarantee (precise or probabilistic) on search cost. This, however, is typically at the expense of maintaining certain additional information. Employing the principle of the mapping, most of the structured P2P systems, including CAN [266], Chord [173], and Pastry [275], adopt the key-based routing (KBR) strategy to locate the desired resource. As a result, a request can be routed to the peer who maintains the desired data quickly and accurately. However, since the placement of data is tightly controlled, the cost of maintaining the structured topology is high, especially in a dynamic network environment, where peers may join and leave the network at will.

Note that there are some systems such as [199] whose overlay network is a mix between unstructured topology and structured topology. The purpose of these systems is to leverage the advantage of search in structured topology while still allowing a good degree of autonomy, and hence keeping an inexpensive maintenance cost as in unstructured topology. The basic idea of a system based on a mixed topology is that the system employs search techniques of unstructured P2P systems such as flooding for locating popular items and search techniques of structured P2P systems (*structured search*) for locating rare items. To serve the purpose of structured search, a small part of nodes are selected to form a structured network for keeping rare items. Since only a small part of nodes forms the structured network, the maintenance cost is not high. In this system, search is executed in two steps. At first, the system performs unstructured search by broadcasting the query to neighbor nodes. If the search item is a popular item, it should be found in the first few steps, and hence the search cost is not expensive. On the other hand, if the search item is a rare item, i.e., there are not enough results returned within a predefined time or a predefined number of search steps, the system performs structured search, which should locate the item if it exists in the system. As a result, the system can alleviate the problems of search in conventional unstructured P2P systems. The problem of this system, however, is that without global knowledge, it is not easy to identify if a data item is a popular item or a rare item for indexing.

2.1.3 Hybrid P2P Systems

The main advantage of centralized P2P systems is that they are able to provide a quick and reliable resource locating. Their limitation, however, is that the scalability of the systems is affected by the use of servers. While decentralized P2P systems are better than centralized P2P systems in this aspect, they require a longer time in resource locating. As a result, hybrid P2P systems have been introduced to take advantages of both centralized and decentralized architectures. Basically, to maintain the scalability, similar to decentralized P2P systems, there are no servers in hybrid P2P systems. However, peer nodes that are more powerful than others can be selected to act as servers to serve others. These nodes are often called *super peers*. In this way, resource locating can be done by both decentralized search techniques and centralized search techniques (asking super peers), and hence the systems benefit from the search techniques of centralized P2P systems.

While it is clearly that different P2P systems belonging to different categories have different advantages and disadvantages, P2P systems in the same category also have different strengths and weaknesses depending on the specific design of the systems. This leads to the fact that different P2P systems are different in the system performance, resource location, scalability, load-balancing, autonomy, and anonymity. In the following sections, we will examine the architectural features of outstanding P2P systems from different categories in detail. Throughout most of our discussion, we shall deal with data sharing applications. However, it should be clear that the systems can also be used for other applications, e.g., sharing of storage, processing cycles and so on.

2.2 Centralized P2P Systems

Napster and SETI@home are two of the earliest and yet very popular P2P centralized-based systems. The success of Napster in digital content sharing and

SETI@home in scientific computation contributes to a proliferation of applications of centralized P2P systems in various other domains: Folding@home [2], Genome@home [130], and BOINC [63] for scientific computation; Jabber [164] in instant message; Openext [246] in digital content sharing; Net-Z [230] and Star Craft [52] in entertainment.

In general, P2P computing by definition emphasizes the equality of functions and responsibilities of all participants, which play the roles of both resource providers and resource requestors. Thus, a node can issue queries (as a client) and answers queries (as a server). Somewhat different from the equality concept, centralized P2P systems inherit some centralized features from traditional client-server architecture. Figure 2.2 illustrates the typical network structure of a centralized P2P system and how it supports data sharing applications. There is one central server in the network. (In general, there may be more than one servers. For simplicity, we restrict our discussion to just one single server.) The central server maintains metadata of files/objects shared by peers in the network. This metadata can be viewed as (objectID, peerID) pairs where objectID and peerID denote the object identifier and peer identifier, respectively. Any query is first directed to the central server that returns a list of nodes containing the desired objects. Then the query initiator communicates directly with these nodes to obtain the objects. At this phase, the central server is no longer needed.

Briefly speaking, a centralized P2P system enjoys two merits: (a) It speeds up the process of resource location, and guarantees finding all possible nodes that maintain the desired files; (b) It is easy to maintain, organize, and administer the whole system through the central server. However, the central server may become the bottleneck of the system's scalability. Even worse, it may result in a single point of failure. Therefore, improving the scalability, robustness, and security of these systems is an important research issue. In the next two subsections, we present Napster and

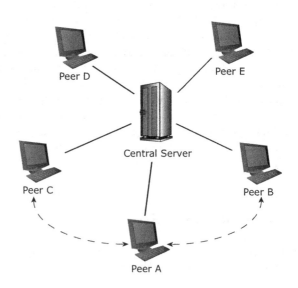

Fig. 2.2 The centralized P2P system. Peer A submits a request to the central server to acquire a list of nodes that satisfy the request. Once Peer A obtains the list (which contains Peer B and Peer C), it communicates directly with the nodes

SETI@home as representative systems to further clarify the advantages and limitations of centralized P2P systems.

2.2.1 Napster: Sharing of Digital Content

Music file sharing is perhaps one of the fastest growing applications in the Internet, and Napster [226] certainly played a critical role in facilitating music file exchange over the net. In Napster, each user (computer) acted as a producer of content. Thus, one can view the system as a collection of MP3 files that are distributed over the personal computers of Napster users. To enable users to locate music files, Napster employed a centralized server that stored the locations of the nodes that own the files. Thus, a request will be channeled to the central server to obtain the list of owner nodes. Actual data exchange between two peers can proceed without any further intervention from the central server.

Generally, Napster provided three basic functions [226]: *search engine, file sharing*, and *Internet relay chat*. The search engine is a dedicated server, which realizes the function of resource location. File sharing provides a mechanism to trade MP3 files among peers, without using the storage space of the central server. Internet relay chat provides a way to find and chat with other online peers. A simple MP3 trading procedure in Napster can be divided into three phases: *joining Napster, resource discovery*, and *downloading files*. First, through various connections (e.g., dial-up or LAN), a user was able to *join* the Napster network by connecting to the central server and completing a registration process on this central server. Second, a peer queries the central server by sending out a lookup message. After receiving the message, the central server first looked up against the index in its local repository and then returned a list of nodes that contained the desired files. Thus, *resource discovery* was accomplished with the help of the central server. Note that the central server maintained an index of metadata of shared files on all online peers and corresponding information (e.g., IP address), but it did not store MP3 files itself. Finally, the query peer established direct connections with the desired peers, and *downloaded files* without the involvement of the central server. The advantages and limitations of Napster architecture can be briefly described as follows.

– *Fault resilience, privacy, anonymity, and security.* Since Napster relies on the central server to record the information about online users and shared files, it is vulnerable to malicious attacks and a single point of failure. A query peer can easily obtain IP addresses of other peers from the central server, which may destroy the anonymity and privacy of peers. Knowing the IP addresses, a malicious user (e.g., a hacker) can attack other peers directly, or steal valuable information from them (e.g., data loss or data leakage). Therefore, potential danger exists in Napster network, and security cannot be guaranteed efficiently. How to improve fault resilience, privacy, anonymous, and security is a critical issues to Napster.
– *Scalability.* In Napster, all peers must connect to the central server and all queries must be processed by the central server firstly. Considering the server has limited capability, no matter how powerful it is. If the number of connections and

queries at one time exceed the permitted capability of the server, the response time may be beyond users' patience or denial-of-service (DOS). Therefore, Napster is weak in scalability and robustness; that is, it can only serve a limited number of connections and queries at one time.

- *Availability.* In P2P environment, we define availability as to what degree or likelihood a query peer can find the desired data on other peers. After a peer downloads MP3 files from other peers, it will keep a copy of these files within its local storage. Assume that the original peers that maintain the desired files all retreat from Napster network in a extreme condition, and these files are still available on the query peers that downloaded the files previously. Thus, the exchange of music files among peers improves data availability of Napster.

- *Decentralization, self-organization and resource location.* The degree of decentralization of Napster is low since a central server is employed to manage the operation of the system. But the searching process is quite efficient, for the mapping between resources and peers can be found directly from the central server. Self-organization refers to the ability of peers to cluster dynamically according to their own interests or optimization objectives. In Napster, peers connect first to the central server, and then interact with each other. So, it is unnecessary for Napster to do self-organization.

- *Cost of ownership.* One attractive feature of P2P system is of lower ownership cost, including the cost to maintain various resources in P2P network. In the case of client-server architecture, a powerful server is used to store sharing resources for clients to download, and provide other services to the clients. It is very expensive to maintain such a powerful server. There is also a central server in Napster. But different from client-server architecture, Napster stores resources on individual peers other than the server. Free from the burden of providing a large amount of storage spaces for resources, maintaining the central server of Napster is much cheaper than that of traditional client-server applications.

- *Efficiency and effectiveness.* The success of Napster has proved that a central control can accelerate resource location with cheaper cost and high efficiency. Also, in terms of effectiveness, peers can obtain expected files by directly exchange among themselves at will.

2.2.2 About SETI@home

Many scientific research projects require tremendous computational power. Following the conventional methodology, they are typically satisfied with a massive number of supercomputers, which of course results in substantive cost of infrastructure, administration, and maintenance. Inspiringly, armed with P2P technology, we can exploit the idle computing resources of the numerous computers (e.g., PCs) at the edge of the Internet, which is not only more economical but also more powerful than the conventional method. The most notable project in this sense is Search for Extraterrestrial Intelligence (SETI) at home (SETI@home), that aims to detect aliens and intelligent life outside the earth. Instead of accomplishing all of tasks with high-end computers, SETI@home splits each computational task into manageable *work units* and incites each peer (i.e., a PC at the edge of the Internet who also is a participant of SETI@home) to process one work unit at one time. After finishing one unit, peers can pick up another. In this way, SETI@home has evolved into the "world's most powerful computer". For example, as reported on their website [288], SETI@home is faster than ASCI White even though the cost of building SETI@home is less than 1% of the cost of building ASCI White. Every day, peers joining SETI@home process an average of 700,000 work units, which works out to over 20 TFLOPS. This success has triggered the expansion of the project into many other areas of scientific computation. The University of California at Berkeley has then developed a general purpose distributed scientific computation project, BOINC [63] of which SETI@home is now part of.

SETI@home consists of four components: *data collector, data distribution server, screensaver (SETI@home client),* and *user database* [247]. Data collector is an antenna that is responsible for gathering radio signals from outer space, and recording these radio signals in digital linear tapes (DLT). Data distribution server receives data from data collector, and divides data into *work unit* from two dimensions: time and frequency. Then the work units will be dispensed to personal computers that have installed screensaver. Screensaver can be downloaded freely and conveniently installed on personal computer, where the software runs in the idle CPU cycles. User database is a relational database that keeps track of SETI@home users information, for instance, tapes, work units, results, user name, and so on. Some important features of SETI@home are as follows:

— *Fault resilience.* SETI@home is also vulnerable to a single point of failure. If servers (e.g., data distribution server or data collector) are down or suffer from malicious attacks, the whole system will break down. While with respect to the validation of computation result of a work unit, a threshold is predefined, and if the computational time span exceeds the threshold, then the result of the work unit is expired. The work unit will be redispatched to another peer.
— *Privacy, anonymity and security.* Peers of SETI@home only fetch work units from data distribution server or send computation results back to user database server. They never need to know about or exchange information with other peers. Thus, SETI@home can assure the privacy and anonymity among peers.
— *Decentralization and scalability.* Similar to Napster, SETI@home has a server for dispatching work units. The bottleneck of SETI@home lies in the capability provided for maximum connections, storage spaces for work units and results. Due to limited capability of the server, SETI@home cannot obtain high decentralization and scalability.
— *Availability.* SETI@home assumes that a work unit can be completed within a given time span. If the time period for calculating a work unit exceeds the given threshold, the result of the work unit is expired, and the work unit will be reassigned to another peer. Therefore, no matter whether a peer can complete a task on time or not, SETI@home always can obtain the corresponding results of the assigned work units.

- *Cost of ownership.* SETI@home pools idle computing power of PCs together, and provides a parallel and distributed computing environment with high performance. As shown by a statistics coming from SETI@home [288], the total number of users in the system are about four millions, and the TFLOPS is about 2.8×10^{21}. By far, SETI@home arms with the most powerful computing capability in the world, but pays for a very cheap cost of ownership.
- *Efficiency and effectiveness.* As reported in [288], SETI@home is faster than ASCI White even though the cost of building SETI@home is much lower than the cost of building ASCI White. Furthermore, peers participating SETI@home can process a huge amount of work each day. Therefore, SETI@home has satisfying efficiency and effectiveness.

2.3 Fully Decentralized P2P Systems

In a P2P system of fully decentralized architecture, each peer is of equal responsibilities and rights, so that none is superior to the other. Furthermore, there are neither centralized servers nor other auxiliary mechanisms, e.g., "supernodes" to coordinate the operations among peers, including resource location, replication and caching, etc. The system can run smoothly while nodes joining or leaving the network at any time.

Several existing P2P systems belong to this category, such as the original Gnutella [133], FreeNet [3], FreeHaven [155], Chord [173], PAST [114], OceanStore [242], etc. As mentioned before, they can be further classified into two subcategories, i.e., unstructured P2P systems and structured P2P systems, based on the criterion of "the structure of overlay network".

- In *unstructured P2P systems*, the content resided on each peer has no relationship to the "structure" of the underlying overlay network. That is to say, each peer chooses the content to store at will. So given a query, it is hard to know precisely the location where the results are. The solution is to search all or a subset of the peers in the network. Usually, a lot of nodes need to be checked before the desired files are found. Most of unstructured P2P systems adopt broadcast-based query routing strategies to discover expected resources, for example, BFS-based (breadth-first search) broadcast in Gnutella. The advantage is that it can easily accommodate a highly transient node population, since the query can be spread to a large number of peers within a short time. The disadvantage is that it widely floods the query to many peers in the network no matter whether they can answer the query or not, which causes heavy network traffic of exponential query messages. Therefore, this routing strategy is efficient as far as network bandwidth consuming is concerned. Consequently, the scalability of an unstructured system is problematic. Examples of the unstructured P2P systems are the original Gnutella, FreeNet, FreeHaven.
- On the contrary, in a *structured P2P system*, there is a certain mechanism to determine the location of files in the network; that is to say, files are placed at

precisely specified locations. For example, by applying a distributed hash function (e.g., SHA-1) on both files and peers' name, files are placed on the peers whose hash values are numerically close to that of the files. Thus, a mapping is built up between files and peers. Given a query, the location of desired files can be decided quickly and deterministically, so it is unnecessary to aimlessly visit unrelated nodes to find the answers to the query. As a result, the efficiency of searching and routing can be improved greatly. Usually, peers need to maintain some data structures (e.g., distributed hash table) to guarantee the correctness and efficiency of query routing. When nodes join and leave the network very frequently, the cost to maintain the routing information is quite high. Systems such as Chord, PAST, and OceanStore belong to this category.

2.3.1 Properties

Fully decentralized P2P systems have no centralized mechanism, such as central servers and "super" nodes, to provide services to others or coordinate the operations of the systems. All participants have the same rights and obligations, and any peer can depart the network without significantly impacting the normal running of the system. Obviously, a single point of failure is avoided, since all tasks and services are distributed throughout the network and no peer is indispensable to the system. Thus, the network has strong immunity to censorship, technical failures of partial network and malicious attacks.

As there exists no central index, routing is also done in a distributed manner. Usually, peers send messages to their neighbors to indicate their requests, decide the path to use, and return feedbacks. In unstructured P2P systems, query routing is often achieved via message-based broadcasting, which involves a large number of peers in the searching process during a short time. To avoid messages flooding in the network, a Time-To-Live (TTL) counter is attached to each message. The TTL value decreases as the message is forwarded among nodes. When it turns zero, the message reaches the end of its lifetime and is no longer forwarded.

Though the broadcast strategy is easy to employ, it is inefficient with regard to the bandwidth consumption and response time. To overcome these limitations, a number of structured P2P systems have been proposed to improve the efficiency of query routing. Since there are precise mappings between the identifiers of the files and those of the peers (or locations), desired objects can be located precisely and efficiently. The cost to pay is some storage space at each peer for the routing table that contains routing information. Also it is the peer's duty to keep the routing information fresh with the change of the network. The difficulty lies in the efficient maintenance of distributed routing tables when nodes join and leave the network at a high rate.

As peers in a fully decentralized P2P system interact with each other without any central coordination, the network is entirely decentralized, self-organizing, and symmetric. In the following subsections, we study two typical fully decentralized P2P systems, Gnutella and Pastry, on various aspects of the design and functionalities.

2.3.2 Gnutella: The First "Pure" P2P System

Gnutella is a purely decentralized P2P system. No central authority is in charge of the network's organization, and there is no discrimination between the client and the server. Nodes in the system connect to each other directly through a specific software application. The Gnutella network expands as new nodes join the network and collapses as all nodes leave the network. In this sense, it is a software-based network infrastructure. Routers, switches, and hubs are not necessary to enable communication at this level.

Briefly speaking, the basic operations of Gnutella include *joining or leaving network, searching and downloading files*:

− *Joining or leaving network.* When a node joins the Gnutella network, it sends a "PING" message to indicate its presence. The "PING" message is forwarded to other nodes by broadcast strategy. When nodes receive the "PING" message, they feed back "PONG" messages as replying, which means they are now aware of the existence of the newcomer. From the "PONG" messages, the newcomer can get the information about those nodes and establish its own neighborhood with some of them. When a node leaves the network, it is not necessary for the node to notify its neighbors. On the contrary, each node needs to probe its neighbors with "PING" messages at regular intervals to confirm whether its neighbors are still online. If no response is returned, the node will take it for granted that these nodes have left the network, and then update the list of its neighbors.
− *Searching and downloading files.* When a node wants to find certain files, it asks its neighbors by issuing a "lookup" message, and its neighbors in turn relay the message to all of their own neighbors in the same manner. Those who have the desired files reply the query initiator with "hit" messages, which are reversely routed back along the same path as the "lookup" message has routed. Through relaying the "lookup" message via nodes' neighbors, a good recall of the searching can be achieved. The broadcasting process goes on until the entire network is covered or the TTL (time-to-live) value of the lookup message reaches zero. Now the original node may have many replies at hand, and can choose some nodes to connect and then download the desired files. Moreover, each message is attached to a unique identifier. When a node receives a message with an identifier it has seen, it will drop the message so that message loops can be avoided. Figure 2.3 illustrates the routing process of Gnutella.

2.3.2.1 Properties

Gnutella has the following properties:

− *Scalability.* The broadcasting mechanism of Gnutella is a two-edged sword. On one hand, because each query may be broadcasted to as many nodes as possible in the network, Gnutella is powerful at discovering all potential results. On the

Fig. 2.3 Gnutella's search mechanism. Peer A requests for some data that Peer D and Peer H have. The query will be broadcasted to the neighbors of Peer A, and gradually, to the other peers in the whole network

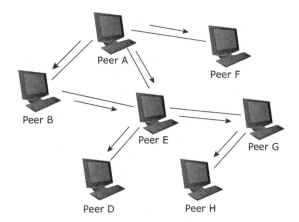

other hand, as more and more nodes join the Gnutella network and the nodes issue queries continuously, the network may be congested with floods of messages. Thus, the scalability of Gnutella is problematic.

— *Self-organization.* When a node connects to the Gnutella network at the first time (or even rejoins after a departure or failure), it is just like a person entering a totally new environment. It randomly chooses a node as its entry point and stays there. As time goes, it becomes familiar with more nodes and builds connections with them. These connections are not permanent. In order to make sure that queries can be best and quickly satisfied, it is up to the node itself to decide which connections are to be established and which established connections are to be severed. Obviously, the node tends to maintain connections with those nodes who have often answered its queries and have enough bandwidth. From the viewpoint of the whole network, high-speed nodes will gradually be placed in the central part of the topology, while low-speed ones will be pushed to the edge of the topology.

— *Anonymity.* Gnutella is a system with good certain degree of anonymity. It uses a message-based broadcasting mechanism to delivery a query. The broadcast-based routing strategy is influenced by the routing tables of quite a lot of Gnutella nodes, which are dynamic and changing all the time. Therefore, it is almost impossible to figure out from which nodes a query came or to which nodes the query would go. However, the anonymity is broken when the original node chooses one or several nodes to establish direct connection and download files. At this phase, the IP addresses of the providers and the requesters are exposed to each other.

— *Availability.* Since a node can connect to and disconnect from the Gnutella network at any time without warning and because there is no mechanism to control the availability and the stability of the replies from other nodes, the availability is not guaranteed. Studies in [21, 284] have shown that only a small fraction of Gnutella nodes will be online long enough to share files with other nodes. Therefore it cannot be guaranteed that queries can be answered well, and the desired files can be downloaded successfully. When it fails, the only available solution is to retry the query or download from other peers.

2.3.3 PAST: A Structured P2P File Sharing System

PAST is a persistent peer-to-peer archival storage utility that enjoys many desirable advantages, including high performance, scalability, availability, and security. It is built on Pastry [275], a DHT-supported overlay that adopts a prefix-based routing scheme. In the PAST system, each node is assigned a 128-bit node identifier that is obtained by hashing the node's public key using a hash function such as SHA-1 [16]. Similarly, each file stored in the PAST is assigned a 160-bit file identifier that is derived from hashing the file name, the owner's public key, and a randomly chosen salt.

When a file is inserted into PAST, it is put on k nodes whose identifiers are numerically closest to the 128 most significant bits of the file identifier, among all live nodes. Given a lookup for a file, a node will forward the request to a node whose identifier has a longer prefix match with the file identifier than itself. If such a node cannot be found, the message will be forwarded to a node whose identifier shares the same length with the file identifier as the present node, but is numerically closer to the file identifier. To achieve this, each node needs to maintain a leaf set and a routing table, whose entry maps a node identifier to its corresponding IP address. Finally, the request will be reliably routed to one of the k nodes that store the file and near to the node issuing the lookup. A simple routing process is illustrated in Fig. 2.4.

2.3.3.1 Properties

PAST has the following properties:

- *Efficiency and cost of ownership.* Since PAST assigns documents to specific nodes according to some predefined rules, the locations of a file are not totally random. As a result, the routing of a request can be well directed. In a steady PAST network, all lookups can be resolved in a number of hops at most logarithmic to the total number of nodes in the system. The property is valid even when

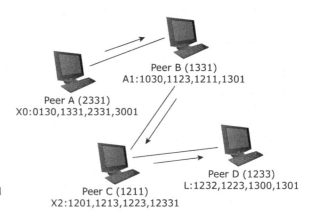

Fig. 2.4 PAST's search mechanism. Peer 2331 issues a query for a file on Peer 1233. Each time, the query is forwarded to a peer closer to the destination. Finally, it will arrive at Peer 1233

Peer B (1331)
A1:1030,1123,1211,1301

Peer A (2331)
X0:0130,1331,2331,3001

Peer D (1233)
L:1232,1223,1300,1301

Peer C (1211)
X2:1201,1213,1223,12331

the number of nodes in the network expands dramatically. The cost of ownership is that each PAST node needs to maintain a table with $(2^b - 1) * \lceil \log_{2^b} N \rceil + 2l$ entries, where N is the number of nodes in the PAST network, while b and l are configuration parameters with typical value 4 and 32, respectively.

− *Availability and persistence.* PAST is an entirely self-organizing overlay network, and provides high availability and persistence. One key factor that may influence system performance is the dynamic nature of the network. Fortunately, the PAST network can be efficiently maintained as nodes arrive frequently or leave without notifying others. Another situation under which performance should be examined is that of extreme operating states, such as when a large fraction of the aggregate storage capacity of all nodes has been occupied. PAST presents two kinds of storage management methods, replica diversion and file diversion, to deal with this situation. With them, free storage space among nodes in PAST network can be well-balanced, and hence PAST can achieve high global storage utilization and graceful degradation when the system approaches its maximal load. Furthermore, PAST will cache copies of popular files on some nodes to minimize the hops count, maximize the query throughput, and balance the workload in the system.

− *Anonymity.* Recall that when a file is inserted into PAST, a file identifier is computed by applying the SHA-1 hash function to the file name, the owner's public key, and a random number. The public key acts as an *initially unlinkable pseudonym* [255] for users to hide their identities. It is also possible that a user uses several pseudonyms to obscure that certain operations were initiated by the same user. It is hard to break the pseudonym to reveal the identity of a user. In addition, other strong mechanisms can be layered on top of PAST to provide higher levels of anonymity.

− *Fault resilience.* In PAST, each file has several replicas on different nodes, and the probability that those nodes fail simultaneously is quite low. Through which, PAST guarantees the availability of files unless all k nodes have failed at the same time. In the case of node failures, all members in the leaf set of the failed node will be notified and updated by the first one that detects this failure. However, routing table entries that refer to failed nodes are repaired lazily: only when the failed node is on a routing path, it will be detected and be replaced by another appropriate node. Experimental results [275] show that Pastry can recover all missing table entries, and the average number of hops is only slightly higher than that before the failures.

− *Security.* In most conditions, PAST nodes and end users use *smart card* to ensure security and do quota management. The smart cards generate identities for nodes and files, and maintain their integrity. Consequently, an attacker cannot forge identifiers of nodes and files to control the identifier space or mislead file insertions. When a file is inserted into the PAST network, a *file certification* is issued and signed with the owner's private key. The file certification should be verified by the stored receipt, which prevents a malicious node from tampering the stored content or occupying extra storage quotas. Analogously, in order to reclaim a file, the file's legitimate owner must issue a *reclaim certificate*, which is verified by a node storing the file by comparison with the file certificate stored with the file itself. The PAST routing scheme is actually randomized to prevent from repeating requests along a path being intercepted by a malicious node. Because of all these measures taken, PAST has a high security level and is resistant to attackers.

2.3.4 Canon: Turning Flat DHT into Hierarchical DHT

As stated in Sect. 2.1, the network structure can be *flat* (single-tier) or *hierarchical* (multi-tier). In a flat structure, the functionality and load are uniformly distributed among the participating nodes. It turns out that most existing decentralized systems are nonhierarchical. On the other hand, recently, Ganesan et al [126] put forward an approach to turn flat DHT into hierarchical one, which takes advantages of both flat and hierarchical structures. Concretely, hierarchical design naturally offers fault isolation and security, efficient caching and effective bandwidth utilization, hierarchical storage, proximity of physical network and so on. In what follows, we discuss the hierarchical DHT design, named as Canonical approach.

The key idea behind of the Canonical approach is that it uses recursive routing structure to construct a hierarchical DHT. For example, Fig. 2.5 shows a part of hierarchical structure of National University of Singapore. In the Canonical approach, all nodes in any domain are interconnected with each other to form a flat DHT routing structure. Notice that "nodes in domain X" refers to all nodes in the subtree rooted at X. However, different from any flat DHT structure, the Canonical approach ensures the nodes located in different sub-domains, will be merged into a new, high-level DHT structure in the current domain by adding some links from each node in one domain to some nodes in other domains. For example, there are three research groups in the SoC domain, i.e., DB, IS, and DS, and all computers of each sub-domain forms a Chord ring. Similarly, in SoC domain, all nodes of DB, IS, and DS domains form a new, high-level Chord ring. In this way, all participating nodes will form a hierarchical DHT according to the hierarchical structure of their domains.

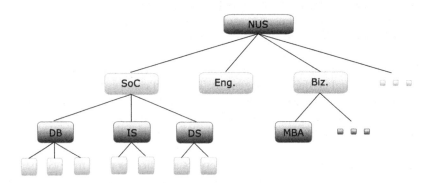

Fig. 2.5 A hierarchical structure of National University of Singapore

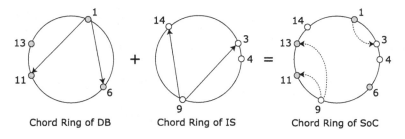

Fig. 2.6 Merging Chord rings of DB and IS into Chord ring of SoC

Obviously, the challenge of the Canonical approach is to design a merging operation in such a manner that the total number of links per node remains the same as in a flat DHT, and that global routing between any two nodes can still be achieved as efficiently as in the flat design. In what follows, we use the Chord protocol [173] as an example to illustrate how to design such a hierarchical DHT (please refer to Sect. 3.3.1 for description of Chord). Specifically, nodes of Chord rings being merged together retain all their original neighborhood. At the same time, they may create some additional links from each node n in its Chord ring to other nodes n' in their Chord rings if and only if (1) for some $0 \leq k < m$ (m is the size of the namespace), node n' is the closest node that is at least distance 2^k away; and (2) n' is closer to n than any other node in n's ring. Condition (1) is indeed the standard Chord rule for establishing neighborhood with other remote nodes, which is used for uniting nodes of different Chord rings. On the other side, condition (2) emphasizes on the fact that each node in one ring need only establish a subset of these links (defined by Chord protocol). That is, only the links to nodes that are closer to it than any other nodes in its own ring.

Figure 2.6 depicts how two Chord rings are merged together into a new Chord ring. Suppose that there are two Chord rings of DB and IS, each with four nodes and its namespace m equals to 4. Let's focus on node 1 of DB ring and node 9 of IS ring. Recall that node 1 builds neighborhood with node 6 and node 11 in DB ring (for each $0 \leq k < 4$, the closest node that is at least distance 2^k away, and hence, node 6 is the closest node corresponding to distance 1, 2, and 4, and node 11 is the closest node corresponding to distance 8). Similarly, in IS ring, node 9's neighbors are node 14 and node 3.

When we merge two Chord rings of DB and IS together, a few new links must be created between nodes of the two Chord rings. Returning to the example above, let's consider the links to be created by node 1 in DB ring. According to condition (1), node 1 will build neighborhood with node 3 (for distance 1 and 2), and with node 9 (for distance 8). However, according to condition (2), node 9 should be ruled out since it is further away than the closest node (node 6) in the DB ring. As such, node 1 only establishes neighboring relationship with node 3. Similarly, node 9 in IS ring should build links with node 11 (for distance 1 and 2) and node 13 (for distance 4), while not with node 1 (for distance 8).

To route messages in such a hierarchical DHT, the Chord protocol is employed. In general, greedy clockwise routing will forward the message to the closest predecessor p of the destination at each level, and p would then be responsible for switching to the next level of Canonical ring and continue routing on that ring. For example, in Fig. 2.6, if node 3 looks for the node with key 13, it first routes the query to node 9 in DB ring. Then node 9 will route the query in the merged ring till node 13 is found. The maintenance of node joining and leaving is similar to the Chord protocol (if interesting, reader can refer to [126] for details).

2.3.4.1 Properties

Hierarchical DHT has the following properties:

- *Efficiency and cost of ownership.* From above, we observe that the cost of ownership of each node in the Canonical ring is $O(\log N)$ irrespective of the structure of the hierarchy. Thus, the efficiency of the Canonical structure is the same as the original one.
- *Fault isolation.* Like DNS system, such a hierarchical DHT can isolate fault efficiently. This is because all nodes in a domain have their own flat DHT. As such, any fault occurring within certain domain would not affect nodes outside the domain.
- *Proximity of physical network.* The likelihood of nodes within a domain being physically close to each other is very high. Hence, such a hierarchical DHT naturally adapts to the proximity of physical network.
- *Hierarchical storage and retrieval.* Compared with the flat DHT, the hierarchical design of a DHT offers more alternatives for content storage. When a node inserts content to the network, it can use domain information to store the content into a specific domain. As a result, the retrieval can be limited within a particular domain and other nodes outside this domain never need to be accessed.

2.3.5 Skip Graph: A Probabilistic-Based Structured Overlay

From the perspective of the *network topology*, there are two main ways in which P2P systems are structured: using DHT and using skip-lists. Distributed Hash Table (DHT) provides a basis for distributing data objects (or just indices) as evenly as possible over nodes in the underlying node space. Well-known systems in this class include Chord [173], CAN [266], Pastry [275], and Tapestry [349]. Though DHT-based systems can guarantee data availability and search efficiency on exact key lookup, they cannot support complex queries (e.g., *nearest neighbor* or *range* queries) as hashing destroys data locality. To solve this problem, Aspnes et al. [31] have proposed a novel structured P2P overlay named *Skip Graph*, which preserves data locality and has the potential capability of supporting complex queries. Typical P2P systems based on Skip Graph are SkipIndex [348] and SkipNet [154].

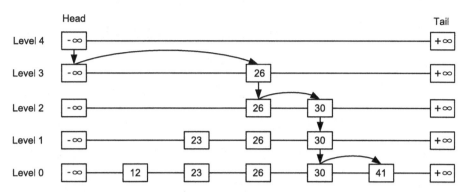

Fig. 2.7 A Skip List with 5 nodes. The *arrow lines* show the process of search node 41 from head, through node 26 and node 30, to node 41

Before presenting the general ideas of Skip Graphs, let us first review the Skip List. A Skip List [260] is a randomized balanced search tree where nodes are organized to a set of sorted linked lists, each of which corresponds to a level of the tree. The list at the lowest level of the tree (level 0) contains all nodes in the Skip List sorted increasingly by the nodes' keys. The list at level $l > 0$ contains a subset of nodes in the list at level $l - 1$ in which each node in the list at level $l - 1$ appears in the list at level l with a fixed probability p and independently on other nodes. In this way, the density of nodes in lists decreases with the increasing of the lists' level, i.e., high level lists are more sparse than low level lists. The purpose of high level links is to provide a jump over a large number of nodes in query processing. In particular, to search the node with a specified key, the nodes in the top level are first traversed, while not overshoot the node compared with the search key. Then the search repeatedly drops down to the lower levels till the desired node is found. Figure 2.7 shows a Skip List with 5 nodes and the process of search node with key 41.

A Skip Graph consists of a set of Skip Lists. Because a fixed probability p is used to determine which level a node will belong to, we thus classify Skip Graphs into *probabilistic-based* structured P2P overlay. Like the Skip List, in the lowest level of a Skip Graph, all nodes are also organized as a linked list in increasing order with respect to the identifier or key of each node. However, unlike the Skip List, in a Skip Graph each node belongs to *several* Skip Lists and the list a node x participates in is determined by its *membership vector* $m(x)$. That is, at each level $i > 0$, there are many linked lists and each node takes part in one of these lists. The highest level of a Skip Graph is the level where each node belongs to a separate list. In other words, the number of lists in the highest level of a Skip Graph is equal to the number of nodes in the Skip Graph.

To build a P2P system based on the skip graph, each resource is assigned to a node and all nodes are ordered according to their resource key. Figure 2.8 shows a skip graph with 7 nodes. Now, we give a formal description of membership vector to determine, for each level $i > 0$, which list a specific node should belong to. Suppose that membership vector $m(x)$ is an infinite random word over some fixed alphabet. Then the membership vector of any list is defined by some finite word w, and any

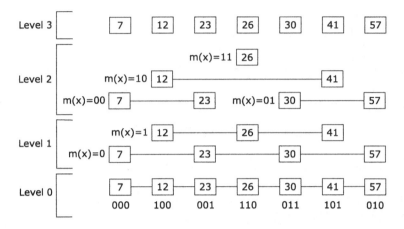

Fig. 2.8 A skip graph with 7 nodes, where level 0, 1, 2, and 3 contain 1 list, 2 lists, 4 lists, and 7 lists, respectively. For example, in level 1, there are 2 lists and their membership vectors are $m(x) = 0$ (node 7, node 23, node 30, and node 57) and $m(x) = 1$ (node 12, node 26, and node 41)

node x in the list labeled by w if and only if w is a prefix of $m(x)$. That is, at i^{th} level, any node in a list has the same prefix of its word w and the length of the prefix equals to i. For example, in Fig. 2.8, level 1 includes two lists $m(x) = 0$ and $m(x) = 1$. In the list $m(x) = 0$, node 7, node 23, node 30, and node 57 have the same prefix "0" whose length is 1, while in the list $m(x) = 1$, node 12, node 26, and node 41 have the same prefix "1".

Since insertions and deletions in a Skip Graph can be supported in the same way as search operations, i.e., locating the node holding a particular key to insert or delete data, we only introduce how to locate the node with a particular key (to see details how insertion and deletions are executed please refer to [31]). Like search in a Skip List, the search begins at the highest level of the node issuing the query. At any step in the search process, it travels along the same level without overshooting the key. In cases the search cannot go further in a level, it travels to the next lower level until it reaches level 0. Since nodes are ordered according to their key, Skip Graphs can support *range queries* that retrieve all nodes whose key is between x and y. To this end, the query node needs only to search the first node whose key is less than or equal to x and then traverses all nodes in level 0 sequentially, till any node whose key is greater than y.

2.3.5.1 Properties

Skip Graph has the following properties:

− *Efficiency and cost of ownership.* As a kind of distributed search tree structure, Skip Graphs guarantees to find all nodes with desired answers in $O(\log N)$ steps using $O(\log N)$ messages, where N is the number of nodes in the system. Similarly, inserting a node in a Skip Graph is expected to incur $O(\log N)$ messages in $O(\log N)$ time. The cost of ownership of Skip Graphs is measured by the number of neighboring nodes and with high probability, is $\Theta(\log N)$.

— *Locality preservation.* Since no hash function is used, similar resources are stored at adjacent nodes in a Skip Graph. As such, resource locality will be preserved. This property benefits some applications such as pre-fetching of web pages, enhanced browsing and efficient searching.

— *Support of complex queries.* Preserving data locality in a Skip Graph is especially useful for database communities to design the novel P2P system that can support range queries, i.e., locating resources whose keys fall into a specified range of values. Further, based on the range search, nearest neighbor queries can also be implemented. Indeed, many subsequent refinement and proposals have used Skip Graph as part of their design.

— *Fault tolerance.* Since each level of a Skip Graph contains several linked lists, the chance that any individual node takes part in a search is not big. Thus, neither single points of failure nor hot spots should exist. Furthermore, all nodes in a Skip Graph are still interconnected even under the circumstances of removal of a large number of nodes selected at random. In particular, if we randomly select an $O(1/\log N)$ fraction of the nodes in a Skip Graph to remove, most of remaining nodes still interconnect.

— *Scalability.* In DHT-based P2P systems, it is necessary to know the size of the system to determine the namespace of nodes. On the contrary, a Skip Graph does not need to have this constraint. As a result, a Skip Graph can be inflate or deflate at will with respect to the number of nodes in the network.

2.4 Hybrid P2P Systems

Hybrid P2P systems draw advantages from the other types of P2P architectures, i.e., centralized and fully distributed ones, while distinguish themselves from the other two types by their elegant auxiliary mechanisms that facilitate resource location. In some P2P systems of hybrid architecture, there are some peers possessing much more powerful capabilities and having more responsibilities than other peers, which are usually referred to as "super" peers (or supernodes). These supernodes form an "upper level" of a hybrid system, which provides similar services for the ordinary peers as the central server does in a centralized P2P system. The common peers, on the other hand, can enjoy much more services from the supernodes in the "upper" layer, especially in the process of resource location. Though supernodes share some similar features to the central server in centralized P2P systems, it is easy to distinguish one from the other based on the following metrics: (i) A supernode is not as powerful as the central server of a centralized P2P system, and it is only in charge of a subset of peers in the network. (ii) A server as in Naspter, just helps peers to locate desired files without sharing any file by itself; however, a supernode has to not only coordinate the operations among the peers under its supervision, but also perform the same operations by itself and contribute its own resources as the common peers do. Interestingly, the determination of a supernode and its connections to other peers are very similar to contacts between persons in human society. For example, in human society, some sociable persons always keep more knowledge and connections than the common persons (e.g., professors, mentors). If one person has some problem, he or she can seek the help of these "mentors". The probability for these latter individuals to settle the matter is greater than that of the average persons.

In some other hybrid P2P systems, there exist some components as their "upper" level. For example, BestPeer [234] has a relatively small number of location independent global names lookup servers (LIGLOs), which serve as the "upper" level of the system. Obviously, the LIGLOs are also distinct from the central serves in centralized P2P systems. Since a LIGLO just generates a unique identifier for the peers under its management, it helps common peers to recognize their neighbors in spite of their dynamic IP, and facilitates peers to dynamically reconfigure their neighbors based on certain metrics (e.g., MaxCount and MinHops). However, a LIGLO is never involved in the resource location of a peer. In such a system, when a peer joins the network for the first time, it can randomly choose a set of nodes as its neighbors and issue queries for desirable information or answer queries from other nodes. With the feature of self-reconfiguration, each peer in a hybrid P2P system manages to directly connect to those that can potentially benefit its later queries. Note that any node can also be chosen as neighbor by other peers. As time passes, queries can probably be answered more efficiently and more precisely due to dynamic reconfiguration. In summary, hybrid P2P systems have many advantages, such as optimizing network topology, improving response time and saving system resource consumption, and avoiding a single point of failure as well. Hence, there are plenty of research focusing on hybrid P2P systems and corresponding applications of such P2P systems in real life, including current Gnutella, BestPeer, PeerDB, PeerIS, CQBuddy.

In the following sections, we introduce a self-configurable P2P system—BestPeer, which exhibits essential features of hybrid P2P systems. Furthermore, BestPeer combines mobile agents and P2P technology into a unified framework gracefully. From the discussions on BestPeer, we can obtain a good understanding of the desirable features of hybrid P2P systems.

2.4.1 BestPeer: A Self-Configurable P2P System

BestPeer is designed as a generic platform to develop P2P applications. Compared to other P2P systems, BestPeer has four distinct features:

1. BestPeer employs mobile agent technology. The system uses mobile agents that contain executive instructions to allow peers to execute operations locally. In this way, raw data can be processed directly at its owner node, and hence the system utilizes network bandwidth efficiently. Furthermore, since agents can be customized, new applications can be extended on BestPeer easily.
2. BestPeer allows peers in the system to share not only data but also computational resources. It is because mobile agent technology can allow a peer to process a request on behalf of another peer.

Fig. 2.9 BestPeer network

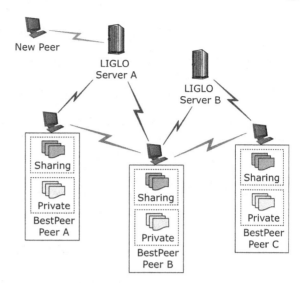

3. BestPeer uses a dynamic method that allows a peer to keep peers having a high potential of answering its queries nearby, and hence the system can reduce the query response time. This feature is actually similar to human behavior.
4. BestPeer introduces a concept of location independent global names lookup (LIGLO). The system uses LIGLO servers to identify peers independently of their IP address. In this way, even though a peer can change its IP address each time it joins the system, the system still recognizes it as a unique peer.

There are two types of nodes in a BestPeer system: peers and LIGLO servers, and a majority of node in the system are peers. As in Fig. 2.9, which shows an example of a BestPeer system, each peer participating the system can share a portion of its data and a peer can only access the sharable data of other peers. A typical procedure of a node joining BestPeer network, accessing sharable resources of other nodes, and rejoining BestPeer network is as follows:

– Joining BestPeer system. For the first time when a peer joins the system, it needs to register itself with a LIGLO server. When a LIGLO server receives a registration request from a peer, it creates a global and unique identifier BPID (BestPeer ID) for that peer. This BPID is then returned to the new node. Additionally, the LIGLO server also returns to the new node a list of BPID and IP address of current online peers registered to the server. The new peer can communicate with peers in this list directly without going through LIGLO servers. However, since a peer can leave the system anytime without notifying the server, the IP address of a peer may be incorrect. In this case, the peer simply removes the unreachable peer from the list. To avoid this case, LIGLO servers often check IP address of their registered peers and discard offline peers from the list. Note that a peer can register to multiple LIGLO servers.
– Accessing sharable resources. When a peer is in the system, it can query and access shared data from other peers. The basic idea of query processing in BestPeer

is similar to that in Gnutella. In particular, when a node wants to issue a query, it simply broadcasts the query to its neighbor peers, which in turn forward the query to their neighbor peers, and so on. When a peer receives a query request, if it contains the queried data, it returns the result directly to the query initiator.

- Rejoining BestPeer network. When a node rejoins the system, i.e., it is not the first time the node joins the system, the node sends its IP address together with its BPID to the LIGLO server it has been registered before. If this IP address is different from the previous registered IP address, the LIGLO server updates the new IP address for the node.

As discussed above, BestPeer can be distinguished from other P2P systems based on four main features. In the following part, we analyze in detail the effect of these features on the performance aspects of BestPeer such as fault resilience, security, anonymity, scalability and so on.

- *Fault resilience.* The use of LIGLO servers helps BestPeer to avoid a single point of failure phenomenon in centralized P2P systems. The main purpose of LIGLO servers is to provide peer registration and auxiliary mechanism for recognizing rejoining nodes. Thus, if a node finds its registered LIGLO server is down, it can still exchange sharable data with others through his neighbors. Additionally, the failure of a LIGLO server does not affect other LIGLO servers or peers registered to these servers. This is essentially different from the centralized P2P architecture, e.g., in Napster a failure at the central server will disrupt all communication between peers. As a result, BestPeer is immune to a single point of failure and has high fault-resilience.

- *Security and trust.* Thanks to combining agent-based technology with P2P computing technology, BestPeer can transform security and trust problems of information exchanging between peers into a secure agent-based routing issue. Pang et al. [251] have discussed two security agent-based routing approaches. One is a parallel dispatch model, the other is a serial dispatch model. In the former model, the route of a mobile agent is predefined, encrypted, and signed at the first step. After that, the agent is dispatched to each new peer to collect information. While in the later model, the peer with which a mobile agent needs to communicate is determined independently by the agent itself and information is collected dynamically when the agent visits peers. For each model, different attack types are considered and the corresponding solutions are discussed. As far as typical attack is concerned, mobile agents can work on behalf of their owner more autonomously, and system scalability, security and performance as a whole can be improved greatly.

- *Scalability.* By use of mobile agent technology, scalability of BestPeer is better than that of the centralized P2P system. Since mobile agents can execute operations locally at peers, agents can be customized for different purposes. As a result, several applications can be deployed on BestPeer easily. Furthermore, an application can provide different functions. For example, an agent can be customized to search files based on file names, another agent can be customized to search files based on file content. On the other hand, BestPeer can easily add a new LIGLO server or remove an existing LIGLO server without affecting the existing system environments.

— *Self-reconfiguration.* BestPeer provides a mechanism that lets each peer keep some most promising peers as close as possible without additional information exchange. In detail, BestPeer employs two approaches: MaxCount and MinHops. The former guarantees that a peer with such neighbor deployment strategy can obtain maximum number of objects from its direct neighbors. In other words, a peer tends to choose those peers that may contain maximum number of potential answers of its queries. While the latter, MinHops, connects peers in a way that minimizes the number of hops for query processing. This indicates how far the query answering peers from the request peer. Through the two strategies, any node in BestPeer network can reconfigure his neighbors in a dynamic manner, which will reduce bandwidth cost for broadcasting queries and return desired answers as quickly as possible. Note that the self-reconfiguration mechanism is irrelevant to the presence of LIGLO servers. Thus, in contrast to static peers network that a peer's neighbors will not change automatically during runtime, BestPeer can adjust peers' neighbors automatically to make good use of existing bandwidth efficiently.

— *Novel applications and extensibility.* Like any infrastructure, it is important for a P2P platform to be able to support a variety of new applications effectively and efficiently. By far, five prototype systems have been developed on Best-Peer to enhance peer data management (PeerDB [235]), information retrieval (PeerIS [196]), continuous query processing (CQBuddy [236]), Web caching (BuddyWeb [330]) and OLAP application (PeerOLAP [169]). PeerDB provides relational data management in P2P environment, while PeerIS combines information retrieval technology with P2P framework to offer high-efficient message routing and resource location. In order to process online analysis processing queries, PeerOLAP, a distributed cache system, is established to facilitate similar queries from different nodes nearby each other. BuddyWeb aims at improving the effectiveness and efficiency of Web searching through applying data caching technology in P2P network, and CQBuddy copes with distributed continuous queries processing in P2P environment. Moreover, to further improve security of BestPeer platform and guarantee privacy and anonymity during data exchange between peers, high security routing issue is studied in agent-based P2P system.

— Efficiency and effectiveness. The former refers to the system performance (e.g., response time), while the latter deals with the quality of the answers(e.g., relevant degree). For example, a request peer can receive answers from other peers quickly after initiating query message, which means a good efficiency. On the other hand, the number of answers may be very few and some of them are irrelevant to query, which means poor effectiveness. Because BestPeer employs MaxCount and MinHops strategies to choose peers' neighbors, Ng et al. [234] have proved that any peer in BestPeer network can obtain a better quantity and quality of answers than Gnutella and traditional client-server architecture.

Notwithstanding, being a system that supports agents, BestPeer has to provide the environment for agents to operate on. While agents bring with them their own definitions and actions such as a new query processing strategy, they also bring problems to the operating environment. As a result, agents increase the complexity of the system, and hence they are not supported in BestPeer 2.0.[1]

2.5 Summary

From the birth of Napster to the current prolific deployment of P2P-based applications, great efforts have been made to address various specific issues of P2P computing. In this chapter, we presented a summary of architectural issues of P2P systems, such that researchers, developers, and users are able to see clearly the potential merits of different P2P systems, identify the key architectural factors that decide the system performance, and make appropriate implementation decisions.

In terms of the degree of decentralization, the architectures of P2P systems can be generally classified into three categories: *centralized P2P systems*, *decentralized P2P systems*, and *hybrid P2P systems*. On one extreme, the centralized P2P systems are supported by one or more centralized servers, where key operations are managed by the servers. On the other extreme, fully distributed P2P systems are completely decentralized. Between these two extremes are hybrid systems where nodes are organized into two layers. The upper layer, such as "super" nodes or other distributed mechanisms (e.g., LIGLO), provide services for the lower layer nodes. The features that distinguish one category from the others are summarized as follows:

- *Centralized P2P systems* inherit centralized features from the client-server architecture, which are composed of one or more central servers and a great number of "clients" (peers). The major point distinguishing it from the client-server model lies in the fact that these P2P servers do not perform sharing operations by themselves or even contribute to the sharing resources. Specifically, in the application of data sharing, the servers never store sharable files and are not involved in the file trading between peers. They only manage resource location by building up metadata index of sharable files. When a peer searches a file, its query is first sent to the central server, which in turn replies to the query initiator with the location of peers that contain desired files. At last, the requestor directly interacts with the answer contributor, without the involvement of the central server. Due to the limited capability of the central server, this type of P2P systems lacks scalability and is vulnerable to malicious attacks and a single point of failure. The most important contribution of centralized P2P systems, such as Napster and SETI@home, is that they arouse great interests from wide application areas, and further incur a wave of research and deployment of the brand new Internet-based applications to make the P2P-based applications successful in real life.
- Even though *fully decentralized P2P systems* can be further divided into subclasses according to either their *structure*: *flat* and *hierarchical* or their *topology*:

---

[1]http://www.bestpeer.com.

structured and *unstructured*, the latter classification is often used. The difference between structured P2P systems and unstructured P2P systems is whether the sharable objects are precisely mapped to their locations or not. In an unstructured P2P system, each peer stores files at will and utilizes heuristic routing strategies, such as routing indices, to facilitate looking up expected files from others. However, these systems might be weak in scalability, since their network might be flooded with query messages if they do not adopt effective searching schemes. In structured P2P systems, such as Chord, CAN, Tapestry, Pastry and Viceroy, peers only contain the sharable objects related to their identifiers, which can be efficiently located through key-based routing (KBR) strategies. Indeed, thanks to the features of the distributed hash tables employed in structured P2P system, queries can reach the locations of the desired objects within $O(\log n)$ or $O(dn^{1/d})$ hops. In addition, it is also advantageous in scalability, fault resilience, anonymity and security over either centralized P2P systems or unstructured P2P systems. However, in structured P2P systems, since the data placement are tightly controlled, their cost to maintain the structured topology is very high, especially in a dynamic environment.

— Different from the other two P2P architectures, *a hybrid P2P system* consists of two kind of nodes and forms a hierarchy of two tiers, where the upper tier serves the processing of the lower one. Actually, hybrid P2P systems can also be considered as a special type of hierarchical unstructured P2P systems. In the current Gnutella, its supernodes form an upper layer, which provides similar services to the ordinary peers as the central server in a centralized P2P system. The common peers, on the other hand, can enjoy much more services from the supernodes, especially in the process of resource location. As aforementioned, the supernodes are different from the servers in client-server systems. In BestPeer and various applications implemented upon it, the upper tier is made up of LIGLOs, which generate an unique identifier for their peers, facilitate peers to recognize and further dynamically reconfigure their neighbors. These desirable functionalities are helpful for peers to naturally evolve into interest communities. In short, hybrid P2P systems combine advantages of both fully distributed and client-server systems.

Besides outlining the categories of P2P system architectures, analyzing their features and comparing their advantages and disadvantages, we have studied how peers in different architectures define their neighbors, i.e., statically or dynamically, and figured out the mechanism supporting dynamic self-reorganization and peers evolving into interest communities.

Chapter 3
Routing in Peer-to-Peer Networks

One of the key operations in a peer-to-peer (P2P) network is the *routing* of messages or requests. To locate desired resources, each peer should be able to forward queries to a subset of neighbor peers that are closer to the destination than any other peer. As such, the design of routing protocols is perhaps one of the most widely researched issues. To some extent, the key differences between the various schemes lie in the amount of information (metadata) that is maintained at each peer, and how this information is organized (see Fig. 3.1). Essentially, if no metadata is maintained at all, then there is really no way in which one can locate information except to broadcast the request to one's neighbors; if the request is met, then the answer can be returned, otherwise, the request may be further routed to the neighbors' neighbors and the process repeats. This is indeed the mechanism adopted in Gnutella [133]. Moreover, given that there is no metadata, the topology of the network is inherently unstructured. On the other hand, one can follow the design of a centralized system that has perfect information. This is exactly what was done in Napster [226]. Such a system is highly (an extreme form) structured. Every peer knows exactly where to turn to look for what they want. Now, depending on the kinds of data that are maintained, we have a continuum of protocols. In this chapter, we focus on the issue of routing in P2P networks. There are three main approaches in which routing is performed in terms of the structure and metadata property of the P2P networks. We, respectively, introduce them as follows.

- In Sect. 3.2, we introduce routing strategies in unstructured P2P networks. The routing strategies in this type emerge from the earliest P2P systems, such as Gnutella and FreeNet. After examining the basic routing strategies, we discuss

Fig. 3.1 An information-oriented perspective of routing protocols

Q.H. Vu et al., *Peer-to-Peer Computing*,
DOI 10.1007/978-3-642-03514-2_3, © Springer-Verlag Berlin Heidelberg 2010

variants of these basic methods that have been invented to enhance their efficiency, bandwidth utilization and so on. Some of these include iterative deepening, expanding ring, and routing indices.

- In Sect. 3.3, we describe routing approaches in structured P2P networks. In this kind of P2P systems, both network structure and data placement are tightly controlled. Each peer uses semantic-free index to forward lookup queries to the peer that is numerically closest to the destination. The most prominent advantage of the structured P2P system is that a theoretical routing bound can be given even in the adverse case. In particular, we discuss in details three categories of structured P2P systems: distributed hash based systems, skip list based systems, and tree-based systems. We also present several well known structured P2P systems including Chord [173, 266, 275, 349], etc.
- Finally, in Sect. 3.4, we discuss routing methods used in hybrid P2P systems. This type of P2P systems combines the advantages of both structured P2P systems and unstructured P2P systems, but avoids their disadvantages.

3.1 Evaluation Metrics

Before we examine the various routing protocols, we shall look at some of the metrics that can be used to compare and evaluate the effectiveness and efficiency of a routing scheme. Some of these include *security*, *anonymity*, *scalability*, *reliability*, *coverage*, *usability*, *storage*, and *efficiency*. In this chapter, we shall focus on just the following ones:

- *Storage.* Each peer may need to incur some storage space for maintaining metadata that are used in directing the search space. Clearly, storing more metadata also implies that it is more costly to keep these data up-to-date.
- *Efficiency.* A system is efficient if it can locate the resource quickly. One metric of efficiency is the response time, which can be measured by the *average query path length*.
- *Usability.* This reflects the ease of use, and the types of queries that can be supported. For example, depending on the metadata maintained, one system may support complex queries, while another can only perform an exact match.
- *Coverage.* By coverage, we refer to whether the search space contains the answers. A scheme with a higher coverage is certainly more useful.
- *Scalability.* The scalability of a system is important for it to be useful in large-scale environments. One measure of scalability is the *number of messages* that need to be routed in order to locate information. For systems that require transmitting a huge amount of messages (e.g., broadcast-based systems), the bandwidth consumption will be high, rendering the system unscalable.

3.2 Routing in Unstructured P2P Networks

The earliest P2P systems are unstructured and peers in these systems are fully autonomic. This means that there is no fixed topology for nodes in these systems. In an unstructured P2P system, each peer typically stores its own data objects and self-maintains a set of links to other nodes (called neighbor nodes) so that the backbone of the system is formed. When a node wants to join the system, it simply contacts an existing node inside the system and copies links of that node to form its own links, which are then maintained at the new node independently on the contact node. The advantage of this type of P2P systems is that the systems allow high autonomy at nodes and hence incur low maintenance cost. However, this advantage comes at the high cost of query processing—since no peers have global knowledge of data placement, queries may be flooded over the entire network. Consequently, the scalability of unstructured P2P systems remains an issue of concern. To alleviate the problem that the system may be flooded with query messages, most unstructured P2P systems attach a Time-to-Live (TTL) value to each query. Based on the TTL value, the system is able to delete the query when a predefined time or a predefined number of search steps has passed. The challenge now is how to optimize query processing in the limited number of search steps constrained by TTL. Several routing strategies have been proposed to target this challenge. In particular, Li et al. [193] have done a survey of existing routing strategies. In this section, we first introduce the two basic routing strategies: Bread-First Search and Depth-First Search. After that, we discuss some outstanding heuristic-based routing schemes.

3.2.1 Basic Routing Strategies

3.2.1.1 Breadth-First Search

BFS (Breadth-First Search) is a simple and straightforward search technique for unstructured P2P networks, such as the original Gnutella [133]. The search depth is specified by a predefined system parameter D, which denotes the maximum TTL of a message during query traversal or search. When a node receives a query message, besides processing the query, it simply forwards the query to all its neighbors except the sender. This process repeats until the length of the query path of the message reaches D. The original Gnutella network is a fully decentralized P2P network and the details could be found in Chap. 2.

3.2.1.2 Depth-First Search

In DFS (Depth-First Search) search scheme, a system-wide search depth D is also specified to denote the maximum TTL of a query message. However, instead of sending a query to all neighbors, each node selects the most promising neighbor that can answer the query and sends the query to only that node. After that, if the node does not receive a reply within a certain period of time or answers of the query cannot be found, the node selects the next promising neighbor to send the query. This process repeats until either the node satisfies with the query result or the node

---

Algorithm 1 : *FreeNet_Search* (Node x, Key k, TTL t)

 1: result = Local_Search(k)
 2: **if** *result = found* **then**
 3:     **return** result to the requester node
 4: **else**
 5:     **if** $t = 0$ **then**
 6:         **return** "not found" to the requester node
 7:     **else**
 8:         **repeat**
 9:             pick a neighbor node y in the routing table of x that has the nearest key
               to k and has not been searched before
10:             result = FreeNet_Search($y, k, t - 1$)
11:         **until** result = found **or** all neighbors have been searched
12:         **return** result to the requester node
13:     **end if**
14: **end if**

---

has no more neighbors to send the query. When a node has an answer for the query, it returns the answer back to the query initiator along the reverse query path and each peer in the query path will cache the answer locally.

FreeNet [3] is an information storage and retrieval P2P system based on the DFS scheme. The system is designed to address the problem of privacy and scalability. In FreeNet, each peer maintains a data repository and a routing table. While the data repository holds shared data, the routing table keeps information of neighbor nodes such as IP Address and keys of shared data possibly stored at these nodes for routing purpose. To limit the use of storage, which is constrained by most nodes, FreeNet employs the Least Recently Used (LRU) replacement policy to discard old shared data and neighbors. In FreeNet, all files are stored and searched with keys. To search a file whose key is k, the query initiator, node x, first searches the key in itself. If k is found, the node retrieves the file and the search process terminates. Otherwise, the node sends the query to a neighbor node y in its routing table that has the nearest key to k. Upon receiving the query, y also first performs a local search for k. If k is found, y returns the result to x and the search process terminates. Otherwise, y continues to send the query to a neighbor z that has the nearest key to k and so on. This search process repeats until the TTL value of the query equals to 0 or the query is satisfied. In general, the search algorithm of FreeNet is described in Algorithm 1.

Figure 3.2 shows an example of query processing in FreeNet. In this example, Peer 1 queries the file with key k that is actually stored at Peer 4. Peer 1 first sends k to Peer 2 that has the nearest key in terms of k. Peer 2 then sends a failure message back to Peer 1 since there is no target file in Peer 2 and Peer 2 has no other neighbors except Peer 1. Upon receiving the failure report from Peer 2, Peer 1 sends k to the second best neighbor Peer 3. Peer 3 relays the query to Peer 4 since Peer 4 is its best neighbor with respect to key k. The target file is found at Peer 4. Peer 4 returns the file to Peer 1 along the reverse path of request. Note that during the return of

Fig. 3.2 An example of query routing in Freenet

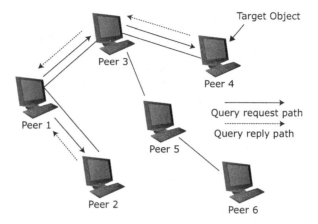

the query result, the information of the key k is also cached (stored) in the routing tables of Peer 1 and Peer 3.

3.2.2 Heuristic-Based Routing Strategies

3.2.2.1 Iterative Deepening

Iterative deepening is a searching technique widely used in many areas more or less related to Artificial Intelligence. Yang et al. [343] applied this technique in P2P searching. In iterative deepening, the query is initiated with a sequence of multiple traditional BFS searches by enlarging search radius gradually. The search process terminates when either the maximum depth is reached or the results for the query satisfy the user's requirement.

In iterative deepening, a system policy P must be provided to specify the sequence of the depths at which the iteration happens. Formally, the policy should be like this: $P = \{D_1, D_2, \ldots, D_n\}$, where $D_1 < D_2 < \cdots < D_n$. In addition, the time period for each iteration, W, should also be determined. In the following, we would give a specific example to explain the use of P and W during query processing.

Suppose we have a policy of three iterations, $P = 2, 4, 7$ and $W = 5$ seconds. Under this policy, the source node S first sends a *query message* to the network via BFS search of depth 2. The nodes that are within 2-hops away from the source node would receive the message. These nodes then evaluate this query message locally and return the results to S. In the meantime, the query would be temporarily stored on the nodes that are 2-hops away from S. After W seconds, S would terminate the query if the results satisfy the user. Otherwise, S issues another *resend query message* with a BFS depth of 4, whose query ID is the same as the query ID of the previous query message. Upon receiving this resend query, the nodes that are less than 2-hops away from the query node would do nothing but forward the query to their neighbors. This process repeats until the *resend query message* reaches the nodes, where the previous query terminates, i.e., the nodes 2-hops away from S. At these nodes, the previous query that has been temporarily stored before is retrieved and forwarded to their neighbor nodes with the new TTL of 4–2. The query message is then processed in the same way as the query message in the first iteration. Similarly, the search for depth of 7 is processed next. However, when the depth of 7 is reached, the messages are not temporarily stored on nodes that are 7 hops away from S since this is the last iteration. S will not issue another *resend message* even if the results do not satisfy the user's requirement.

3.2.2.2 Directed BFS and Intelligent Search

The difference between BFS and directed BFS [343] is that in BFS each node sends the query to all of its neighbors, while in directed BFS each node only queries a subset of its neighbors. Those neighbors that receive the query from the source node, then forward the query by using the standard BFS technique. The key point in directed BFS is how to intelligently choose "good" neighbors that would potentially contribute more relevant results for the query. To achieve this goal, each node maintains some statistics of its neighbors such as the number of times previous queries can be answered through a neighbor node, the number of results obtained for the queries and the latency in receiving the results. Based on these statistics, the node can choose the neighbors "intelligently". Some heuristics include:

— Choose neighbors that returned the largest number of results previously.
— Choose neighbors that incurred the least hop-count messages previously.
— Choose neighbors that forwarded the largest number of messages previously.
— Choose neighbors that have shortest message queues.

The advantage of directed BFS is that since a node only sends the query to a limited number of neighbors instead of all neighbors, the number of query messages in the network is greatly reduced. In the meantime, if a node is able to choose "good neighbors" to send the query, the quality of query results can be maintained.

One disadvantage of this technique is that the statistics each node stores of its neighbors are too simple. These statistics do not contain the information related to the content of query. To alleviate this problem, Kalogeraki et al. [170] have presented a similar but more complex approach called *intelligent search*. In this method, each peer ranks its neighbors based on their relevances to the query and only routes the query to those neighbors that have high relevances. To implement this technique, two components are presented in the paper, one is the *profile mechanism*, the other is the *Relevance Rank* function.

— In the *profile mechanism*, the peer builds a profile for each neighbor. The profile contains the most recent queries processed by its neighbors along with the number of query hits. To limit the use of storage, the peer employs the Least Recently Used (LRU) replacement policy to discard old cached queries.
— In the *Relevance Rank* (RR) function, the peer p_l performs an online ranking of its neighbors to choose the nodes the query q should be forwarded to. To compute

the rank of each neighbor p_i, p_l collects the information from the profiles and computes the relevance of p_i and q as follows:

$$RR_{p_l}(p_i, q) = \sum_{j=\text{queries answered by } p_i} Q_{\text{sim}}(q_j, q)^{\alpha} * S(p_i, q_j). \tag{3.1}$$

In the above equation, $Q_{\text{sim}}(q_j, q)$ represents the similarity between queries q_j and q, which is the cosine of the angle between the representative vectors of these two queries. $S(p_i, q_j)$ is the number of results returned by p_i for query q_j. In addition, α is a configurable parameter that is used to add more weight to the most similar queries. This equation is based on the intuition that those nodes that returned more highly similar results should have higher relevances.

Intelligent search provides a more exact ranking of peers than directed BFS since it takes the content of the query into account. It has good performance in networks that exhibit a high degree of query locality. The problem associated with intelligent search is that the search space might be limited to a small part of the network and thus fails to explore other parts of the network. To address this problem, a small amount of random peers are also added into the set of high-relevance peers to forward the query.

3.2.2.3 Local Indices Search

In the local indices search method [343], each node creates indices for both its local data and the data on neighbor node that are within a radius of k hops from it (if $k = 0$, this method is similar to BFS search, since each node only indexes its own data). In this way, the result returned by processing a query with data indices at a node is the same as the result returned by processing the query with local data at all nodes within a radius of k hops from the node. The purpose of this method is to reduce the number of nodes processing a query while still getting the same result as BFS search. In particular, this method processes queries based on a global policy P that specifies a list of depths in the search tree where the query is processed. When a node receives a query, if it is located at the depth specified in P, it processes the query. Otherwise, it simply forwards the query to its neighbor nodes without processing it. The search process terminates when the specified maximum depth in P is reached. For example, if global policy is $P = \{1, 4, 7\}$, queries should be processed at nodes located at the depths 1, 4, and 7 in the search tree and be forwarded at nodes located at the depths 2, 3, 5, and 6, and the search terminates at nodes located at depth 7.

In this method, the indices of a node need to be updated when a new node joins the system, an existing node leaves the system, or when there are changes in the data stored at neighbor nodes within a radius of k hops from it. In particular, when a new node joins the system, it creates and broadcasts its data indices to all neighbor nodes within a radius of k hops from it so that these neighbor nodes can add new data indices for the new node. Additionally, when a node receives a data index message from a new node, it also replies the new node its data indices. Based on replied indices, the new node then constructs its own data indices. In cases of node departure, when a node realizes the absence of a node, which has left the system or failed, it simply removes data indices from that node. In cases of data update, when a node modifies its data, it needs to broadcast the modification to all nodes within a radius of k hops from it so that these nodes can update their data indices to reflect the modification.

It is important to note that while the local indices approach reduces the processing cost by limiting the processing to fewer nodes, it incurs a higher storage cost since more indices need to be stored at a node and a higher update cost for these indices. Furthermore, due to the dynamics of the network, the indices may be obsolete or inconsistent.

3.2.2.4 Routing Indices-Based Search

In routing indices (RI) search [88], documents are classified into topics and each peer stores information about topics and the number of documents in each topic that can be retrieved through its neighbors. During query processing, this information is used to guide the search. This type of search is actually similar to intelligent search in the sense that both methods use the indexed information about neighbors to direct the search. But the information of neighbors in these two methods are different. In intelligent search, each peer stores the statistics about past queries answered by each of its neighbors, while in routing indices search the information is about the number of documents that can be found through each neighbor on each topic. There are three specific types of RI search, as follows.

− *Compound RI (CRI).* In this type of RI, each node keeps both the total number of documents and the number of documents in each topic that can be retrieved through each neighbor. Using this information, the "goodness" of a neighbor i for a query could be evaluated by the number of documents NUM_i that could be found through neighbor i. With the assumption that document topics are independent, the value of NUM_i could be estimated by the following formula: $n_i \times \prod_j \frac{CRI(n_{ij})}{n_i}$, where $CRI(n_{ij})$ is the number of documents on topic j that could be found through neighbor i and n_i is total number of documents that could be found through neighbor i. During query processing, each peer computes the goodness for each neighbor with the above formula and forwards the query to the "good" neighbors. The CRI uses the following strategy to create the indices. When a node x connects to another node y, each of them summarizes its RIs and sends aggregated indices to the other one. When either of them receives the other's indices, it creates a new RI, and updates their other neighbors accordingly. The mechanism of CRI update and deletion are similar to the creation of CRI.

− *Hop-count RI (HRI).* A weakness of CRI is that the indexed information only contains the number of nodes that can be retrieved through each neighbor node. This information does not reveal how many hops that are required to find documents. The HRI aims to address this limitation by incorporating the hop count.

In this method, each node stores a CRI for each hop going through a neighbor node from 1 to h, where h is the *horizon* of the index, i.e., the maximum number of hops in query processing. In particular, a HRI of a neighbor node at a node consists of a set of CRI, each of which specifies the number of documents that can be retrieved though the neighbor after a number of hops. Given a query, the goodness of the neighbor to a query is evaluated by not only the number of the returned documents for the query per message, but also the number of hops required to find such number of documents.

— *Exponentially aggregated RI (ERI)*. A disadvantage of the HRI is that it incurs high storage and transmission costs. Additionally, each peer becomes "blind" for those nodes beyond the horizon. The ERI alleviates these shortcomings by scarifying the accuracy of indices. In particular, the method accepts some incorrectness in the indices by applying the regular-tree cost formula to HRI.

3.2.2.5 Random Walk

The basic idea of a *random walk* algorithm is that when a peer issues or receives a query, each *randomly* selects a neighbor to send or forward the query and this process repeats until the search result is found. The query message in this case is called a "walker". The advantage of this algorithm is that it significantly reduces the network communication cost since it uses only one message each time. The disadvantage, however, is that it incurs a long delay in query processing. Moreover, if TTL is applied, the search result may not be found. To alleviate this problem, authors of [210] suggested that the query initiator could send k query messages to its neighbors instead of one, each of which is a walker. It means that when a node receives a query message, it just follows the basic random walk to randomly select a neighbor to forward the query. To distinguish the basic random walk algorithm from this variant random walk algorithm, the former is called 1-walker random walk algorithm while the later is called k-walker random walk algorithm. The expectation of k-walker algorithm is that it can reach the same number of nodes after H hops as 1-walker after $k \times H$ hops. In this way, the network delay in 1-walker is cut down by a factor of k. The experimental results in the [210] confirm this expectation. There are two mechanisms that are applied to terminate a query in the random walk algorithm: time-to-live (TTL) and "checking". Similar to other methods, in TTL mechanism, each query message is attached a TTL that limits the searching scope. In "checking" mechanism, each walker periodically refers to the query source and checks if the query should be terminated before it walks to the next node.

Another search method, called random breadth first search (RBFS) [170], is very similar to the k-walker random walk algorithm. In this method, the query initiator first randomly selects a subset of its neighbors to send the query. Each of these neighbors then randomly selects a subset of its neighbors to forward the query. The process repeats until the termination condition is satisfied, e.g., TTL is expired or the result is found. The main difference between the k-walker random walk algorithm and the RBFS is that as search progresses, the number of messages as well as the number of visited nodes in the k-walker random walk algorithm increase linearly while those in the RBFS increase exponentially, and hence RBFS has a higher query success rate than the k-walker random walk algorithm.

3.2.2.6 Adaptive Probabilistic Search

The *adaptive probabilistic search (APS)* [321] is a search method that combines techniques of both k-walker random search and probabilistic search. This method is based on an assumption that both the storage of objects and the number of the queries follow a certain distribution, which cannot be affected by the query process. The main difference between APS and random walkers method is that given a query random walkers method sends the query randomly to neighbor nodes while APS sends the query to neighbor nodes based on some probabilities. In particular, in APS, each peer contains a probability for each neighbor with respect to each object. The probability of a neighbor node to receive a query from a node is determined from past results returned to the node via that neighbor node. The higher the number of cases a query is successfully processed when it is forwarded through a neighbor node, the higher the probability of that neighbor node is, and the higher the change that neighbor node is selected to send a query in the future. Initially, the probability associated with each neighbor and each object is the same. There are two approaches to update the probabilities as follows.

- *Optimistic approach.* In this approach, the system proactively increases the probabilities for selected neighbors associated with the queried object along the search path and decreases their probabilities only if the walker passing through them terminates with a failure.
- *Pessimistic approach.* In this approach, the system proactively decreases the probabilities for selected neighbors associated with the queried object along the search path and increases their probabilities when the walker passing through them terminates with a success.

To further improve the performance of APS, Tsoumakos et al. [321] have presented two optimization techniques: swapping-APS (s-APS) and weighted-APS (w-APS). In s-APS, each peer swaps between optimistic method and pessimistic method based on the observation of the ratio of the successful walkers for each object. The w-APS takes into account the location of objects when probabilistically selecting neighbors.

3.2.2.7 Bloom Filter Based Search

In *attenuated bloom filter based search* [270], each peer uses the attenuated bloom filter to summarize the names of nearby documents and then forwards the query to the nodes that potentially have matching documents. To some extent, this approach is similar to the Routing Indices-Based Search presented in Sect. 3.2.2.4. In this method, each peer stores an attenuated bloom filter for each neighbor. An attenuated bloom filter of depth d consists of d regular bloom filters from level 1 to level h, h is the *horizon* of the index. The ith bloom filter in the attenuated bloom filter at node x for neighbor y summarizes the documents that can be retrieved though y after a number of i hops. The accuracy of the information in the bloom filters is attenuated from the lowest level to the highest level. Similar to the Hop-count Routing Index scheme (HRI), a limitation of this method is that it cannot find documents, which are far away from the query initiator ($>h$ hops in distance). Another limitation of this method is that it can only support title-based search rather than content-based search.

PlanetP [92] is an information retrieval P2P system based on gossiping the global state in the form of bloom filters. Specifically, each peer uses the bloom filter to summarize its local inverted index and distributes this bloom filter into the network. The global index is obtained by gossiping the bloom filters of different peers in the network. Given that each peer has the bloom filters from other peers, it can forward the query to the nodes that potentially have more answers. Upon receiving the query, these peers perform the local search using the vector space model. Even though PlanetP does not suffer from the two problems associated with attenuated bloom filter search, it is not scalable since the gossiping protocol is used.

3.2.2.8 Interest-Based Shortcuts

Sripanidkulchai et al. [301] have introduced a method where each peer adds additional links on top of existing searching network (e.g., Gnutella) to improve the search performance. The additional links are links connecting two peers having a similar interest. The basic idea of this method is based on an observation that if a peer x is interested in some contents of a peer y, with high probability x is also interested in other contents of y. These additional links are called *interest-based shortcuts* since they represent interest-based locality for content search. The main advantage of this method is that using shortcuts, the method improves not only the search performance but also the scalability of the system. In the meantime, the method still retains the good nature of Gnutella. Figure 3.3 shows an example of interest-based shortcuts used by nodes in a system.

When a peer issues a query, it first employs interest-based shortcuts to forward and process the query. After this step, if the peer satisfies with the returned results, the search is terminated. Otherwise, the peer continues to process the query by using the normal query processing algorithm over the Gnutella overlay. Shortcuts of a peer in the system are constructed in the following way. At first, when a peer joins the system, it has no shortcuts. After each successfully processed query, the peer adds shortcuts to peers providing answers for the query. Due to space constraint, each peer only stores a limited number of shortcuts that have the highest utility.

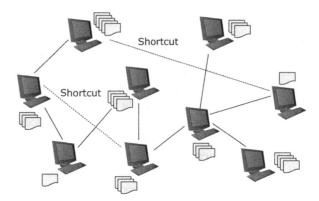

Fig. 3.3 Interest-based shortcut

3.3 Routing in Structured P2P Networks

Even though the unstructured P2P systems are the most popular ones because they are simple and easy to deploy they suffer from the problem of low efficiency, i.e., the systems cannot guarantee that a result of a query is found even if it exits in the system. This problem inspired the development of *Structured P2P Systems*. Unlike unstructured P2P systems, participant nodes in a structured P2P system are required to organize into some fixed topologies such as a ring as in Chord [173], a multi-dimensional grid as in CAN [266], a mesh as in Pastry [275] and Tapestry [349], or a multiple list as in Skip Graph [31]. This means that in a structured P2P system, when a node joins the system, it has to follow some strict procedures to set up its position in the system according to the topology the system adopts. The advantage of this requirement is that based on a fixed topology, the system is able to index data in some order so that the data can be found easily later. As a result, the system can provide an effective and efficient search. In particular, the system can guarantee that if a result of a query exists in the system, it has to be found. Moreover, most structured P2P systems can provide an answer for a query within $O(\log N)$ steps where N is the number of nodes in the systems and each step takes exactly one message. This result implies that the problems of search in unstructured P2P systems are totally eliminated in structured P2P systems. Nevertheless, the disadvantage of structured P2P systems is that the need for a network topology incurs high maintenance cost. In general, we can classify existing structured P2P systems in three main categories based on their overlay network structure: distributed hash table based systems, skip list based systems, and tree based systems.

– Distributed hash table based systems use distributed hash tables (DHTs) [35] to organize nodes and index data. In this kind of systems, each participant node is responsible for a range of values and each data item is assigned a single value obtained by a uniform hashing function such as SHA-1 [16]. As a result, these systems can support exact match query efficiently. Moreover, by employing uni- form hashing, these systems inherit good properties from this kind of hashing, such as uniform load distribution among nodes in the systems, and hence their good performance is ensured. Several existing P2P systems belong to this category. These systems are based on a variety of structures such as a ring as in Chord [173], a multi-dimensional grid as in CAN [266], a Plaxton mesh [258] as in Tapestry [349] and Pastry [275], a butterfly as in Viceroy [213], de Bruijn graphs as in Koorde [175], or a XOR-based metric topology as in Kademlia [218]. The weakness of these systems, however, is that they cannot support range query since uniform hashing destroys the ordering of data. To solve this problem, variants of the distributed hashing methods such as locality sensitive hashing [141, 281] and locality preserving hashing [29] have been proposed.

– Skip list based systems including Skip Graph [31], Skip Net [154], and Skip Index [348] utilize the skip-list structure, which is a multiple sorted double linked list. However, different from Skip List, these systems have many lists at a level and a node participates in a list at each level. By preserving the order of data in the list structure and partitioning data into ranges of values, these systems are able to support both exact match queries and range queries.

– Tree based systems employ different types of trees to index data. The purpose of using tree structures is to support range queries efficiently. P-Grid [17], which employs a binary prefix tree structure, can be considered as the first P2P system building on a tree structure overlay network. Later, there are proposals of using an arbitrary multi-way tree [194], a balanced tree structure (BATON [166]), a B^+-tree structure [86, 87], and an R-tree [167, 192, 225].

Even though different structured P2P systems employ different topologies to organize and connect nodes, [262, 265], and [207] have observed that most of them have Cayley graphs as their static architecture. These abstract algebra graphs have been studied in the late 1980s and early 1990s in the context of parallel computers (processor interconnection networks), but properties that are considered important in that context, like planarity—the possibility to arrange the nodes without intersecting the edges, are not relevant in P2P overlays. Lupu et al. [207] have proved that by choosing different sets of generators and operations, we can form different Cayley graphs corresponding to different structured P2P systems. For example, by applying two different generating sets $S_1 = \{2^i, i = 0, \ldots, m - 1\}$ and $S_2 = \{\pm 2^i, i = 0, \ldots, m - 1\}$ with the same binary operation $+ \pmod{2^m}$ over same the group of positive integers smaller than 2^m, we form two Cayley graphs corresponding to two structured P2P systems: Chord [173] and Skip Net [154]. Furthermore, even if a structured P2P system is not generated from a Cayley graph, by adding some limited extra nodes and connections, it can form a Cayley graph. As an example, Lupu et al. [207] have shown that even though BATON [166] is a structured P2P system not generated from a Cayley graph, by adding just one node and corresponding connections to that node, the tree structure can be easily converted to a Chord ring, which is in a form of a Cayley graph as in Fig. 3.4. Since so many structures can be represented as Cayley graphs (e.g., Chord, CAN, Viceroy, SkipNet) and others can be mapped to them (e.g., Pastry, BATON) it is worth while studying the architecture of these underlying graphs (how to connect nodes and how to route messages between them) in order to obtain good estimates

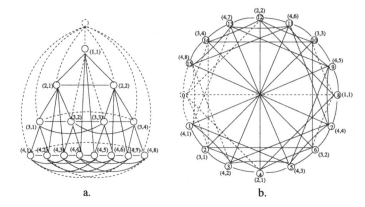

a.   b.

Fig. 3.4 Mapping BATON (**a**) to a Cayley graph (**b**)

of the performance of the networks in terms of query success rates [207]. A common conclusion of these works is that hamiltonicity (i.e., the existence of a hamiltonian cycle) is an important property of the structures. This is mainly because it provides a "default" route in the network. [207] goes a bit further with the analysis of the properties of these networks and identifies the node bisection width (the number of nodes that need to be removed to split the network in equal subnetworks) as a significant measure of quality for the underlying structures. Through extensive tests over the different networks mentioned above in this section, [207] shows that the higher the node bisection width of the underlying graph, the higher the success rate of the queries.

In the remaining part of this section, we introduce some well-known systems of the above three categories. These systems include representative systems from the first category: Chord [173], CAN [266], Tapestry [349] and Pastry [275], Viceroy [213] and Crescendo [126]; typical systems of the second category: Skip Graph [31], Skip Net [154]; and outstanding systems of the third category P-Grid [17], P-Tree [86], and BATON [166].

3.3.1 Chord

Chord is one of the most widely known structured P2P systems in the P2P literature. The system uses a one-way consistent hash function to map each node and data item to an identifier in a single-dimensional identifier space. In particular, the hash function uses the node's IP address to generate an identifier for a node and uses the data item (or the key of the data item) to generate an identifier for a data item. For example, if we use the SHA-1 [16] algorithm, the identifier of a node IP = "202.120.224.102" is SHA-1(202.120.224.102) and the identifier of a data item "12345" is SHA-1(12345). An important characteristic of this system is that the identifier space must be chosen large enough so that the probability of assigning the same identifier to different nodes is negligible.

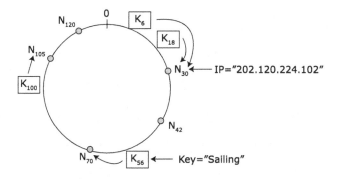

Fig. 3.5 An identifier circle based on consistent hashing

Chord orders identifiers of nodes and data items in an identifier circle modulo 2^m i.e., the identifier space is a circle of numbers from 0 to $2^m - 1$. This is the reason why we call Chord a ring structure. The system assigns a key k to the first node n whose identifier is equal or follows the identifier of k in the circle space. In other words, k is assigned to the first node clockwise from k. In this case, n is called the successor node of k, denoted as $n(k)$. Figure 3.5 shows a graph representing a Chord ring where two keys K_6 and K_{18} are assigned to the same node identifier N_{30} obtained by hashing the IP address "202.120.224.102"; Key K_{56} obtained by hashing the word "Sailing" is assigned to node identifier N_{70}; Key K_{100} is assigned to node identifier N_{105}; Two nodes N_{42} and N_{100} store no data items.

Simple Lookup Algorithm. In this algorithm, each node in the system only needs to know its immediate successor node to perform lookup operations. When a node receives a query request, it first checks its local storage to see if it holds the queried data item. If yes, it returns the result to the query requester. If no, it forwards the query to its immediate successor node. Note that in a special case where the node does not hold the queried data item while the identifier of its immediate successor node exceed the identifier of the queried data item, that queried data item does not exist in the system. Since this algorithm forwards a query step by step through successor nodes, the complexity of the algorithm is $O(N)$, where N is the number of nodes in the system. For example, assume that node N_{30} wants to lookup for key K_{56} stored at node N_{70} as in Fig. 3.6. Since node N_{30} does not hold the key, it first sends the query request to node N_{42}. Then, since N_{42} also does not hold the key, it forwards the query to node N_{70}. Finally, when N_{70} receives the query request, since it holds key K_{56}, it returns the result to node N_{30} along the reverse of the path followed by the query.

Scalable Lookup Algorithm. To expedite lookups, instead of maintaining only one immediate successor node, each node can maintain additional routing information. In particular, each node identifier n maintains a finger table consisting of m successor nodes and an immediate predecessor node. Each entry i in the finger table of a node n contains information of the identifier and IP address (and port number) of the first node whose identifier succeeds or equals $n + 2^i$, where $0 \leq i \leq m - 1$ (all arithmetic is modulo 2^m). Before presenting the scalable lookup algorithm, let

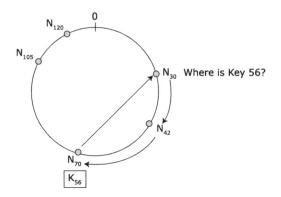

Fig. 3.6 The query path from node 30 for key 56

Algorithm 2 : *Chord_Lookup* (Node n, Key-Id k)

1: **for** $i = m$ down to 1 **do**
2:      $n' = n$.routingtable.get(i)
3:      **if** n.id $< n'$.id $< k$ **then**
4:          Chord_Lookup(n', k)
5:          **return**
6:      **end if**
7: **end for**
8: $n' = n$.successor
9: **if** n.id $< n'$.id $< k$ **then**
10:      Chord_Lookup(n', k)
11: **else**
12:      result $=$ Local_Search(k)
13:      **return** result to the query issuer node
14: **end if**

---

us consider an example that will help clarify the meaning of entries in the finger table. Consider the network (logically) and the finger table shown for node N_7 in Fig. 3.7(a), where the identifier space is $[0, 127]$. The first entry in this finger table contains information of node N_{30} since node N_{30} is the first node that succeeds $(7 + 2^0) \bmod 2^7 = 8$. Similarly, the last entry in this finger table contains information of node N_{81} since node N_{81} is the first node that succeeds $(8 + 2^6) \bmod 2^7 = 72$.

Now we present the lookup algorithm in Chord with finger tables as in Algorithm 2. The procedure is executed when a node n wants to find the key-id k. At first, node n searches its finger table for a node n' with highest node identifier that satisfies the condition n.id $< n'$.id $< k$. If such a node exists, n asks n' to find the k, recursively. Otherwise, n asks its immediate successor to find k. The basic idea of this algorithm is that the closer n' is to k, the higher possibility n' contains k or knows the node holding k. As an example, assume that node N_7 wants to search key K_{117} as in Fig. 3.7(b). At first, node N_7 searches its finger table to find the farthest node that precedes K_{117} in the identifier space. Since node N_{81} is such the

Fig. 3.7 Scalable lookup
algorithm

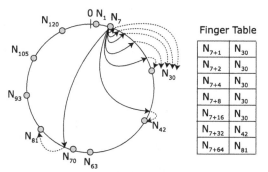

N_{7+1}	N_{30}
N_{7+2}	N_{30}
N_{7+4}	N_{30}
N_{7+8}	N_{30}
N_{7+16}	N_{30}
N_{7+32}	N_{42}
N_{7+64}	N_{81}

(a) The finger table entries for node 7.

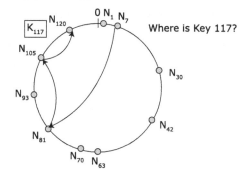

(b) The query path for key 117 starting at
node 7.

node, node N_7 asks node N_{81} to resolve the query. In turn, node N_{81} determines
node N_{105} as the farthest node in its finger table that precedes K_{117} in the identifier space. As a result, N_{81} forwards the query to N_{105}. Node N_{105} then discovers
that its immediate successor, node N_{120}, succeeds key K_{117}, and hence it continues
to forward the query to N_{120}. Finally, since N_{120} holds the queried key, it returns
the result to node N_7. It is shown that the expected number of routing hops in this
search algorithm is $O(\log N)$ steps, assuming accurate finger tables and no recent
node failures.

System Construction. In Chord, when a new node n joins the system, it needs to
(1) find its position in the Chord ring and obtains keys it is responsible for, (2) initialize its finger table and (3) update finger tables of other nodes to reflect the presence
of the new node. To do the first task, n needs to know an existing node x in the system and sends a request to find its immediate successor to x. x then uses the lookup
algorithm to find the immediate successor y of n. Upon finding y, n is put between
y and its predecessor z and y passes to n keys n should be responsible for. Now,
n replaces y to become the new immediate successor of z and replaces z to become
the new predecessor of y. When a node has set up its position in the system, the second task can be done simply by sending lookup requests to find successor nodes of
specific finger table entry values. However, the third task cannot be done easily. It is
because the new node does not know which nodes should update their finger tables

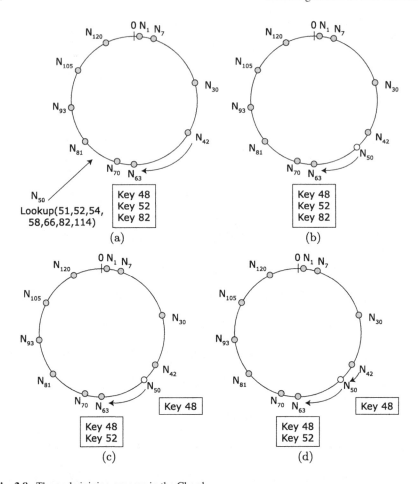

Fig. 3.8 The node joining process in the Chord

due to the presence of the new node. The given solution is that each node in the system needs to periodically run a stabilization protocol that updates Chord's successor pointers and finger tables. As a result, soon after a new node joins the system, finger tables of affected nodes should be updated. This stabilization protocol also makes it easy for node departure. When an existing node leaves the system, it needs to do nothing. The changes in finger tables of nodes that are affected by the departed node are corrected later by the stabilization protocol. As an example, Fig. 3.8 illustrates the join procedure of a new arrival node N_{50}.

3.3.2 CAN

CAN [266] (Content Addressable Network) is a structured P2P system built on a virtual d-dimensional Cartesian coordinate space. The system partitions the coordi-

Fig. 3.9 A two dimensional space CAN system with 5 nodes

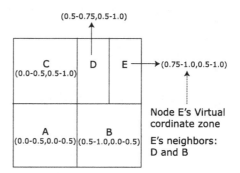

nate space into different zones, each of which is assigned to a node. Each node in the system stores all data items belonging to the zone it is responsible for. To insert a new data item, the system uses a uniform hash function to map the key value of the data item to a point p in the coordinate space and finds the node n whose zone covers p to store the new data item. To process a query, the system also uses the same hash function to map the query to a point p' in the coordinate space and find the node n' whose zone covers p'. If the query's result exists, it should be stored at n'. To find a node whose zone covers a point, the system starts at the requester node and follows immediate neighbor nodes step by step until it reaches the destination node. As a result, for routing purpose, each node in CAN needs to maintain the information of its neighbor nodes that are nodes holding adjacent coordinate nodes to the node's zone. Information of a node's neighbor nodes forms the routing table of that node. Figure 3.9 shows an example of a CAN system with 5 nodes in a two dimensional space.

Routing in CAN. Basically, CAN routes query messages in the system by following the most direct path through the Cartesian space from the source node to the destination node. As mentioned above, each node in CAN has a routing table storing information of its neighbor nodes in the coordinate space. The information of a neighbor node includes the IP addresses of the neighbor node and the coordinate zone that node in charge of. In a d-dimensional coordinate space, two nodes are neighbors if they share the borders at all d dimensions but 1 dimension. Based on routing tables of nodes, a system can forward a message between two arbitrary points in the coordinate space. In particular, similar to CHORD, CAN employs a simple greedy forwarding algorithm that always routes the message to the neighbor having the closest coordinate zone to the destination zone. Algorithm 3 displays the search algorithm of CAN.

It is shown that in a system of N nodes in a d dimensional space, the average routing path length between two arbitrary points is $(d/4)(N^{1/d})$ steps and each node maintains approximately $2 \cdot d$ neighbors. The later result implies that the routing table size of nodes in CAN is independent of the network size, i.e., in a fixed dimensional space, the number of nodes in CAN can be increased without increasing the routing table size. Furthermore, since there are many different routes between two points in the coordinate space, CAN provides strong fault tolerance: even if one

---

Algorithm 3 : *CAN_Lookup* (Node *n*, Point *p*)

1: **if** *n*.zone covers *p* **then**
2:    result = Local_Search(*p*)
3:    **return** result to the query issuer node
4: **else**
5:    find a neighbor node *n'* whose zone is closer to *p*
6:    CAN_Lookup(*n'*, *p*)
7: **end if**

---

or more neighbor nodes of a node fails to work, the node can automatically selects the next best available path to route the message.

System Construction. In CAN, when a new node joins, the system must find the location for the new node and set up neighbors for that node. The join process operates in three steps as follows.

1. *Retrieving existing nodes in the system.* In this step, the new node sends a request to the system's bootstrap node to find an existing node in the system. The bootstrap chooses an arbitrary existing node and returns this node to the new node.
2. *Finding a location:* When the first step is done, the new node randomly chooses a point in the coordinate space and sends a JOIN request towards the node *n* holding this point using the routing algorithm. Upon receiving the JOIN request, *n* splits its zone into two parts. It keeps one part and assigns the other to the new node.
3. *Setting up the routing table:* After setting up its position in the coordinate space, the new node needs to construct its routing table. To do this, the new node just copies the routing table of node *n* in the previous step. The set of neighbor nodes in the routing table of the new node is a subset of nodes in the copied routing table and node *n*. Besides, node *n* and neighbor nodes of the new node also needs to update their routing table to reflect the existing of the new node.

3.3.3 PRR Trees, Pastry and Tapestry

In this subsection, we will first introduce PRR trees [257] followed by two schemes based on PRR trees: Pastry and Tapestry. We will describe how to route message in Pastry and handle the node joining and leaving a Pastry network. After that, we will present routing and object location in Tapestry.

Plaxton, Rajaraman, and Richa introduced PRR trees in 1997. They were interested in object sharing in a distributed network, where several copies of each object may exist at any given time. Their goal was to ensure both fast access to the objects and efficient utilization of network resource based on a probabilistic algorithm for accessing shared objects that satisfy each access request with a nearby copy. They used a novel mechanism to maintain and distribute information about object loca-

Fig. 3.10 Neighbors of a
node under PRR

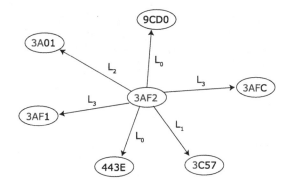

tions, and their scheme requires only a small amount of additional memory at each
participating node. But PRR tree was designed only for static networks and had no
existing implementation. Later, two P2P networks have been proposed, based on
PRR trees: Pastry and Tapestry. Both extend to support dynamic node membership
and have several implementations.

The Basic Idea. In PRR scheme, each node is assigned a unique t-bit identifier
(nodeID) randomly from identifier space (below we denote it as ID-Space). We can
divide the nodeID into l levels of $w = t/l$ bits each; let w bits represent a digit and
$b = 2w$ be the basis of node identifier. Each node i has $(b-1)\log N$ neighbors
$l = \log N$ levels of $2w$ neighbors each, such that each level k, $0 \le k \le l$, will have
nodes with identifiers as follows: k common digits with i's identifier, followed by all
possible 2^w values for the $(k+1)$st digit, and any of the 2^w possible values for each
of the remaining digits. These sets of neighbors form a routing table. An example of
routing table is given in Fig. 3.10. In the figure, at level L_1, 3AF2 has one neighbor
3C57 (these two nodes share the common first digit), and at level L_3, 3AF2's two
neighbors (3AF1 and 3AFC) share the same first three digits. For each node i in the
ID-Space, we define closest(i) as the node whose nodeID is "closest" to i, where
the definition of "closest" varies, but subject to the ID-Space.

Routing in PRR Tree. It is essential to find closest(i) of each node i. In general, we
can find closest(i) from node with identifier j by greedily forwarding the message
to a node k in the routing table of j that (1) has the longest matching prefix with
i among neighbor nodes and (2) has the longer matching prefix compared to the
matching prefix between i and j. In the case where k does not exist, j is the closest
node (root) to i. The routing algorithm is described in Algorithm 4. To see how
to route message in PRR trees, we consider an example like the one depicted in
Fig. 3.10. In this example, for node $3AF2$ to search for $47E2$, it first searches its
routing table to locate a node closest to $47E2$. In our example, this node is $443E$.
When node $443E$ receives the message, it continuously resolves the second digit by
routing to another node with $47**$ (where $*$ denote any digit), which in turn routes
to $47E*$ and finally reaching $47E2$.

In a network of N nodes, routing takes $\log_b N$ time for exact matches. However, for inexact match, it is unclear how it works. Let's consider the example in
Fig. 3.11(a). Suppose we are looking for owner of node identifier 3701. Now, sup-

---

Algorithm 4 : *PRR_Routing* (Node *j*, Node *i*)

1: find a neighbor node *k* having the longest matching prefix with *i*
2: set *p* = length of matching prefix between *i* and *j*
3: set *q* = length of matching prefix between *i* and *k*
4: **if** *q* > *p* **then**
5:      PRP_Routing(*k*, *i*)
6: **else**
7:      *j* as the closest node to *i*
8: **end if**

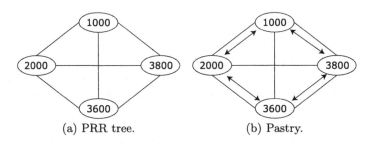

(a) PRR tree.   (b) Pastry.

Fig. 3.11 Routing in PRR and Pastry

pose that the network is well formed (i.e., every routing table spot that can be filled is filled, and can route to all node identifiers). If the query starts at node 1000, it will be routed to node 3800. On the other hand, if the query starts at node 2000, then it will be routed to the node 3600.

Intuitively, what we want is that every node/key has a unique closest node. That is we must have a way to resolve inexact matches. In what follows, we will introduce the method used in Pastry (where every node chooses numerically closest node) and Tapestry (where every node chooses next highest match on per digit basis).

Pastry. Pastry is an application layer service that provides object location and routing services. The system architecture is a mix architecture of a PRR tree and a Chord-like ring. The special design of Pastry compared to other P2P systems is that Pastry considers the network locality in message routing. The purpose of this design is to minimize the network distance of messages in traveling in terms of proximity metrics such as the number of routing hops via different IP zone. To achieve this purpose, Pastry employs a prefix-based scheme where each node has a unique 128-bit node identifier and maintains a routing table consisting of:

  — A set of *leaf nodes*. Leaf nodes are nodes having identifiers numerically closest to the node identifier in which half of them have identifiers smaller than the node identifier and half of them have identifiers greater than the node identifier. This set of nodes plays an important role in routing messages.
  — A set of PRR-style *neighbor nodes*. Neighbor nodes are nodes sharing the same prefix with the node identifier at different degrees and are organized in a structure that is very much like the finger table in Chord [173]. Together with leaf nodes,

neighbor nodes are used in routing messages. However, they are only used if the search key cannot be found at leaf nodes.

— A set of *neighborhood nodes*. Neighborhood nodes of a node are nodes that are closest to the node according to some proximity metrics. Neighborhood nodes are used in complementary with leaf nodes and neighbor nodes in routing messages. In particular, they are employed to select the closest nodes among satisfied nodes to forward the query. This case happens when replication is applied in the system, and hence given a query, there may be multiple routes to different replication sites.

Routing in Pastry. Similar to other PRR-based systems, when a node receives a query message, it selects a neighbor node whose identifier is the closest number to the key and forwards the query to that neighbor node. In particular, the routing algorithm works as follows. Given a query message received at a node, the node first checks to see whether the search key can be found in the set of leaf nodes. If so, it then chooses the numerically closest node and forwards the message directly to that node. Otherwise, if there exists an appropriate PRR-style neighbor having a common prefix with the key longer than the common prefix between the node and the key by at least one digit, that neighbor node is selected to forward the query. Finally, in the very rare case if a neighbor in the above case does not exist or it is unreachable, the node forwards the query to a neighbor having the same common prefix length with the key as itself or a node whose identifier is numerically closer to the key than the node identifier. This routing procedure ensures that the routing always converges, though not necessarily efficiently. It is because in each routing step, the query is always forwarded to a node whose identifier is numerically closer than the current node identifier. Note that to give Pastry strong robustness, each node can stores up k predecessors and k successors instead of just 1 predecessor and 1 successor as in Chord. To see how Pastry routing algorithm works, we consider an example like the one depicted in Fig. 3.11(b). In the figure, the PRR neighbors are depicted by the lighter lines, while the leaf set neighbors are in bold arrows. Now we will see that the closest node of 3701 is well defined. From node 1000, it will resolve the first digit routing to 3800. After that at 3800, we are done because it is numerically closer than 3600. On the other hand, if the query starts at node 2000, it will resolve first digit routing to node 3600. Then at node 3600, it checks to see that 3701 is in leaf set because 3701 is in the range 2000–3800. Now node 3600 will route the message to the numerically closer node, 3800.

Tapestry. The Tapestry network [349] is another peer-to-peer overlay routing infrastructure, which is based on PRR Trees just like Pastry network. Both Pastry and Tapestry can maintain locally optimal routing table to reduce routing stretch. The main difference between them is the method of dealing with inexact match. Pastry chooses numerically closest node when routing identifier in the overlay. In contrast, Tapestry chooses the next highest match node on per digit basis.

Routing and Object Location in Tapestry. There is a global identifier space in the Tapestry, which can be represented as a PRR trees based overlay network. Every node is assigned an identifier and every object has a unique identifier in the same identifier space. Tapestry maps each object identifier to a unique live node dynamically, which is called the object's root. It is the same with Napster, Gnutella, and DNS, that the root maintains a mapping from the object's identifier to its host instead of storing the object itself. To deliver messages to or find the object in the overlay network, each node maintains a routing table containing information about identifiers and IP addresses of its neighbors. Messages are forwarded across neighbor links to the object's root node.

The structure of Tapestry's routing table called *neighbor maps* is similar to the longest prefix routing scheme that is used by Classless InterDomain Routing (CIDR) IP address allocation. There are several levels in the neighbor maps of a node, denoted as $L_1, L_2, \ldots, L_b$ (b is the basis of identifiers). Each level has many link entries pointing to the node's neighbors. All the neighbors in L_i share $i - 1$ prefix digits with the node identifier, and the jth link entry of the ith level points to a *closest* node that the ith position of that node's identifier is j. There are variant definitions of closest node, such as the node with lowest latency or highest next digit. Figure 3.10 shows some link entries of the neighbor maps of a single node in Tapestry network, where the node 3AF1 is the first entry of the fourth level for node 3AF2. All the neighbor maps of a node construct a routing table. In a real implementation of Tapestry, each link entry may have several backup links for performance and availability. For the purpose of maintaining Tapestry's integrity, each node also keeps reverse references(*backpointers*) to other nodes that have a link entry pointing to it.

The mechanism of object location used in Tapestry is DOLR (Distributed Object Location and Routing), which service model is: *route_to_ object(ID, message)* and *publish(ID)*. DOLR can be implemented based on simple owner service. However, the main problem of this method is not taking network distances into account, which will cause bad performance in some situations, e.g., even if a object is stored nearby, it's owner node might be far away. A message sent to the object may be routed through the diameter of the network. In Tapestry, the *closest nodes* provide the locality property to reduce routing stretch.

Given an object identifier O_{id}, node N routes it to its root node. Let p is the length of prefix digits shared by O_{id} and ID of N, Tapestry searches the $(p + 1)^{\text{th}}$ level neighbor map of N for the best matched link. Let n is the digit at O_{id}'s $p + 1$ position, if the nth link entry is not empty, node N routes O_{id} to the node pointed by the link. Otherwise, Tapestry chooses a *closest* link entry for routing. It is called *surrogate routing*, where every identifier is mapped to a live node. For the identifier that has no exactly matched node ID, a similar node ID is chosen as its root. Figure 3.12 gives an example of Tapestry network including three nodes: 0700, 0F00, and FFFF. Node 0F00 is defined as the closest to node FFFF. For identifier 0000, node 0700 is its root node.

In Tapestry network, both objects and nodes have identifiers and each identifier has a unique root node. An object O is stored in node S, whose identifiers are O_{id} and S_{id}, respectively. The root node of identifier O_{id} is node R, whose identifier is R_{id}. A publish message of object O is routed from node S to node R periodically, it will pass through several nodes that construct a publication path. To improve routing performance, each node in the publication path stores a reference to object O. For

Fig. 3.12 A simple example of Tapestry network

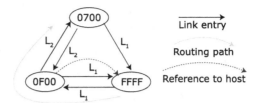

example, in Fig. 3.12, node FFFF is the host of object 0000, so the routing path is also the publication path. Node 0F00 is an intermediate node of the publication path, which has a reference to 0000's host (node FFFF) indicated by the dashed line. If there are several replicas of object O on different nodes, each node publishes its own copy independently. Tapestry nodes can store references to object O according to network latency from their perspective. To locate object O in the Tapestry network, a client routes a message to object O's root node R to get the reference to O. If there is a reference to object O in a node of the routing path, the message is redirected to node S.

3.3.4 Viceroy

Viceroy [213] is a multi-level DHT-based routing network approximating to a butterfly network. In Viceroy, every node maintains five outgoing links besides linking to its predecessor and successor on the ring, which is formed like Chord. For a node in level l, it holds a down-right edge and a down-left edge that are linked rigidly to the close-distance node and $1/2^l$ away node of level $l + 1$, as well as a "up" link to a close-by node at level $l - 1$ and two "level-ring" links to the next and preceding nodes of the same level. The routing procedure of a message consists of three steps as follows.

1. *Going up*: the system forwards the message to a level-1 node using "up" links. In some cases, the system may forward the message to the root by repeatedly going up.
2. *Going down:* the system routes the message downward low levels of the tree using the down links. In particular, depending on whether the destination is at a distance more than $1/2^l$ or not, the system follows either the link to the close-by down link or the far-away down link to forward the message. This process repeats until the system reaches a node with no down links, which should be adjacent to the target.
3. *"Vicinity" search:* the system uses the ring and level-ring links to find the destination node (which may not be a leaf in the tree).

It is shown that in a random network construction, the whole routing process is bounded by $O(\log N)$ steps with high probability. Figure 3.13 depicts an ideal Viceroy network and a routing path from node A to node B. To route to node B, node A first climbs up to its up node C of level 2. Then node C gets down along its

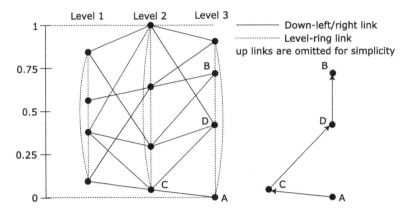

Fig. 3.13 Viceroy network and the routing path

down-right link to node D. At last node D issues a "vicinity" search to the destination node B using its level-ring link.

3.3.5 Crescendo

Canon [126] is a kind of hierarchical DHT schemes for structured P2P overlay, and Crescendo is a canonical version of Chord. The members of Crescendo system form a conceptional hierarchy that is constituted by multiple domains in different levels. In each level of the hierarchy, all nodes in one domain maintain a Chord-like ring and add links to outside nodes. In addition, two separate Chord rings in low level can be merged into a large Crescendo ring of upper level according to the following conditions that, besides retaining all its original links each node n in one ring establishes a link to node m in the other ring iff: (a) m immediately succeeds n at least distance 2^i away for some $0 \leq i < N$ (the space size is N-bit), and (b) m is closer to n than any node in n's ring.

For the example shown in Fig. 3.14, node 0 holds the links to nodes 2, 6 and 12 in standard Chord protocol in its local ring (real arrows). When its local ring is merged with the other ring in which nodes 1, 10, and 14 exist, node 0 creates links to node 1 and node 10 (dashed arrows) following above conditions, for that node 1 and node 10 are closer than its original successor node 2 and node 12 for least distance 2^0 and 2^3, respectively.

As in Chord, Crescendo also adopts a greedy clockwise routing policy. In detail, if a node requests for a destination d, it first routes the query to the closest predecessor p of d in the ring of its lowest level. Then p is responsible for looking for d by switching to the higher ring in which routing is continued. Such routing proceeds from a lower level to an upper level, switching from small ring to merged ring continuously until arriving at d. Back to the example in Fig. 3.14, if node 0 requests the resource at node 10, it would first route along its ring of the lowest level

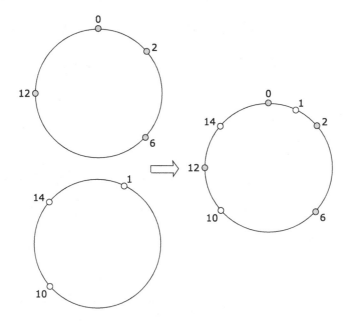

Fig. 3.14 Merging two rings in one Crescendo ring

to node 6. Then node 6 switches routing to the merged ring of the next higher level of the hierarchy, and in turn routes to node 10 using the greedy clockwise algorithm.

3.3.6 Skip Graph

Skip Graph is based on the well known Skip List [260] structure, which is a multiple sorted double linked lists. However, unlike Skip List, which has only one list at each level, a Skip Graph has many lists at a level. In Skip Graph, each node in the system participates in a list at each level. The system controls the lists in which a node belongs to by a randomly membership vector that is created when the node joins the system. In this way, a Skip Graph can be considered as a set of many skip lists all of which share the same lowest level. As an example, a Skip Graph with 6 nodes is illustrated in Fig. 3.15. Note that this Skip Graph has one list at level 0, two lists at level 1, and 4 lists at level 2.

When a node x joins a Skip Graph system, based on its membership vector $m(x)$, x joins the lists of nodes whose membership vector shares the same prefix with $m(x)$ at different lengths. In particular, x first joins the list at level 0 in which x links to nodes containing keys closest to the node's key. For level $i \geq 1$, x links to the closest node y satisfying the condition: $m(x)_i = m(y)_i$, where $m(x)_i$ and $m(y)_i$ are, respectively, the prefix of length i of the membership vectors of x and y. The insertion process continues until x cannot be inserted into any list. At this point x creates its own list.

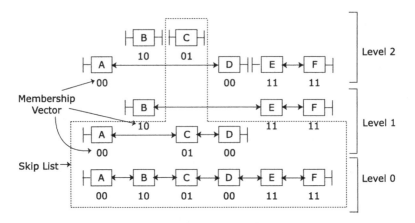

Fig. 3.15 Skip Graph

Algorithm 5 : *SkipGraph_Search* (Node *n*, Key *k*)

1: *l* = the highest level of *n*
2: **while** *l* ≥ 0 **do**
3:     find a neighbor node *n'* at level *l* that is closer to *k*
4:     **if** *n'* exists **then**
5:         SkipGraph_Search(*n'*, *k*)
6:         **return**
7:     **end if**
8:     *l* = *l* − 1
9: **end while**
10: result = Local_Search(*k*)
11: **return** result to the query issuer node

Searching in Skip Graph is based on the same principle as searching in Skip List except with a minor difference. Instead of sending a search query from a low level node to a high level node, in a Skip Graph, when a node issues a query, the search process always starts at the highest level of that node. At each step, if there is a neighbor node at the same level that keeps a closer value to the search key, the node forwards the query to that neighbor node. Otherwise, the node continues the search process at a lower lever. The destination node containing the result is found when the search process reaches the bottom level. The search algorithm of Skip Graph is shown in Algorithm 5. As in Skip List, it takes approximately $O(\log N)$ steps to process a query in an N node system.

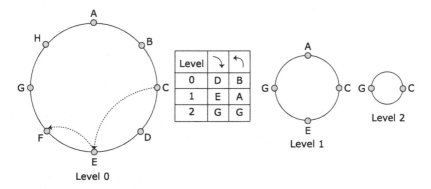

Fig. 3.16 Level rings of SkipNet and the routing table

3.3.7 SkipNet

SkipNet shares the same underlying inspiration with SkipGraphs [31] that originates from the SkipList structure. As its novelty, SkipNet combines two separate but related address spaces: string name ID space and numeric ID space, which endow nodes uniformly distribution in address space as well as the organizational clustering. Nodes in SkipNet are arranged into address rings of multiple levels rather than lists, and each node maintains a two-direction routing table (R-Table) storing $2 \log N$ (N is network size) pointers to the neighbors in different levels. There are two kinds, i.e., "perfect" SkipNet and "probabilistic" SkipNet being partitioned based on the different fashions of nodes participating in the rings. E.g., the SkipNet in Fig. 3.16 is a "perfect" SkipNet containing 8 nodes, in which every node maintains a R-Table pointing to the neighbors bidirectionally. As node C's R-Table indexes the neighbors in clockwise and anticlockwise directions of 3 levels, of which each level h entry points exactly to 2^h away nodes.

Routing either by name ID or by numeric ID follows a search path advancing to the node whose name/numeric ID is the closest to the destination using R-Table from level 0 to top level, i.e., from coarse granularity to fine granularity. Because R-Tables are bidirectional, a node can use the left or right pointers depending on whether target ID is smaller or larger than local when routing. For the example in Fig. 3.16, if node C searches name ID F, it forwards the query to node E using the pointer in level 1 of clockwise direction for F is greater than C in name ID. Then node E routes to node F in its level 2 ring. Such a Chord-like routing mechanism achieves $O(\log N)$ search time as well as the tolerance to uncorrelated and independent failures, that is detailed in [154] as a salient property.

3.3.8 P-Grid

P-Grid is based on a *virtual* binary tree structure in which each peer maintains a leaf node of the tree. In the tree structure, for each connection between a node and

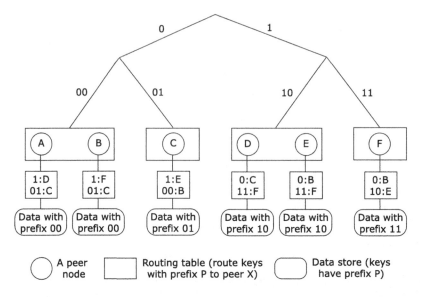

Fig. 3.17 P-Grid

its child, the system labels a binary value. Based on labels, the system assigns each peer an identifier, which is the binary bit string representing the path from the root to the leaf node of which the peer is in charge. Each peer is responsible for all data items whose prefix is equal to the peer identifier. An example of a P-Grid with 6 peers is shown in Fig. 3.17. In this example, since the binary bit string representing the path from the root to A is 00, the identifier of A is 00. As a result, A stores data items, whose prefix is 00. Note that the peer identifier is not unique. For fault-tolerance purpose, multiple peers can be assigned the same identifier, and hence they are responsible for the same position in the tree structure. As in Fig. 3.17, nodes A and B have the same identifier 00. For routing purpose, each peer maintains a routing table. For each level from the root to the node, the routing table contains at least a reference to a peer that is in the other size of the tree rooted at the internal node at that level. For example, the routing table of A in Fig. 3.17 contains two entries: one points to D, which is located in the other side of the root; the other points to C, which is located in the other side of the tree rooted at the middle level.

Based on the tree structure, an exact match query is processed as in Algorithm 6. The algorithm can be explained as follows. When a peer n receives an exact match query with key k, if its identifier $n.id$ is a prefix of k, the peer is in charge of k, and hence it searches its local storage to find the result. On the other hand, the peer looks up its routing table to find a closer neighbor node to forward the query. Since each time the query is forwarded from a node to another node, the length of the common prefix between the node identifier and the search key increases by at least one, the maximum number of search step is bounded by the height of the tree, which is $\log_2 N$, where N is the number of nodes in the system. For example, assume node A in Fig. 3.17 issues a query whose key is 11. Since A is not in charge of the key, it has

---

Algorithm 6 : *PGrid_Search* (Node n, Key k)

1: **if** n.id $\subseteq$ k **then**
2:     result $=$ Local_Search(k)
3:     **return** result to the query issuer node
4: **else** {find a closer neighbor node to forward the query}
5:     find l such that Prefix(k, l) = Invert(Prefix(n.id, l))
6:     $n' = a$ randomly selected node from Routing(n) at level l
7:     PGrid_Search(n', k)
8: **end if**

---

to forward the query to D, which is a neighbor node at level 1 since Prefix(11, 1) = Invert(Prefix(A.id, 1). After that, D continues to forward the query to F, which is the destination node. To support range query, in addition to having a routing table, each node also has an adjacent link to its adjacent node, which is a node maintaining the range of values next to the node's range of values [97]. In this way, a range query is processed simply by finding a node containing a data item belonging to the search range. After that, adjacent links are followed to retrieve remaining results. The cost of query processing now is $\log_2 N + T$, where T is the number of nodes containing the query's result. Note that by not mapping peers to the root and internal nodes while using routing table for query processing purpose, P-Grid is not potential to the bottleneck problem at the root in the tree structure.

3.3.9 P-Tree

Different from P-Grid, which is based on a *virtual* binary tree and the balance of the tree structure cannot be guaranteed, P-Tree is based on a *virtual* balanced B^+-Tree built on top of a Chord ring (or in other words, the Chord ring forms the base of the P-Tree). The key idea of P-Tree is that each peer maintains a Chord node, which is a leaf node of the tree structure, and a semi-independent B^+-Tree, which is a part of a fully independent B^+-Tree in the view of the peer. A fully independent B^+-Tree at a peer is a B^+-Tree, where the value stored at the peer is considered as the smallest value in the Chord ring. A semi-independent B^+-Tree contains all nodes in the left-most root-to-leaf path of the corresponding fully complete B^+-Tree. An example of a P-Tree with 8 nodes is shown in Fig. 3.18 in which Fig. 3.18(a) displays semi-independent B^+-Trees maintained at nodes in the system while Fig. 3.18(b) displays the fully independent B^+-Tree in the view of node A. Note that to make it easy for maintenance, ranges of B^+-Tree nodes can be overlapped. As in Fig. 3.18(a), the root node of the B^+-Tree at node C has four sub-trees in which the first and the second sub-trees have overlapping ranges because the first sub-tree covers values in the range of 13–30 while the second sub-tree covers values in the range of 29–42. This is in contrast to the traditional B^+-Tree.

Query processing in P-Tree is similar to that of B^+-Tree except that when a query traverses from a level to the next level, it actually jumps from a peer to another

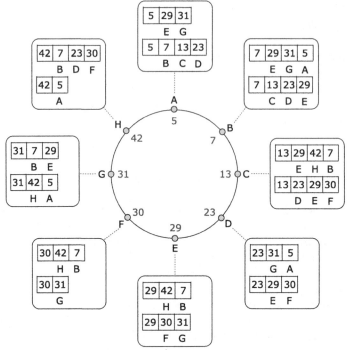

(a) Semi-independent B$^+$-Trees maintained at nodes

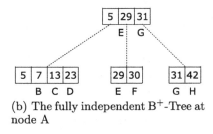

(b) The fully independent B$^+$-Tree at node A

Fig. 3.18 P-Tree

peer. When the query comes to the lowest level of the tree, it follows the successor lists of peers in the Chord ring to reach the destination node. The query process-ing algorithm is displayed in Algorithm 7. As an example, consider a range query $30 \leq$ value ≤ 35 issued at peer A in Fig. 3.18. At A, there exists a node E at the first level, second position, whose value falls in between A's value and the query's lower bound. As a result, the query is forwarded from A to E. At E, a similar process is conducted and the query is continuously forwarded from E to F. Since F contains the value 30, which falls in the search range, F returns the result to A, the query ini-tiator. Additionally, F also forwards the query to its immediate successor node G. The search process terminates at G since the value of the immediate successor node of G does not fall in the search range.

Algorithm 7 : PTree_Search(Node n, Range_Query q)

1: Find a neighbor node n' at the lowest level l and the maximum number j such that n'.value $\in (n$.value, q.lowerBound)
2: **if** n' exists **then**
3:     PTree_Search(n', q)
4: **else**
5:     **if** n covers the search key **then**
6:         result = Local_Search(q)
7:         **return** result to the query issuer node
8:     **end if**
9:     n' = successor of n
10:     **if** n'.value $\in (n$.value, q.upperBound) **then**
11:         PTree_Search(n', q)
12:     **end if**
13: **end if**

3.3.10 BATON

While P-Tree constructs a balanced tree structure bottom up from a Chord ring, BATON [166] builds a balanced tree structure top down. The overlay network in BATON, however, is different from the standard tree structure by two main features. On the one hand, in the network, data is stored at both leaf nodes and internal nodes. On the other hand, in addition to parent and child links, nodes in the network also have adjacent links and neighbor links. An adjacent link is used to connect a node to an adjacent node, which is a node maintaining an adjacent range of values of the range of values the node is maintaining while a neighbor link is used to connect a node with a selected neighbor node at the same level in the tree structure having a distance 2^i, $i \geq 0$, from the node. The purpose of these links is to avoid the bottleneck problem at the root of the tree structure in query processing. As a result, each node in the network stores a link to its parent, a link to each of its children, a link to each of its two adjacent nodes, and a link to each of its neighbor nodes. Note that neighbor links pointing to nodes on the left side of the node is stored in a left routing table while neighbor links pointing to nodes on the right of the node is stored in a right routing table. BATON maintains the tree structure balanced by forcing each node to have both its left and right routing tables full before it has a child node. Figure 3.19 shows an example of BATON.

In BATON, when a node x processes a query, if the searched key does not fall into the range of values managed by x, x forwards the query to the farthest neighbor node in the routing table that is nearer to but not overshooting the searched key. In particular, if the searched key is greater than x's upper bound, x forwards the query to the farthest neighbor node, whose upper bound is still less than the searched key. Similarly, if the searched key is smaller than x's lower bound, x forwards the query to the farthest neighbor node, whose lower bound is still greater than the searched key. In cases such neighbor node does not exist, x forwards the query to either a

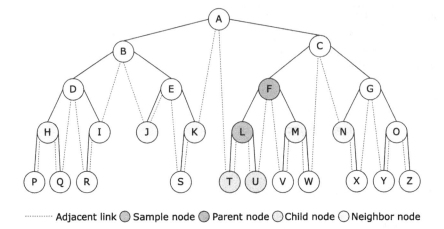

.... Adjacent link ◐ Sample node ● Parent node ○ Child node ○ Neighbor node

Fig. 3.19 BATON

Algorithm 8 : BATON_Search(Node n, Key k)

 1: **if** n covers the search key **then**
 2:     result $=$ Local_Search(q)
 3:     **return** result to the query issuer node
 4: **else**
 5:     **if** there exists a neighbor n' of n that is closer to k **then**
 6:         BATON_Search(n', k)
 7:     **else**
 8:         **if** there exists a child n' of n that is closer to k **then**
 9:             BATON_Search(n', k)
10:         **else**
11:             n' is an adjacent node of n that is closer to k
12:             BATON_Search(n', k)
13:         **end if**
14:     **end if**
15: **end if**

---

child (if it exists) or an adjacent node of x in the search direction. In a special case, if x is a leaf node without a full routing table on the search direction, x always forwards the query to its parent node for processing. The overall search algorithm of BATON is shown in Algorithm 8.

It is important to note that the search request is always forwarded via neighbor nodes or child nodes. The request is only needed to forward to higher level nodes in two cases: the higher level node contains the searched value, or the processing node does not have two children (a leaf node or a node near the leaf). This property helps the root to avoid receiving more requests than other nodes. For example, assume that node H wants to search for a data item that is stored in node C and whose value is

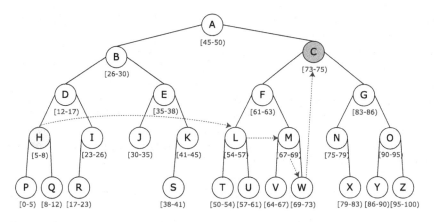

Fig. 3.20 Query processing in BATON

74 as in Fig. 3.20. Since the searched value is greater than H's upper bound, H first sends the query to L, the farthest neighbor node nearer to but not overshooting the searched key. Similarly, L then forwards the query to M. Since there is no neighbor node of M whose upper bound is less then the searched key, M continues to forward the query to its right child W. Finally, following right adjacent link from W to C, the query is forwarded to the destination node.

3.4 Routing in Hybrid P2P Networks

Though unstructured and structured P2P systems are fully decentralized, both represent two completely different extremes. The former does not put any control on both network structure and data placement, and peers are fully autonomic for selecting their neighbors and storing data objects, while the latter puts tight control on both network structure and data placement, and peers are in a semi-autonomic state. The difference between them results in two extremely different routing efficiency and effectiveness, i.e., unstructured P2P network floods user queries blindly to most of peers, while structured P2P network always locates destinations within limited hop bound.

To overcome their shortcomings and make better use of their advantages, hybrid P2P systems have been invented. In this section, we will discuss the design philosophy of hybrid P2P networks and introduce the basic routing scheme of typical systems.

3.4.1 Hybrid Routing

In a real-life P2P network, peers are of heterogeneity in terms of computational and bandwidth resource and storage capacity. However, traditional P2P systems treat all peers equally and overlook these differences. For the purpose of making better use of heterogeneity of peers, both academic and industry communities have invented hybrid P2P systems that beautifully combine the advantages of both unstructured and structured P2P system together. The hybrid P2P systems take heterogeneity of peers into consideration and organize all peers into a hierarchical network, where powerful peers lie in high level and common peers lie in the lower level. These powerful peers are called superpeers or supernodes and all of them are organized as a small P2P network. Each common peer, also named client peer, belongs to a supernode and does not connect with any other common peer that does not belong to the same supernode. Typical hybrid P2P systems include KaZaA network [200], BestPeer [234], Edutella [228, 229], and related research work include search in power-law network [20], structured superpeers [224] and designing superpeer networks [344].

Since a supernode will answer queries on behalf of its client peers, the routing scheme in a hybrid P2P network is very simple and straightforward. In general, the routing scheme in a hybrid P2P network follows four steps. First, a client peer sends a query to its supernode. Second, the supernode searches its directory to determine which client peer or supernode has the desired answers. Third, the query is sent to the supernode that may have the desired answers, and the supernode will use its directory of all its client peers to answer the query. Last, the IP address of the client peer having the desired answers is returned to the query peer and the query peer will exchange resources with that peer.

From the above description, the detailed network structure among supernodes is not given. This reason is that either unstructured or structured network overlay can be used for the supernodes network. For example, Edutella uses HyperCuP as its supernodes network, while KaZaA organizes its supernodes arbitrarily. Another point we should notice is that the selection strategies of the supernodes, i.e., which peers can be selected out as supernodes for the remainder peers. There are two ways to address this problem: static and dynamic. As for a static superpeer selection, once a peer is chosen as supernode, its role will not change any more. As for a dynamic supernode selection, a few of heuristics are used, such as, sufficient online duration, sufficient bandwidth, free of firewall and so on. In this section, we do not touch this topic.

In what follows, we discuss three typical hybrid P2P systems with different design philosophy. The first one is Edutella, which is a RDF- and Schema-based P2P system and its supernode network is organized as a HyperCuP. The second one is Ultrapeers, which aims at solving the scalability of the original Gnutella network by using supernodes. The last one is built upon the well-known Chord network and all supernodes are also organized as another ring in the center of the whole network.

3.4.1.1 Edutella

Edutella [228, 229] is a RDF and Schema-based P2P system based on JXTA [10] project. All educational organizations in the Edutella network publish their information and resources (including documents, papers, and videos) via their defined RDF

Fig. 3.21 The Edutella network structure. Query routing in Edutella is first directed to superpeers in HyperCuP, where suffix-based routing scheme could be employed

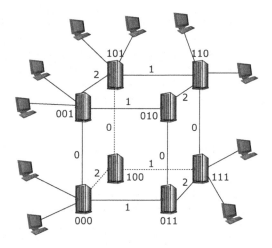

schema. As such, all organizations can use the standard query language RDF-QEL-i to find their desired resources and process raw materials for their further purposes.

The core Edutella network is a HyperCuP [286] network that is composed of superpeers. All common peers will select one of superpeers as their access point for the whole network. In order to route queries on behalf of client peers, each superpeer is also responsible for indexing its client peers' RDF schemes, which is defined as *superpeer-peer routing indices*. To route queries among superpeers, all superpeers then exchange these indexed RDF schemes to build a high level index, which is defined as *superpeer-superpeer routing indices*.

Based on the above statement, the Edutella supports three types of query routing schemes: semantic-free, semantic-based, and broadcast. As for scheme-free routing scheme, the HyperCuP structure is used for routing user queries. For example, Fig. 3.21 shows a typical Edutella network with 8 superpeers that construct a Hyper-CuP network. To route a user query with a specific identifier, the query peer needs only send the query to its superpeer, and then the superpeer will be responsible for routing the query to the desired superpeer in terms of the query identifier. For example, if a superpeer "000" wants to locate a superpeer with identifier "101", it relays the query to its neighbor "001" and then the superpeer "001" relays the query to the destination "101".

As for the semantic-based query routing scheme, both superpeer-peer and superpeer-superpeer routing indices will be used. In this case, the query peer will send its query to its superpeer, then the superpeer searches both routing indices to determine which directions the query should be forwarded to. Note that in this case, the RDF schemes in the routing indices are used to decide the direction of query traversal, and hence we refer this scheme as semantic-based query routing.

Last, different from the query flooding in unstructured P2P networks, broadcast in the Edutella network only involves $N - 1$ messages, where N is the number of superpeers. The broadcast algorithm works as follows: Each link between superpeers is tagged with the dimension. A node can broadcast the query message to all its neighboring superpeers and each broadcasting message is tagged with the label of the link, along which the message is traversed. Any node receiving the broadcasting message only forwards the query message to its neighboring superpeers whose links' label values are greater than the current one. For example, if the superpeer "000" broadcasts a message, then the broadcast paths are $000 \rightarrow 011 \rightarrow 111$, $000 \rightarrow 001 \rightarrow 101$, $000 \rightarrow 100$ and $000 \rightarrow 001 \rightarrow 010 \rightarrow 110$. Another advantage of this scheme is that the last nodes are reached after $\log N$ forwarding steps.

3.4.1.2 Ultrapeers

The original Gnutella [133] blindly floods user queries in the whole network for desired answers. Though this search scheme is efficient in terms of query response time, it wastes a lot of valuable bandwidth at peers. Hence, the scalability is problematic. Further, the lack of considering heterogeneity of peers aggravates this problem. To alleviate this problem, Anurag et al. [295] have proposed a method by splitting the peers into two levels by taking peers' capabilities into account. The peers, named ultrapeers, in the high level have faster computational and bandwidth resources and storage capacity. The peers, named leaf peers, in the low level are thought of as equal capability. For example, Fig. 3.22 shows a typical hybrid network with ultrapeers, where ultrapeers lie in the center of the network and leaf peers are around ultrapeers.

In the ultrapeer network, all ultrapeers form an unstructured P2P network. To locate desired resources, a leaf peer should send a search query to its ultrapeer. The ultrapeer will propagate the query to all neighboring ultrapeers and each neighboring ultrapeer then propagates the query to its neighboring ultrapeers and so on. Once receiving the query, the ultrapeer will search the query with its reflector indexing to locate which leaf peer has the desired resources. If a leaf peer is found, then the IP address of the leaf peer will be returned to the query peer. Here, we notice the concept of "reflector indexing", which is a kind of index for meta data of shared

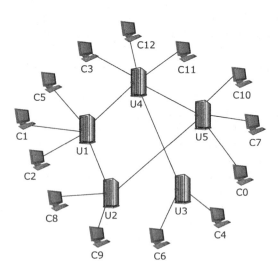

Fig. 3.22 The modified Gnutella network with ultrapeers. Suppose that the resources requested by peer C12 is at the peer C9. The peer C12 first requests its ultrapeer U4, then U4 floods the query to U2 via U1. U1 searches its reflector index and finds C9 has the desired answers, then it sends the IP address of C9 back to C12

files of its leaf peers. That is, when a leaf peer joins the network, it first chooses a ultrapeer and then sends all metadata of its shared files to its ultrapeer. The ultrapeer will construct an index (similar to Napster) according to these meta data of its leaf peers, in order to facilitate resource location.

3.4.1.3 Structured Superpeers

Structured superpeers [224] combines the well-known Chord protocol and the concept of supernodes together to design a constant-time lookup P2P system. Structured superpeer network considers the heterogeneity and chooses k most powerful peers as superpeers to speed up query routing (to some extent, the concept of superpeer here is similar to the concept of ultrapeer mentioned in the previous subsection). As such, given an N peers Chord network, there are k superpeers at the center of the network and the left $N - k$ peers form a Chord ring. Figure 3.23 shows a typical structured superpeer network with 13 peers, where 4 superpeers form an "inner-ring" and the other 9 peers form an "outer-ring".

Each common peer maintains its predecessor and successor, which are the same as those of Chord protocol. Each superpeer also keeps its successors, which refers to the first peer within the range that the superpeer controls. For example, peers P1 and P5 are the successor of the superpeers S0 and S1 respectively and each common peer maintains a pointer to its superpeer and each superpeer maintains a superpeer table that records the range partition of all superpeers. These invariants are maintained by superpeers and common peers respectively in terms of node arrival, departure and failure.

To locate the peer with a specific key, the query peer first requests its superpeer and the superpeer checks whether the key falls into its own range. If so, the query peer will use the Chord protocol to locate the peer. Otherwise, the lookup key will be forwarded to the superpeer whose range contains the key, by using the super-peer table. Last, the superpeer sends the lookup query to its successor and then the successor uses the Chord protocol to locate the desired peer.

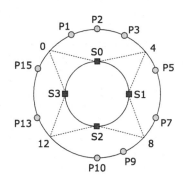

Fig. 3.23 The structured superpeers. The superpeers S0, S1, S2, and S3 control ranges (0,4], (4,8], (8,12], and (12,0], respectively. If the peer P1 requests $key = 10$, it first sends the lookup key to S0. S0 relays the key to S2 since S2 controls the range of (8,12] that contains 10. Last, S2 passes the key to its successor P9 and then P9 uses Chord protocol to locate P10

3.5 Summary

In this chapter, we only focus on the typical routing protocols of current P2P systems. We do not emphasize on the properties of these P2P systems because the other chapters (e.g., Chap. 2) also refer to the related content of these P2P systems. From the perspective of network structure, we classify the typical routing protocols into three types: unstructured, structured, and hybrid.

In unstructured P2P networks, there is no global control on both network overlay (i.e., neighborhood among peers) and data placement. As such, the maintenance of network overlay is simple and easy since each peer only needs to update its routing table by adding new neighbors and/or removing offline peers. This type of P2P systems is very suitable for the transient Internet users to share content with each other. However, the flexibility of unstructured P2P systems brings inconvenience of locating desired resources in such a dynamic environment. That is, since every peer has no global knowledge of data placement, locating desired resources becomes a big problem. To solve this problem, academic community has invented dozens of heuristics to facilitate the resource location in order to make such P2P systems more scalable in terms of bandwidth consumption during query traversal among peers.

On the contrary, structured P2P systems make a tight control on both network structure and data placement. In this way, peers cannot share arbitrary data objects as they like, but have to store the predetermined data objects according to the global knowledge. The advantage of structured systems is that they provide a simple and efficient way to locate the peers with desired answers within a theoretical bound. In general, there are three categories of structured P2P systems: distributed hash table (DHT) based systems, skip list based systems and tree based systems. While systems in the first category can only support exact match queries well, systems in the two remaining categories can support both exact match and range queries. However, by employing DHT, systems in the first category are better than those in other categories in terms of load balancing. The disadvantage of structured P2P systems is that they incur high cost in maintaining routing tables.

The hybrid P2P systems take advantages of both structured P2P systems and unstructured ones. On the one side, the hybrid P2P systems locate desired resources more efficiently than those used by unstructured P2P systems, which makes them more scalable than before. On the other side, the hybrid P2P systems loose the control of data placement and network structure compared with structured P2P systems, which makes them more adaptive to real applications. Furthermore, with the help of both agent technology and network reconfiguration, the performance of hybrid P2P systems can be improved greatly and the network resources (e.g., bandwidth and computational resources) can be made better use of.

We can observe a common idea in all the routing methods across different types of peer-to-peer networks: an attempt to "jump" as much as possible and as long as you can, and then go with finer steps towards the exact destination. This is explicit in some routing methods, like the one used in Chord (i.e., use the furthest pointer that does not overshoot the target), or it is one way in which we can see others. For instance, we might consider the prefix-based routing in Pastry as a version of the traditional phone number resolution: the first few digits give you a country code—so

you have the largest "jump" resolving those, then an area code—a smaller "jump"
and so on. The same point of view may be taken in the case of hybrid P2P systems: a regular peer contacts a super-peer, which then contacts another super-peer.
This higher level can be regarded as a way to by-pass large areas of the [virtual]
space. Translated into graph theory, maintaining these sets of "hyper-jumps", either
in structure or hybrid networks, means maintaining a low diameter of the underlying graph. For unstructured networks, the underlying graph may be thought of being
that of a random graph.[1] In this case, the diameter is statistically low. In conclusion,
we summarize features of existing routing methods employed in P2P systems in
Table 3.1.

Table 3.1 Summary of existing routing methods in P2P systems

System	Overlay network	Routing table	Routing method
Gnutella	Unstructured, Random topology	Random neighbors	Breadth First Search with Time-to-Live
FreeNet	Unstructured, Random topology	Random neighbors	Depth First Search with Time-to-Live
Chord	Structured, Ring topology	Neighbors at distances 2^i in the ring	Repeatedly jump to the farthest node in the routing table whose id is still less than the search key
CAN	Structured, Mesh topology	Neighbors at adjacent positions in the mesh	Repeatedly travel through the neighbor that is closer to the destination
Pastry & Tapestry	Structured, PRR tree topology	Neighbors sharing common prefix identifier at different levels	Repeatedly forward the message to the neighbor having the longest matching prefix identifier
Viceroy	Structured, butterfly topology	Five neighbors: one at the upper level, two at the lower level, and two at the same level	Three steps: going up, going down, and vicinity search
Crescendo	Structured, hierarchical ring topology	Chord-like neighbors at different ring levels	A combination of Chord-like routing and the routing between rings at different levels

---

[1]Though in general that is not the case: it has been shown that unstructured networks more often
have a "small worlds" structure, where highly connected subgraphs are sparsely interconnected.

Table 3.1 (continued)

System	Overlay network	Routing table	Routing method
Skip Graph	Structured, multiple linked lists topology	Neighbors sharing common prefix membership vector at different lengths	Travel from the highest to the lowest level of the list. At each level, jump to the neighbor closer to the destination if such a neighbor exists
SkipNet	Structured, hierarchical ring topology	Neighbors are predecessors and successors at different ring levels	Skip Graph-like routing, traveling from the highest to the lowest level of the ring.
P-Grid	Structured, binary tree topology	A neighbor at the other side of the tree rooted at each internal node from the root to the leaf	Travel from the root to the leaf. At each level, jump to the neighbor closer to the destination
P-Tree	Structured, a combination of a B^+-Tree and a Chord ring topology	Neighbors are nodes in the left-most root-to-leaf path of the B^+-Tree	Travel from the root to the leaf. At each level, jump to the neighbor closer to the destination
BATON	Structured, balanced tree topology	Neighbors are parent, children and Chord-like neighbors at the same level	If not having full routing tables, go to parent. Otherwise, go to the neighbor or the child closer to the destination
Edutella & Ultrapeers	Hybrid, a combination of structured and unstructured topology	Neighbors exist only at superpeer level. At client side, each client peer connects to a superpeer	A client peer always routes its requests to its superpeer while routing at supper peer level depends on the topology employed at that level

Chapter 4
Data-Centric Applications

In this chapter, we discuss different types of data sharing applications that run on P2P networks. The basic and most popular data sharing applications are file sharing applications. This type of applications enables users to find and download files shared by other users in the network. There have been numerous commercialized P2P systems supporting file sharing over the Internet such as Morpheus, Kazaa, Gnutella, and BitTorrent. In these systems, various files (textual documents, movies, songs, etc.) are shared as a whole and the typical type of queries is to look up files in the network based on their names (i.e., given the name of a file, the systems find the peer nodes storing the file). The challenge of processing these type of queries is just on how to locate the queried files. This is actually the problem of how to route queries from the source node to the destination node, which has been discussed in Chap. 3. However, since people may want to issue queries at finer granularities, a bigger challenge in query processing is to look up files based on file description or file content (content-based search).

In file sharing applications, files are often described by a set of attributes. The challenge for supporting search on file description is actually the problem of how to index file attributes and process queries from these indices. A straight-forward solution to this problem is to use multiple indices for a file; each index is for a descriptive attribute. In other words, the system indexes each descriptive attribute independently. As a result, queries can be processed from indices of any attribute. Alternatively, the challenge of supporting search on file description can be considered as a problem of supporting search in multi-dimensional space if we consider each descriptive attribute as a dimension in a multi-dimensional space. In Sect. 4.1, we will present solutions for both of these approaches. Additionally, we will also discuss skyline query, a related type of queries in multi-dimensional space, and its solutions in P2P systems.

In general, the challenge for supporting content-based search is the problem of either textual information retrieval (for textual files) or multimedia information retrieval (for multimedia files). Textual information retrieval focuses on the problem of keyword search in textual files. For example, given a keyword, a set of keywords or even a whole sentence, the system needs to find nodes storing the file having queried

Q.H. Vu et al., *Peer-to-Peer Computing*,
DOI 10.1007/978-3-642-03514-2_4, © Springer-Verlag Berlin Heidelberg 2010

keyword(s) or sentence. Multimedia information retrieval deals with the problem of similarity search in multimedia files, i.e., given an image/song/movie, the system needs to find nodes storing the image/song/movie or similar images/songs/movies. A basic solution for content-based search is to consider it as a search in multi-dimensional space in which the content of each file is summarized as a feature vector in the space. However, the dimensionality of feature vectors is often very high, and it is a challenge is how to index data in high-dimensional space efficiently. Section 4.2 discusses solutions for this challenge. Additionally, we dedicate Sect. 4.3 to address a different class of techniques for textual information retrieval.

In addition to unstructured data, there is also a need to share structured data, such as relational databases or semi-structured data such as XML documents, in P2P networks. Supporting structured data sharing applications poses more difficulties than supporting the previous type of applications because there often exist plenty of structural and data heterogeneities among data sources residing at different, autonomous peers. Although the problem of data or schema mapping is not new, the decentralization and dynamism requirements of P2P paradigm make it especially tough, and consequently traditional approaches cannot be directly applied. In Sect. 4.4, we will describe current state-of-the-art techniques for modeling and building schema mappings between the databases shared by different peers. After that, we will present various query processing methods for both keyword queries and structured queries by exploiting the built schema mappings.

4.1 Multi-Dimensional Data Sharing

While most existing file sharing P2P systems can only support queries on file titles, it is desirable to support queries on file descriptions. To explain why this desire exists, let us consider an example of a music file sharing system where a song file may contain description about the title of the song, the singer performing the song and the album of the song. Since different people may name the same file with different names while the file description remains relatively similar, a search on the file description can return a better result than a search on the file title. Additionally, compared to file title, file description contains more information and describes the content of file better. Intuitively, we can support search on file description by two basic approaches. On the one hand, we index values of each descriptive attribute to the overlay P2P network separately and process queries from indices of any attribute (multi-attribute index based approach). On the other hand, we consider each descriptive attribute as a dimension in a multi-dimensional space and process queries as multi-dimensional queries in this multi-dimensional space (multi-dimensional index based approach). In the subsequent subsections, we will present how to support multi-dimensional index and multi-attribute index in P2P networks.

– Multi-dimensional index: CAN [266], which has been discussed in the previous chapter, can be considered as the first P2P system supporting multi-dimensional index, although the original intention of the system is to hash data uniformly into multi-dimensional space such that a certain degree of fault tolerance can be guaranteed. Even though CAN can support multi-dimensional point queries well, by employing uniform hashing, CAN cannot support multi-dimensional range query. Being a structure that resembles the kd-tree [42] and grid-file [156], CAN can be used to directly index multi-dimensional data in its natural space. Following CAN, subsequent systems also adapt traditional multi-dimensional index tree structures such as the R-Tree [145], X-Tree [44], or M-Tree [77] to support multi-dimensional index. In particular, Skip Index [348] utilizes the kd-tree [42] to partition the data space, and then maps the data space into Skip Graph overlay network by encoding it into a unique key. The P2PR-Tree [225] proposes a tree structure, which integrates the R-Tree. The VBI-Tree [167] and DP-Tree [192] are designed as frameworks that can employ different types of index structures such as the R-Tree, X-Tree, M-Tree and their variants. In employing tree structures in P2P systems, it is important to avoid the potential bottleneck occurred at the root or nodes near the root. The basic solution used by these systems is to assign each peer node to a leaf node and let the leaf node keep information about all internal nodes from itself to the root for routing purpose. To some extent, this technique is similar to the technique used by the P-Tree [86], which was discussed in the previous chapter.

- Multi-attribute index: MAAN (Multi-Attribute Addressable Network [61]) supports multi-attribute index simply by indexing all attributes to a Chord [173] ring. This means that given a data item having m attributes, the system simply creates m indices corresponding to values of these attributes. To process a query, the system needs to choose a *dominate attribute* of the query and processes the query based on constraints on that attribute. For constraints of other attributes, they are still carried along query processing, but they are only used for filtering purpose. Different from MAAN, where the same Chord ring is used to index all attributes, in Mercury [49], each attribute is indexed to a separate Chord ring called a routing hub. In this way, a data item needs to be sent to all routing hubs for indexing while a query is always forwarded to the routing hub corresponding to its *dominate attribute* for processing.

To enhance the quality of retrieval, data may be retrieved based on ratings provided by other users. Such features are common in social network and community based systems. For example, in addition to maintaining descriptive information of the file content, a description of a song file may contain information about ratings of the song in different aspects from listeners. In this case, users may be interested in searching for songs, which are not "dominated" by any song. A song is dominated by another song if it is not better than that song in any aspect. This special type of queries is called skyline query. To support skyline queries in P2P systems, SkyPeer [323], a super-peer based P2P network, proposes that subspace skyline queries can be effectively answered by storing and scanning the super-set of skyline whose attribute set is the super-set of all subspace skylines. The system uses a threshold based algorithm to optimize local skyline computation at peers and reduce the amount of unnecessary data transmitting on the network. Alternatively,

DSL [337] parallelizes the search for skyline and progressively returns skyline answers by enforcing a partial order on query propagation based on CAN. In this way, the succeeding nodes have to wait for preceding nodes' completion to start their computation. As a result, it slows down the query response time. Furthermore, since the query search boundary is not refined, DLS incurs unnecessary return overhead. To alleviate these problems, SSP [329] proposes a solution where the search space is first defined at the most dominant node whose local results are guaranteed to be in the final skyline. After that, in each processing step, the system partitions the search space into subspaces adaptively. These subspaces are then searched in parallel.

In the next part, we will present concrete systems supporting multi-dimensional index (VBI-Tree [167]), multi-attribute index (Mercury [49]), and skyline queries (SSP [329]).

4.1.1 VBI-Tree

VBI-Tree [167] is a framework that can adapt different types of multi-dimensional index tree structures including R-Tree, X-Tree, SS-Tree, M-Tree, and their variants. The system is based on a binary tree structure where each peer manages a pair of adjacent tree nodes: one leaf node and one internal node (the leaf node is the left adjacent node of the internal node in the in-order traversal of the tree). The leaf node is a data node that is in charge of holding indices of data belonging to a specific multi-dimensional region. The internal node is a routing node that has associated a region that covers all regions managed by its children. For routing purpose, in addition to parent and child links, the internal node also keeps links to other nodes in the tree structure. In general, each internal routing node has five types of links.

- Parent link: pointing to the parent node of the internal node.
- Child links: pointing to child nodes of the internal node.
- Adjacent links: pointing to adjacent nodes of the internal node in the in-order traversal of the tree.
- Neighbor links: pointing to neighbor nodes at the same level having distances 2^i from the internal node in both left and right directions.
- Upside links: pointing to ancestor nodes of the internal node in the tree.

Note that these links maintain not only pointers to destination nodes but also information about multi-dimensional regions covered by these nodes. An example of a VBI-Tree is shown in Fig. 4.1 where nodes with the same name are maintained at the same peer. Based on this tree structure, when a peer issues or receives a query, it checks if the region in charged by its corresponding routing node n intersects with the searched region. If this is true, the peer checks child links of n and forwards the query to n's children that are in charge of regions intersecting with the searched region. Additionally, n finds the nearest ancestor a that is in charge of a region that totally covers the searched region. If such an ancestor a exists, for each ancestor a' in the path from n to a (including a), n forwards the query to a neighbor node

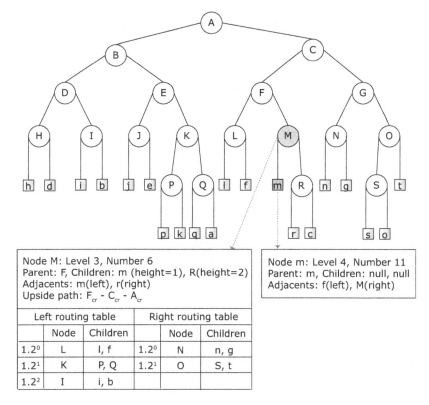

Fig. 4.1 VBI-Tree structure

that is in the other side of the tree rooted at a'. In this way, VBI-Tree can search all nodes whose region intersects with the searched region without causing bottle neck at the root or nodes near the root. Algorithm 9 displays the basic search algorithm of VBI-Tree. It is important to mention that (1) to avoid search loop, the system keeps track the search path and (2) to avoid frequently update of upside links due to changes in covered regions at ancestor nodes, VBI-Tree proposes a new concept of *discrete data*. Discrete data are data that are stored at internal nodes and do not fall into any regions covered by children of internal nodes.

For example, assume that node H wants to search data in the shaded region as in Fig. 4.2. At first, H executes the query locally since the region it is in charge of intersects with the searched region. After that, H tries to forward the query to other nodes. Since the nearest ancestor of H, which is in charge of a region totally covering the searched region, is A, H needs to forward the query to all nodes in the other side of the tree rooted at D, B, and A, i.e., I, e, and J. However, H actually forwards the query to only I and J. In the case of node e, since it is not a routing node, H just forwards the query to its parent D. Thereafter, D forwards the query to E, J forwards the query to G though F. Finally, at destination nodes I, E, and G, the query is forwarded to data nodes b, a and l. Furthermore, since discrete data

---

Algorithm 9 : VBI_Search(Node n, Region r)

 1: **if** n.region intersects r **then**
 2:   **if** n has no children **then**
 3:     result $=$ Local_Search(r)
 4:     **return** result to the query issuer node
 5:   **else** {n has children and hence it is a routing node}
 6:     **if** n.left_child.region intersects r **then**
 7:       VBI_Search(n.left_child, r)
 8:     **end if**
 9:     **if** n.right_child.region intersects r **then**
10:       VBI_Search(n.right_child, r)
11:     **end if**
12:   **end if**
13: **end if**
14: find the nearest ancestor a of n whose region totally covers r
15: **for** each ancestor a' of n in the path from n to a **do**
16:   let n' be a neighbor node in the other side of the tree rooted at a'
17:   VBI_Search(n', r)
18: **end for**

---

may exist at internal nodes, nodes E and J also forward the query to routing nodes B, C for discrete data search.

We observe that even though discrete data is introduced as a solution to reduce the cost of updating upside links, this cost is still high in dynamic systems where data is frequently inserted or deleted. Furthermore, while the bottom-up search strategy helps to avoid the potential bottle neck problem at high level nodes, it incurs a high cost in query processing since the system always needs to check a large number of leaf nodes once the searched region intersects with a region covered by a high level node.

4.1.2 Mercury

To support multi-attribute index, Mercury [49] distributes nodes in the system into hubs each of which is in charge of indexing data values for an attribute. Each peer joining in the system participates in one or more hubs. Nodes in a hub are arranged in a circular form, which is similar to Chord [173]. However, instead of setting neighbor links of a node to nodes at distance 2^i as in Chord, Mercury nodes set up neighbor links in their routing table by using a harmonic probability distribution function. Additionally, for routing purpose among hubs, each node in a hub needs to hold an cross-hub link to a node in each of remaining hubs. In other words, a node in Mercury maintains two types of links.

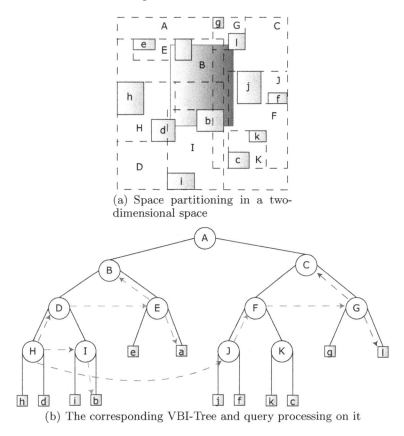

(a) Space partitioning in a two-dimensional space

(b) The corresponding VBI-Tree and query processing on it

Fig. 4.2 Query processing in VBI-Tree

— Intra-hub links: connecting to nodes in the same hub.
— Cross-hub links: connecting to nodes in different hubs.

In Mercury, when a data item is inserted to the network, for each attribute a of the item, its attribute value is indexed to the hub H_a. As an example in Fig. 4.3, the data item ($x = 160$, $y = 80$, $z = 470$) is inserted to three hubs H_x, H_y and H_z at corresponding nodes C, F and L. Mercury processes query by selecting an attribute as the dominant attribute and executes the query on the hub correspondent to the dominant attribute. Since every node of a hub has links to nodes in all other hubs, it takes only one step to forward the query to the hub in charge of the dominant attribute. After that, the query is executed locally within the hub according to the search algorithm of the Chord ring. As in Fig. 4.3, query q involves three attributes x, y, and z. However, only the hub H_x correspondent to the attribute x executes the query. In this case, the conditions on attributes y and z are used to filter results found on H_x. It is important to note that in this method the selection of the dominant attribute affects to the performance of query processing. If the search on dominant

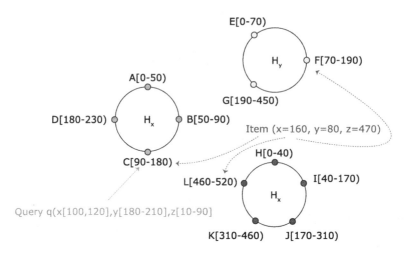

Fig. 4.3 Mercury

attribute produces a lot of results, the system performance degrades significantly.
Therefore, it is important to choose the dominant attribute wisely.

The disadvantage of Mercury is that it incurs a high cost in data insertion and
deletion especially when the number of index attributes is big. It is because when a
new data item is added to the system, it is inserted to all hubs corresponding to index
attributes. Similarly, when an existing data item is deleted, all hubs are checked to
delete the corresponding data item.

4.1.3 SSP

Skyline Space Partitioning, SSP [329], is a method for supporting skyline queries
over P2P networks. The basic idea of this method is to partition the multi-
dimensional space into multi-dimensional regions each of which is in charge by
a peer node. Peer nodes in the system are arranged in BATON [166], a P2P system supporting one-dimensional index, according to the positions of their covered
regions ordered by the z-curve method. For routing purpose, in addition to information of links to other nodes in BATON, each node also needs to maintain information
of the region it is in charge of. This information includes:

– Region Number: a 0–1 string that identifies the position of the region in the z-
  curve order.
– Data range: the range of values covered by the region.
– Split history: a list of entries of split value and dimension from the start to the
  creation of the region.
– Next partition dimension: the next dimension that will be split when the region
  is partitioned.

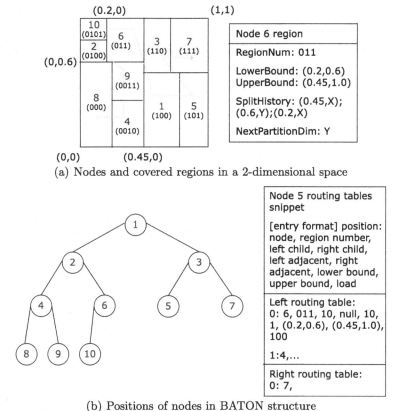

(a) Nodes and covered regions in a 2-dimensional space

(b) Positions of nodes in BATON structure

Fig. 4.4 Mapping nodes on BATON

An example of a system with 10 nodes using SSP method is shown in Fig. 4.4. In this figure, we can realize that the in-order traversal of the tree structure is corresponding to the z-curve order of regions in the multi-dimensional space.

In SSP, a skyline query is processed in four steps.

– At first, the system finds the node whose local results are guaranteed to be in the final skyline. This node can be found by searching the most dominating point that dominates all other points in the data space such as points (0.0, 0.0), (1.0, 0.0), (0.0, 1.0), or (1.0, 1.0) in a two-dimensional space. Let this node be the STARTER node.
– Once the STARTER node is reached, it computes local skyline results and selects the most dominating point p_{md} that has the largest dominating region. The skyline search space is then determined by pruning the region that is dominated by p_{md}.
– After that, the STARTER node routes the query to nodes covering the search region. These nodes compute their local skyline points and return the result to the query initiator.

- Finally, the query initiator computes global skyline points from the local skylines points had been returned.

A weakness of SSP is that the query processing speed depends much on the STARTER node. As a result, when the STARTER node has not been reached or p_{md} has not been found, any bad thing happening at the STARTER node will decrease the speed of query processing.

4.2 High-Dimensional Indexing

File description can provide some information of the file content. However, it cannot completely represent the file content. As a result, it is still desirable to provide a search at a finer granularity: content-based search. As discussed before, the general solution to support content-based search is to construct feature vectors for sharing files and index these vectors to the system. However, since the dimensionality of feature vectors is often very high, conventional multi-dimensional index structures such as the R-Tree [145] may not be efficient due to high overlap of boxes in high-dimensional spaces. Consequently, new mechanisms have been proposed for indexing high-dimensional space data, and they can be broadly classified into three categories: mapping-based approach, distance-based approach, and hashing-based approach.

- In mapping-based approach, high-dimensional objects are mapped to a lower dimensional space (usually one-dimensional space) before being indexed. Multi-dimensional queries are also transformed to this space for processing. In particular, many systems [29, 190, 287, 293] use space filling curves (SFC) [278] such as Hilbert curve or Z-curve (Z-order) to map multi-dimensional data to one-dimensional data. After that, an overlay network supporting single-dimensional query search is used to index that one dimensional data. For example, CISS [190] and the work of Schmidt and Parashar [287] share the same idea of using Hilbert curve to convert data in a multi-dimensional data space to a single-dimensional value, and then index the resulted values on a Chord ring while ZNet [293] uses Z-curve as the mapping method and Skip Graph as the overlay network. Besides SFC, other solutions such as Pyramid [43] and iMinMax [245] can also be used to map multi-dimensional data into one-dimensional data for indexing and can also be adapted for P2P systems.
- Different from mapping-based approach, distance-based approaches such as the VP-tree [345] and iDistance [165] index high-dimensional objects directly to the system based on their distances to a predefined set of points called reference points where each point has a unique index value. The index value of an object is calculated as the summation of the distance between the object and the nearest reference point and the index value of that reference point. As discussed in iDistance, the system can choose reference objects in different ways either uniformly or accordingly to data distribution. Examples of P2P systems employing this index approach are mChord [240] and SimPeer [112].

– In cases where a system can suffer a small error rate of the search results, it can apply locality-sensitive hashing (LSH) scheme [160] for indexing data objects. The basic idea of this hashing-based approach is to hash similar objects to the same place (index bucket). In this manner, a search query can be processed by searching indices around its hashing value. Even though this approach cannot always return the exact search results, the error rate of search results is guaranteed to be within a predefined ϵ value. LHS Forest [39] is a P2P system applying this approach.

In general, P2P systems can apply techniques that have been well studied in centralized systems, to support high-dimensional data indexing. The systems, however, need to adapt these techniques to suit the properties of distributed P2P environment. For example, a typical centralized algorithm to process a kNN query is to first estimate an initial radius for a range query. The system then executes the range query to find results. If there are not enough k objects in the returned results, the system iteratively increases the radius of the range query and re-executes the query. This process stops when at least k objects are returned from the query. The final k nearest objects are selected from these results. Nevertheless, this algorithm cannot be applied directly in P2P systems because it incurs a high cost in query processing due to high number of query messages (this problem does not happen in centralized systems where the search process is done locally at a computer). In other words, this kNN algorithm should be modified for P2P environment. In the following subsections, we will introduce five P2P systems supporting high-dimensional indexing, namely CISS [190], ZNet [293], mChord [240], SimPeer [112], and LHS Forest [39].

4.2.1 CISS

To support high-dimensional indexing, CISS [190] employs the idea of using Hilbert Space Filling Curve (SFC) [278] to map data points in a multi-dimensional space to data points in a single-dimensional space, and then index these one-dimensional data points in Chord [173]. The system first encodes each dimension value to a set of bit keys, and a multi-dimensional data point is represented by sets of bit keys. The system then uses Hilbert SFC to convert these sets of bit keys to a single key value. Finally, the system indexes this single key value to Chord. An example of the conversion process is shown in Fig. 4.5(a). This example shows a two-dimensional system where each dimension is encoded by three bits. Using Hilbert SFC, the point in the shaded region is converted to a single value 33. The point is then indexed to the Chord node identifier 40.

To process a query, the system first needs to convert the multi-dimensional searched value to a one-dimensional value. After that, this one-dimensional value is searched from indices in Chord. Note that since there are some regions in the Hilbert Space where nearby points are not mapped to nearby values in one-dimensional space, a multi-dimensional query may be converted to one or more segments of

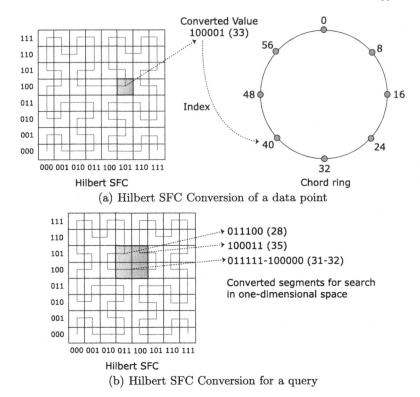

Fig. 4.5 CISS

values in one-dimensional space. As an example, Fig. 4.5(b) shows a query corresponding to the shaded region in the Hilbert space. This query is converted to three different search segments in the one-dimensional index space. This is indeed a common problem with the use of curves in data mapping. In particular, the higher the dimension is, the higher the possibility of having more search segments in query processing is and hence the higher the cost of query processing is.

4.2.2 ZNet

To map multi-dimensional data to one-dimensional data, instead of using Hilbert curve as in CISS [190], ZNet [293] employs Z-curve. In this system, the whole data space is recursively partitioned in a quad-tree like manner to subspaces, each of which is assigned a unique address corresponding to its position in the Z-curve ordering and the level of subspace partitioning. Each node in the system is in charge of a subspace and indices of data belonging to the subspace. The system arranges nodes in a Skip Graph structure where the position of a node is determined by the address of the subspace it is maintaining. In other words, the position of a node

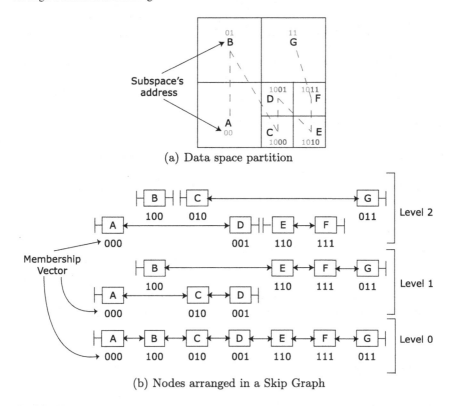

(a) Data space partition

(b) Nodes arranged in a Skip Graph

Fig. 4.6 ZNet

in a Skip Graph structure is determined by the position of its holding subspace in the Z-curve ordering. An example of ZNet structure is shown in Fig. 4.6, where the partition of the data space is displayed in Fig. 4.6(a) and the positions of ZNet nodes in a Skip Graph structure are displayed in Fig. 4.6(b).

When a node issues or receives a query from another node, it needs to find the address of the subspace containing the search data and forwards the query towards the node maintaining that subspace. Even though in some cases a node may not be able to fully resolve the address of the destination subspace due to incomplete knowledge about space partitioning, it is still able to know the prefix of the address. In these cases, the node forwards the query to a neighbor node maintaining a subspace closer to the destination subspace. This node should be able to further resolve the address of the destination subspace. As a result, the address of the destination subspace will be refined after each routing step. Algorithm 10 illustrates the search algorithm of ZNet. As an example, assume that node A wants to look up a data belonging to the subspace maintained by node F in Fig. 4.6. Since A only knows that the address's prefix of the destination subspace is 01, it forwards the query to either C or D (assume that D is chosen). Since D maintains a subspace that is partitioned in the same level with the destination subspace, it should be able to fully resolve the address of the destination subspace, which is 0111. As a result, D simply forwards

---

Algorithm 10 : ZNet_Search(Node n, Search_Space s)

  1: **if** n.subspace covers s **then**
  2:     result $=$ Local_Search(r)
  3:     **return** result to the query issuer node
  4: **else**
  5:     resolve the address a of the destination search space
  6:     **if** a can be fully resolved **then**
  7:         let n' be a neighbor node whose subspace is closer to a
  8:         ZNet_Search(n', s)
  9:     **else** {a cannot be fully resolved}
 10:         compute the longest prefix address l of a
 11:         let n' be a neighbor node whose subspace is closer to l
 12:         ZNet_Search(n', s)
 13:     **end if**
 14: **end if**

---

the query to E, which is a closer node to the destination node. Finally, E forwards the query to F, the destination node.

4.2.3 M-Chord

M-Chord [240] is a P2P system supporting similarity search in high-dimensional metric spaces. The system is built on top of the Chord [173] overlay network. M-Chord employs two steps to index multi-dimensional data.

1. The system uses iDistance [165], a distance-based method, to map high-dimensional data to one-dimensional data. The basic idea of iDistance is to use a set of globally known reference points to divide the entire data space into partitions and index data by the distance between them and their nearest partition/reference point.
2. The one-dimensional value returned in the first step is indexed to the Chord ring.

In particular, based on iDistance method, the system needs to pre-partition the data space into a set of partitions $S = \{P_1, P_2, \ldots P_n\}$. Each partition P_i is represented by a reference point O_i and a radius r_i. A constant c is selected so that each partition $P_i(O_i, r_i)$ is mapped to a nonoverlapping range of values $[i \cdot c, i \cdot c + r_i]$ ($key_{O_i} = i \cdot c$ is the one-dimensional mapping value of O_i). When a data object D is indexed to the system, M-Chord first finds the nearest reference point O_j to the data object. The index value of D is then computed as $j \cdot c + dist(D, O_j)$, where $dist(D, O_j)$ is the distance between D and O_j. Finally, this one-dimensional index value is inserted to the Chord ring. For example, as in Fig. 4.7, the index value of data object A, whose nearest reference point is O_i, is $key_A = i \cdot c + d_1$, where d_1 is the distance between A and O_i. Similarly, the index value of data object B is

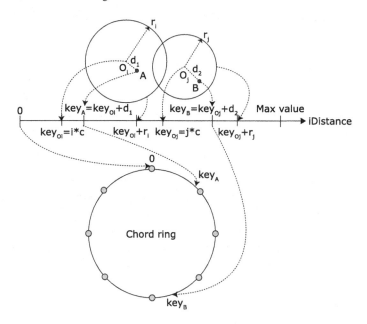

Fig. 4.7 M-Chord

$key_B = j \cdot c + d_2$. These two index values, key_A and key_B, are inserted to corresponding positions in the Chord ring.

To process a range query $Q_R(o, r)$, where o and r are the center and the radius of the search region, M-Chord follows the algorithm of iDistance. At first, the system determines partitions that intersect with the search region. After that, for each intersecting partition $P_i(O_i, r_i)$, the system creates a one-dimensional range query $q[key_{O_i} + dist(O_i, o) - r, max(key_{O_i} + dist(O_i, o) + r, key_{O_i} + r_i)]$ and sends the query to the Chord ring for execution. Finally, the results returned from executing one-dimensional range queries are filtered to retrieve final results.

To process a kNN query $Q_{kNN}(o, k)$ where o and k are the center and the number of wanted nearest objects, the algorithm of iDistance is not suitable for P2P environment because the repeat of executing range queries with increasing of radius incurs a high number of query messages in the system. Instead, M-Chord employs a different algorithm that aims to save the network communication cost. This algorithm consists of two steps as follows.

1. The system uses a low-cost heuristic to find k objects that are near o. The maximum distance δ between these k objects and o is computed.
2. The system executes a range query $Q_R(o, \delta)$ and selects the k nearest objects from the returned results.

A weakness of M-Chord is that if the number of objects in the system is large, it incurs a high cost of indexing because the system needs to index objects separately.

4.2.4 SIMPEER

To avoid the high cost of indexing every object, SIMPEER [112] proposes that peers should summarize their objects before indexing and only index these summaries in the system. In this way, the system can significantly reduce the cost of indexing. SIMPEER is a super-peer based system utilizing a three-level index structure as follows:

− At the lowest level, each peer indexes its sharing objects. Additionally, the peer clusters its own objects to create cluster summaries and sends these summaries to the super-peer in charge of it.
− At the super-peer level, on the one hand, each super-peer indexes summary clusters submitted from its client-peers. On the other hand, it clusters these summary clusters to create hyper-clusters and broadcast these hyper-clusters to other super-peers.
− At the highest level, each super peer builds routing indices from its own hyper-clusters and hyper-clusters received from other super-peers.

In this structure, when a peer issues a query, it sends the query to the super-peer that is in charge of it. At the super-peer, based on local indices of summary clusters and hyper-clusters, the query can be forwarded to client-peers who may hold the query results or to other super-peers, which will continue to forward the query to other client-peers. To index summary clusters, SIMPEER generalizes the idea of iDistance [165] for distributed environment. The basic idea of indexing summary clusters using iDistance is to index the clusters based on special points of the clusters. In particular, like iDistance, SIMPEER uses a set of globally known reference points that divide the entire data space into partitions. To index a summary cluster C_x, SIMPEER first assigns this cluster to a partition P_i—the one whose reference point is closest to the center of the cluster. It then maps the *farthest* point of C_x to a one-dimensional index value based on the reference point O_i of partition P_i. To process a range query, for each partition P_i that is formed by a reference point O_i and intersects with the query, SIMPEER has to search from the nearest point of the query to O_i to the boundary of P_i. An example of SIMPEER's range query processing based on iDistance is illustrated in Fig. 4.8.

There are two disadvantages of SIMPEER. First, since the search space of SIMPEER depends on the nearest point of the query to reference points of intersecting partitions, if the nearest point of the query is close to reference points, the system always needs to search a large space no matter how big the query size is. Second, since partitions need to be enlarged to encompass the furthest point (the index) of each cluster, large overlaps among data partitions may be generated, incurring a bigger search space, and hence a higher search cost.

Fig. 4.8 SIMPEER

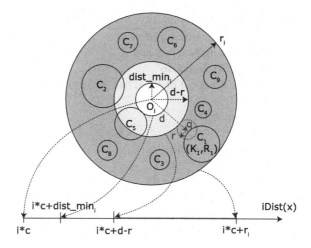

4.2.5 LSH Forest

LSH Forest [39] is an index structure containing a set of l LSH Trees, each of which is a prefix tree. For indexing purposes, the system uses a family $\mathcal{H}$ of locality sensitive hash functions. In this index structure, each inserted object O is indexed l times to l LSH Trees. At each LSH Tree, O is assigned a variable length x-digit identifier, which is the concatenating result of $\{h_1(O), h_2(O), \ldots, h_x(O)\}$, where $h_1(O), \ldots, h_x(O)$ are hashing functions chosen from $\mathcal{H}$. This identifier determines the position of O in the LSH Tree where O is a leaf node and each digit in the identifier of O represents a part of the path from the root to O's position. An example of a LSH Tree containing 4 objects is shown in Fig. 4.9 where the identifiers of these objects are 00, 01, 110, and 111. It is important to note that the length of object identifiers should be long enough so that each object can have a distinct identifier, and hence a distinct position in the LSH Tree.

To process a similarity search query, LSH Forest first uses hash functions selected from $\mathcal{H}$ to generate the identifier of the query point. This process is actually similar to the process of assigning an identifier for an inserted object. After that, the

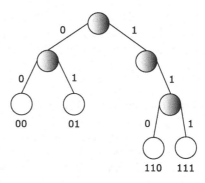

Fig. 4.9 A LSH Tree
containing 4 objects

Algorithm 11 : LSH_Similarity_Search(Query q)

1: generate the identifier qId of q
2: initiate two empty sets S and R
3: **for** each LSH Tree t **do**
4:     find a leaf node n of t that has the largest prefix match with qId
5:     S.add(n)
6:     R.add(n.object)
7: **end for**
8: **while** R.size $< M$ **do**
9:     initiate an empty set S'
10:    **for** each node n in S **do**
11:        let n' be parent of n
12:        S'.add(n')
13:        **for** each descendant leaf node d of n' that has not been reached **do**
14:            R.add(d.object)
15:        **end for**
16:    **end for**
17:    $S = S'$
18: **end while**
19: retrieve the top nearest objects from R

---

system searches l LSH Trees top-down to find leaf nodes having the largest prefix match with the query identifier. From these leaf nodes, the system travels LSH Trees bottom-up step by step synchronously to collect similar objects, which are descendant leaf nodes of the reaching internal nodes. This iteration process stops when the system returns at least M objects. Finally, from these M objects, the top nearest objects to the query object are retrieved. Algorithm 11 illustrates the similarity search algorithm over LSH Trees.

To support similarity search on P2P systems, assume that LSH Trees in LSH Forest are binary trees, i.e., hash functions in $\mathcal{H}$ return only two values: either 0 or 1. In this case, LSH Forest can be implemented in P2P systems naturally by employing P-Grid [17], a binary prefix tree structure where each peer maintains a leaf node of the tree and each connection between a node and its child is represented by a binary value (details of P-Grid are discussed in Chap. 3). The only variation is that LSH Forest is built on a set of l P-Grid overlay networks, one for each LSH Tree. Note that if the domain of hash functions in $\mathcal{H}$ has more than two values, a P-Grid like structure can be implemented to support LSH Forest in P2P systems.

4.3 Textual Information Retrieval

Content-based search in centralized systems has been extensively studied throughout the literature of Information Retrieval (IR). Several methods have been proposed to support this type of search. Most methods use the Vector Space Model [336] to represent documents as term vectors [283] in the Cartesian Space. Each element of a term vector is associated with a term t and has a weight $w(t) = tf(t) \cdot idf(t)$, where $tf(t)$ is the *term frequency* of t in the document and $idf(t)$ is the *inverse document frequency* reflecting the general importance of t in the entire corpus. Basically, *inverse document frequency* decreases the weight of terms that occur in many documents, and hence they have a low discriminating value (these terms are called as *popular terms*). However, it is not straightforward to employ these methods in P2P context since it is difficult to maintain global knowledge of existing terms in the whole system to calculate *inverse document frequency* of terms. A popular solution for global knowledge management is to rely on a set of super peers (or centralized servers) as a directory service. Alternatively, gossiping algorithms can be used to propagate global knowledge among all nodes in the system. Another difficulty in IR in P2P systems is that since the number of terms in shared files in P2P systems is typically very large, there is a need of building an effective and scalable indexing structure for them. According to the way global knowledge is managed and term indices are constructed, we can classify IR methods in P2P systems in three main categories.

- In the first category, P2P systems manage global knowledge locally at each node in the system [91, 92, 306]. As a result, every node can process queries based on its own global knowledge. To keep global knowledge at nodes up-to-date, these systems often employ gossiping algorithms to propagate new information among nodes. The main difference between these systems, however, is in the way they design gossiping algorithms to avoid message flooding so that they can keep the cost of data update as low as possible. Even though variants of gossiping algorithms have been proposed, since a change at a node will eventually be propagated to all nodes in the system, the cost of maintaining global knowledge is still high.
- In the second category, P2P systems manage global knowledge in a hierarchical summary index tree structure where global knowledge is accumulated from the leaf to the root of the tree. In particular, in the summary index tree structure, each leaf node, which is a peer node, first creates a summary index for documents it is sharing and submits the summary index to the parent node. Each internal node then creates a summary index from summary indices submitted by its children. Step by step, summary indices from all nodes in the system are gathered at the root node to build global knowledge. In this basic structure, since only the root maintains global knowledge, it poses a potential bottleneck problem. To leverage the problem, all methods [201, 202, 208, 268, 290, 320] propose a use of a super peer network consisting of several connected super peers to work as the root. In particular, as proposed in Overcite [305], the super peer network can be built from volunteer peers. Even though the use of a super peer network can leverage the bottleneck problem, it loosens some properties of P2P systems such as decentralization and scalability. Furthermore, it incurs a high cost to maintain the consistency of global knowledge among super peers. It is interesting to realize that most methods [201, 202, 268, 290, 320] only build a summary index tree structure at two levels: the leaf-peer level and the super-peer level. On the other hand, in an excepted case, Lupu et al. [208] suggest a use of a multi-level

binary tree structure where the number of nodes in the system determines the number of levels in the tree. Nevertheless, summary indices in the binary tree are constructed and maintained in almost similar fashion as other systems.

– In the third category, P2P systems manage global knowledge in a decentralized manner by employing P2P overlay networks to index terms extracted from sharing documents. For example, pSearch [311] uses CAN [266] for its index purpose while other methods [269, 310, 351] index terms in a Chord [173] ring. Additionally, in cases the system supports "AND" keyword in queries, Bloom filters [53] can be used [269] to improve the efficiency of query processing. Nevertheless, these systems still require some "special" nodes to maintain global information (e.g., the total number of documents in the system) that is needed in information retrieval techniques. Alternatively, in Minerva, Bender et al. [41] suggest to index terms both globally and locally, where global knowledge exists in the form of global indices. In this system, when a node issues a query, local indices are used to process the query first. After that, if the returned result is not good enough, i.e., the result does not satisfy some requirements, the system will retrieve global indices to process the query. To avoid overlapping in query processing, the system penalizes peers holding overlapping documents. Along a different line, Luu et al. [209] propose a solution to reduce the cost of indexing documents by using only metadata and discriminative keys. While this method may be able to decrease the index cost, it may also decrease the quality of query results. Furthermore, it is not easy to identify discriminative keys in highly dynamic systems. Along a different line, Sahin et al. [279, 280] assume that they are able to obtain global knowledge in advance and use this knowledge to first create global *reference vectors*. After that, sharing documents are indexed in a Chord ring based on their similarity to *reference vectors*. The challenge of using this method, however, is that, it is not easy to know global knowledge in advance.

In what follows, we should first introduce basic textual information retrieval techniques. After that, we should present applications of IR methods in P2P systems such as PlanetP [92], Summary Index [290], pSearch [311], and eSearch [310], for global knowledge management and term indexing for supporting content-based search in different P2P systems: unstructured, super-peer based, and structured P2P systems.

4.3.1 Basic Techniques

4.3.1.1 Query and Document Representation

Vector model is widely used in text retrieval systems [33]. Let $\{k_i\}$ be the set of index terms that are used in information retrieval, $\{d_i\}$ be the set of shared documents, and q be the user query. A weight $w_{i,j}$ is associated with a pair (k_i, d_j), and $w_{i,q}$ is associated with (k_i, q). Both $w_{i,j}$ and $w_{i,q}$ are nonnegative. Thus, the query vector $\vec{q}$ and document vector $\vec{d_j}$ are defined as $\vec{q} = \{w_{1,q}, w_{2,q}, \ldots, w_{t,q}\}$

and $\vec{d}_j = \{w_{1,j}, w_{2,j}, \ldots, w_{t,j}\}$, respectively, and they are used as representatives of the query and the document. Note that both $\vec{q}$ and $\vec{d}_j$ are vectors of t dimensionality. Here, t is the number of index terms. The similarity between the query q and a document d_j is defined as the cosine of the angle between the vectors $\vec{q}$ and $\vec{d}_j$, i.e.,

$$sim(d_j, q) = \frac{\vec{d}_j \cdot \vec{q}}{|\vec{d}_j| \times |\vec{q}|}$$

$$= \frac{\sum_{i=1}^{t} w_{i,j} \times w_{i,q}}{\sqrt{\sum_{i=1}^{t} w_{i,j}^2} \times \sqrt{\sum_{i=1}^{t} w_{i,q}^2}}.$$

Therefore, given a query q, all documents can be ranked based on their similarities to the query. The larger the similarity is, the more relevant the document is to the query.

Many different term weighting schemes exist [33], and the *term-frequency and inverse document frequency* (TF-IDF) scheme is the most commonly used. Term frequency of term k_i in document d_j is defined as $f_{i,j} = \frac{freq_{i,j}}{\max_l freq_{l,j}}$. Here, $freq_{i,j}$ is the number of occurrence of term k_i in document d_j, and $\max_l freq_{l,j}$ is the maximum occurrence of any index terms in the document d_j. The inverse document frequency of term k_i is defined as $idf_i = \log \frac{N}{n_i}$, in which N is the number of documents in the corpus, and n_i is the number of documents that contain the term k_i. Thus, the weight $w_{i,j}$ according to the (k_i, d_j) pair is defined as the product of the term frequency and inverse document frequency:

$$w_{i,j} = f_{i,j} \times idf_i$$

$$= \frac{freq_{i,j}}{\max_l freq_{l,j}} \log \frac{N}{n_i}.$$

Furthermore, the query term weights can be defined as

$$w_{i,q} = (0.5 + 0.5 f_{i,q}) \times idf_i$$

$$= \left(0.5 + \frac{0.5 freq_{i,q}}{\max_l freq_{l,q}}\right) \times \log \frac{N}{n_i}.$$

This vector model is widely used in centralized information retrieval systems and consequently in P2P systems (e.g., pSearch [311], PlanetP [92], SummaryIndex [290]).

4.3.1.2 Directory Management

Directory management is a key problem in P2P-based IR systems. Different information is kept in directories of different systems. Typically, the summary of the corpus is stored in the directory. Two types of directory management methods adopted in P2P-based IR systems are as follows:

– Bloom-Filter-Based Approach: PlanetP employs a Bloom filter based approach for the management of the indexed terms [92]. A Bloom filter is an array of m bits, and K independent hash functions $h_1, h_2, \ldots, h_K$, each with range $1, \ldots, m$. Initially, all the bits are set to 0. For a term k, it is hashed by all the hash functions. The bits $h_i(k)$ are set to 1 for $1 \leq i \leq k$. To check if a term k appears in a peer, all bits of $h_i(k)$ are checked. The term is in the corpus only when all these bits are set to 1. Bloom filter produces false positives but it never causes any false negative. This solution is efficient for summarization of data and has been widely used in network applications [53, 56].

  In PlanetP, each peer generates its own Bloom filter based on the indexed terms of its corpus. The Bloom filter is then distributed in the whole P2P network based on a gossiping-based method. A peer may store a Bloom filter from other peers stand-alone or merge it with some Bloom filters it receives, as a trade-off of space cost and accuracy. When the peer receives a query, it judges if the keywords in the query appear in the documents on a set of peers based on the Bloom filters it stores. It is assumed that the majority of the documents are fully static and change slowly. Therefore, the Bloom filters do not have to be distributed frequently. The advantage of distributing the Bloom filters in the whole network is that even when a peer is temporarily offline, the querying peer may still know the existence of the potential answer, and may schedule a later visit to the offline peers.

– Classification Hierarchies: Semantic Overlay Network (SON) is designed for P2P semantic-based search [90]. SON differs itself from traditional overlay networks in that the connection between peers are labeled and peers connected by the links with same label form a semantic network. Intuitively, a semantic overlay network is constructed by a set of peers with documents of similar topic. A peer may belong to several SONs. Classification hierarchy is used to build the SONs. First, it is assumed that each document can be classified into at least one category in the classification hierarchy. A peer can choose the SONs to join based on the categories its documents belong. When a query comes, it is also classified into a specific category. Based on the classification, the query is sent to the related SONs to retrieve the answers. This method assumes that the classification hierarchy is relatively stable, and hence each peer has a copy of the hierarchy.

  Triantafillow and his colleagues [318] propose a P2P-based system architecture for information retrieval, which is also based on document classification. However, different from SON, only one level of categories is used. Each peer maintains a Document Table, which stores the category of each document, a Document Category Routing Table, which maps each document category to a cluster identifier, and a Node Routing Table, which maintains the list of peers belonging to each cluster. For query processing, a query is firstly classified into one or several categories and is then routed to peers in the corresponding cluster. As it is in SON, each peer must keep a copy of category list.

4.3.1.3 Ranking of Results

Traditional IR systems may rank the documents based on their similarity to the query. However, for some similarity measurement, the TF-IDF-based measurement introduced in Sect. 4.3.1.1, cannot be applied easily. For example, the information needs to calculate the similarity is hard to be obtained by the querying peer. Instead, a general approach is to first rank peers based on the number of documents they have that is relevant to the query. Based on the ranking list, the query is sent to top relevant peers for processing. For example, PlanetP [92] presents a two-phase method for solving this problem [92]. It introduces a new concept: *inverse peer frequency* (IPF). IPF is calculated for each indexed term t by using $IPF_t = \log(1 + \frac{N}{N_t})$, where N and N_t are the number of nodes and the number of nodes containing term t in the system. Based on IPF, each peer i is assigned a score $R_i(Q) = \sum_{t \in Q \wedge t \in BF_i} IPF_t$ according to the query Q, where BF is the Bloom filter of the peer. After that, the peers are sorted in the order of their $R_i(Q)$ scores, and accessed one-by-one until a peer does not contribute any of its documents to the top-k documents with highest $sim(d_j, q)$ scores. The final top-k documents in the list ordered by similarity to the query are returned as the answer with corresponding ranks.

4.3.1.4 Improving the Performance of Information Retrieval

Besides basic information retrieval techniques introduced before, there are two important techniques to improve the performance of information retrieval: Latent Semantic Index and Peer Clustering.

— Latent Semantic Index (LSI) Approach: Latent semantic index is widely used for dimensionality reduction [47]. pSearch [312] introduces LSI into P2P-based information retrieval. pSearch is designed as a text retrieval system over CAN [266]. It is assumed that documents semantically similar to each other are mapped to identifiers close in the CAN identifier space. In this approach several problems exist if the dimensionality of CAN identifier space is set to be equal to the dimensionality of vectors after LSI processing. First, the vectors are not uniformly distributed in the identifier space. Second, the dimensionality of vectors is typically very high and search in high dimensional space is affected by the so called *curse of dimensionality*. Last but not least, global information is needed.

    A series of enhanced techniques are applied to overcome the shortcomings listed above. First, the vectors after LSI processing are transformed so that they are approximately uniformly distributed in the CAN identifier space. Furthermore, for a newly added peer, its join request is first routed to a peer corresponding to a certain document the added peer contributes. Similarly, a query is routed to such peer first. However, the query is then flooded in the neighboring peers. Recall that documents semantically similar to each other are assigned identifiers close in the CAN identifier space. This approach leads to quite efficient search. To overcome the curse of dimensionality problem, multiple CAN identifier spaces are used. Respectively, the vectors are partitioned into several subvectors, each is located in one CAN identifier space. When a query is issued, the corresponding vector is also partitioned into subvectors, and they are used to search in the CAN identifier spaces respectively. The results found in different CAN identifier spaces are retrieved and ranked by using their original vector. Finally, it is proposed that the information, e.g., dictionary and IDF, can be computed in advance based on samples. These information can be updated when it is needed. It is noted that the statistics is relatively stable, so that reexecuting the computation and the subsequent redistribution of documents rarely happens.

– Peer Clustering: To group the similar peers together, i.e., to connect the peers with similar documents, can decrease the hops needed to find answers to a specific query and improve the performance of information retrieval. This is in fact a peer clustering task. Several P2P-based information retrieval systems share the same idea of peer clustering [90, 232, 318].

In the work of Triantafillow [318], the clusters are determined based on the document categories. Each document category can only belong to one cluster. Each peer is assigned to the clusters corresponding to the categories its documents belong to. Furthermore, to achieve high performance, the system should satisfy *inter-cluster load balancing*, *intra-cluster load balancing*, and *global load balancing*. Here, *load* means the number of requests served by a peer storing the documents. Inter-cluster load balancing ensures a fair distribution of document categories to different clusters, intra-cluster load balancing causes the peers in one cluster approximately having the same load while global load balancing tries to balance the load of each peer as uniform as possible.

Each SON [90] can be treated as a peer cluster. Similar to the architecture proposed by Triantafillow [318], the peers join the clusters based on the categories of their documents. When the percentage of documents on a peer belonging to a specific category exceeds a given threshold, the peer should join the corresponding SON. In this way, with appropriate threshold setting, small size of SON can be achieved, and the query performance can be improved significantly.

Another peer clustering method suggests a test-and-verify approach under the assumption that no predefined category is available [232]. Each new added peer randomly connects to a peer. Then, it finds another set of peers within a certain hops from the peer it connects, and calculates the similarity between each of those peers to itself. The most similar one is chosen to be connected by the new added peer. Different from above two methods, the similarity is calculated *on-demand*, and no category information is needed.

4.3.2 PlanetP

PlanetP [92] is an unstructured P2P system supporting content-based search. In PlanetP, each node creates and maintains a local index of its shared files. This local index stores information about terms extracted from local shared files. Additionally, a gossiping algorithm is employed to replicate a term-to-peer index to other

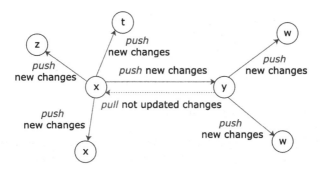

Fig. 4.10 Gossiping Algorithm

nodes in the system so that all nodes can obtain global knowledge of the system. The gossiping algorithm works in two modes, *push* and *pull*, as follows.

— *Push*: when there is a change in global knowledge at a node x, at interval, x randomly selects a neighbor node y to *push* this change. If y has known this change before, it ignores the notification. Otherwise, y updates its global knowledge and *pushes* the change to a random neighbor node as x does. The *push* process at x stops if none of n consecutive neighbor nodes that are *pushed* the change from x needs to update its global knowledge.
— *Pull*: if n is set to a small value, it is possible that the *push* process may stop before its global knowledge is updated at all nodes in the system. As a result, at interval, a node x also tries to *pull* new changes from a random neighbor node. If y has changes that have not been updated at x, x needs to update its global knowledge with these changes.

The operating of the gossiping algorithm is illustrated in Fig. 4.10. In PlanetP, since global knowledge is maintained at all nodes in the system, a node can process content-based search locally in the following steps.

— Let $(t \rightarrow n)$ denote the existence of a term t at a node n. At first, the node ranks nodes containing queried keywords in the system according to their similarity score. The similarity score between a node n and a query q is calculated as:

$$S_{\text{sim}}(n, q) = \sum_{t \in q | (t \rightarrow n)} IPF_t$$

where IPF_t is the inverse peer frequency and is computed as $\log(1 + \frac{N}{N_t})$, N is the number of nodes in the system and N_t is the number of nodes having documents containing term t.
— After that, the node repeatedly sends the query to nodes from the top to the bottom of the ranking list, m nodes each time (m is a configurable parameter representing a trade off between parallelism in query processing and the potential of getting unimportant results). When a node receives a query, it returns a set of

documents and their similarity score to the query. The similarity score between a document d and a query q is calculated as:

$$S_{\text{sim}}(d, q) = \frac{\sum_{t \in q} IPF_t \cdot (1 + \log(f_{d,t}))}{\sqrt{|d|}}$$

where $f_{d,t}$ is the appearance frequency of t in d and $|d|$ is the total number of terms in d.

— Assume that the user is only interested in top-k documents. When the node receives a query result, it recalculates the current top-k documents result list and updates the result list if the new result contains a document having a higher similarity score compared to existing documents in the result list. The process stops when the query results from a number of n' consecutive nodes fail to modify the result list.

As we have mentioned before, a weakness of this system as well as other systems employing the gossiping algorithm is that it always incurs a high cost in broadcasting messages in the system.

4.3.3 Summary Index

Summary Index [290] is a super-peer based indexing system supporting content-based search. The system employs a two-level tree structure to build a three-level hierarchical summary index structure. The first level of the tree structure is the *leaf-peer* level containing peer nodes that share documents. The second level is the *super-peer* level containing super-peer nodes. In Summary Index, each peer node is attached to a super-peer node while each super-peer node is responsible for a set of peer nodes. Based on this two-level tree structure, Summary Index builds a three-level hierarchal summary index structure as follows.

— The first summary index level called *document summary* level is built at the leaf-peer level of the tree structure. In this level, each peer node constructs local indices for its shared documents. These document indices are then summarized to create a summary index, which is sent to the super-peer in charge of the peer node.

— Two other summary index levels are built at the super-peer level. In this level, from summary indices received from peer nodes a super-peer node is in charge of, the super-peer node first builds indices for these peer nodes. These peer indices form the second summary index level called *peer summary* level. After that, the super-peer node creates a summary index of peer indices to exchange with other super-peers. This summary index together with summary indices received from other super-peers form the third summary index level called *super-peer summary* level at the super-peer node. This summary index level provides global knowledge of the system.

Fig. 4.11 Summary Index
Architecture

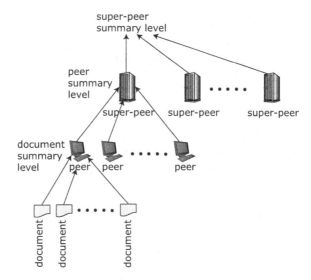

The tree structure and summary index structure are illustrated in Fig. 4.11. Based on this summary index structure, when a peer node issues a query, it first sends the query to its super peer. The super-peer then checks the *super-peer summary* level to find super-peers holding relevant indices to the query. These relevant super-peers are forwarded the query. When a super-peer receives a query from another super-peer, it checks the *peer summary* level to find suitable peers to forward the query. Finally, at peer nodes in the leaf-peer level, *document summary* level is referenced to process the query and the results are returned to the query issuer. Algorithm 12 shows the overall search algorithm.

While the three-level hierarchical summary index structure is able to process queries effectively, the main disadvantage of this structure is that it incurs a high communication cost among super-peers. It is because super-peers need to communicate with each others frequently to maintain up-to-date global knowledge (or super-peer summary). In particular, any change at a peer will lead to an update at its super-peer and then at other super-peers.

4.3.4 pSearch

pSearch [311] is a CAN [266] based P2P system supporting content-based search. In pSearch, the system selects a set of stable and strong nodes to build its search engine. These nodes are organized into an overlay network, which is CAN. For each shared document of a node, its retrieved terms form a semantic vector, which is a point in a multi-dimensional space. This point is indexed directly into the overlay network since CAN supports multi-dimensional data indexing. To process a query, the node issuing the query first creates a multi-dimensional query point from queried keywords. This query point is then sent to the overlay network. Finally, since similar

---

Algorithm 12 : SummaryIndex_Search(Node n, Document d)

1: **if** n is a super-peer **then**
2:   **if** the search request is sent from a normal peer **then**
3:     check super-peer summary level
4:     **for** each super-peer n' whose summary index is relevant to d **do**
5:       SummaryIndex_Search(n', d)
6:     **end for**
7:   **else** {the search request is sent from a super-peer}
8:     check peer summary level
9:     **for** each peer n' whose summary index is relevant to d **do**
10:      SummaryIndex_Search(n', d)
11:    **end for**
12: **end if**
13: **else** {n is a normal peer}
14:   check document summary level
15:   **for** each document d' that is relevant to d **do**
16:     **return** d' to the query issuer node
17:   **end for**
18: **end if**

Fig. 4.12 pSearch

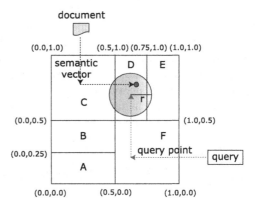

documents are indexed in nearby regions, the overlay network returns all document indices with in a radius r from the query point (r is a configurable parameter determined by either the similarity threshold or the number of wanted documents). A pSearch engine constructed on a 6 CAN nodes is illustrated in Fig. 4.12. Note that in pSearch global knowledge is created and maintained at each node in the overlay network. The way global knowledge is managed is independent with the way documents are indexed.

The biggest challenge in pSearch is to solve the mismatch between the dimensionality of index space created by documents and the dimensionality of index space which CAN can support. It is because the semantic vector, which is a multi-dimensional point $V = (v_0, v_1, \ldots, v_l)$, created by a document is often in a high-

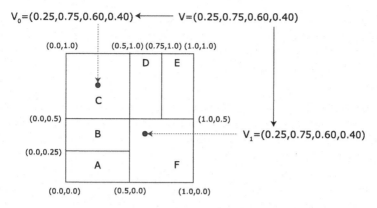

Fig. 4.13 A rotation of a 4-dimensional points to two 2-dimensional points

dimensional space while the dimensionality of index space supported by CAN is much lower. A solution proposed in pSearch to this challenge is to rotate repeatedly the semantic vector p times. Each time, the semantic vector is rotated m dimensions, where $m = 2.3, \ldots, \ln(n)$, n is the number of nodes in the system. This rotation process generates a series of p new vectors $V^i = (v_{i \cdot m}, \ldots, v_0, v_1, \ldots, v_{i \cdot m - 1})$, $i = 0, \ldots, p - 1$. These p rotated semantic vectors are indexed independently into p places in the overlay network. Similarly, when a node issues a query q, it also rotates the query point p times to create p rotated queries. These new rotated queries are processed independently to retrieve results. Since the similarity between two vectors is measured by their inner product, if a document is satisfied a query, its rotated semantic vectors should be close to the rotated query points. An example of rotating a 4-dimensional data point with $m = 2$ dimensions each time to create two 2-dimensional data points to index in a 2-dimensional CAN is shown in Fig. 4.13. Even though the solution of rotating data points and queries is able to reduce the dimensionality of index space to a value that CAN can support, since it creates data duplications, it incurs a high cost in data insertion, data deletion as well as query processing.

4.3.5 PRISM

Similar to pSearch, to support content-based search efficiently, the basic idea of PRISM [280] is to index similar documents to the same node. However, instead of using CAN as in pSearch [311], PRISM employs a Chord ring for its overlay network. PRISM indexes documents and processes queries based on a set of reference vectors $R = \{R_0, R_1, \ldots, R_n\}$, which are created at the system startup time and are kept for references at all nodes in the system. To index a document, the system calculates the distances between the document and reference vectors from which indices are created for the document. Since similar documents usually have similar distances to reference vectors, they should be indexed at the same nodes. Similarly, to process a query, the system calculates the distances between the query and reference vectors from which nodes holding indices of similar documents are targeted. The processes of indexing documents and processing queries are described in details as follows.

- Document indexing: when a node indexes a document to the system, it first computes the semantic vector of the document. After that, the node calculates the distances between this semantic vector and reference vectors. The reference vectors are then sorted based on their distance with the semantic vector increasingly. Finally, the top k reference vectors in the sorted list are selected to create C_k^2 indices for the node. For each pair of selected reference vectors, an index is created for the document by concatenating the binary representations of the two vectors to create high order bits of the index and setting remaining low order bits randomly. For example, assume that a set of 4 reference vectors $R = \{R_0, R_1, R_2, R_3\}$ are used, their binary representatives are $00, 01, 10$, and 11, the sorted list of reference vectors based on their distance to a document d is $R_2 R_0 R_3 R_1$, the top 3 reference vectors are selected to create indices and each index has 6 bits, the system will create 3 indices for d: $1000xx$, $1011xx$, and $0011xx$, where xx are random bits. Figure 4.14 illustrates the three indices of the document in this example.
- Query processing: when a node issues a query, it also calculates the distances between the query vector and reference vectors and sorts reference vectors based on their distance with the query vector increasingly. After that, the top k reference vectors in the sorted list are used to create C_k^2 query points in the same way as indices are constructed for a document. Finally, these generated query points are sent to the Chord ring for processing.

Note that in the above processes, k is a configurable parameter and is set depending on the system. If k is big, more indices are created, and hence more storage is

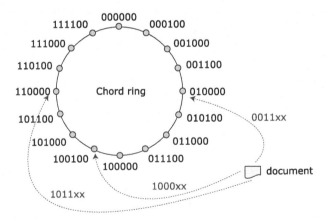

Fig. 4.14 PRISM

consumed. However, having more indices can help to get a high recall rate in query processing because it provides more changes for a query to meet an index. This is a trade-off. Another important note is that PRISM requires global knowledge for constructing reference vectors when the system starts. Since such a requirement is difficult to satisfy, it is a weak point of the solution.

4.4 Structured Data Management

Besides content-based search over unstructured textual documents, it is also important to support sharing of structured data sources such as relational databases or XML documents in P2P systems, since there are many emerging online data sources with rich structures. However, this type of application poses a big challenge due to the heterogeneity of data sources. Since different data sources may have different schemes, a local query issued at a data source cannot be executed at others. As a result, to process a query at different data sources, the query has to be modified according to the data sources. The most popular solution to solve this problem is to employ schema mediation that creates mappings between pairs of data sources. An example of a P2P system employing this solution is Piazza [148, 149, 212, 313]. By using schema mediation, a query can be reformulated to different queries to execute in different data sources. This basic solution, however, does not work if schemes of data sources cannot be shared. In this case, an alternative solution is to create mapping tables from stored values as in Hyperion [30, 178, 180, 273]. These mapping tables can be created by domain experts first and are regenerated automatically later. Nevertheless, since this solution requires the availability of domain experts, PeerDB [235] suggests another solution, where mappings are inferred automatically from annotations of tables and columns based on information retrieval techniques. The only requirement of this solution is to ask users to input annotations for tables and columns when they are created. In addition to the mapping problem, it is also a challenge to process queries efficiently across multiple data sources. PIER [159] proposes to use distributed hash tables to process equi-join queries across multiple relational databases while Papadimos, Maier, and Tufte [253] introduce an approach based on distributed catalog to process mutant query plans across multiple XML documents. In a different approach, to make it easy for users to issue queries over relational databases without knowing the data manipulation language and the database schemes, M-KS [346] and G-KS [324] propose a solution to summarize relationships of keywords locally at each data source based on the data source's schema. Using databases' summaries, these systems are able to support unstructured keyword queries. In this solution, two keywords having a relationship if they are in the same tuple or in different tuples but these tuples can be connected together in a meaningful way. Based on keyword relationships, these systems are able to process unstructured keyword queries. Finally, to speed up query processing, PISCES [339] presents a partial indexing scheme. In the remaining part of this section, we first present all these above solutions in detail. After that, we respectively introduce three well-known P2P projects supporting relational database sharing: Piazza [148, 149, 212, 313], Hyperion [30, 178, 180, 273], and PeerDB [235].

4.4.1 Query Processing in Heterogeneous Data Sources

In this section, we first analyze semantics of queries. After that, we introduce three popular methods for solving the problem of mapping heterogeneous data sources. Then we present two basic query processing techniques over relational databases and XML documents. Finally, we discuss indexing techniques that can be used to speed up query processing.

4.4.1.1 Semantics

Above all, the semantics of data and queries should be defined. In PIER [159], the authors introduced the data semantics that is called *dilated-reachable snapshot*. Additionally, they define a *reachable peer* as a peer that can be reached by multicast of a query. A *local snapshot* is the data on a peer when a query arrives. A *reachable snapshot* is the union of all local snapshots of reachable peers according to the query. Thus, the correct behavior of the system should be the correct behavior of queries on reachable snapshots.

In the Hyperion project [179, 181], the semantics issue is discussed based on the model named *Local Relational Model* (LRM) [46]. In the LRM model, the *relational space* consists of a complete set of local databases *DB* and a set of mapping functions specifying the relation between pairs of local databases. This model assumes that different local databases can support different languages and uses L_i to represent the language supported by local database $i \in DB$. In this way, the set of *coordination formulas RF* on the family of relational languages $\{L_i\}_{i \in DB}$ is defined as

$$RF ::= i : \phi | RF \rightarrow RF | RF \wedge RF | RF \vee RF | \exists i : x.RF | \forall i : x.RF$$

where $i \in DB$ and ϕ is a formula of L_i. Given a query on a family of relational languages $\{L_i\}_{i \in DB}$, the *global answer* for this query is retrieved by first executing it in all local databases and then using mapping functions to recursively compose and map the local query results.

The Hyperion project implements the mapping functions by using *mapping tables*. A mapping table contains pairs of attributes X and Y in two different local databases, in which each tuple is a mapping associating a pair of values (x, y) where x is a value in X and y is a value in Y. For a value x of X appearing in the mapping table, it is called to follow the *open-world* semantics, if x can be associated with any possible value y in Y. Otherwise, it is called to follow the *closed-world* semantics, i.e., x can only be associated with the indicated value y of Y in the mapping table. For a value x of X being absent in the mapping table, it is called to follow the

Table 4.1 Alternative
open/closed world semantics

	Open-world	Closed-world
A present of value x	Any value y	Indicated value y
An absence of value x	Any value y	No value y

open-world semantics, if x can be associated with any value y of Y, or it is called
to follow the *closed-world* semantics, if x cannot be associated with any value of Y.
Thus, the alternative open and closed semantics are listed in Table 4.1 [181].

4.4.1.2 Mapping Heterogeneous Data Sources

There are three basic solutions for mapping heterogeneous data sources. The first
solution is based on mapping rules (schema mediation based approach). The second solution is based on mapping tables (mapping table based approach). The third
solution is based on annotations of tables and columns (information retrieval based
approach). Three P2P systems employing these three methods are, respectively, Piazza [148, 149, 212, 313], Hyperion [30, 178, 180, 273], and PeerDB [235]. Details
of these three solutions are as follows.

— Using mapping rules: this is a traditional method to integrate and exchange data
  between heterogeneous data sources used in Piazza project [148, 149, 212, 313].
  In this method, for each pair of heterogeneous data sources, the system defines
  a set of mapping rules between the two data source schemes. These rules are
  built from two types of views: *global-as-view* (GAV) and *local-as-view* (LAV).
  In GAV, the schema of the mapping data source (the mediated schema) is defined
  as a set of views over the schema of the other data source. On the other hand, in
  LAV, the content of the other data source is described as views over the mediated
  schema. Based on GAV and/or LAV, the system is able to reformulate a query to
  be executed in different schemes of different data sources.

  Alternatively, Katchaounov et al. studied the problem of mediation in P2P
  systems from another point-of-view, which is named as view expansion [176].
  Here, a view can be treated as a shared schema on a peer. A view is called expanded, if it is rewritten according to the remote views. Three different view
  expansion strategies, i.e., black-box, full expansion, and selective expansion, are
  discussed and compared. Using *black-box* strategy, remote views are treated as
  black-boxes. Thus, a peer only rewrites a local query into a query using the stored
  relations and schema shared by neighboring peers. From the point-of-view of
  query optimization, this may lead to a suboptimal query plan. When using *full
  expansion*, it is assumed that a peer knows the shared schemes of all peers. Thus,
  the peer can rewrite a query to a query using those schemes directly. However, in
  a P2P system, the information of all peers is usually not available. Furthermore,
  some peers may only share its schema to some trusted peers. When *selective
  expansion* strategy is used, only some views are expanded. Katchaounov et al.
  argue that this strategy leads to a trade-off between compilation cost, which is

the cost to generate the rewritten query plan, and execution plan quality, which means the efficiency of evaluation of the query plan.

- Using mapping tables: in some cases where database schemes cannot be shared due to privacy reasons, it is infeasible to set up mapping rules via definitions of views as in the previous solution. In these cases, using mapping tables may be a choice. Basically, mapping tables map corresponding identifiers from different schemes. Based on mapping tables, a local query at a database source can be translated to a set of queries that can be executed in different database sources. In general, the mapping tables are first created by domain experts. After that, they are developed and maintained automatically by the systems. Hyperion project [30, 178, 180, 273] employs this solution.

- Using annotations: the above two solutions cannot be applied if database schemes cannot be shared while we have no domain experts to create initial mapping tables. In this case, we need a more flexible solution. As proposed in PeerDB [235], a feasible solution is to let users specify metadata in terms of descriptive keywords for tables and columns when they are created. Since matching tables and columns of different peers should have similar descriptive keywords, an information retrieval method can be applied to find and match them in query processing. This solution is implemented by a mechanism called agent assisted query processing as follows.

In PeerDB, each peer has a *master agent*. The master agent is responsible for monitoring statistics and managing the user queries. It may clone and dispatch *worker agents* to neighboring peers, and receive answers. When a query is issued by a user, it is parsed. Then the local directory is searched and an information retrieval method is applied to find related relations to report to the user. Meanwhile, a *relation matching agent* is cloned and dispatched to each neighboring peer. The master agent waits for the answers returned by remote peers. The user can select the relations that are interested from the relations found in both local dictionary and remote peers. The above process forms the first phase of agent assisted query processing. For each relation selected by the user, a *data retrieval agent* is cloned. If the relation resides on a remote peer, the agent is dispatched to that peer. If the time-to-live (TTL) threshold has not been reached, the agent is cloned and dispatched further to neighboring peers. In any cases, the data retrieval agent reformulates an SQL query according to the schema of the corresponding relations. Then, the query is executed by the local query engine on the corresponding peer. The answers are returned to the master agent of the peer that initiates the query, and presented by the master agent to the user. Thus, the second phase of the query processing is finished. For searching in both local and export dictionaries, a simple SQL query is transformed into a triple, constructed by relation names, attribute names, and conditions. The triple is used to search in dictionaries in an information retrieval fashion. The result relations are directly returned to the peer that initiates the query.

This two-phase query processing approach is able to partially solve the problem of lack-of-schema problem in self-organizing P2P environments. By providing an interface for users to interact with the process of query executing, the agent assisted approach can support the join of data from two or more relations. To achieve this, in the first phase, i.e., relation selection phase, not only individual relations, but also related relation combinations are returned to the user. Thus, the data retrieval agent may reformulate the query according to the relationships between the relations, so that the join capability is implemented. Currently, the join of data from more than one peer is not supported by PeerDB. Developing more intelligent peers that can determine the strategies at runtime, and find relations with similar schema remain as further research problems [235].

Based on these mapping techniques, a query issued at a node can be reformulated to be executed at neighbor nodes of the node. In particular, when a query Q is issued at a node, it is reformulated into a set of queries $S_Q = \{Q_1, Q_2, \ldots, Q_n\}$, each of which corresponds to a neighbor node and is rewritten according to the mapping between the node and that neighbor node. While Q is evaluated locally and queries in S_Q are sent to the neighboring nodes. These neighbor nodes then continue to apply the mapping methods to transform and forward the query to their neighbors and so on. The union of their results is the final answer to the query [147]. In fact, gossiping algorithm is often applied to bring the query to far-away nodes. However, when the query goes through a long distance, information-loss may occur. Chatty Web [18] proposes a solution to detect this problem. The solution is based on both syntactic analysis of reformulated queries and semantic analysis of query results. In particular, syntactic analysis is done when a query is reformulated along a mapping cycle. At this point, the system analyzes the syntactic similarity between the original query and the reformulated query from which the level of agreement among peers in the cycle is determined. On the other hand, semantic analysis is based on the comparison of the data dependencies appearing in the query result and the data dependencies in the local data.

4.4.1.3 Query Processing over Relational Databases

Distributed Hash Table (DHT) based query processing is first proposed in PIER [153], and detailed techniques are studied under variant environments [129, 141, 159]. The main function of DHT in query processing is shown in Fig. 4.15. Data objects, similar to files in file sharing applications, are hashed into the identifier space, while peers are hashed to the same space using a different hash function.

Besides locating and routing, DHT is employed in join algorithms implemented in PIER. Two join algorithms are proposed for P2P-based query processing [159]. *DHT-based adaption of pipelining symmetric hash join* is designed as a general-purpose equi-join algorithm. The data to be joined should be *rehashed* based on the join attribute, since data objects are hashed first based on resourceID, as it is stated before. The rest of this join algorithm is similar to traditional symmetric hash join and it is performed on the querying peer. *FetchMatches* is another join algorithm designed for conditions that one of the joining tables has already been hashed on the join attributes. Suppose $S \bowtie N$ is a join operation to be performed on tables S and N, and S has already been hashed on the joining attributes, FetchMatches

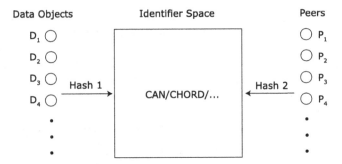

Fig. 4.15 Matching of the data objects and peers in DHT-based query processing

scans peers containing data in N, and fetches corresponding data in S for each tuple in N. FetchMatches has the disadvantage that selections on non-DHT attributes cannot be pushed into the DHT layer [159]. It is because if the selection functions are integrated into the DHT layer, they may *dirtying* the DHT APIs. To solve this problem, two improved algorithms, namely *symmetric semi-join* and *Bloom join*, are studied [159].

Locality sensitive hashing (LSH) is a hash method for *locality preserving*, which means for hash function h, it satisfies that $\Pr[h(A) = h(B)] = sim(A, B)$ [141]. Min-wise independent permutations are proved to be a family of hash functions that are locality preserving according to Jaccard set similarity measure [141]. LSH is suitable for range selection query processing, since similar data objects and queries have high probabilities to be hashed to the same identifier in the identifier space.

PeerCQ employs another simple DHT scheme, which is called to be *peer aware* and *CQ aware* [129]. Intuitively, by peer awareness, it means that a peer containing more data is assigned more identifiers than other peers, so that queries have more chances to be mapped to this peer. By CQ awareness, it means similar queries have more chances to be mapped to the same peer. To achieve CQ awareness, the data source and objects to be queried in a query is hashed standalone, the result of which forms the first part of the identifier of the query. The second part of the identifier is obtained by hashing properties of the peer and the query. Thus, the second part of the identifier can be expected to be uniformly random. The identifier space used in PeerCQ is organized in a circle. Thus, the larger the first part is, the higher the probability it has that two similar queries are mapped to the same peer.

4.4.1.4 Query Processing over XML Documents

Papadimos, Maier, and Tufte [253] introduce a multi-hierarchical-namespaces approach, which is employed to cooperate with mutant query processing. The categories are organized in several hierarchies. An object belonging to a child category also belongs to all the parent categories. Each namespace is treated as a dimension.

Thus, the query can be represented by interested cells that are defined by the categories in different namespaces. It is assumed that peers take different roles in the system. Some peers maintain data belonging to specific interested cells, which are called *base servers*. Some peers maintain information about base servers and other peers whose interests or indices are overlapped with its own. These peers are called *index servers*. Furthermore, some index servers maintain only the multi-hierarchic namespace index. They are called *meta-index servers*. Finally, the peers that maintain the detailed information, i.e. the hierarchies, of namespaces are called *category servers*.

A *mutant query plan* is a query plan graph that is capable of using URLs and URNs as references of resources. The mutant query plans are represented by XML documents, and are sent from one site to another to *resolve* the URNs [252]. The mutant query plan is routed from one peer to another to resolve the URNs or evaluate the subplans after which the results are inserted into the corresponding node in the plan. Thus, to answer a query is to resolve all the URNs in the mutant query plan. A mutant query plan is evaluated serially by the peers. Therefore, mutant query processing may be inefficient when it is compared with using other pipelined plans. Nevertheless, mutant query plan gains more robustness and site autonomy. Furthermore, the plan can be reoptimized on each peer, while the coordination overhead is saved. Since peers are usually fully autonomous, mutant query processing fits in with the P2P environment well.

4.4.1.5 Unstructured Keyword Query Processing over Relational Databases

The requirement of knowing both the database schema and the data manipulation language such as SQL to issue queries limits the use of relational databases to only advanced users. To make it easy for normal users, M-KS [346] and G-KS [324] propose a solution to support unstructured keyword query over relational databases. The basic idea of this solution is to build a summary of keyword relationships for each relational database in the system and keyword queries are processed based on the summaries of databases. In this solution, two terms have a relationship if they are in the same tuple or they are in different tuples but these tuples can be connected in a meaningful way (via Primary Key—Foreign Key relationship). Given a keyword query, this solution checks the existence of queried keywords and their relationships in the summaries of databases to select the top-k databases that are most likely to contribute to results. The query is then sent to only these top-K databases for processing. The main difference between M-KS and G-KS is in the way these systems maintain summaries of databases. While M-KS employs a matrix for this purpose, G-KS utilizes a graph. Furthermore, while M-KS simply counts the number of occurrences of term relationships in database summaries, G-KS employs information retrieval techniques to weight nodes and edges in summary graphs according to their importance compared to other nodes and edges in the graphs.

4.4.1.6 Indexing Schemes

Data indexing is a popular technique to improve the query processing speed. A straightforward solution to index relational databases in a P2P system is to index every tuple of the database (fully indexing scheme). To index a tuple, the system first creates a set of indices for all indexed attributes in the tuple (a tuple can be indexed on all attributes or a subset of attributes). After that, these indices are inserted in the system. The problem with this method is that since the accumulate amount of data from different relational databases is often large, it incurs a significant cost in creating and maintaining indices. To alleviate this problem, PISCES [339] proposes a use of partial indexing scheme. This method does not index every tuple. Instead, it selects a subset of tuples to index based on some criteria such as query frequency, update frequency, etc. To determine if a tuple should be indexed, PISCES employs histograms to keep statistics of the system. Furthermore, to support query processing on tuples that are not indexed, PISCES employs an approximate range index scheme in which each node containing a relational table with an indexed attributed a_i publishes a range index $[I(a_i)_{min}, I(a_i)_{max}]$, where $I(a_i)_{min}$ and $I(a_i)_{max}$ are, respectively, the minimum and maximum values of the attributed a_i of the table. In particular, the system first indexes tuples with the approximate range index scheme. After that, if some range indices receive a significant number of queries (according to the histograms), individual indices are created for tuples containing data in these ranges. To ease the index maintenance, each index is assigned a timestamp and the system will delete the index when its timestamp is expired.

4.4.2 Piazza

Piazza [148, 149, 212, 313] applies a traditional method to integrate and exchange data between heterogeneous data sources. In Piazza, each peer maps its schema of stored relation (local schema) to its neighbors' schema. Users initiate queries based on local schema. The query is rewritten according to the schema mapping, and sent to the neighbors, so that it can be answered by other peers. The query is roaming in the P2P network and continuously sending result back in its lifetime.

Figure 4.16 shows the architecture of Piazza system [146]. Each peer shares its data in the form of *stored relations*. The peer defines its *peer schema*, according to which other peers can access its stored relations. The peer maintains two kinds of schema mapping. The first is the mapping between the stored relations and peer schema. The second is the mapping between its peer schema and its neighbors' peer schema [149].

Currently, it is reported that PIAZZA supports sharing XML/RDF data for supporting Semantic Web applications [147]. Accordingly, the schema is described using XML-Schema or OWL ontologies [100] for XML data and RDF data respectively. Furthermore, the mapping language and query language is XQuery [54] based [147]. Note that so far PIAZZA has only reported results that focus on semantic issues in peer data management systems (PDMS). The results on issues such

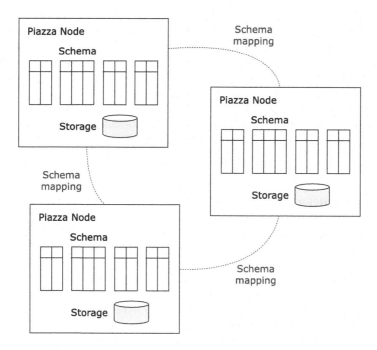

Fig. 4.16 PIAZZA architecture

as how to find interested data sources in a large PDMS have not been reported yet [138, 146, 147, 149].

Piazza creates a language called Peer-Programming Language (PPL) for mapping heterogeneous data source schemes. PPL allows users to specify mapping rules from two types of views: *global-as-view* (GAV) and *local-as-view* (LAV). In the following parts, we first present PPL. After that, we introduce the query reformulation algorithm in detail.

4.4.2.1 Peer-Programming Language

The syntax of PPL focuses on two main concepts: storage description and peer mapping. While storage description of a peer specifies which data the peer stores in its relations, peer mapping provides semantic connection between schemes of different peers. Storage description and peer mapping are described and classified through the following definitions.

- *Equality storage description*: appears in a formula of $A : R = Q$. This formula describes that the result of a query Q over peer A is stored at relation R.
- *Containment storage description*: appears in a formula of $A : R \subseteq Q$. This formula describes that a subset of the result of a query Q over peer A is stored at relation R.

- *Equality peer mapping*: appears in a formula of $Q_1(\bar{A}_1) = Q_2(\bar{A}_2)$. This formula describes that the result of a query Q_1 over a set of peer $\bar{A}_1$ is equal to the result of a query Q_2 over a set of peers $\bar{A}_2$.
- *Inclusion peer mapping*: appears in a formula of $Q_1(\bar{A}_1) \subseteq Q_2(\bar{A}_2)$. This formula describes that the result of a query Q_1 over a set of peer $\bar{A}_1$ is a subset of the result of a query Q_2 over a set of peers $\bar{A}_2$.
- *Definitional peer mapping*: appears in a formula of a datalog rule whose relations in both head and body are peer relations. This formula describes that the data stored in peer relations of the head is equal to the data stored in peer relations of the body.

4.4.2.2 Query Reformulation Algorithm

Given a query Q, a set of storage descriptions and a set of peer mappings, the process of query reformulation is a construction of a rule-goal tree where rule nodes (or internal nodes) are labeled with entities of peer mappings, goal nodes (or leaf nodes) are labeled with peer relations and links are rules (peer mappings or storage descriptions). The algorithm starts at the root of the tree, which is Q. It then expands Q to sub queries $Q_1, Q_2, \ldots, Q_n$ as children of Q. After that, it repeatedly applies peer mapping rules to expand the existing nodes to generate new nodes until no nodes can be further expanded. Finally, it uses storage descriptions to generate goal nodes. The new query is reformulated from these goal nodes. The resultant query is a union of conjunctive queries over goal nodes (or peer relations). Each conjunctive query represents a way to get the query result from peers. The query reformulation algorithm is illustrated in Algorithm 13 and an example of the query reformulation is illustrated in Fig. 4.17. The goal of the query in the example is to find researchers who work in the same department of a university and on the same research direction.

Algorithm 13 : Query_Reformulation(Query q)

1: set q as the root node
2: initialize a queue Q containing the root node
3: **while** not Q.empty( ) **do**
4:    $n = Q$.pop()
5:    **if** n is expandable by applying a mapping rule R **then**
6:       apply R to expand n to a list L of child nodes
7:       add all nodes n' in L to Q
8:    **else**
9:       use storage descriptions to generate goal node n'
10:   **end if**
11: **end while**
12: set reformulated query $q' = \{\}$
13: **for** each goal node n' **do**
14:    $q' = q' \wedge n'$
15: **end for**

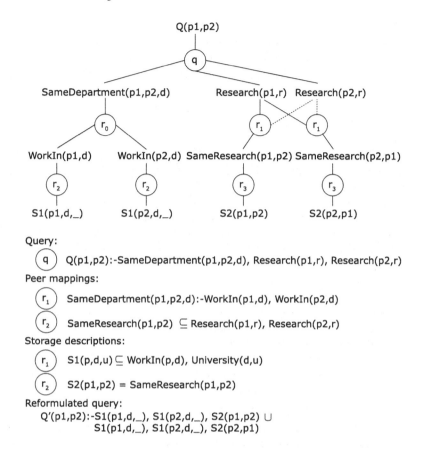

Fig. 4.17 Reformulation rule-goal tree

4.4.3 Hyperion

Different from Piazza, Hyperion [30, 178, 180, 273] employs mapping tables to solve the problem of mapping heterogeneous data sources. There are two main issues in this method: how to create mapping tables and how to process queries based on mapping table. We, respectively, discuss these issues in the following parts.

4.4.3.1 Mapping Table Construction

Mapping tables are first constructed by domain experts. A mapping table needs to record both the mapping values and the confidence of experts about the mapping. The confidence of experts can be expressed in four different modes corresponding to Table 4.2.

Table 4.2 Expert confidence modes

	A presence of value x	An absence of value x
Open-open-world	Any value y	Any value y
Open-close-world	Any value y	No value y
Close-open-world	Indicated value y	Any value y
Close-close-world	Indicated value y	No value y

– Open-open-world (OO-world): this mode has the lowest confidence. The mapping implies that a value x can be associated with any value y whether x exists in the mapping table. This mode is used when the mapping table creator has no glue about the mapping at all. Actually, this mode is not interested in practice.
– Open-close-world (OC-world): this mode implies that if a value x does not exist in the mapping table, there is no associated value y. However, if x exists in the mapping table, x can be associated with any value y. This mode is used when the mapping table creator only knows the domain value of X. As a result, it does not help much in query processing.
– Close-open-world (CO-world): this mode implies that if a value x exists in the mapping table, it is associated with an exact value y. However, the mapping table creator does not know the mapping values of missing values. In general, this mode represents partial knowledge of the domain.
– Close-close-world (CC-world): this mode has the highest confidence. It represents the complete knowledge of the domain. If a value x exists in the mapping table, it is associated with an exact value y while if x does not exist in the mapping table, there is no associate value y.

Since no experts can have complete knowledge of the domain especially when the system involves several peer nodes, it is necessary to infer new mapping tables automatically from existing mapping tables and to check consistency of mapping tables created by different experts. Basically, new mapping tables can be inferred by combining existing values in data sources and using mapping tables as constraints to filter invalid mapping values. On the other hand, consistency of mapping tables can be checked on the fly from mapping tables and values of related data sources. The algorithm for generating new mapping tables automatically consists of two phases: information gathering and computation. Assume that existing mapping tables in the system appear in a chain $P_1, P_2, \ldots, P_n$. The two phases of the algorithm are described as follows.

– Information gathering phase: starts at P_1 and ends at P_n. In this phase, each peer computes and sends to the next peer in the chain information about mapping values. The purpose of this phase is to collect information from peers to reduce computation in the next phase and to determine which computations can be done in parallel.
– Computation phase: starts at P_n and ends at P_1. In this phase, each peer actually computes new mapping tables from existing one and check consistency of mapping tables as discussed above. The results are sent back to the previous peer in the chain.

4.4.3.2 Query Processing

Using mapping tables, a local query at a data source can be transformed to different queries to be executed in other data sources. In particular, when a node issues a query, it first executes the query locally. After that, it uses mapping tables to transform the query to other queries and sends the transformed queries to its neighbor nodes. These neighbor nodes then execute the query at their data sources and continue to transform and forward the query to their neighbor nodes. This process continues until either a prefixed number of execution steps or a prefixed time has passed. While the algorithm for query processing is straightforward, it is important to note that query transformation has to be sound and complete according to the two definitions introduced by Kementsietsidis and Arenas [178] as follows.

Definition 4.1 (Sound Translation) Let $q_1 = \sigma_E(R_1 \bowtie \cdots \bowtie R_k)$, where E is a selection predicate, be a query over P_1 and q_2 be a query over P_2. q_2 is a sound translation of q_1 with respect to mapping table m if for every relation instance r_2 of P_2 and $t_2 \in q_2(r_2)$, there exists a valuation ρ of m and a tuple $t \in \sigma_E(\rho(m))$ such that $\pi_{att(q_2)}(t) = t_2$.

Definition 4.2 (Complete Translation) Let q_1 and q_2, respectively, be queries over P_1 and P_2. q_2 is a complete translation of q_1 with respect to mapping table m if for every q_2' over P_2, q_2' is a sound translation of q_1 with respect to mapping table m, for every instance r_2 of P_2, $q_2(r_2) \supseteq q_2'(r_2)$.

4.4.4 PeerDB

PeerDB [235] is a query processing engine for querying data in P2P environment. PeerDB is developed on top of BestPeer [234] whose details were discussed in Chap. 2. Different from Piazza and Hyperion, PeerDB requires neither database schema sharing nor mapping tables. Instead, the system lets user specify descriptive keywords for tables and columns when they are created. These keywords are used to find matching tables for a query in query processing. The basic idea of this solution is to apply an information retrieval method to find tables, whose descriptive keywords and column descriptive keywords are best matched to queried tables and columns. Based on retrieved relevant tables, corresponding queries can be created for execution. The architecture of a PeerDB node is shown in Fig. 4.18. Each peer in PeerDB has an local *Object Management System* for management of local data, which is implemented based on MySQL [235]. The metadata information that include the schema, keywords, etc. are stored in *Local Dictionary*, while the sharable part is also stored in *Export Dictionary*. The query functions are supported by the module *DB Agent*. Furthermore, each peer has a *Cache Manager* that is in charge of the caching and replacement policy. Finally, the system provides a graphical user interface (GUI), so that users may manage the system or issue the queries easily. In

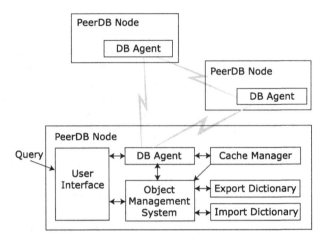

Fig. 4.18 PeerDB Architecture

the following parts, we will present in details how to find relevant tables (in terms of measuring the similarity between a table and a query) and how to process a query in the context of P2P system.

4.4.4.1 Table-to-Query Similarity Measurement

Let T and C, respectively be a set of tables and columns appearing in a query q; t and c be a table and its columns. The similarity between t and q is calculated as follows.

$$Sim(q,t) = \frac{(wt_t \cdot r) + (wt_c \cdot N_{\text{match}}(C,c))}{wt_t + (wt_c \cdot N(C))}$$

where wt_t and wt_c are predefined weights reflecting the importance of matching table and column names; r is set to 1 if there are some descriptive keywords of t that match descriptive keywords of tables in T. Otherwise, r is set to 0; $N_{\text{match}}(C,c)$ is the total number of descriptive keywords in c that match queried columns; and $N(C)$ is the total number of distinct queried columns.

4.4.4.2 Query Processing

In PeerDB, a query is processed in two main steps.

- When a user issues a query, the system first passes the query to extract queried tables and columns. After that, the system uses a gossiping algorithm with time-to-live (TTL) to broadcast the query to other nodes in the system. When a peer node receives a query, if it is not the first time the node receives the query, it just

discards the query. Otherwise, the node calculates the similarity scores between its shared tables and the query. Tables whose scores are greater than a threshold value are considered relevant tables. They are returned to the user.
— From returned relevant tables, the user selects some of them for further process-ing. In this phase, the query is sent directly to the node holding relevant tables and queries are created for execution at these nodes. The results of query execu-tion are returned to the user.

To improve the efficiency and effectiveness of query processing, PeerDB self-reconfigures the connections between peer nodes so that a node only keeps connec-tions to nodes that have most recently provided answers. This feature improves the performance of query processing because if users have a tendency to issue similar queries (this tendency often happens in practice), with high probability, the results of subsequent queries can also be found at peers that provide the most answers for previous queries.

In conclusion, the architecture of PeerDB has several advantages in query processing in an unstructured P2P network. First, it employs the export dictionary, which is an analog to the corresponding part in traditional file sharing P2P systems. Export dictionary enables the similarity-based search in the local database of a peer, even the detailed schema of the database is unknown. Second, agent assisted query processing supported by DB Agent provides a facility for executing queries on re-mote peers. Third, by allowing users to interact with the process of query executing, the system is able to decrease unnecessary data transmitting. Fourth, with the tech-nique of query rewriting the join of data from two or more peers can be processed. Last but not the least, agents implemented in DB Agent monitor the statistics from the directly or indirectly connected peers. The peers with stable and high-quality result to the specific queries are maintained as direct neighbors. This feature is es-pecially important to a data management system over unstructured P2P network, in which the peers are usually dynamic, and self-organizing of peers can usually improve both the effectiveness and efficiency of query processing in a number of factors.

4.5 Summary

In this chapter, we have introduced different techniques to support data sharing at different granularities. We started with techniques to support searching on file de-scription including multi-dimensional indexing, multi-attribute indexing, and sky-line query processing in Sect. 4.1. After that, we introduced techniques to support content-based search. In particular, since file content is often summarized as a data vector in a high-dimensional space, the challenge to support content-based search turns into a challenge of supporting high-dimensional index. This challenge was addressed in Sect. 4.2. We further presented special techniques for information re-trieval over text files in Sect. 4.3. Finally, in Sect. 4.4, we introduced techniques to support structured database sharing in P2P systems.

The basic solution to support multi-dimensional index in P2P systems is to apply conventional multi-dimensional indexing structures used in centralized systems such as the kd-tree [42], R-Tree [145], X-Tree [44]. Several P2P systems such as CAN [266] and VBI-Tree [167] have adopted such an approach.

Supporting multi-attribute indexing is difficult not only in P2P systems but also centralized systems. So far, the basic approach to solve this task is to index each attribute separately. MAAN [61] and Mercury [49] are two P2P systems supporting multi-attribute indexing along this direction. MAAN uses the same identifier space to index all attributes while Mercury uses separate identifier spaces or hubs to index separate attributes.

The challenge of supporting skyline queries in P2P systems is in how to optimize skyline computing in P2P environment. In particular, proposed solutions optimize the search space to reduce the amount of hopping and data transmission in the network, and parallelize the search process to reduce the query response time. For example, both DSL [337] and SSP [329] propose algorithms that parallel the search process by participating it to subsearch regions. To optimize the search space, SSP proposes a solution that defines the search space from a point that has the largest dominating region at the most dominating node.

To support high-dimensional indexing, the popular solution is the mapping-based approach, which converts data in a high-dimensional space to a lower dimensional space (usually one-dimensional space) before indexing. Several P2P systems such as CISS [190] and ZNet [293] employs space filling curves for this purpose. Otherwise, in distance-based approach, high-dimensional data objects are directly indexed to the system based on their distance to a predefined set of referenced objects (mChord [240] and SimPeer [112]). Finally, in hash-based approach, similar objects are hashed to similar buckets for query processing (LSH Forest [39]).

Textual information retrieval methods are classified into three main categories based on the way the systems manage global knowledge (that is used in information retrieval methods) and the way the systems construct term indices. In the first category, global knowledge is maintained at every node in the systems and gossiping algorithms are used to distribute and synchronize information among nodes [91, 92]. In the second category, P2P systems employ a hierarchical index tree structure to aggregate global knowledge at the root node, which is constructed as a set of super-peers to avoid bottleneck [201, 202, 208, 268, 290, 320]. Finally, in the third category, terms are extracted and indexed directly to the networks [269, 310, 311, 351].

Even though there are several aspects that need to be studied to support structured data sharing, so far, researchers have focused on the mapping problem between heterogeneous data sources. Other problems such as how to construct a query plan to execute the query or how to optimize a query plan are still open. In general, there are three approaches to solve the mapping problem: using mapping rules (Piazza project [148, 149, 212, 313]), using mapping tables (Hyperion project [30, 178, 180, 273]) and using metadata specified by users in conjunction with information retrieval method (PeerDB project [235]).

Chapter 5
Load Balancing and Replication

In previous chapters, we have presented several designs of Peer-to-Peer systems to support different kinds of queries. In this chapter, we continue to present two essential aspects that need to be considered in the design in order to bring efficiency to query processing: *load balancing* and *replication*.

There are two reasons why load balancing is critical in Peer-to-Peer systems: First, nodes in the systems usually have different resources and hence it is necessary to distribute load to nodes proportional to their capabilities. Second, if file identifiers are correlated with the contents of the files, their distribution will often be skewed. It is necessary then to have more nodes managing a smaller area of the identifier space. With a good load balancing strategy, the system can reduce the query latency and avoid the problem of failure due to overloaded nodes. Consequently, a good load balancing strategy maximizes the throughput the system.

Complementing load balancing, replication deals with the problem of *bottleneck* in query processing at nodes keeping popular data items. It makes sense that if we have a document that is frequently retrieved, we should replicate it on several nodes to improve access to it. With a good replication strategy, the most important benefit is that the system can reduce overloaded nodes. Additionally, replication improves the performance of query processing since it shortens the routing path of a query (the result may be replicated to a node near the node that issued the query). By shortening the query path, the system can also reduce the cost of bandwidth consumed by forwarding queries. Finally, replication increases the availability of data, essential in the Peer-to-Peer environment, where the system is often dynamic and unstable due to the fact that nodes can join and leave at any time.

In general, load balancing and replication are orthogonal and complementary to each other. They are important aspects to any system. Details of load balancing techniques are presented in the first part of the chapter, while the second part is used to introduce replication techniques.

Q.H. Vu et al., *Peer-to-Peer Computing*,
DOI 10.1007/978-3-642-03514-2_5, © Springer-Verlag Berlin Heidelberg 2010

5.1 Load Balancing

Load balancing methods try to balance the use of resources (generally, but not only, storage space) across nodes in the system, such that nodes are neither overloaded nor underloaded. In particular, if nodes have similar capabilities, the expected load distribution should be equal to all nodes. On the other hand, if nodes are heterogeneous, the load distribution should be proportional to the distribution of the needed resources. In general, it would of course be desirable to have load balancing achieved by the data publication process, but even though this is attempted at the moment when the data is inserted into the network, the appearance and disappearance of nodes may lead to unbalances. We must then trigger a specific load balancing process.

There are generally two questions needed to be answered for any load balancing technique: (1) when should load balancing be triggered and (2) how can load balancing be done amongst nodes in the system. This section will answer these two questions step by step.

5.1.1 When Load Balancing is Triggered

5.1.1.1 Dynamic Load Balancing

The basic and straight-forward answer for this question is that load balancing should be triggered when a node becomes overloaded or underloaded. However, the real question now is how a node knows that it is overloaded or underloaded. To answer this question, there are three solutions:

- The most popular method is based on the random choices paradigm [132, 174, 182, 264]. In this method, one node periodically asks for the load of a number of random nodes and compares the received results with its own load. If the number of queried nodes is large enough, the node can approximate the average load of the system, and hence it can decide if it needs to do load balancing for being overloaded or underloaded. Usually, if the node is overloaded, the lightest loaded node amongst those contacted in the sampling step is selected to share the load with the current node. On the other hand, if the node is underloaded, the heaviest loaded node amongst those contacted is selected. An issue of this method is how to determine the number of nodes to contact in the sampling phase. If this number is too small, an incorrect decision can be drawn, i.e., a node is considered as overloaded even though it is not, and hence load balancing is triggered although it is not necessary. If the number of contact nodes is big, the cost of querying is high since each contact node incurs a cost equal to the cost of searching a data item in the network (usually $O(\log N)$). In other words, the issue of this method is establishing the correct tradeoff between the benefit of load balancing and its cost.

- In a different way, Mercury [49] employs histograms to maintain an image of the load distribution on nodes in the system. However, the construction of these histograms with load information is similar to the previous method: asking for the load of a number of random nodes and estimating the load distribution of other nodes. In particular, each node periodically asks for the load of neighbor nodes in its vicinity and exchanges the local load information with random far away nodes to build as well as to maintain histograms. In some sense, Mercury simply adds "memory" to the sampling process presented before. In this method, a node determines if it is overloaded or underloaded by comparing its load with the load information in the histogram. Once load balancing is triggered, load information in histograms can also be used to find lightly loaded nodes or heavily loaded nodes for the process.
- The weakness of the above two methods is that they cannot guarantee the balance of nodes across the system since they are based on the random choices paradigm for querying node load. In order to control the load balance, Ganesan, Bawa, and Garcia-Molina [125] use a *threshold value*. A node is considered to be potentially overloaded if its load is higher than the upper bound of the threshold value. Similarly, it is considered to be potentially underloaded if its load is lower than the lower bound of the threshold value. To check if the node is really overloaded or underloaded, it needs to find the lightest loaded node or the heaviest loaded node for comparison. If it is true, load balancing is done between the node and either the lightest loaded node or the heaviest loaded node, which is found. However, if it is not true, the node needs to adjust its threshold value. In particular, if the node is not overloaded, it increases its threshold value while if the node is not underloaded it decreases its threshold value. The issue of finding the lightest loaded node or the heaviest loaded node is solved by using a separate Skip Graph to keep the load of every node in the system in order. The disadvantage of this method is that the cost of keeping a separate Skip Graph is high, especially in systems with a significant churn rate.

Note that the third method can also be used together with the first method [174]. In this way, instead of periodically asking the load of other nodes, a node only needs to trigger that process when its load goes out of the threshold value. After getting the load of other nodes, if the node is overloaded or underloaded, load balancing is done. However, if the node is neither overloaded nor underloaded, threshold parameter is adjusted to the new value. Nevertheless, similar to the first two methods, this mixed method has no guarantee about the balance of the system since it is still based on the random choices paradigm.

5.1.1.2 Static Load Balancing

Instead of waiting until the system becomes imbalanced to do load balancing, it could also be done preemptively, to avoid an imbalanced load. Such a technique is called *static load balancing*. Static load balancing is usually done at the time a new node joins the system or an existing node leaves the system. In particular, a new node always tries to join next to a heavily loaded node to share a part of the heavy work load. On the other hand, a departing node always tries to find a lightly loaded node to pass its current load to. The way in which a heavily loaded node is found for a new node to join, or a lightly loaded node is found for a departing node to pass its load is similar to the method used in dynamic load balancing. For example, if a histogram or a skip graph is maintained inside the system, the node receiving the first join request from the new node, assists the new node to find a heavily loaded node based on load information in its histogram or skip graph. On the other hand, if the random choices paradigm is used, the new node needs to send multiple join requests to multiple existing nodes in the system and selects the heaviest loaded node amongst them.

In another approach, Byers, Considine, and Mitzenmacher [58] suggest that static load balancing can also be done when new data is inserted. In this system, each new data item is hashed by multiple hash functions to get multiples hash values. Among the nodes that are in charge of these hash values, the one with the lightest work load is selected to insert the data item. However, this method incurs a very high cost in data insertion, data deletion and data search because several nodes need to be searched/contacted for each of these operations.

5.1.1.3 The Power of Two Choices

In general, since these two methods are complementary to each other [174, 223] they should be used together to achieve the desired load balance. To further understand the advantages of combining these two methods, let us consider what may happen if only one of the two load balancing methods is used.

- If only static load balancing method is used, the system is not strong enough to deal with the dynamic change in work load of nodes. If a node becomes overloaded or underloaded when no new nodes come or existing nodes depart, the system still becomes imbalanced. Note that even if we accept the high cost of Byers's solution [58] that uses multiple hash functions to avoid overloaded at nodes when data is inserted, this solution still cannot avoid underloaded at nodes when data is deleted. As a result, dynamic load balancing is needed to solve this problem.
- If only dynamic load balancing method is used, let us consider a case where a new node comes and joins next to a lightly loaded node. In this case, with high probability, these nodes become underloaded, and hence, sooner or later, load balancing has to be triggered for them. Since it takes some cost for doing load balancing, it would have been better if the new node could have joined next to a heavily loaded node. In this way, the new node could have taken some load of the heavily loaded node and consequently the probability of needing another load balancing process would have been decreased.

In general, Algorithm 14 shows the combination of the two methods: static load balancing and dynamic load balancing.

Algorithm 14 : Static_And_Dynamic_Load_Balancing()
1: /*Static Load Balancing*/
2: **if** a new node n joins the system **then**
3:    find a heavily loaded node n'
4:    n shares a part of the load being in charged by n'
5: **end if**
6: **if** an existing node n leaves the system **then**
7:    find a lightly loaded node n'
8:    n' is responsible for the load of the leaving node n
9: **end if**
10: /*Dynamic Load Balancing*/
11: **if** an existing node n becomes overloaded **then**
12:    find a lightly loaded node n'
13:    perform load balancing between n and n'
14: **end if**
15: **if** an existing node n becomes underloaded **then**
16:    find a heavily loaded node n'
17:    perform load balancing between n and n'
18: **end if**

5.1.2 How Load Balancing is Performed

As discussed in the previous section, load balancing is done between a lightly loaded node and a heavily loaded node. In order to balance the load between these nodes, the heavily loaded node needs to pass a part of its load to the lightly loaded node. In general, there are two ways to do this.

— Instead of being in charge of only one position in the system or one virtual node, as suggested in some of the works described in [134, 174, 264], each peer node may keep several virtual nodes at the same time. In particular, Chord [173] suggests that if each peer keeps approximately $\log N$ virtual nodes, with high probability, the load of peers in the system is balanced. In this method, when a node is overloaded, it simply assigns some of its virtual nodes to a lightly loaded node. Furthermore, the load balancing process can happen not only between a heavily loaded node and a lightly loaded node but also between several heavily loaded nodes and several lightly loaded nodes at the same time [264].

  In situations where an overloaded peer cannot find any virtual node to pass to other lightly loaded nodes because the virtual nodes are too big, it is necessary to split the virtual nodes into smaller ones and pass some of them to lightly loaded nodes. The weakness of this method is that it requires more storage at a node for keeping additional virtual nodes. Furthermore, having more virtual nodes leads to higher bandwidth consumption overhead for node maintenance. This method may also cause an increase in the latency of the query, since the number of steps in query processing is often proportional to the number of virtual nodes in the network (if not handled properly, a message may hop between two real nodes multiple times simply because its path follows a set of virtual nodes that reside on the same two real peers).

— To avoid the problem of the virtual nodes method, some systems [49, 125, 166] suggest that a lightly loaded node should leave its position and rejoin next to the heavily loaded node to balance the load. In this way, each peer still needs to keep exactly one virtual node. Furthermore, they also propose that an overloaded or underloaded node should try to do load balancing with its adjacent nodes first before looking for a far away lightly or heavily loaded node [49, 125, 166]. This is because load balancing with adjacent nodes is always cheaper than load balancing with a far away node. To distinguish between these two load balancing approaches, these systems call the former *global load balancing*, since it can happen between two distant nodes, while the later is called *local load balancing*, since it only happens between two adjacent nodes.

5.2 Load Balancing in Concrete Systems

5.2.1 Basic Load Balancing Schemes with Virtual Nodes

Rao and his colleagues [264] discuss in detail three basic load balancing schemes in systems that employ the concept of virtual nodes. These schemes are different from each other in the number of nodes that can participate in the process at the same time. In particular, in the simplest scheme, only two nodes, one lightly loaded node and one heavily loaded node, invoke the load balancing process while in the most complex scheme there may be several lightly loaded nodes and several heavily loaded nodes joining the load balancing process at the same time.

5.2.1.1 One-to-One Scheme

This is the simplest scheme, taking place between a lightly loaded node and a heavily loaded node. Basically, the heavily loaded node iteratively selects a virtual node to pass to the lightly loaded node. The virtual node selected at each step is subjected to the following conditions:

— If transferred, it will not overload the lightly loaded node. This is the most important principle because if we make the lightly loaded node become overloaded, then load balancing will continue to be required at that node. As a result, it causes a ripple effect of load balancing, incurring a very high cost or even the collapse of the network.

— The transferred virtual node is the lightest virtual node that makes the heavily loaded node become normal. This means that the process tries to balance the load by transferring a minimum amount of load.

Fig. 5.1 One-to-One load
balancing scheme

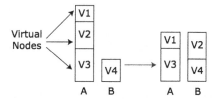

— If there is no virtual node that can be transferred to make the heavily loaded node
become normal, the heaviest virtual node is selected to transfer (given that the
first principle is still satisfied). This principle makes it easier for subsequent steps
to balance the load with smaller virtual nodes.

An example of load balancing using this scheme is illustrated in Fig. 5.1 in which
A is a heavily loaded node and B is a lightly loaded node.

5.2.1.2 One-to-Many Scheme

This scheme is a variant of the previous scheme. Instead of doing load balancing
between a lightly loaded node and a heavily loaded node at each time, this scheme
allows a heavily loaded node to do load balancing with many lightly loaded nodes
at the same time. Nevertheless, the principles of selecting a virtual node to transfer
from a heavily loaded node to a lightly loaded node are similar to those of the
previous scheme. An example of load balancing using this scheme is illustrated in
Fig. 5.2 in which A is a heavily loaded node while B and C are lightly loaded nodes.

5.2.1.3 Many-to-Many Scheme

This is the most complex scheme involving many lightly loaded nodes and many
heavily loaded nodes in the load balancing process. To serve the process of moving
virtual nodes, this scheme creates a pool to keep virtual nodes temporarily while
they are not assigned to any node. The scheme is executed in three phases:

— Unload: In this phase, heavily loaded nodes select virtual nodes to put in the pool
so that they all become normally loaded nodes. At the end of this phase no nodes
are overloaded. However, there are virtual nodes in the pool, which need to be
assigned to nodes.

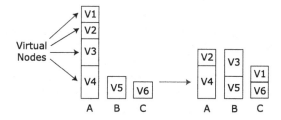

Fig. 5.2 One-to-Many load
balancing scheme

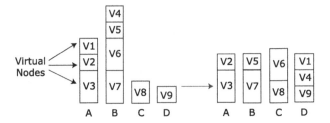

Fig. 5.3 Many-to-many load balancing scheme

— Insert: In this phase, best-fit heuristic is used to transfer virtual nodes from the pool to lightly loaded nodes in the load balancing process. This is done step by step such that no nodes become overloaded. This phase stops when either the pool is empty or no more virtual nodes can be assigned without overloading a node. If this phase stops because the pool is empty, the load balancing process is finished. Otherwise, the next phase is executed.

— Dislodge: In this phase, nodes try to swap remaining big virtual nodes in the pool with smaller virtual nodes they are holding. After that, the process comes back to the insert phase. Since the pool contains smaller virtual nodes, it is easier to assign them.

An example of load balancing using this scheme is illustrated in Fig. 5.3 in which A and B are heavily loaded nodes while C and D are lightly loaded nodes.

Note that in the above schemes, in the worst case, if no virtual nodes can be selected to transfer between heavily loaded nodes and lightly loaded nodes, it is necessary to split a big virtual node into smaller virtual nodes and transfer some of them to the lightly loaded nodes. However, as analyzed in the previous section, having more virtual nodes degrades the performance of the system. As a result, whenever it is possible, if a node maintains adjacent virtual nodes, it merges these virtual nodes into one to reduce the number of virtual nodes in the system.

5.2.2 Y_0 Protocol

Since the high cost of maintaining multiple virtual nodes comes from the cost of maintaining their routing tables, Godfrey and Stoica [134] suggest a method to reduce such a cost. As in Chord [173], each peer is required to maintain $O(\log N)$ virtual nodes, such that, with high probability, the load of peers in the system is balanced. However, instead of selecting these $\log N$ nodes randomly, the Y_0 protocol selects $\log N$ virtual nodes from a $\log N$ of consecutive intervals of length $\frac{1}{N}$. The advantage of this selection is that it allows the system to consider these $\log N$ virtual nodes as a big cluster and create only one routing table for the whole cluster instead of having a routing table at each virtual node. As a result, even though a peer keeps $\log N$ nodes, the cost of maintaining the routing table is still as if it keeps only one

Fig. 5.4 The Y_0 protocol

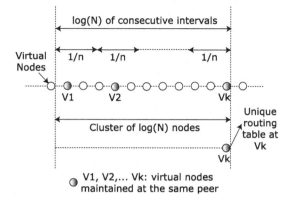

node. The problem now is how to direct a query, given that the routing table keeps only one entry for $\log N$ nodes. Y_0 deals with this problem by modifying the search algorithm a little: A node still tries to forward the search request to the farthest node in its routing table not overshooting the searched key and the message stops when it arrives at a node whose range of values covers the search key, as in Chord. However, that node may not actually keep the key because there are internal nodes between the virtual nodes that are actually maintained at the node. At this point, the successor link of the virtual node, which is the nearest with respect to the searched key, is selected for forwarding the request. The next node receiving the request repeats the same process to forward the query through a successor link towards the destination node. In particular, if a virtual node keeps $O(\log N)$ successor links (the main purpose is fault tolerance[1]), the query processing only takes $O(1)$ additional steps. The Y_0 protocol is illustrated as in Fig. 5.4.

5.2.3 The S&M Protocol

Based on the random choices paradigm, Giakkoupis and Hadzilacos [132] propose two versions of a load balancing protocol called S&M: one is used for homogeneous systems, and the other, the *weighted* S&M protocol, is used for heterogeneous systems. These protocols work under the assumption that data is uniformly distributed over the system. It means that the load of a node is proportional to the size of the range of values of which the node is in charge. As a result, this protocol only uses the static load balancing technique. Note that this assumption is only true if consistent hashing is used to distribute data uniformly. However, in many applications that need to support range queries, such a hashing does not work. As a result, dynamic load balancing is also necessary as analyzed in the above section.

---

[1] Another advantage of selecting $\log N$ nearby virtual nodes to keep at a node is that even though each node may keep $O(\log N)$ successor links, the number of distinct successor nodes, which are needed to maintain at a peer is still bounded by $O(\log N)$.

5.2.3.1 The Design of the S&M Protocol

The two versions of the S&M protocol work in the same way except that the weighted version takes into account the capacity of nodes and, consequently, is splitting or merging the load, function of this capacity. The S&M protocol balances the load of nodes when a new node joins the system or when an existing node departs from the system, as follows:

– When a new node joins the system, it first contacts an existing node inside the network. Through that node, the new node sends a lookup request to a number of random nodes in the system and selects the heaviest loaded node amongst contact nodes to join next to it. The heavily loaded node now splits a part of its load to the new node. In particular, if nodes are homogeneous, the load is simply split into two equal parts. However, if nodes are heterogeneous, the load has to be split proportionally to the capacity of the heavily loaded node and the new node.
– When an existing node leaves the system, it also contacts a number of random nodes in the system. The lightest node amongst the contact nodes is selected for further processing. This lightest node needs to check the load of its sibling, which is either the node splits the load to it when it joins the system or the node receives the split load from it depending on which action happens later. If the load of its sibling has not been split further, these two nodes are merged together. One of them replaces the departure node. On the other hand, if the load of the sibling node has been split with another node, the load of the sibling node must be lighter than the load of the current lightest node. As a result, the sibling node takes the role of the former lightest node and repeats the checking process with its other sibling. This process continues until two lightest sibling nodes are found and merged together. Note that if the load of the departure node is lighter than the load of the lightest node amongst contact nodes, the previous process is executed at the departure node to find a pair of the lightest nodes to merge.

We can observe that this protocol is similar to constructing a binary tree such that the gap between the highest level leaf node and the lowest level leaf node in the tree is as small as possible: The narrower the gap between these nodes, the better the load distribution. As a result, when a new node joins the system, it tries to split a high level node in the tree, which is a heavily loaded node. On the other hand, when an existing node leaves the system, a pair of low level leaf nodes that are lightly loaded nodes should merge together. After that, one of them replaces the position of the departed node. For example, as in Fig. 5.5, assume that a new joining node contacts and obtains information about the load of nodes A, C, and J. Since A is the highest level, or the heaviest, node among the three nodes, the current load of A is split into two parts and the new node takes one part. On the other hand, assume that node I wants to leave the network and it contacts three nodes B, D, F. Since F is the lowest level or the lightest node amongst three nodes, F checks its adjacent node. Since the adjacent node of F, G, has been split before, G replaces F as the lightest node. Finally G and H are merged together, and one of them takes the merged load while the other comes to replace the position of I.

Fig. 5.5 A binary tree
formed by S&M protocol

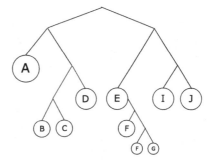

5.2.4 A Combination of Both Local and Random Probes

In order to reduce the cost of random choices paradigm, some authors [182, 215] suggest that the node should ask for the load of not only random nodes (random probe) but also neighbor nodes surrounding them (local probe) to estimate the load distribution of the system. Since it is much cheaper to ask for the load of an adjacent node of a contact node than to ask for the load of a contact node (1 message compared to $O(\log N)$ messages), the node can reduce the cost of load querying by decreasing the number of contact random nodes and increasing the number of contact neighbor nodes in the vicinity of contact nodes while still achieve the same performance.

5.2.4.1 Load Imbalance Boundary

Under the assumption that the data is uniformly distributed over the system and nodes are inserted step by step to the system, Manku [215] shows that if the kth node joining the system asks for the load of one random node and $O(\log k)$ neighbor nodes in the vicinity of that random node, with high probability, the maximum imbalance of the system that is the ratio between the heavily loaded node and the lightly loaded node is just 4. Later, Kenthapadi and Manku [182] prove that if the kth node asks for the load of r random nodes and v neighbor nodes of each random node so that $r \cdot v \geq c \cdot \log k$, where c is a suitable large constant, with high probability, the maximum imbalance of the system is 8. An issue here is how a new node knows k, its order in the insertion sequence. The solution is that k can be deduced from the number of nodes in the system, which can be estimated from the number of bits in the identifier of any node in the system. An example of a combination of local and random probes is shown in Fig. 5.6 with $r = 3$ and $v = 4$.

5.2.5 Mercury

Mercury [49] suggests the use of histograms to maintain the load distribution of nodes in the system. In Mercury, each node periodically samples nearby nodes to

Fig. 5.6 A combination of both local and random probes

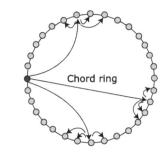

Fig. 5.7 Histogram construction in Mercury

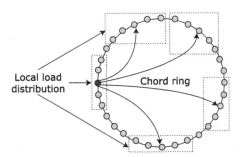

get local load distribution. The node also periodically samples a number of random distant nodes, to ask for the local load distribution of these nodes. The process of sampling distant nodes is based on random walk algorithm. In particular, the node first sends sampling requests with $\log N$ hops time-to-live to random neighbor nodes. After that, at each node along the sampling path, a random neighbor node is selected to forward the request. In this way, the process finally sends sampling requests uniformly to nodes in the system, with high probability. The node at the end of the sampling path returns to the requester node its local load distribution. Based on the received samples, a load distribution histogram is constructed at the node. The process of constructing and maintaining the histogram of a node is illustrated as in Fig. 5.7. As discussed before the method to construct and maintain the histogram is based on the combination of local and random probes presented in the above section. In particular, in the figure of the example, values of random probe (r) and local probe (v) are respectively, 4 and 5.

5.2.5.1 Load Balancing with Histograms

From the information given by a histogram, a node can calculate the average work load of the system. Additionally, by calculating the average work load of itself and adjacent nodes, a node can determine its status as normally loaded, overloaded or underloaded. In particular, if the ratio between the average local work load and the average work load of the system is smaller than $\frac{1}{\alpha}$, the node is underloaded. On the other hand, if this ratio is greater than α, the node is overloaded. If the node is overloaded, information in the histogram is used to find a lightly loaded node. Once the lightly loaded node is found, that node leaves its current position and joins next to the current node to share the heavy load. On the other hand, if the node is underloaded, the information in the histogram is used to find a heavily loaded node. The node then leaves its position and comes to join next to the heavily loaded node. Here, α is set depending on applications.

5.2.6 Online Balancing of Range-partitioned Data

Ganesan, Bawa, and Garcia-Molina [125] propose a model for load balancing in which load balancing in the system is controlled by a threshold function T: $T_i = \lfloor c \cdot \delta^i \rfloor$. Whenever the load of a node passes the threshold value, load balancing is triggered as follows: At first, the node tries to do local load balancing with its adjacent nodes by comparing the threshold value of itself and that of its adjacent nodes. If there is at least one level difference between the two threshold values, local load balancing is done between the node and its correspondent adjacent node. If not, the node tries the next step to do global load balancing. To do global load balancing, the node needs to find the lightest node in the system and compares its threshold with the threshold of the lightest node. If there is at least a two level difference between the two threshold values, global load balancing is done. Otherwise, the node is not actually overloaded, but the entire network is considered to be having a heavier load, and consequently the threshold level is increased. The complete algorithm is shown in Algorithm 15. The process of local load balancing and global load balancing are illustrated in Fig. 5.8.

In this algorithm, in order to find the lightest load node, a separate Skip Graph is dedicated to keep the load of every node in the system ordered by the load of nodes.

Algorithm 15 : Online_Load_Balancing()

1: set $T_n = c \cdot \delta^n$ be threshold value of the current node
2: set $T_l = c \cdot \delta^l$ be threshold value of the left adjacent node
3: set $T_r = c \cdot \delta^r$ be threshold value of the right adjacent node
4: **if** $n - 1 \geq l$ **or** $n - 1 \geq r$ **then**
5:     perform local load balancing with adjacent nodes
6: **else**
7:     find the lightest loaded node K in the system
8:     set $T_k = c \cdot \delta^k$ be threshold value of K
9:     **if** $n - 2 \geq k$ **then**
10:         perform global load balancing between the current node and K
11:     **else** {increase the threshold value}
12:         $n = n + 1$
13:     **end if**
14: **end if**

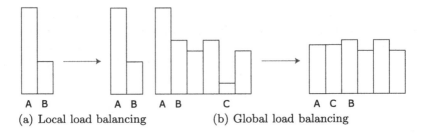

(a) Local load balancing   (b) Global load balancing

Fig. 5.8 Online load balancing

Even though maintaining such a Skip Graph is expensive, since any of operations
from node join, node departure to data insertion or data deletion can make nodes
in the Skip Graph change their positions, this method can achieve the maximum
imbalance ratio load, which is the ratio between the heavily loaded node and the
lightly loaded node in the system, by δ^3. Note that, depending on applications, δ can
be set to a low or a high value. The lower value the δ is, the better the load balance
of the system is and certainly the higher the cost of load balancing is.

5.3 Replication

Replication is a technique in which data can be stored at multiple nodes in the system.[2] The benefits of replication are that it can improve availability of data in case
of failure, avoid hotspot problem due to many queries targeting to the same node,
and improve performance of query processing since a replica may be found at a
node nearer to the query node than the node holding the original data. Nevertheless, the benefits do not come for free. Replication requires some costs for creating
and maintaining replicas. Since it is costly to blindly replicate data in Peer-to-Peer
systems, where the amount of data is huge, a challenge in replication is how to determine which object should be replicated, how many replicas are needed, where
replicas are stored, and how to maintain consistency of replicas with their original
data. This section gives a detailed view of all the above problems.

5.3.1 Replica Granularity

There are two levels of replica granularity: *Full replication* and *Block replication*.

---

[2]If the data is only replicated at the query node, the technique can be called caching.

5.3.1.1 Full Replication

The simplest way in replication is storing the entire data object. Gnutella [133] and Napster [226] use or used this method for file replication. In particular, when a node downloads a file, it automatically creates a replica stored at itself. The advantage of this method is that it is simple to implement and easy to maintain consistency of data. However, it is not efficient to replicate the entire object in one operation, especially when the object size is large.

5.3.1.2 Block Replication

In some applications, users do not require to retrieve the entire data object. They only need a part of it or they need the whole object but only a part of it at each time. For example, video applications only need a part of file to play at each time. As a result, the second type of replication is block-level replication. In this way, each data object is divided into several parts, and replication is done for each part individually. This method brings several advantages compared to the previous method:

— By dividing the object into separate parts, it is easier to find a place to keep the object's replicas. In some cases, a big object cannot be stored in any peer. However, by splitting it into smaller pieces, they can be stored at several peers.
— Since individual parts can be distributed or collected simultaneously, this method can reduce the time of replicating as well as the time of collecting replicas to rebuild the original data object. To some extent, this method can provide a faster response to users than the previous method, which replicates the whole object.
— The replication cost of small parts can be smaller than the replication cost of the whole big object since it does not require a long and stable network connection.

However, there are also some disadvantages of using the method:

— In order to reconstruct the original object, it is required that all parts of the object be available. As a result, it is necessary to maintain statistics about replicas and the number of blocks in an object. This puts some extra cost in replication.
— In the worst case, if any part of an object cannot be retrieved, the whole object cannot be reconstructed completely. In case of the full replication method, the object once retrieved should be complete.
— Compared to the full replication method, it is harder to maintain data consistency in this method as the higher number of replicas has to be updated in case of change in the original data object.

The second problem mentioned above requires a good strategy in distributing replica parts of an object so that we can collect at least one replica for each part every time. As an effort to reduce the number of blocks, that has to be collected to reconstruct the original object, Erasure codes such as Reed-Solomon [259] and Tornado [59] are proposed. These codes have an interesting feature: the original n-block object can be reconstructed from a number of blocks m less than n (m is close to n). These m blocks are taken from a set of $k \cdot n$ coded blocks, which are encoded from the n original blocks (k is a small constant).

5.3.2 Replica Quantity

5.3.2.1 Uniform Replication

This is a simple method in which each object has the same number of replicas. Since objects are treated equally, this method is often used in two cases:

− To guarantee the available of data in the system in case of node failure.
− To provide a high probability that any data can be found within a boundary number of steps, if it is used in unstructured Peer-to-Peer systems (as discussed in Chap. 2, under normal condition, there is no guarantee to find an existing data in unstructured Peer-to-Peer systems within a boundary number of steps).

However, this method cannot deal with the bottleneck problem caused by popular objects. Since the method always creates the same number of replicas for both frequently queried objects (popular objects) and infrequently queried objects (unpopular objects), if the storage capacity of the system is limited, there may be a case where popular objects are lack of replicas to deal with the bottleneck problem while there are redundant replicas of unpopular objects. By keeping unnecessary replicas for unpopular objects, it also means that the method is not efficient if the two above cases are not considered (i.e., if it is used in structured Peer-to-Peer system and there is no worry about node failure).

5.3.2.2 Proportional Replication

To solve the bottleneck problem caused by extremely popular objects, this method suggests that the number of replicas of a data object should be proportional to the number of queries looking for that object. As a result, a popular object with a large number of queries has a large number of replicas while an object with a small number of queries has a small number of replicas. By replicating data objects following query distribution, the more popular a data object is, the higher the number of replicas it has, and hence the bottleneck can be avoided. Furthermore, this method can improve the efficiency of query processing in the system, since replicas of popular objects are pervasive and consequently queries about them are answered quickly. Nevertheless, this method can neither guarantee the availability of data nor the boundary of search steps in unstructured Peer-to-Peer systems as in the previous method because unpopular objects may only have a few of replicas or no replicas at all.

5.3.2.3 Square-root Replication

Although the two previous methods, uniform replication and proportional replication, apply different strategies in creating the number of replicas for an object, they produce the same average performance on successful queries. As pointed out by Cohen and Shenker [80], this performance is actually worse than that of any replication strategy falling between them in which the performance of square-root replication is the optimal one. In square-root replication, the number of replicas of a data object is proportional to the square-root of its number of queries. In other words, replica distribution of objects in the system is proportional to the square root of query distribution. As indicated by Cohen and Shenker [80], let m be the number of different objects, n be number of peers, R be the total number of replicas, q_i be the query distribution of object i, and $p = \frac{R}{n}$ be the average number of objects stored at each peer, both uniform replication and proportional replication take the average search size of $\frac{m}{p}$ while the optimal value achieved by square-root replication is $\frac{1}{p}(\sum \sqrt{q_i})^2$. It is interesting to realize that even though proportional replication is based on query distribution, the average search size is similar to that of uniform distribution and does not depend on query distribution at all. It only depends on the number of objects, the number of peers, and the number of replicas. On the other hand, the average search size of square-root distribution really depends on query distribution.

5.3.3 Replica Distribution

There are five general strategies used to select locations for distributing replicas: owner replication, path replication, random replication, preceding replication, and successor replication.

— *Owner replication:* this method places a replica at the requester node when a search is successful.
— *Path replication:* instead of putting replica at only the requester node as the previous method, this method puts replicas at nodes along the search path between the requester node and the destination node. Even though it incurs additional costs (storage, bandwidth), this method has the advantage that replicas can be put at nodes near the source node, and hence it can help the source node to avoid the bottle neck problem if the searched data is a hot data object.
— *Random replication:* Lv et al. [210] have pointed out that path replication has a tendency to distribute objects to nodes following the topological order. As a result, it is not as effective as the method that creates the same number of replicas but distributes them in random order to nodes that have been visited by the search process (i.e., not only nodes in the search path between the requester and the destination node).
— *Preceding replication and successor replication:* while the first three strategies only replicate data objects upon search requests, the last two strategies replicate data objects equally to preceding nodes or successive nodes in the search path. In particular, the preceding replication distributes replicas of a data object to all preceding nodes when the object is popular, and hence avoids the bottle neck problem. Conversely, the last strategy, the successor replication, replicates data objects to successor nodes since if a node fails, its immediate successor node is

the node taking responsibility for all data stored at itself. As a result, the system increases availability of data objects, and hence is more resilient to failures.

5.3.4 Replica Consistency

Guaranteeing the consistency of replicas is an important aspect of replication. However, most of the current Peer-to-Peer systems assume that replicated data is read only and hence they can avoid this problem. Only a few of Peer-to-Peer systems consider this aspect and give solutions. Generally, these solutions can be classified into two main categories.

5.3.4.1 Replication with Expiration

The simplest solution to guarantee consistency of replicas with the source data is keeping them only for a period of time. Depending on the frequency of object modification, an expiration time can be adjusted. For example, if the data object is often modified, the expiration time can be set to a small value. Otherwise, it can be set to a high value. When replicas expire, they can either be discarded or be refreshed by soliciting the resource owner for an update.

5.3.4.2 Immediate Updates

A difficulty of the previous method is the determination of a suitable expiration time. It is inefficient if an unsuitable value is chosen for expiration time. For example, if a data object is persistent while we discard its replicas or refresh them at frequent time intervals, it is unnecessary and costly. On the other hand, if a data object is modified frequently while the expiration time is set to a high value, stale replicas may be retrieved. To overcome this problem, this method suggests that replicas can be used as long as possible, no expiration time is set. However, when the original data object is changed, an update request should be sent to all nodes keeping replicas for updating. In order to update replicas, there are generally two solutions. The easiest one is broadcasting the replica update request to all nodes in the system. The weakness of this solution is that it is expensive. On the other hand, the second solution suggests that the system should keep links between the node holding the original data object and nodes keeping its replicas. Nevertheless, this solution also incurs a high cost for maintaining these links, especially in high churn rate systems.

5.3.5 Replica Replacement

In some cases, due to the limitations of storage capacity, it is necessary to remove less efficient replicas, to reserve space for new coming replicas. As a result, replica replacement policies have to be considered. In general, all popular replacement policies such as Least Recently Used, Most Recently Used, Least Frequently Used, Most Frequently Used, Minimum Size, Maximum Size. . . can be applied for replica replacement in P2P systems. However, replicas in P2P file-sharing system may need special policies due to their special characteristics [335]. As an example, a special replacement policy called Minimum Relative Size has been proposed.

5.3.5.1 Minimum Relative Size

This replacement policy can be used in systems that create replicas at block level. Since the whole data object can only be reconstructed completely if all replicated parts of the objects are found, this replacement takes into account the total amount of replicas of a file in the policy. In other words, the policy considers how much content existing replicas contribute to reconstruct the whole file. In particular, this replacement policy tries to replace replicas that contain the smallest percentage of content in a replicated file. For example, if a node keeps all replicated parts of a file, it is better to keep all of these parts since they can be used to serve subsequent requests with the least cost (the query does not need to be forwarded to other nodes to find remaining parts).

5.4 Replication in Concrete Systems

5.4.1 Replication in Read-only Unstructured P2P Systems

Owner replication is the most popular replication strategy, which is used in read-only unstructured P2P systems such as Gnutella [7] and Napster [12]. This strategy works efficiently because the search strategy in unstructured systems allows the query to be sent to any node so that replicas have a potential to be reused. However, this strategy cannot be applied in structured P2P systems because in these systems, queries always traverse though specific paths and replicas on certain nodes are unlikely to be encountered during the course of a query, and thus such replicas are useless.

5.4.2 Replication in Read-only Structured P2P Systems

5.4.2.1 Past

PAST [114] is a read-only file sharing system, which employs the uniform replication to create k replicas for each data file. These replicas are placed on k nodes, whose node identifiers are closest to the file identifier. This strategy has two important properties:

- With high probability, k replicas are widely spread across the physical network. As a result, the system is resilient to massive node failures as well as to network partition.
- Since identifiers of nodes and files in the system are generated uniformly, the number of files stored at each node is approximately equal.

The biggest advantage of this method is its simplicity. However, as analyzed before, it is not efficient to deal with the bottleneck problem since the popularity of files is very different.

5.4.2.2 Cooperative File System

Cooperative File System (CFS) [93] is a Peer-to-Peer read-only storage system built on top of Chord [173], in which data files are stored and managed at block-level. Clients see the storage system through a file system (FS) layer that is similar to those used by common operating systems. It is structured in blocks and a block can be either a part of a file or a part of the file system metadata. The FS accesses blocks by interacting with the distributed hashing table (DHash) layer under it. In turn, the DHash layer uses the Chord layer to access concrete file blocks from servers. Different from clients, servers do not have the FS layer, they only have the two bottom layers: DHash and Chord. The system architecture of CFS is illustrated in Fig. 5.9. In CFS, replication is done at the DHash layer at servers to improve the performance of the system. Two replication techniques are used in CFS:

- The first technique uses the successor replication scheme. Each block stored at a node is replicated to k following nodes in the Chord ring to increase availability of the block. This technique is based on a property of Chord ring that if a node fails, the immediate successor node will take responsibility for all data belonging to the failed node. As a result, using this replication technique, blocks are always available to retrieve even thought the block owner fails. Furthermore, this technique can help clients to select the fastest download server from a group

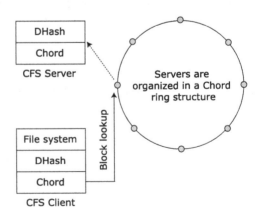

Fig. 5.9 CFS architecture

of servers holding the resource, provided that additional statistics of servers in the successor list are also maintained at the nodes.

— The second technique employs the path replication scheme. Replicas of a block are replicated through the search path to avoid bottle neck at the block owner node if that block is a popular block or in order words, that block belongs to a popular file.

5.4.3 Beehive

Beehive [263] proposes the use of proactive replication to achieve $O(1)$ average-case lookup performance on structured Peer-to-Peer systems such as Pastry [275], Tapestry [349], Chord [173], or P-Grid [17]. It is based on an interesting property of structured Peer-to-Peer systems: "the length of the lookup path will be reduced by one when an object is replicated to all neighbor nodes having links to it" and "this lookup path length can be further reduced if the object is also replicated at all nodes preceding neighbor nodes in the search path and so on". As a result, by replicating data objects to an enough number of levels in their lookup paths, the system can achieve a constant average lookup performance. Figure 5.10 illustrates replication in Beehive. Note that similar to other systems, popular queried objects should be replicated to deep levels while rare queried objects may be replicated only at narrow levels.

5.4.3.1 Analytical Model

At the center of Beehive there is an analytical model, which helps to identify optimal replication levels for objects based on the query distribution. Let α be the parameter of the query distribution in which the ith most popular object has the number of queries proportional to $i^{-\alpha}$; M and N be the number of objects and the number of nodes in the system; b be the fan-out of the search tree structure in the system; $k = \log_b N$ be the maximum number of search steps; C be the desired lookup constant.

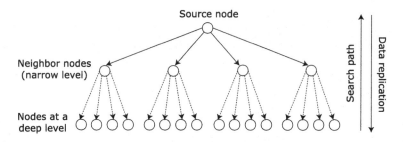

Fig. 5.10 Replication in Beehive

Let x_i be the fraction of objects replicated at level i or lower. The closed-form solution of x_i is

$$x_i^* = \begin{cases} [\frac{d^i(k'-C')}{1+d+\cdots+d^{k'-1}}]^{\frac{1}{1-\alpha}} & \forall 0 \le i < k', \\ 1 & \forall k' \le i \le k. \end{cases}$$

In which $d = b^{\frac{1-\alpha}{\alpha}}$, $C' = C(1 - \frac{1}{M^{1-\alpha}})$ and k' has to satisfy the condition

$$x_{k'-1} < 1 \quad \text{or} \quad \frac{d^{k'-1}(k'-C')}{1+d+\cdots+d^{k'-1}} < 1.$$

The above formula is used only in the case of $\alpha < 1$. If $\alpha > 1$, there is no optimal value since the space is not convex. However, this formula can still be used simply to improve lookup performance. In the special case $\alpha = 1$, the close-form solution of x_i is

$$x_i^* = \begin{cases} \frac{M^{\frac{-C}{k'}} b^i}{b^{\frac{k'-1}{2}}} & \forall 0 \le i < k', \\ 1 & \forall k' \le i \le k. \end{cases}$$

Beehive estimates the value of the α parameter in two steps. In the first step, the popularity of data objects is calculated by aggregating query hits at nodes in the replication paths. After that, the calculated result is broadcasted back to all nodes in the second step. The gossiping algorithm is used to forward messages in both steps. In details, at interval time, nodes report query hits counted at them and lower level nodes in the replication path to higher level nodes. Step by step, these counts are aggregated at the resource owner node. The aggregated result is then propagated back to other nodes. By getting popularity of data objects, each node estimates the α parameter locally in the second step. The estimated value is further refined by exchanging knowledge between nodes.

5.4.3.2 Replication

Based on the results of the estimation of α, replication is performed asynchronously. Each node has a responsibility to manage replicas of data objects stored at itself. If the analyzed results show that it is necessary to create more replicas of a data object at lower level nodes, the node replicates the data object to nodes preceding it on the search path. On the contrary, if the popularity of a data object is decreased, and hence it is not necessary to keep a replica of that object at the node, the node automatically deletes the unnecessary replica. Data consistency in the system is achieved by propagating changes in data objects from the resource owner node to other nodes through the replication path. In particular, each data object is associated with a version number. When a data object is modified, a new (higher) version number is assigned for it, and the modification is propagated to nodes keeping replicas. By comparing version numbers, a node can determine the latest version of data object it should keep among different versions.

5.4.4 Symmetric Replication for Structured Peer-to-Peer Systems

The basic idea of the symmetric replication method for structured Peer-to-Peer systems [131] is simple: nodes in the system are split into groups in which every node keeps replicas of all data stored at other nodes in the same group. Depending on the system, the size of groups can be smaller or larger.

5.4.4.1 Node Grouping

The biggest challenge of this method is how to gather nodes into groups and distribute data among them. One simple solution is to partition the identifier space into equal zones. Nodes in the same zones are located in the same group. For example, if N is the number of nodes in the system and f is the intended size of groups, then nodes whose identifier modulo f is the same can be put in the same group. Figure 5.11 shows 16 nodes organized in a Chord ring structure with the group size of 4. As a result, nodes whose identifier is 0, 4, 8, and 12, are put in the same groups, and data stored at these nodes is replicated to all others. Similarly, nodes 1, 5, 9, and 13 are in a group; 2, 6, 10, and 14 are in a group; 3, 7, 11, 15 are in a group.

5.4.4.2 Data Replication

Based on the fact that data is stored at the immediate successor node in the identifier space, it can be replicated in an opposite way of node grouping. In particular, replicas of a data object are created with identifiers $i' = (i + j \cdot f) \bmod N$, where i is the original data identifier, $0 \le j < r$, $r = \frac{N}{f}$ is the number of groups in the system. Having data replicas and their identifiers, they can be concurrently inserted into the system.

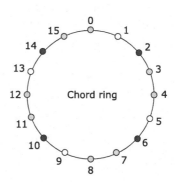

Fig. 5.11 Symmetric replication in a Chord ring

5.4.5 CUP: Controlled Update Propagation in Peer-to-Peer Networks

CUP [274] is a protocol employing the path replication method. However, instead of blindly replicating data objects along the search path, in CUP, a node has its own right to decide if it needs to keep a replica of the data object or not. A node only keeps a replica if that replica brings benefits to it. For example, if the node receives queries for a data object frequently, it is reasonable to keep a replica for that data object.

5.4.5.1 System Architecture

To manage replication, in addition to the traditional link that is used for search purpose (called *query channel*), CUP maintains a separate channel called *update channel* for distributing and controlling replicas. Queries for a data object are forwarded along the query channel to the destination node. If there is any node in the query channel, which wants to keep a replica, a replica of the object is created and sent through the update channel to that node. Note that the update channel only exists if there are replicas of an object in that channel. Based on the update channel, CUP can promptly update replicas when the original object is changed. The system architecture is illustrated as in Fig. 5.12.

5.4.5.2 Data Replication

To determine if a replica should be kept at a node or not. CUP introduces the concept of *investment return*. Investment return is based on the popularity of a data object. For every query a node receives, the node keeps track of its popularity, which can be determined by the query frequency. Note that since the popularity of data objects may be changed by time, the node only keeps track of queries either in a sliding time window or since the last time the object is modified. Knowing the popularity of a data object, a node can then decide to keep a replica of it or not. CUP controls the process of updating data by using an "interest" bit vector for each data object. An update is only sent to a neighbor node if the interest bit corresponding to that neighbor node is set. If the interest bit is clear, it means that the correspondent neighbor node does not need to keep the replica and hence it is not necessary to send the update request.

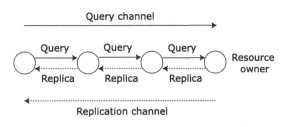

Fig. 5.12 CUP system architecture

5.4.6 Dynamic Replica Placement for Scalable Content Delivery

Another variant of the path replication technique is to select the most suitable node satisfying some system constraints[3] along the search path to place a replica on it [72]. Replication is managed through disseminating trees. A disseminating tree is constructed at a node whenever a replica is created for a data object stored at that node. Nodes keeping replicas are represented as tree nodes in the disseminating tree. As a result, data updates can be done to guarantee the consistency of replicas simply by distributing update requests along the tree starting from the root node and ending at leaf nodes. The architecture of a disseminating tree is shown in Fig. 5.13.

5.4.6.1 Disseminating Tree Construction

There are two methods for constructing disseminating trees. In the following descriptions, assume that there is a node, called *client*, that needs to duplicate a data item it has on another node that satisfies some system constraints.

— *Naive placement:* if, by issuing a query, it finds a node x, keeping the resource or a replica of the resource, and x satisfies the system constraints, then the replica already exists and no further copying is performed. Instead, node x becomes the parent of the client in the tree structure. However, if x does not satisfy the constrains, then a node y along the search path, satisfying the constrains, is selected to store the replica. If no node satisfies the constraints, the node nearest to the client node is chosen. Once the replica is created, x takes y as its child in the disseminating tree structure.

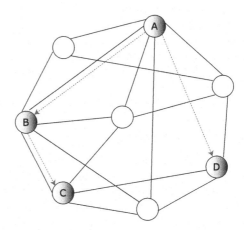

Fig. 5.13 Dissemination tree architecture

---

[3]Constraints can be the maximum query latency from clients, the minimum server storage capacity, or the minimum network bandwidth speed.

— *Smart placement:* if the node x, found as before, keeps a replica, it is already a node in the disseminating tree. However, instead of only checking constraints at x, surrounding nodes (parent, siblings and children) are also checked to select the best node satisfying the constraints. If such a node is found, the client node becomes a child of that node in the tree structure. Otherwise, the same process as the naive placement is performed.

The tradeoff between the two methods is that the naive placement method requires less cost in the tree's construction than the smart placement method does. However, the smart placement method is more efficient than the naive placement method in the aspects of number of replicas, load distribution, query latency, and bandwidth consumption (for query processing).

5.4.6.2 Disseminating Tree Maintenance

The tree structure is maintained in a simple way: At interval times, "heartbeat" messages are sent from the root node downwards to all nodes in the tree. If a node does not receive such a message within a time interval, it knows that it is no longer in the tree structure, and has to rejoin the tree. On the other hand, each child node has a responsibility to send a "refresh" message to its parent periodically. If the parent node does not receive such a message within a time interval, it assumes that the child has died and removes the link to that child.

5.4.7 Updates in Highly Unreliable, Replicated P2P Systems

Instead of using a dissemination tree for replica update as before [72], Datta, Hauswirth, and Aberer [96] suggest that each node only needs to keep a replica list, which contains nodes holding replicas. Nodes in the replica list of a node can include the nodes from which it received the replica, nodes to which it has sent the replica, or other nodes that it happens to know by random search or by the process of replica update, which is discussed later. In other words, if we consider the set of all nodes holding the same replica, each node in this set knows an arbitrary portion of remaining nodes in the set. Based on the replica list, replica update can be propagated in two phases.

1. *Push phase:* when a data item that has been replicated to other nodes is updated, the push phase starts. At first, the node holding the original data item selects randomly a number of nodes in its replica list (not all nodes in the list) to send the update request. The update request contains four pieces of information: the new updated data item U, its version V, the list of nodes that have received the same update request R_f, and a counter t that count the number of push round that has been executed. When a node receives an update request, it updates its current data item and continues to select a number of nodes in its replica list to forward

the update request. Before forwarding the update request, the node needs to add the selected nodes to R_f and increases t by 1. Note that in this phase, nodes can also add more nodes into its replica list using the nodes in R_f.

2. *Pull phase:* during the push phase, some nodes holding replicas may be offline, and hence they do not receive update requests. Consequently, the replica stored at these nodes may be out of date. The pull phase is proposed so solve such a problem. In particular, when a node that was offline before, comes online, it issues a pull request to a portion of online nodes in its replica list to ask for an update. When a node receives a pull request, it sends its stored replica version to the requester if it is sure that it currently holds the latest version of the data. Otherwise, it joins the pull phase, and continues to ask other nodes.

Figure 5.14 shows an example of these two phases. In this figure, the replica list of a node contains all nodes to which it has a link. For example the replica list of node A contains C, D, G, and H, while the replica list of node B contains C, G, and H. Note that to make the figure clearer, we just assume the links are symmetric. However, they can be asymmetric in practice. Now, assume that node A is the node holding the original data item and the data item is updated. As a result, A starts the push phase. We further assume that C is offline at this time. Following the push phase, replica update can be propagated from A to D and H; from D to E; from H to B and G; from E to F and G to F. Since C is offline, it cannot receive the update request. As a result, its holding replica is out of date. However, when C goes online, it has to start the pull phase. As a result, sooner or later, it will receive an update of the latest replica version. In this figure, C sends a pull request to B and gets the latest version from B (assume that B is sure that it currently holds the latest version).

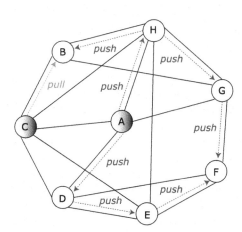

Fig. 5.14 Updates with push and pull

5.4.8 Proactive Replication

As discussed before, replication can help to improve the availability of data in case of failure. Usually, to achieve this property, for each data item stored in the system, a number of k replicas of it are created and maintained, where k is configured depending on applications. In particular, when a new data item is inserted into the system, k replicas are created and distributed to other nodes in the system. On the other hand, when a node fails, the system must recreate new replicas for all data items stored at the failed node in order to keep enough number of necessary replicas of a data item. This process may cause overhead in bandwidth usage at that time. As a result, Sit and his colleagues propose Tempo [297], a proactive replication protocol, which replicas data items constantly at regular time intervals instead of failure time. If the replication rate is equal to the failure rate, the system can still guarantee the same number of k replicas for each data item.

5.4.8.1 Replication Protocol Design

A concern with Tempo is how to determine the replication rate, since if this rate is smaller than the failure rate, the system cannot guarantee the availability of a data item. On the other hand, if the replication rate is greater than the failure rate, the system will eventually run out of storage space. The basic solution is to greedily select the largest possible replication rate at first and control the rate later. In particular, replicas can be created constantly at the maximum bandwidth capacity, which is allowed at nodes. Usually, this replication rate is much greater than the failure rate. After that, the rate is gradually adjusted when the number of replicas reaches k. Tempo also applies this solution with a little modification based on three parameters specified by nodes:

- μ: bandwidth budget used for replication.
- C_{max}: storage budget used for replication.
- R_{max}: total number of replicas, which is needed for an object.

Using these three parameters, in Tempo, replicas are created constantly at nodes at the rate of μ until the storage at nodes used for replicas reaches its maximum capacity C_{max}. However, if a data item does not have enough replicas (i.e. it has less than R_{max}), replicas continue to be created at nodes. The purpose of this strategy is to achieve the minimum requirement to provide availability of data by using R_{max}. Nonetheless, whenever it is possible, it also improves availability of the system by using all granted resources. Additionally, to avoid many concurrent uploads at nodes, which may slow down the system, it is suggested that each node may only replicate data items to a fixed number of other nodes. A potential problem of this replication protocol is that there may be situations where nodes are out of storage space due to keeping several replicas of some data items while not having enough replicas of others, and hence they have to delicate more storage to keep new replicas for these data items to satisfy R_{max} constraint. Nevertheless, such a case is unlikely because when a node decides to create a new replica for a data item, it always gives preference to data items having the least replicas, and hence the number of replicas of data item should be approximately equal.

5.5 Summary

In this chapter, we have introduced in details load balancing and replication techniques. They are important techniques that increase the efficiency of P2P systems. In particular, load balancing helps to balance the load of nodes proportional to their capability. As a result, nodes in the system can avoid being overloaded. On the other hand, replication helps to avoid hotspots at nodes holding popular data items, to reduce query latency, and to improve the availability of data in the system. In general, these two techniques, load balancing and replication, are orthogonal and complementary to each other.

Basically, there are two load balancing strategies: static load balancing and dynamic load balancing. Static load balancing happens at the time a new node joins the system or when an existing node departs from the system. In the former case, the new node gets a part of the load from some heavily loaded node. In the latter, the departing node passes its load to some lightly loaded node. On the other hand, dynamic load balancing happens when an existing node in the network becomes overloaded or underloaded. It is "dynamic" in the sense that even if the network does not suffer changes in its set of nodes (but only in the data that they make available), it still acts upon it by a continuous process of self diagnose. If a node somehow detects it is overloaded, it needs to find a lightly loaded node to balance the load, while if the node is underloaded, it needs to find a heavily loaded node. To balance the load between a lightly loaded node and a heavily loaded node, there are two solutions. The first solution is to use the concept of *virtual node*. In particular, a node may keep several virtual nodes. As a result, the overloaded node only needs to pass some virtual nodes to the lightly loaded node to balance the load. The second solution is to let the lightly loaded node pass its load to its adjacent node and join next to the heavily loaded node to share the load.

A significant issue in this process is how to find a lightly loaded node or a heavily loaded node. Currently, there are three main methods. They show a spectrum of choices as to when to incur some overhead. The first method is based on random choices paradigm: a node needs to sample a number of random nodes in the network. The node having the lightest load is considered a lightly loaded node while the node having the highest load is taken as a heavily loaded node. This method has a high overhead each time a rebalancing is triggered, but it does not need to maintain an image of the state of the network. The second method is to use histograms to maintain the load distribution of nodes in the system. It balances the overhead at the time of the rebalancing with the overhead in maintaining metadata on the load distribution. The last method is to use a separate Skip Graph to keep the load of nodes in the system in order. As a result, the heaviest loaded node and the lightest loaded node are two nodes at two heads of the skip graph. Obviously, this method incurs a high maintenance overhead, as links in the skip graph are constantly adjusted, but at the time of the rebalancing process, there is little or no overhead in identifying one or more lightly or heavily loaded nodes.

Replicas of a data item can be created at two levels of granularity: file level and block level. At file level mode, the whole data item is replicated while at block level mode, only a part of data item is replicated. In this second case, it is necessary to collect all pieces of replicas of a data object in order to reconstruct it. Again, this is a design decision: the smaller the replication units, the better the chances of a uniform spread, but the chances of not being able to retrieve one of the pieces also grow. Of course, we could have multiple copies, but then consistency is an issue to take into account.

A simple solution for maintaining the consistency of replicas is to set timeout, such that after a limited time, replicas are discarded. As a result, there is no worry about inconsistency of replicas with the original data. Another solution is to create links between nodes holding replicas and the node keeping the original data. In this way, replica updates can be disseminated through these links.

Finally, the number of replicas to be created could also depend on the number of queries issued for each data item. Such replicas could be stored at the query requester node, at a node along the query search path, a node preceding or following the data item owner node, or a random node in the system. To decide, a system designer should consider what is likely to be more frequent: data querying, in which case store a replica closer to nodes likely to issue the query, or data updating, in which case, store the replica closer to the nodes generating the data.

Chapter 6
Security in Peer-to-Peer Networks

For P2P systems to be widely accepted and adopted, they must be secure. Unfortunately, securing applications in a P2P environment is much more challenging than the already hard problem of securing client-server or traditional distributed applications. This follows from the openness and autonomous nature of a P2P network. For example, as nodes can join and leave the network, this could turn out to be a potential (denial-of-service) threat that can disrupt the operations of the system. As another example, given that a (malicious) node may change its identity whenever it rejoins the network, it becomes more difficult to trust a newly joined node. Yet another example of security threat is that (malicious) nodes may not be operating according to the prescribed protocols—a node may not route requests, another may not store data, yet another may not serve requests even if it has the data, etc.

In this chapter, we will endeavor to survey some of the works in the literature that attempt to address some of the security issues mentioned above. Our focus will be on (a) Routing attacks, (b) Storage and retrieval attacks, (c) Denial-of-service attacks, (d) Verification of data and computation, (e) Free riding, (f) Privacy and anonymity, and (g) PKI-based security. We defer the issues of trust and reputation to the next chapter.

6.1 Routing Attacks

Structured P2P systems such as Chord [173], CAN [266], Pastry [275], and BA-TON [166] apply the same principle in query processing: when a node receives a query request, if it does not contain the query result, it always forwards the query to a node in its routing table that is "closer" to the node holding the query result and the process stops when the responsible node is reached. This means that given a fixed overlay network where no new nodes join and no existing nodes leave, the same query starting at the same node always follows the same route (via the same series of nodes). In these systems, it is important to guarantee the correctness of routing functions, and hence *routing attacks* must be adequately dealt with. In routing attacks, the malicious node plays an active role in the system—it not only participates in routing, but its information is in the routing tables of other nodes. In [298], routing attacks are classified into three types.

6.1.1 Incorrect Lookup Routing

Incorrect lookup routing arises when a malicious node forwards a query request to an incorrect node or returns an incorrect result to the query requester node e.g., returns a random node as the node holding the query result. For the former attack, a solution is to let the query requester node monitor the search process. In this way, if a node forwards the query to another node that is not "closer" to the destination node while such a node exists, it is identified as a malicious node. Additionally, to recover from this attack, the query requester node can backtrack the routing path to the last trustworthy node to ask for an alternative route. For the latter attack, the query requester can check the range of values managed by the destination node to verify the result. For example, the query requester can look at the identifier of a node to justify whether this node is the correct destination node. This scheme, however, requires that the identifier of a node should be assigned in a verifiable way e.g., using the IP address of the node.

6.1.2 Incorrect Routing Updates

Incorrect routing updates happen when a malicious node damages the routing tables of other nodes by providing them incorrect information. The consequence of this is that "good" nodes in the system end up misdirecting queries to inappropriate, or nonexistent, nodes. A solution to this attack is to verify that the remote node can be reached before incorporating the update into the node's routing table. A more subtle attack can occur when the system provides added flexibility by offering server selection (i.e., provide alternative routes). This attack does not affect the correctness of the routing but it may affect the desired quality of service. For example, instead of picking the fastest node, the malicious node may route the query to a node with low bandwidth and highly unreliable. In this case, an effective trust model may offer a good solution.

6.1.3 Incorrect Routing Network Partition

Incorrect routing network partition occurs when a new node joining the P2P network is "hijacked" to another network partition formed by a group of malicious nodes. This can happen because when a new node joins a system, it needs to bootstrap via some known (existing) node in that system. Such a node may be a member of the malicious network partition. Alternatively, a malicious node in a legitimate network partition may also divert new nodes to the malicious network partition. Such attacks not only may deny service to the new node, but more importantly, may observe the behavior of the new node. One solution is for a new node to bootstrap only to trusted nodes. In this solution, each node maintains a list of trustworthy nodes that the node has known in the past and only contacts nodes in this list to join the network (if the node joins the network in the first time and does not know any trustworthy node, it can ask some publicly known nodes). Additionally, the new node can perform cross-checking of routing tables to detect a malicious partition. This can be done by initializing random queries at random neighbor nodes of the node and compare the returned result to the result returned by initializing these queries at the node. If the two results are not the same, there is a potential that the node falls into a malicious partition. Actually, as discussed by Sit and Morris [298], a simple but effective solution to avoid malicious nodes is to assign identifiers for nodes using their public key. Even though the overhead incurred by this solution may be high, with this solution malicious nodes cannot easily cripple the system.

6.1.4 Secure Routing Scheme

Castro et al. [64] addressed routing attacks by proposing a *secure routing scheme*. The scheme exploits redundancy and replication to ensure that a message sent from a nonmalicious node will, *with very high probability*, eventually be delivered to all target nonmalicious nodes. In particular, a key is replicated and stored at multiple nodes. Moreover, each node may maintain more than one routing table, and messages may be broadcast to a set of neighbors (despite the fact that the basic architecture is a structured P2P system). The scheme achieves this by providing solutions to three subproblems:

— *Secure assignment of node identifiers (nodeID) to nodes.* Basically, attackers should not be allowed to have control over nodeID assignments. Otherwise, the attacker can potentially position itself to be on the path of a victim node in order to monitor all traffic to or from it. For example, in Chord [173], the nodeID is a function of the IP address. A malicious node can pick an IP address that meets its need. Similarly, in Pastry [275], nodeIDs are randomly chosen 128-bit numbers, and hence a node can choose its nodeID maliciously. The proposed solution to ensure that nodeIDs are assigned securely is to employ a trustworthy server to generate nodeIDs from the public keys of nodes. This server is only consulted whenever a new node joins the P2P system, and does not participate in other actions of the system. As such, there is little concern about the potential bottleneck at this node, and hence it does not have any effect on the scalability of the system.

— *Secure maintenance of routing tables.* The routing table of a nonmalicious node must be protected in order to ensure that it does not contain too many malicious nodes (e.g., the ratio between malicious nodes and trustworthy nodes in a routing table should not be large). Otherwise, the node is effectively being controlled by these malicious nodes. A solution to secure routing tables is to constrain the entries in the routing tables. For example, in Chord, the nodeIDs need to be the nearest nodeIDs following some calculated values in the identifier space. Given that the node-IDs of nodes are secured with the previous scheme, the probability that a malicious nodes takes an entry in a routing table is small. In particular, this probability would be equal to the ratio between the number of malicious nodes and the total number of nodes in the system.

- *Secure message forwarding.* To ensure that a query could be sent, with high probability, to the correct destination node holding the search key, a solution is to send the query over multiple and diverse routes. The rationale is that given enough copies of the message being disseminated over different routes, at least one copy of the message should go through the correct route, and hence reach the correct destination node with high probability. In particular, when a node wants to issue a query, it should send the query to all its neighbor nodes since the neighbors are expected to be a sufficiently random and geographically diverse sample of the nodes in the network. When a node receives a query request from another node, it just follows the normal procedure to forward the query to the destination node. A performance study based on modeling and simulation [64] concludes that the probability of successfully sending a copy of a query to the destination node in this scheme is 99.9% if the number of malicious nodes in the system is less than 30%.

Routing attacks may also take place in unstructured P2P systems, for example, a node that receives a forward request may simply drop it or forward to incorrect nodes. However, since such systems typically broadcast to a number of neighbors, unless all its neighbors are malicious, the system is less vulnerable to these attacks.

6.2 Storage and Retrieval Attacks

P2P systems (structured or unstructured) deployed as distributed data repositories are liable to a number of storage and retrieval attacks, including the following:

- A malicious node may refuse to store data it should be responsible for.
- A malicious node may agree to store data but delete it later. This is a critical problem since the data may be lost permanently.
- A malicious node may claim to be responsible for the data but refuse to serve to clients; or worse, it may serve an altered copy.
- A malicious node may coordinate attacks with other peers.
- A malicious node may masquerade as a different peer.

The above attacks also apply to systems where metadata (instead of the actual data) are stored. In particular, the most common metadata are those used in routing indexes, and are critical to ensure the correctness and completeness to requests. A solution to the these attacks was proposed in PIPE [82], a Peer-to-Peer Information Preservation and Exchange network. PIPE is essentially a distributed system designed to protect documents from failures and malicious nodes. Assuming k peers will fail, and m peers are malicious, PIPE offers several services to a peer:

- *Discover()*. This service is used by a new node joining the system. The service is responsible for announcing the existence of the new node to online nodes in the system, and helping the new node to obtain a list of at least k peers where it can store its documents. To ensure that any document to be stored (or replicated) at other peers is not lost, at least $(m + 1)$ peers must be contacted to ensure that at least one of the peers is nonmalicious. PIPE assumes that the new node knows the identity of these peers in order to bootstrap the process of learning the identifier of other nodes in the system. In fact, it may be necessary to contact up to $(m + k + 1)$ peers if k peers fail. From these $(m + 1)$ (or more) peers, the new node will merge the lists of peers provided by each peer. These are the peers where the new node needs to store its document in order to be able to retrieve a valid copy at a later time.
- *publish(D,i)*. This operation will store document D at peer i. Since malicious nodes may delete D or even refuse to serve D, and nodes may fail, P must publish to at least $(m + k + 1)$ peers. In this way, there will be at least one valid copy in at least one active node.
- *recover(D,i)*. This operation is used to publish extra copies of a document into the PIPE network when malicious or failed nodes have been detected, so that there will always be at least one active copy around.
- *search(q)*. The search operation broadcasts the query q to all nodes. Nodes containing documents that match q will return the id of the documents and their own peer id. The challenge here is to be able to filter out junks or even altered versions.
- *retrieve(D,i)*. This operation retrieves document with id D from peer i. To guarantee that the retrieved document is a valid copy (and not an altered version), one solution is to securely bind the id of the document to the content of the document. This can be done by representing the id as a signature (using one-way hash functions such as SHA or MD5). A document is therefore authentic as long as its signature matches its id (obtained from search()).

The effectiveness of PIPE depends on accurate prediction of m and k, which is very difficult, if not impossible. While the most straightforward solution is to introduce extra redundancy (replicate the document over a larger number of nodes), an alternative solution is to raise the barrier to maliciousness a little. The latter can be achieved by employing mechanisms to detect some obvious malicious behaviors. In PIPE, two mechanisms were proposed for a *challenger* to query the node that is supposedly storing a document. The first scheme—*detect-servecopy*—requires a peer to serve a document that it has been allocated. Clearly, if it is unable to return the document, then it is treated as being malicious. The second strategy—*detect-has-copy*—requires a node storing a document to return a portion of the document (randomly selected by the challenger). Again, if the node is unable to return the portion or the returned portion is not the expected content, the node is likely to be malicious. Once a malicious node is detected, the system would *recover* by further replicating extra copies (since those at the malicious nodes are no longer valid).

Besides the challenging scheme, an *incentive-based* strategy was also proposed [82]. The basic idea is for nodes who store a document to prove that they are storing the document before they can retrieve other documents. For example, imagine peer P_2 wants to retrieve document D_2 from peer P_1. Suppose P_1 knows that P_2 is storing a document D_1, then P_1 can send $D_3 = D_1$ XOR D_2 to P_2 (instead of sending D_2). Thus, P_2 can only retrieve D_2 (by decoding $D_2 = D_3$ XOR D_1) if it did not maliciously remove D_1. Thus P_2 has an incentive to keep D_1 in its original version. However, this scheme cannot guarantee that P_2 will serve the correct version of D_1. Moreover, it requires P_1 to have a copy of D_1 as well.

Sit and Morris [298] also recognized the need to employ replication to handle storage and retrieval attacks. They proposed that the storage layer in structured P2P employs replication to avoid a single point of failure and that replicas be equally distributed among nodes in the system. Additionally, all nodes holding replicas should be able to ensure that at least a certain predetermined number of copies exist at all times, and no single node should facilitate access to the replicas. However, clients should be able to determine the location of replicas, and hence they can verify where data is available or unavailable at replica sites.

6.3 Denial-of-Service Attacks

In a P2P network, participating nodes should be available to contribute their data or resources to each other. However, a node may become unavailable as a result of attacks. One such form of attacks is the denial-of-service (DoS) attack. In a DoS attack, a node is overloaded by useless messages and its resources are wasted to perform meaningless tasks so that the node cannot serve its intended purpose. For example, a malicious node can continuously send (or route) messages to a particular node. In this way, the targeted node's bandwidth is consumed just to transfer messages, rendering its shared resources (CPU and storage) unavailable to other nodes in the P2P network even though they may be under-utilized.

DoS attacks come in two flavors: *network-layer* attacks and *application-layer* attacks. While network-layer attacks [127, 227, 231] attempt to cripple a node by flooding and subsequently overwhelming it with huge amounts of traffic, application-layer attacks render a node unavailable by large numbers of application requests. The latter can be more damaging since the node must also expend resources to serve the requests.

This section will examine some of the existing methods designed to (a) detect when a DoS attack is taking place, (b) manage the attack so that the node can maintain its service to other nodes, (c) recover from the attack by disconnecting the malicious nodes.

6.3.1 Managing Attacks

In [95], Daswani and Garcia-Molina studied *application-layer* DoS attacks in the context of a super-node P2P architecture. In such an architecture, there are two levels of nodes: local nodes connect to the P2P network through a super-peer node; super-peer nodes communicates in a Gnutella-like manner where a query is broadcast from a super-peer to all its neighbor super-peers. The work focused on *managing* DoS attacks where it is difficult to distinguish between legitimate and attack queries. The basic solution is to load balance the system by giving every client a "fair share" of the resources, i.e., no matter how many messages/requests need to be processed from a node, the serving node only dedicates a fix amount of resources for that node. In this way, the effect of the attack on the victim node is minimized since the node is still able to contribute to the P2P network by serving other queries.

Given the super-node architecture, each super-node has two classes of queries—local and remote queries. To minimize the effect of a DoS attack without being able to tell whether a query is an attack query, the authors introduced a parameter called *reservation ratio*, ρ ($0 \leq \rho \leq 1$), to determine the ratio of local queries and remote queries to accept. For example, if a node has capacity to serve only k queries in a time unit, then it will accept $\rho \cdot k$ local queries, and $(1 - \rho) \cdot k$ remote queries in the time unit. In addition, since a node is willing to accept only $(1 - \rho) \cdot k$ remote queries, this gives rise to two issues. The first issue is how many queries a node should accept from a neighbor node. The second issue is what to do if the number of remote queries is larger than $(1 - \rho) \cdot k$. To handle these two issues, the paper proposed the *incoming allocation strategy*, and the *drop strategy*.

- *Incoming allocation strategy (IAS).* There are two schemes used in this strategy. The first scheme is the *Weighted* IAS scheme, which sets the probability of being accepted of each query equally. As a result, the neighbor nodes that submit more queries will have a higher proportion of queries being accepted. For example, if a node has n neighbor nodes, and each submits α_i, $1 \leq i \leq n$, queries, then the node will accept $(\frac{\alpha_i}{\sum_{j=1}^{n} \alpha_j}(1 - \rho) \cdot k)$ queries from the ith neighbor. The second scheme is the *Fractional* IAS that treats each neighbor as having equal "right". In other words, a node with n neighbors will accept $\frac{(1-\rho)\cdot k}{n}$ queries from each neighbor. For neighbors with fewer than $\frac{(1-\rho)\cdot k}{n}$ queries, the unused capacity will be assigned to other neighbors.
- *Drop strategy (DS).* While a node's IAS decides to accept m queries from its neighbor that submits $(m + \delta)$ queries, the drop strategy (DS) is employed to determine which m (out of $m + \delta$) queries should be picked (or rather which δ queries should be dropped). Let node x be the node that is accepting queries from its neighbor y. Let there be j distinct queries from y, and the number of each distinct query be $q_1, \ldots, q_j$. There are three schemes used in this strategy. In the *Proportional* DS scheme, each query type is given equal weight, and hence x will accept $(\frac{q_i}{\sum_{l=1}^{j} q_l} \cdot m)$ queries from query type i. In the *Equal* DS strategy, queries are selected based on the originating node, and each originating node is

equally likely to be selected. Thus, if there are s distinct sources of origin, then x will accept $\frac{m}{s}$ queries from each of these origins. The unused capacity will be channeled to queries from other sources. Finally, the *OrderbyTTL* DS scheme is used to drop queries based on their time-to-live (TTL) values. There are two flavors here: PreferHighTTL will drop those queries with lowest TTL first, and PreferLowTTL will drop those with highest TTL first.

Daswani and Garcia-Molina report results of an extensive simulation study on different network topologies (including line, cycle, grid, power-law, star, wheel, and complete) [95]. These results showed that the (Fractional IAS, Equal DS) pair is an effective mechanism to handle application-level DoS attacks. It not only minimizes *damage* (degradation in *service*, i.e., the number of queries that are processed) independent of network topology, but also minimizes flood damage distributed throughout the network. The results also showed that under the (Fractional IAS, Equal DS) policy, the complete topology has the strongest resistance to damage. The (Weighted IAS, PreferLowTTL DS) pair is shown to be the least effective combination that maximizes damage independent of network topology.

6.3.2 Detecting and Recovering from Attacks

In a Gnutella-like P2P system, it has been observed that the system's topology follows a power law distribution where a small fraction of nodes hold a large number of connections to other nodes while the remaining large number of nodes only maintain a small number of connections [284]. This means that a majority of traffic in the network go through a small fraction of highly connected nodes. As a result, attacks on these nodes can easily partition the network into isolated fragments, rendering the system ineffective. To survive these attacks, mechanisms to detect attacks and to recover from them are critical.

Attacks that partition the network are different from failures. Failures of peers resulting from nodes dropping out of the network unexpectedly (either due to the nodes leaving or from other forms of attacks, e.g., application-layer DoS attacks) are largely more random. On the other hand, attacks that attempt to split the network target the highly connected nodes. As such, the typical failure detection mechanism that regards a neighbor as failed when it stops responding to a message is inadequate. Keyani et al. [183] proposed a solution to detect an attack that minimizes coordination between nodes. In this solution, it is required that a node maintains information of not only its direct neighbor nodes but also indirect neighbor nodes, i.e., nodes two hops away from the node. The solution is based on an observation that an attack on a node will remove the most highly connected neighbor node of that node with high probability and hence disconnect a large number of neighbor nodes of the removal neighbor node. Thus, to detect an attack, at interval time, each node monitors the number of direct neighbor nodes and indirect neighbors that are disconnected. If the percentage of disconnected indirect neighbor nodes is greater than the percentage of disconnected direct neighbors, and is greater than a predetermined threshold, there is a chance that an attack is happening. The rationale for introducing the threshold is to filter out false positives due to random failures.

To restore the network after an attack has been detected, Keyani et al. [183] also proposed a recovery mechanism. The basic idea is straightforward but effective: the system maintains an alternative *virtual* overlay network besides the active network so that when the active network breaks, nodes from the virtual overlay network can be used to replaced the broken links. To provide such an alternative virtual overlay, several issues have to be addressed: (a) what should the virtual overlay network be like? (b) how to maintain this virtual network? (c) how to employ the virtual network during an attack? Keyani et al. also propose an *exponential network* [183]. In this network type, all nodes have approximately the same number of links, and hence nodes in the network are less probable to be holding the entire network together. This means that an attack on a small number of nodes cannot easily partition the network [23].

To ensure an exponential network can be maintained without excessive overhead, a *random node discovery* scheme is proposed: a node issues a ping message, called a random discovery ping (RDP), randomly picks a neighbor node to send the message. When a node receives a RDP, it also selects a random neighbor node to forward the message. This process repeats until the message has traveled a number of predefined hops. The last node receiving the RDP will reply a pong message to the initiator of the ping message and is thus discovered. To cover the entire network, the number of hops must be sufficiently large to cover the diameter of the network (in Gnutella, this corresponds to a TTL of 20). Moreover, two heuristics were adopted in picking the neighbors to send the RDP. The first heuristic applies to the initial number of hops, and selects neighbors randomly with probability proportional to the number of neighbors they have. This heuristic allows the message to be forwarded as far as possible from the originating node to prevent the occurrence of cycles. The second heuristic applies to the remaining number of hops, and favors nodes with fewer number of neighbors. This strategy is adopted to minimize the preferential attachment property of the active network. Thus, each node in the network will maintain a number of active neighbors for the active network, and a number of virtual neighbors for the virtual networks.

In the event that the network breaks, the virtual network will be used: a node will select nodes from the virtual neighbor list to replace its failed neighbors. Note that during the replacement process, the system does not look for new virtual neighbors since doing this incurs additional traffic in the network, and hence put more burden on the already failed networks. Finding new virtual neighbors can be done later when the network is not busy.

The simulation study [183] showed that the proposed detection and recovery method can reduce network partitioning by a factor of 25 times compared to the standard approach. As a result, query effectiveness is also improved both during and after the attack. The 20% overhead in terms of additional traffic on the network is deemed to be acceptable considering the benefits the scheme brings to the system.

For structured P2P system, Sit and Morris [298] proposed that DoS attacks on a single node be treated as failures so that the system can employ the failure recovery mechanism to isolate the targeted node. However, to minimize the effect of attacks (and failures), some degree of replication is necessary.

6.3.3 Other Attacks

There are many other attacks that affect the availability of a P2P network. For example, in the *rapid joins and leaves attack* [298], a node will repeatedly join the network only to leave immediately. In structured P2P systems, this may cause some network segment to overload as such operations require rebalancing of information/data into for the routing procedures to operate properly. A possible solution is to let only nodes that have been active or alive in the system for a sufficiently long period of time, to participate in the network routing protocol. In other words, newly joined nodes will only be allowed to query through other nodes, but will not participate in facilitating the querying process. Yet another attack is the *Sybil* attack where a malicious node can forge multiple identities. Douceur [111] shows that, without a trustworthy server, it is always possible to create Sybil attacks except under some unrealistic assumptions.

6.4 Data Integrity and Verification

With the rapidly increasing available resources at individual computers, P2P systems such as Freenet [3], Publis [326], OceanStore [242], and CFS [93] provide solutions for an inexpensive, highly available storage without centralized servers. However, P2P environments are essentially hostile in the sense that one can expect malicious nodes to exist (even if most of the nodes can be trusted). A malicious node may corrupt the content, replace it by a harmful one (e.g., that has a virus), or may not return the complete answers to requests (e.g., in the context of database applications, it may choose to return k objects while the answer contains $k + j$ objects for $j \geq 1$). While it is easy for the owner to verify his own data, it is not straightforward for any other users who need to query the data on untrusted nodes.

A straightforward solution is to only store data on trusted nodes, i.e., nodes that have been certified by some authorities to be trustworthy. However, such an approach not only incurs significant overhead, it also severely hinders the wide adoption of P2P technologies. A more viable solution is to remove the need to trust any nodes. Instead, a node will generate some verification objects in response to queries. These verification objects are used by the query nodes to validate that the answers are correct. The two important properties of such a scheme are: (a) it must allow the query node to verify that the answers returned by the untrusted node indeed belong to the answer set; (b) it must allow the query node to verify that the answers are complete, i.e., no answers are intentionally withheld.

6.4.1 Verifying Queries in Relational Databases

Devanbu et al. [105] propose a scheme that facilitates the storage of relational databases in untrusted nodes. The basic idea is as follows:

- The owner distributes a *digest* to nodes that would query the relation. This digest is obtained from the root of a Merkle hash tree [220] built on top of the relation. A Merkle hash tree is a binary tree whose ith leaf node is a hash value H_i obtained by applying a hash function h on the ith tuple, i.e., $H_i = h(h(t_i.A_1)||h(t_i.A_2)|| \ldots h(t_i.A_n))$ for a relation with n attributes. Internal nodes are also obtained by computing the hash value of its child nodes. Figure 6.1 shows an example of a Merkle hash tree. Here, there are four tuples. H_1 to H_4 are the hash values of four tuples t_1 to t_4, respectively. The parent node of t_1 and t_2 has hash value computed as $H_{12} = h(H_1||H_2)$. The digest for these four tuples is H_r.
- Given a query, the untrusted node evaluates the query and returns together with the answer tuples a *verification object*, $\mathcal{VO}$. Essentially, $\mathcal{VO}$ is a sub-tree obtained from the Merkle hash tree on the relation. For an exact match query that retrieves a single tuple, the path from the tuple to the root, along with other intermediate nodes that are necessary to compute this path, form the $\mathcal{VO}$. For example, to retrieve t_2, the $\mathcal{VO}$ comprises the nodes H_1 and H_{34}. For a range query, say q in Fig. 6.1(b), the $\mathcal{VO}$ is more complex. Here, $GLB(q)$ and $LUB(q)$ represent the largest value smaller than the answers of q and the smallest value larger than the answers of q. $LCA(q)$ is the least common ancestor of the subtree that bounds the answers from $GLB(q)$ to $LUB(q)$. The $\mathcal{VO}$ comprises the nodes that are needed to determine three paths: from $GLB(q)$ to $LCA(q)$, from $LUB(q)$ to $LCA(q)$ and from $LCA(q)$ to the root.
- Upon receiving the answers and the $\mathcal{VO}$, the query node will verify the correctness of the answers by recomputing the digest using the answers and the $\mathcal{VO}$.

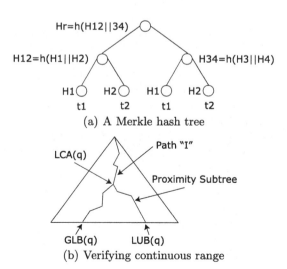

(a) A Merkle hash tree

Fig. 6.1 Using Merkle hash tree for verification

(b) Verifying continuous range

We note that the $GLB(q)$ and $LUB(q)$ values are necessary to verify the completeness the answers. If the resultant digest is the same as that provided by the owner, then the answers returned by the untrusted node is correct and complete. Continuing with our example, to verify that t_2 has not been tampered with, the client does the following: it first computes H_2'; with H_1 and H_2', H_{12}' can be determined; and finally, combining H_{12}' and H_{34} results in H_r'. t_2 is correct if $H_r = H_r'$. Note that the client is assumed to have obtained H_r from the owner separately. Alternatively, H_r may be signed by the owner (with his private key) and be included as part of the $\mathcal{VO}$; in this case, the client can verify if H_r' is the same as the signed H_r (with the owner's public key).

Devanbu and his colleagues [105] also show that $\mathcal{VO}$s for SQL operators such as selections, projections (in a limited way), joins and sets (union and intersection) can be computed using this scheme. The scheme, however, poses three main weaknesses:

1. Since different orders of tuples in a table lead to different Merkle trees, when the order of tuples changes, it is necessary to reconstruct the Merkle tree of the table. As a result, the system incurs a high cost in data update. Furthermore, if the table is sorted in different ways, it is necessary to have different Merkle trees, and hence the storage overheads of holding Merkle trees is big.
2. Since a $\mathcal{VO}$ of a query result covers all nodes in the path from the query result to the root, the size of the $\mathcal{VO}$ is proportional to the size of the query result and logarithmically to the size of the table. As a result, the size of the $\mathcal{VO}$ can be large if the query result is large.
3. Since the hash function is applied on the whole tuple, to verify a $\mathcal{VO}$ of a query result, it is necessary to send complete tuples of the query result to the query issuer. This means that projection operations can only be done at the query issuer, and hence it may waste a lot of efforts in transferring filtered attributes. Additionally, the requirement of sending complete tuples of the query result limits this scheme in supporting access control at the granularity of column level i.e. the scheme cannot allow a user to access some columns while not to access others.

To overcome the above limitations, Pang and Tan [250] propose the Verifiable B-Tree (VB-tree). This solution can create a $\mathcal{VO}$ of a query linear to the size of the query result and independent of the size of the table and allows the projections to be executed at the query result provider instead of at the query issuer. Additionally, the solution also allows updates to be executed dynamically without violating data consistency. An example of a VB-tree is shown in Fig. 6.2. This tree structure is built on three basic ideas as follows.

– First, VB-tree creates signed digests for all attributes in a tuple and uses these signed digests to compute the signed digest of the tuple. In particular, to create a signed digest for an attribute, the system first uses a one-way hash function such as MD5 [271] or SHA-1 [16] to hash the concatenation of the names of database, table, tuple, tuple key, and the attribute value. This result value is then

Fig. 6.2 Verifiable B-Tree

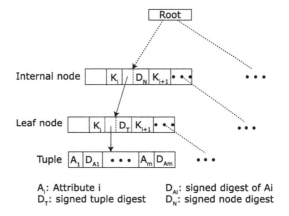

A_i: Attribute i
D_T: signed tuple digest

D_{Ai}: signed digest of Ai
D_N: signed node digest

signed with the private key of the database. In this way, the system needs to have a trusted server to store public keys of databases and an authenticated channel such as the X.509 Public Key Infrastructure Certificate and CRL Profile [158], to allow users to retrieve public keys of databases for the reverse computation.

- Second, this solution employs the hash function $h(x) = g^x \bmod q$ to create hash values for nodes in the VB-tree. Since this hash function has an important property that is $h(x + y) = h(y + x)$, using this hash function allows the system (1) to compute the digest of tree nodes in an arbitrary order, and hence avoid the first problem of the Merkle tree (2) to perform projections at the node holding query result and hence avoid the third problem of the Merkle tree.
- Finally, to alleviate the second problem of the Merkle tree, a $\mathcal{VO}$ of a query result in a VB-tree only needs to contain tree nodes belonging to the smallest subtree covering all the results of the query. This solution is feasible because the system maintains a signed digest for each node in the VB-tree. An example of how a verification object is created is shown in Fig. 6.3.

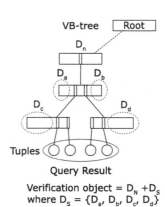

Fig. 6.3 Verification Object for Selection

Verification object = $D_N + D_S$
where $D_S = \{D_a, D_b, D_c, D_d\}$

6.4.2 Self-verifying Data with Erasure Code

Weatherspoon et al. [334] integrated the concept of a Merkle hash tree and erasure code to design a self-verifying scheme for data storage in a P2P context. The data can be a document, an object or a block. We shall use the term data object here. With erasure code [333], a data object can be split into m fragments and subsequently re-coded into n fragments ($n > m$) such that it is able to reconstruct the original data object from the combination of *any* m fragments. In a P2P environment, each fragment is stored in a node, which can be a malicious node. In this case, the malicious node may modify the fragment to damage it (a damaged segment is call *erasure*). Obviously, if the system is unable to recognize damaged fragments, the reconstruction process becomes very computationally expensive, i.e., we may need to try $\binom{n}{m}$ combinations.

A solution to this problem is to build a Merkle hash tree for the data object and its fragment i.e., the data object and its fragments form the leaves of the tree (in a similar manner as that described in Sect. 6.4.1). Figure 6.4(a) shows an example of a Merkle hash tree for data object with 4 fragments. Here, fragment F_i has hash value of H_i and the data object has hash value of H_d. The digest *GUID* is the unique identifier that can be used to identify and verify the object. Each fragment is made self-verifiable by storing in each fragment all necessary information to verify the fragment's hash value i.e., hash values of sibling nodes in the path from the leaf fragment to the root. Figure 6.4(b) shows the self-verifiable fragments' content for the example in Fig. 6.4(a). When a node receives a fragment to reconstruct the object, the node verifies the fragment by first computing the hash value of the fragment, and then repeating the process of hashing the result computed the previous step with the correspondent hash value in the Merkle hash tree until the hash value of the root is obtained. If the final hash value matches the GUID, the fragment is a valid fragment and can be used for reconstruction; otherwise, it is a corrupted version and another fragment has to be obtained.

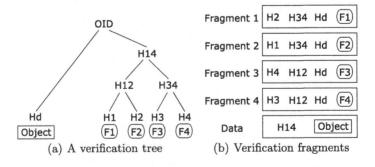

(a) A verification tree   (b) Verification fragments

Fig. 6.4 Self-verification scheme

6.5 Verifying Integrity of Computation

We have witnessed the success deployment of P2P technologies for distributed computation. Notable projects include the SETI@home [288] (BOINC [63]) and the Folding@home [2] projects where compute intensive operations are distributed across peers. For example, the number of participants in SETI@home is more than 4.5 million. They contribute unused processing power of their computers to process an average of 65 TeraFLOPS.

Unfortunately, not all peers that are tasked to perform certain computations can be trusted. For example, some peers may perform only a subset of the tasks assigned and claim that they have done all the computations. Actually, there have been reports about donors of resources to SETI@home have forged the amount of time they have contributed. The purpose of this forgery is to increase the contributed time of the peer so that it is listed as one of the top contributors in the SETI's website [40]. As another example, some peers may intentionally return wrong answers (even if they have done the computations). If undetected, the consequences may be disastrous. A straightforward solution to detect incorrect answers is to exploit redundancy—to assign each task to multiple peers, and then compare their results returned by these peers. The disadvantage of this simple solution is that it incurs a high cost in computation since it wastes some processing cycles and bandwidth to repeat computations. An improved solution is to just double check the computations of some randomly selected *sample* tasks. With proper choice of the number of samples, we can reduce the probability that a dishonest peer can get away without being detected to be very low. For example, if the dishonest peer computes only half of 1000 assigned tasks, and 50 samples are picked, then the probability of getting away is only $1/2^{50}$. By picking a sufficiently large sample size, it is almost impossible for cheating to go undetected. However, this scheme still requires a high communication overhead to transmit all results.

More recently, some work have been done to address the *semi-honest cheating problem* [115]. Du et al. [115] proposed a *commitment-based sampling* (CBS) scheme that further reduces the overhead in communication—instead of returning results of all tasks, only the results of samples need to be returned. The CBS scheme operates in four phases (assuming peer A assigns T tasks to peer B): (a) Peer B performs the allocated tasks; builds a Merkle hash tree where each leaf node corresponds to a task, and the hash values at the leaf nodes correspond to applying a one-way hash function on the result of the task; and peer B transmits the hash value of the root node of the Merkle hash tree to A. (b) Peer A randomly selects m sample tasks for peer B to proof its honesty. (c) For each of the m tasks, Peer B determines the path $\mathcal{P}$ from the leaf node for that task to the root node, then for each node $v \in \mathcal{P}$, the hash value of the sibling node is sent Peer A. The hash value of the result of the task is also transmitted to Peer A. (d) For each of the m tasks, Peer A can easily verifies whether Peer B is honest by recomputing the hash value of the root: If the value of the computed root is the same as that of the committed root hash value, then Peer B is honest with respect to this task; otherwise, Peer B is dishonest. Since the scheme is based on one-way hash functions, it is therefore computationally infeasible for Peer *B* to be able to determine the set of hash values along the path of each sampled task to enable the same committed root hash value be obtained had the result of the task been incorrect. The authors also proposed a noninteractive version of CBS that allows Peer B to generate the samples. To ensure that the scheme does not compromise integrity, larger number of samples can be used; alternatively, the process of generating samples can be made to be more costly.

6.6 Free Riding and Fairness

Cooperation is the central strength of peer-to-peer systems. Nodes participating in the P2P network are expected to contribute their resources (e.g., data, CPU cycles, bandwidth, or storage space) in order to realize the full potential benefits of P2P technologies. Unfortunately, in reality, many users consume the P2P system's resources (e.g., in Napster, Gnutella, and Kazaa) without contributing their own resources to others [21]. Moreover, there is a natural disincentive to cooperate—allowing some other nodes to use one's resources may reduce one's own computing capacity. For example, in file sharing applications such as Gnutella, allowing uploads may increase the delay in one's own file downloads. As another example, sharing one's CPU cycles means it will take a longer time to run one's own tasks locally. As pointed out by Feldman and his colleagues [120], a disincentive to cooperate leads to the "tragedy of the commons" [152] where free-riding from self-interested participants affects the performance of the system (even though free-riding brings benefits to those doing that). In particular, Feldman's study [120] shows three interesting results.

- As the level of cooperation increases, the system performance improves; however, there is a certain "sweet spot" beyond which the improvement in performance is not significant.
- The disincentive for sharing is potentially high at nodes having heterogeneous bandwidths. It is because when these nodes allow data to be uploaded, they suffer a significant delay in their download.
- Prioritization of TCP acknowledgement packages over data packets helps to eliminate the potential cost of sharing, and hence it can potentially increase the sharing level of the system.

The study results show clearly that it is necessary to design incentive techniques to "encourage" cooperation. Previous works have addressed the cooperation problem using game theoretic approaches [32, 241] and economic "mechanism design" theory [118, 119]. However, a P2P system imposes several unique challenges that must be addressed.

- *Asymmetry of interests.* Asymmetry of interests arises when peers with different interests require one another's resources. In this way, it may be difficult for the server (the peer providing the service) to determine if it will benefit from the system if it serves the requests.

— *Zero-cost identity.* A peer in the P2P system can continuously change its identities. As such, it is difficult to monitor whether a *stranger* is indeed a new participant who has not received any service, or is a free-rider who is exploiting the holes in the system.

— *Collusion and other attacks.* Peers in the system may collude so that they vouch for one another to raise each other's reputation (e.g., claiming that they have shared their resources when they have actually not done so). Similarly, peers may also lie that they have provided some service when they have actually not done so. Being able to deal with such attacks is important.

— *Traitor.* A peer becomes a traitor when it turned into a defector after successfully gaining the trust of other nodes in the system. Since the traitor already has established a good reputation, it may be hard to detect when it decides to become noncooperative.

To exploit P2P technologies to the fullness, there must be incentives for peers to contribute, as well as mechanisms to enforce fair sharing to prevent any abuse. The remaining of this section looks at some of the techniques that have been proposed recently.

6.6.1 Quota-Based System

In quota systems [237, 327], each peer is associated with a quota that reflects the amount of resources that a peer can consume from the system. Whenever a peer provides a service, the quota may be increased, and whenever it consumes some resources, the quota is decreased. For example, if peers share storage space, then the quota can reflect the amount of space that a node can utilize from the system. In this way, the more a node needs to utilize the distributed storage, the more it has to provide storage for remote peers. The key issue lies in managing the quota information. Some possible schemes include:

— A trusted centralized authority can be deployed to manage the quota. In this case, every request for service would also generate a query to the centralized server. While effective, the server may become a bottleneck and single point of failure.

— Smart card can also be used to enforce quota [276]. In this system, each node in the network has its own smart card that is used to track a node's usage of remote resources as well as local resources the node provides for other nodes to use. In particular, when a node asks for a service/resource from another node, its quota stored in the smart card is decreased. On the other hand, when the node provides a service/resource for another node, its quota is increased. However, the practicality of this scheme is questionable since it may not be possible to issue every user a smart card. Moreover, the integrity of the data stored within smart card may be compromised by malicious users.

— Another scheme is to employ nodes in the system to be *quota managers*. A node will distribute and/or replicate its quota information across these managers. The managers manage all requests for services/resources from the node to other nodes and all services/resources the node provides for other nodes in the same manner as that of a smart card. To handle the inconsistency in decision among quota managers, the majority vote policy is applied. It means that any decision related to the quota of a node must be agreed by a majority of manager nodes. The disadvantage of this scheme, however, is that the scheme incurs additional overhead on the network. Moreover, there is a lack of incentives for a node to be another node's manager, and a lack of punitive measures for handling a manager who misbehaves.

6.6.2 Trading-Based Schemes

In trading-based schemes, the system is structured as an *exchange* or *barter* economy. Essentially, a set of peers trade resources among themselves so that every one in the group is satisfied. One such exchange scheme for file sharing systems [27] implements N-way exchanges as *rings* of N peers where each peer serves its successor in the ring, and is in turn served by its predecessor. In Fig. 6.5(a), we have peer P_i requesting for object o_{i+1} owned by (and stored at) peer P_{i+1} $(1 \leq i \leq n - 1)$, and peer P_n requesting for object o_1 owned by P_1. As such, though P_i does not benefit directly from P_{i-1}, each peer eventually gets what it wants. Note that the N-way cycle is valid only if every peer has sufficient (upload) bandwidth to serve the requests. (In the work of Anagnostakis and Greenwald [27], this is less of a problem, as it assumes that the system supports partial transfers and that the upload link is organized into fixed-size slots. Thus, as long as one slot is available, the transfer request is considered to be satisfiable.) Nonexchange transfers are allowed only if there is no trading partner encountered.

The key issue in the scheme is for a node P to determine when a cycle occurs. This can be done by constructing a *request tree* as follows. Each request from a neighboring node is tagged with its request tree. A request tree is empty if there are no incoming requests; otherwise, P's tree has an implicit root that serves as the

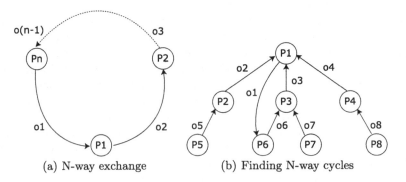

(a) N-way exchange   (b) Finding N-way cycles

Fig. 6.5 Exchange-based scheme

parent of the request trees from the incoming requests and their corresponding trees. A cycle is formed if there exists a peer P_S in the request tree that owns an object that P currently requested. This cycle is a *potential* N-way exchange ring. Note that while P can initiate a request to P_S, it does not mean that there is an N-way exchange since P_S or other nodes in the cycle may not participate in the N-way exchange. One solution proposed in the paper is for P to circulate a token through the proposed ring to determine if all peers along the ring are still willing to participate. This process can also be used to negotiate transfer rate.

Now, it is possible that more than one cycle is detected. In this case, P picks a subset to serve its requests. Intuitively, larger rings may be more beneficial to the entire system as more peers can be served. However, peers with smaller rings incur shorter search cost. Smaller rings are also likely to be more stable—fewer disconnections during the searching. In addition, smaller rings would mean that the overhead to transmit the request trees can be kept small—if the ring size of k is preferred, then a request tree can be pruned to a depth of k before being transmitted. A simulation study [27] showed that a ring size of no more than 5 provides good overall performance.

While the exchange scheme is fair, it cannot prevent cheating—a peer can initiate an N-way exchange by claiming to possess a file that it does not actually have. One solution is to blacklist such peers. Unfortunately, this cannot solve the problem completely since a peer can always assume a new identity each time it is blacklisted. Another solution is to exchange blocks synchronously and to validate each block before the next block is transferred. This will require a mechanism (e.g., valid checksums) to facilitate validation of blocks.

The scheme may also lead to free-riders in the following sense. A peer P may receive requests from peer P_1 for item x and P_2 for item y. Though P may not own both items, it can claim to own them and initiate transfers of x and y between P_1 and P_2 via itself. As a result, it can potentially download objects from P_1 and P_2 without contributing any of its own objects (or rather without having anything to contribute). This can be handled with tighter control that requires a trusted third party (another peer) as a mediator. The blocks are encrypted together with some header information (e.g., the owner identifier of the block), and sent through the mediator (who is assumed to know the secret key for the block). The mediator can then verify the validity of the blocks (by checking the header information).

6.6.3 Distributed Auditing

In quota-based and trading-based systems, cheating is still possible. For example, consider the sharing of disk storage space. Suppose a node agrees to store a file, and as such effectively increases its quota on remote storage. However, the node may then choose to delete the file and free the space for other use. Essentially, what is needed is an auditing system. One such *distributed auditing* scheme is proposed by Ngan, Wallach, and Druschel [237] for sharing of disk storage (the scheme can be easily generalized for sharing of other resources). In the scheme, each node maintains a *usage file* containing (a) the amount of storage space set aside for the system, (b) a *local list* of (ID, F) pairs for the file F that the node is storing on behalf of remote node with identifier ID, and (c) a *remote list* of files that other nodes are storing for the node. In some sense, we can view the two lists as representing the credits and debits to the node's account. A node is allowed to store new files in remote nodes if the size of all files in the remote list is smaller than the storage space set aside, i.e., the node is using less remote storage than it is willing to provide.

When a node L wants to store a file F in a remote node R, R must examine L's usage file to verify that L is indeed allowed to store a file remotely. If so, two new entries are created: L adds F to its remote list, and R adds (id of L, F) to its local list. Clearly, both L and R can cheat. L can fabricate the contents of its usage file, by inflating its storage capacity or inflating (deflating) the number of entries in the local (remote) list. On the other hand, R can drop F quietly after claiming to store it.

Since nodes are sharing storage, they have the incentives to make sure that any malicious node be removed. An auditing procedure can be used to prevent fraudulent behaviors. When a node R is storing a file F for a node L, then R has an incentive to audit L to make sure that it is "paying" for the remote space. If L does not list the file in its remote list, then it is not "paying" for its storage, and so R can delete F. To make the auditing process effective, every node that has a relationship with L should audit it at random intervals and all communications should be anonymous. Likewise, L gains by auditing R: to make sure that R is actually storing the file instead of quietly dropping the file. To prevent colluding among nodes, e.g., A claimed to store some files for B, B for C, and so on, more comprehensive auditing that involves checking the nodes reachable from the local list recursively is required.

6.6.4 Incentive-Based Schemes

Sun and Garcia-Molina [307] propose an incentive mechanism called SLIC (Selfish Link-based InCentives). The goal is to allow each peer to behave *selfishly* (the "you-scratch-my-back-and-I'll-scratch-yours" philosophy) such that it will share resources with those that have helped it in some ways, and ostracized others that it has not benefited much from. SLIC operates in an unstructured P2P context, and is based on a key property in disseminating queries: as each query is flooded in unstructured network, a peer's neighbor would have control over its reach to the network. In other words, a peer can (a) refuse to serve a neighbor's request (if it contains the resources that the neighbor requested), (b) drop its neighbor's requests (if it does not contain the desired resources but will not pass it on), (c) serve the request and/or pass it on. SLIC exploits this relationship as follows. A node N rates its neighbor M based on how much M has contributed to N (M serves N's queries directly or indirectly through its neighbors). If M is rated well, then N will in turn serve M's requests favorably. On the other hand, if M is rated unfavorably by N (because M

did not serve N's requests), then N will also not share much with M. Thus, nodes are incentivized to provide content and/or connection to nodes that provide content.

SLIC works based on a weighted scheme. Consider a peer N with M neighbors. Each neighboring peer is assigned a weight W_i where $0 \leq W_i \leq 1$ ($1 \leq i \leq M$) based on its quality of service perceived by N. $W_i = 1$ means that the neighbor is providing excellent service, while $W_i = 0$ implies an useless neighbor. The resources or services that N will offer neighbor i is proportional to W_i. Note that the capacity of N is used for both local and remote requests, and only the remaining capacity of N (after servicing local queries) will be split across the neighbors. Periodically, the weights are updated to capture any changing behavior of neighbors. For SLIC to be effective, there are several issues that need to be addressed. First, there is a need to determine the weights of neighbors to distinguish between good and bad neighbors, and to update these weights periodically. In SLIC, the service provided by a neighbor is measured by the fraction of query *hits*, i.e., number of data that satisfies a search query. There are three ways to assign initial weights to (new) neighbors: *average*—the weight of a new neighbor is initialized to be the average of the weights maintained by the node; *average_inverse*—the weight is computed as the average multiplied by $\frac{1}{AvgHits_i}$ where $AvgHits_i$ is the average hits per query generated by a node during the ith period; *average_exponential*—the weight is given by the average multiplied by $e^{-AvgHits_i}$. The *average* scheme is fair in that it does not bias against a new comer, but it may be susceptible to free-loaders—a node can simply disconnect from and rejoin the network each time in order to exploit the good service of its new neighbors. The *average_inverse* and the *average_exponential* schemes, on the other hand, are based on how much a node is satisfied with its current neighbors. Essentially, if the current neighbors are already providing good service, then it may not be worth the risk to accept a new neighbor; on the contrary, if a node is dissatisfied with the services of its current neighbors, then a new neighbor may improve its satisfaction. The two schemes differ in their aggressiveness in accepting new neighbors. Weight adjustment is straightforward in SLIC by using an exponential decay mechanism to update weights, i.e., $W_i(t) = \alpha \cdot W_i(t-1) + (1-\alpha) \cdot I(t)$ where $W_i(t)$ denotes the weight of peer i during period t, $I(t-1)$ denotes the quality of service during period $t-1$, and $0 < \alpha < 1$.

Sun and Garcia-Molina [307] also introduce three mechanisms to study how neighbors' decisions can be influenced. First, a node can increase its *answering power*. This may mean sharing more data or offering more computational services. Clearly, by so doing, one's neighbor will be satisfied and will in turn offers equally good service to the node. Second, the number of neighbors can be increased—by having more neighbors, there is a higher likelihood that a node can provide the data that satisfies a request (indirectly through its larger pool of neighbors). Third, a node can increase its capacity used to service neighbor's queries either itself or through its neighbors. Their simulation study shows that the SLIC's approach leads to a good incentive structure for the system as a whole, and nodes though selfish are encouraged to share in order to gain from the system.

6.6.5 *Adaptive Topologies*

In an unstructured P2P network, it has been recognized that the overlay topology cannot be static, and that an adaptive topology that changes based on interaction between peers would improve the efficiency and robustness of the system [81, 234, 235]. For example, if a peer always finds useful files from another peer (that it is not directly connected to), then it is likely that this peer will continue to find useful files. Thus, it may benefit the system if the two peers are linked together in the overlay network so that subsequent searches do not have to pass through other intermediate nodes. Moreover, being able to adapt the overlay network will also allow peers to change their neighbors periodically as their interests (access patterns) change. While the earlier work focused on efficiency issues, Condie et al. [81] show that by deploying such adaptive topologies, P2P systems are able to reward for active peers and punish malicious peer and freeriders, and hence the systems can benefit by increasing their resistance to certain kinds of attacks. In particular, each peer in the system should maintain some past history that allows the peer to estimate the potential downloads from other peers in the future. As a result, when the peer rejoins the system after being offline, it chooses to connect to peers for which it has the highest probability of downloading files from. The history information of a peer is encoded into a vector of *local trust vector* in which the ith entry in the vector indicates the peer's trust (measured by the difference between the number of satisfactory and unsatisfactory transactions) of its ith peer. The protocol maximizes the *trustworthiness* of the network given by

$$Q = \sum_{i=1}^{k} \sum_{j=1}^{k} connection(i, j) \times s_{i,j}$$

where k is the number of nodes in the system, $connection(i, j) = 1$ if peer i is connected directly to peer j and 0 otherwise; $s_{i,j}$ is the trust value that peer i has on peer j. When a peer i joins the network, it attempts to connect to N random connections. When there is at least one connection, peer i will download a file from peer j (peer j must not already be a neighbor of peer i), and then upon receiving an authentic file, peer i will connect to peer j. Note that if peer i is allowed a certain maximum number of connections, say T_i, then if there are already T_i connections, the connection is made only if peer j leads to a higher trust value than one of the existing neighbors of peer i. Clearly, peer j will only accept the connection if peer i is beneficial to it: either peer j has fewer connections than the maximum number of connection T_j or the trust value of peer i at peer j, $s_{j,i}$, is greater than that of an existing neighbor of peer j. In this case, peer j will replace that neighbor with peer i. Even though this basic scheme seems to work well, it has two potential problems:

- It is possible for a malicious peer to disseminate inauthentic files. One scenario reported by Condie, Kamvar, and Garcia-Molina [81] is for a malicious peer i to be connected to an *altruistic* peer j. Peer j is altruistic in the sense that it serves queries but does not issue queries, i.e., it allows others to download files from it, but it does not download any files from other peers. As a result, its local trust vector has all 0 values, and it will accept connections from all nodes. By connecting to peer j, peer i receives queries forwarded by peer j, and hence can answer these queries with inauthentic files. The proposed solution is to associate with each connection between two peers a *connection trust* value. The connection trust value $c_{i,j}$ reflects how much peer i benefits through peer j, and is determined from the number of authentic (or inauthentic) answers obtained from nodes that responded as a result of queries being disseminated via peer j. Thus, peer i can disconnect itself from peer j (even if peer j is an altruistic peer) if peer j's acquaintances are malicious. Peer j can also free itself from the malicious peers by breaking from all its connected nodes and start building up its connections all over again. Now, for this scheme to work, the queries sent out by peer i through peer j must be tagged with an encrypted identifier that encode peer j. Peer j's acquaintances must extract this tag and return it together with the answers. In this way, peer i will know the acquaintances of peer j. Moreover, an answer without a tag cannot be trusted.

- It is also possible for a peer to be stuck in a *local maxima* where the peer continuously suffers a long delay in receiving its query reply and/or has no reply at all. A solution to this problem is to replace problematic connections with new connections to random peers. In particular, in the worst case, a peer may discard all existing connections and create a totally new set of connections.

Simulation results [81] show that by using the API protocol, malicious peers that provide inauthentic files and freeriders will be moved to the fringe of the network sooner or later. In the former case, since a peer will discard its connection to another peer if that peer provides an inauthentic file, malicious nodes are forced to move to the fringe of the network. In the latter case, since the local trust value of freeriders is 0, they are likely to be disconnected by peers who favor other peers that provide it good service, and hence they are also pushed to the fringe of the network. Additionally, using the APT protocol also helps the system to perform well even under threat models where (a) malicious peers refuse to answer queries from a specific neighbor, (b) malicious peers avoid a loss of connection by providing a few authentic files to its neighbors, and (c) malicious peers are partitioned into two groups—one that issues authentic files, while the other that connects only to the first group (and hence never risk being disconnected) and flood the network with inauthentic files.

6.7 Privacy and Anonymity

One critical aspect of security in P2P systems is *privacy*. There are two possible manifestations of privacy—in *data privacy*, the content of the communication should be protected from eavesdroppers, and in *anonymity*, the participants in the communication should be hidden from eavesdroppers. We shall focus on anonymity in this section. In P2P systems, anonymity comes in two flavors [243]: *requester anonymity* protects the privacy of the initiator of a message and *storage anonymity* hides the eventual destination of a message.

While some P2P systems (e.g., Freenet [79]) are designed with anonymity as one of its goals, most of the existing P2P systems (e.g., Chord [173]) do not explicitly consider anonymity as a design objective. For the latter category of systems, it is possible that some information is leak to even "passive observers". In other words, messages (e.g., routing or query) that pass through certain intermediate nodes may disclose certain information (e.g., query tendencies) of other nodes in the system. O'Donnell and Vaikuntanathan [243] evaluated the anonymity of Chord, assuming a stable Chord network (i.e., one in which no node joins or leaves). In this work, two versions of Chord are examined. The *iterative* mode of querying works as follows: The initiator of a request queries nodes that are successively closer to the data item. When a query is received at a node, it replies with the entry in its finger table that is the closest preceding node of the data item. Finally, the initiator of the request queries the node that actually stores the data, at which point, the data item is returned. The *recursive* mode, on the other hand, requires an intermediate node that receives the request to forward it (rather than returning to the initiator node) to the node corresponding to entry in its finger table that is the closest preceding node of the data item. Moreover, once the node storing the data is reached, some information about the data (either the data itself or the IP address of the node storing the data) is passed back along the reverse path.

As shown by O'Donnell and Vaikuntanathan [243], the iterative version of Chord does not provide any storage anonymity. This is because an adversary could request for a data item, and be returned the IP address of the node that stores the data. Likewise, the iterative version of Chord also does not provide any request anonymity as the query initiator will communicate directly with the node that stores the data.

For the recursive version of Chord, while it also does not provide any storage anonymity (same reason as that for iterative mode), it turns out that it can provide a high degree of anonymity against passive observers. The intuition is as follows. If an adversary node N is far away from where the data is stored, say D, then there will be fewer messages going through it. This would also mean that it can be more certain about where the request originate. However, if N is close to D, then it sees more requests but these requests come from a larger pool of possible query initiators.

O'Donnell's and Vaikuntanathan's study [243] also showed that several extensions to Chord can further increase its degree of anonymity. For example, by allowing data to be cached (either at query initiator node or along the query path), there will be fewer messages passing through the network (and the passive observer), and hence it becomes more difficult to determine the requestor of an item. Similarly, by increasing the successor lists (the basic Chord protocol maintains only one successor node), the lookup performance can be improved since a node will search its successor list to see if any of them is an owner of the requested data before forwarding the request using the finger table. Clearly, this also means fewer messages will be sent over the network, and hence increases the degree of anonymity of Chord. Surprisingly, increasing the finger table size does not improve the practical anonymity.

Freedman and Morris [123] proposed a peer-to-peer anonymizing *network layer* called Tarzan. In Tarzan, each participating node installs a software that performs several tasks: (a) to discover participating nodes; (b) to establish a tunnel with these nodes; (c) to anonymize data packets if the applications desired to do so; (d) to route data packets through the established tunnel.

The anonymizing process works as follows. First, the source node (the node whose data packets are to be anonymized) selects a set of Tarzan nodes to establish a tunnel through which data packets will be routed. To ensure that different sets of nodes are selected each time, nodes are randomly selected. Thus, it is difficult for a malicious node to figure out which nodes will be used and when they will be used. It turns out that this random selection process can be done easily by turning the node selection problem into a key searching problem—by randomly generating a lookup key, one can find a random node. In Tarzan, this search process is done locally at the source node; this is because each node maintains information (e.g., IP address and public key) of nodes in the network through *gossiping*. In addition, to minimize threats from malicious nodes that may have gained control over some subnet, only those nodes with different IP prefix are used. This works under the assumption that the adversary does not have the ability to observe traffic throughout the Internet.

Once a set of nodes has been selected, the source node will establish a tunnel to route data packets. Tarzan employs layered encryption similar to Chaumian mixes [70] for data exchanges. Essentially, each node along the path of the tunnel will receive an encryption key and a decryption key. At the source node, the data packets are recursively encrypted by a set of keys (whose decryption keys have been sent to the nodes along the path of the tunnel). As a packet passes through a node, it peels off a layer of encryption (using the decryption key). Likewise, for packets that are to be routed to the source node, a layer of encryption is added. Thus, it is not possible for h_i to know whether its data packet comes from h_{i-1} or its predecessor. Likewise, h_i also cannot determine if h_{i+1} is the originator of a data packet received from it.

Finally, in Tarzan, the source and destination nodes need not be Tarzan nodes, in which case, Tarzan nodes operate a network address translator (NAT) to forward other participants' packets onto the Internet.

6.8 PKI-Based Security

To provide confidentiality, integrity, authentication, and authorization of data (files), techniques based on the X.509 public-key infrastructure (PKI) can be used. One such approach is adopted in the *scishare* system [45] to facilitate secure collaboration in a P2P setting. *scishare* has two key objectives: (a) to ensure queries are securely broadcast to a peer group (i.e., both the query message and the query response message are to be confidential), and (b) the transfer request message and the information transfer are to be protected. To ensure secure group communication, Secure Group Layer (SGL) [22] is used. SGL employs shared group key for securing messages, while providing an efficient mechanism to generate and distribute new keys whenever the membership of the group changes. Communication between pairs of peers are secured through TLS [314]. With SGL, the same group authorization policy can be enforced on the entire group. In order to facilitate a finer grained access control that allows different peers to have different privileges, the Akenti [315] authorization scheme was used. In Akenti, resource owners can remotely and independently specify the constraints that need to satisfied to use their resources. While peers having X.509 certificates issued by a verifiable certification authority (CA) are trustworthy, *pseudo user* is employed to minimize delay in accessing resources. A pseudo user is a user having basic privileges and is created automatically when there is a request to access public resources.

6.9 Summary

This chapter has provided an insight into some of the existing work on securing data in a peer-to-peer network. As we have seen, security is a very broad topic covering attacks that are beyond what traditional system have encountered (e.g., routing attacks, storage and retrieval attacks, free riders, etc.). The basic and straightforward solution to avoid attacks from malicious nodes is to employ trusted entities or trusted servers to control activities in the system. Alternatively, public keys can be used to identify nodes, and hence malicious nodes can be avoided; activities can be monitored to guarantee their correctness and backtrack whenever it is necessary; redundant computation can be made to guarantee the correctness of computation results. Even though these proposed solutions seem to work well under certain conditions or assumptions, they are still far from completely solving the problems and concerns in practice. This is because no conditions or assumption should be applied in real systems. A lot more work needs to be done before we can be comfortable with deploying peer-to-peer technologies for mission critical applications.

Chapter 7
Trust and Reputation

Trust can be seen in every aspect of daily life. Whenever we do something, we expect a good result from such an action. In other words, we trust our action. No one except crazy people wants to do harmful things. On the other hand, whenever we do business with someone, we trust them on the success of our business. For example, we trust doctors for their advice on our health; we trust mechanics for maintaining our cars; we trust structural engineers for building our houses. To some extent, our society cannot exist without trust. Since trust plays an important role in our life, it has been extensively researched in many sciences ranging from sociology, psychology, philosophy to economics, political, and computer sciences [216].

In business dealings, we trust our business partner, but how can we know that our partner is trustworthy? Let us see an example. Assume that we want to set up a new company and look for a skillful director to manage the company on behalf of us since we are busy. We further assume that we have a list of candidates and know everything they have done in the past. In this case, the chosen candidate should be the one who used to manage one or many companies successfully and has high integrity. We certainly do not want to select a candidate who had failed to manage companies before or who is known as a cheater. The criterion we used to measure our trust in a partner in this example is the reputation of our partner, formed through past behaviors.

A computer system or Peer-to-Peer system can be considered as a small society in which each computer or peer is an individual in the society. In this society, trust is a belief of one computer or peer towards another one, in the successful completion of a transaction, while the reputation of a computer or peer is evaluated from transactions it has done in the past. The purpose of trust management in Peer-to-Peer systems is to manage trust values of peers from which the system can distinguish good peers, that usually have high trust values, from bad peers, that often have low trust values. As a result, the system can avoid problems discussed in the previous chapter. Additionally, this technique can help to encourage good transactions between peers in the system since good transactions increase the trust values of peers. A good survey of trust management in Peer-to-Peer systems can be found in the work of Suryanarayana and Taylor [308]. In this chapter, we first give definitions of trust, its properties, types, and values. After that, we present trust models and concrete systems using these models. Finally, we focus on the way the reputation of peers is managed in a system.

7.1 Concepts

7.1.1 Trust Definitions

7.1.1.1 What is Trust

Everyone knows about trust and what trust is. In general, trust can be simply defined as a "belief or confidence in the honesty, goodness, skill, or safety of a person, organization or thing". However, different approaches, different points of view, give rise to different trust definitions. To have a deeper understanding of trust, in the remaining of this section, we would like to introduce major trust definitions from different viewpoints: psychology, sociology, to biology, and economics. These definitions come from Morton Deutsch [103, 104], Niklas Luhmann [204], Bernard Barber [37], and Diego Gambetta [124], who have significantly researched aspects of trust.

7.1.1.2 Trust in the View of Psychology

Probably, amongst several given definitions of trust, the definition proposed by Morton Deutsch in 1962 is the most popular [103]. The definition is based on the view of psychology. It says that "a trusting behavior occurs when an individual is confronted with an ambiguous path, a path that can lead to an event perceived to be beneficial or to an event perceived to be harmful. In this person's perception, the occurrence of these events is contingent on the behavior of another person and the strength of a harmful event to be greater than the strength of a beneficial event. If this person takes the ambiguous path, he makes a trusting choice on another person. He trusts that the other person can do the actions leading to a good result. Otherwise, he makes a distrustful choice". Later, in his book, "The Resolution of Conflict" [104], the definition of trust is further expanded as confidence that one will find what is desired from another, rather than what is feared. The definition of Morton Deutsch shows an interest property of trust: autonomy. Each individual has his own perception about trust. In other words, trust is subjective and dependent on the views of the individual.

7.1.1.3 Trust in the View of Sociology

Approaching trust from the sociological perspective, Niklas Luhmann [204] points out a problem of the society: the complexity of the relation between the society as a whole and the individual identities within it. As a result, the definition of trust is given "as a means for reducing complexity of society; complexity created by interacting individuals with different perceptions and goals". Like Niklas Luhmann, Bernard Barber also relies on sociology in his definition [37]. In particular, he states that trust is "predominantly as a phenomenon of social structural and cultural variables, not as a function of individual variables". In general, these definitions go beyond the definition of Morton Deutsch since they suggest that trust has to be seen from both individual aspect and social aspect.

7.1.1.4 Trust in a Broader View

Diego Gambetta [124] views trust ranging from biology to economics aspects. He defines trust "as a particular level of the subjective probability with which an agent will perform a particular action, both before he can monitor such action and in a context in which it affects his own action". This definition reinforces that trust is subjective to individual. In other words, the same trust value may mean different levels of trust to different individuals or, in short, trust is probability. The definition also implies that the information, that an individual can monitor, has an effect on its trust level. In a similar approach, Stephen Paul Marsh, in his thesis [216], presents trust in different aspects from psychology, sociology to biology. Details of all of the above definitions and discussion about them can also be found in this thesis.

7.1.2 Trust Types

In general, there are two types of trust: trust in an agent's action or trust in an agent's recommendation.

7.1.2.1 Trust in Action

The first type of trust reflects the basic definition of trust: trust in a behavior of another. For example, we trust surgeons on their operations for our health or we trust mechanical engineers for maintaining our car. An important note here is that trust in action is always specified with a concrete action, not in general. For example, we do not trust doctors to repair cars, nor mechanics to perform surgeries.

7.1.2.2 Trust in Recommendation

The second type of trust, on the other hand, takes into account the relationship between individuals in the society: trust in recommendation. An agent may trust another agent's action, but does not trust its recommendation at all. For example, we may trust a doctor on his advice since we know him well. However, if he introduces us to see another doctor whom we have never known, we may not trust his introduction. This type of trust may also be divided further into two subtypes if we make a deeper analysis: trust in recommendation of an agent, and trust in recommendation of another agent who is introduced by an agent.

Note that although there exists different types of trust, in most computer systems, in order to maintain simplicity, people do not differentiate them. In general, if an agent trusts another agent, it also trusts that agent's recommendation as well as recommendations of other agents, that are introduced by this agent. In other words, a single value could be used to represent all types of trusts in computer systems.

7.1.3 Trust Values

In general, we can classify four types of values used in trust: single value, binary values, multiple values, and continuous values.

7.1.3.1 Single Value

In the simplest type, trust values are presented by a single value: either trust or nontrust. For example, in an article by Aberer and Despotovic [19], a trust value can only be specified as a claim. When a peer is not satisfied in a transaction, it sends a claim to the system. Otherwise, it does nothing. By using a single value, this method cannot distinguish trusted agents with unknown agents.

7.1.3.2 Binary Values

To overcome the problem of the previous type, this type employs two values, one value represents for trust while the other represents for nontrust. With this way, trusted agents and unknown agents can be distinguished. However, if we consider more complex situation, an agent still cannot distinguish between agents with whom it has never done transactions with, agents from whom it has done transactions, but it neither trusts nor distrusts them.

7.1.3.3 Multiple Values

Using multiple values seems to be the best way. It provides a flexible way for an agent to specify different levels of trust about others. For example, an agent can specify another agent as "very low trust", "low trust", "average trust", "high trust", and "very high trust" in which "very low trust" and "low trust" can be considered as distrust, "high trust" and "very high trust" can be considered as trust while "average trust" can be consider as unknown or undetermined. This type of values is applied in most systems.

7.1.3.4 Continuous Values

All of above types of values are discrete values. As a result, they always limit the number of trust values an agent can give for its partner. To provide a wider range of selection, a continuous range of values can be used. For example, an agent can rate its partner with a trust value falling between 0 and 1. In this way, an agent can determine a value as trust if it is greater than an upper threshold value or as distrust if it is smaller than a lower threshold value. Values between the lower threshold value and the upper threshold value are considered undetermined. Note that in this way, to be flexible, threshold values are also determined by agents depending on situations.

7.1.4 Trust Properties

There are four main properties of trust: autonomy, asymmetry, transitivity, and composability.

7.1.4.1 Autonomy

As stated in the definitions of trust by Morton Deutsch and Diego Gambetta in the previous section, trust strongly depends on the individual's view. It is the property of autonomy. For example, if we ask two people about whether they trust in the development of the world's economy, we may receive two very different answers. If the one we ask is an unemployed person, the answer may be no. However, if the one we ask is a wealthy person, the answer may be yes. Even if we may receive a yes answer from both of them, each person may have a different level of belief in their answer: one may strongly confirm the answer while the other may weakly confirm the answer. It means that the same answers rarely exist.

7.1.4.2 Asymmetry

Asymmetry is an interesting property of trust. It further confirms the autonomy of individuals in the society. Individuals have different ideas not only about the third party but also about each other in their relationship. A person may strongly trust his friend. However, his friend may not trust him at the same level. The difference between trust levels of partners in a relationship may vary depending on situations. In some cases, a person may totally trust the other while the other does not trust him at all. In other words, if we want to display individuals in a society and their trust relationship in a graph, the graph has to be a directed graph.

7.1.4.3 Transitivity

Trust has a transitivity property. However, it is not a perfect transitivity. For example, a person always trusts a mechanical engineer for fixing his car, and hence whenever his car has problems, he takes it to the mechanical engineer. One time, assume that the car has a problem while the mechanical engineer is so busy that he cannot fix the problem immediately. As a result, he gives two options for the person. The first option is waiting for a day since he can probably fix the problem a day later. Otherwise, he suggests that the person can take the car to his friend, another mechanical engineer, to fix the problem. In this situation, if the person absolutely trusts the mechanical engineer's introduction, he can follow the suggestion. However, this case rarely happens. In most cases, the following action is more likely to occur. The person only takes his car to the mechanical engineer's friend if the car's problem needs to be fixed immediately. Otherwise, he may prefer to wait for a day. The reason is that the person does not trust the mechanical engineer's friend in the same manner as he trusted the mechanical engineer. In other words, the person trusts the mechanical engineer's friend at a lower level. Since complete trust rarely happens, if an introduction is done through many agents, the trust value should be significantly decreased. It is because the trust value is decreased after each step of introduction. For example, if we are looking for a house keeper, and he is introduced via a long chain of our friends, we may not trust him at all.

7.1.4.4 Composability

As mentioned above, since trust is individualized (i.e., has the property of autonomy), different agents can have different ideas about the same thing. As a result, by transitivity, an agent can receive different trust values about one thing. To draw a final conclusion from these received values, it is necessary that these values may be integrated. In other words, trust has to have the composability property. Nevertheless, the way these values are merged to get the final result depends on the situation. For example, if we make a simple survey about whether people trust in development of the world's economy and receive a result in which half of surveyed people says yes while the other half says no. What is the final conclusion? If we cannot draw the final result, the answer is unknown. However, assuming that most people saying yes are economists while most people saying no are not economists, the answer may be yes. Otherwise, if all people saying no are economists while all people saying yes are not economists, the answer may be no. It is because in our knowledge, we may trust economists more than noneconomists.

7.2 Trust Models

In general, we can classify trust models into two categories: one is based on credentials, while the other is based on reputation. Systems in the first model are simply based on credentials to verify trust. For example, if we meet a person who has a drivers license, we can trust him in driving a car. However, in some cases, even though a person holds a drivers license, it does not mean that we should trust him in driving a car since he may be a careless driver, and it is dangerous to sit in a car driven by him. In this case, we should also judge based on his reputation or his previous actions. This is what trust systems based on the second model use to verify trust. Details of these models are discussed in the following.

7.2.1 Trust Model Based on Credentials

A straightforward trust model is based on credentials. When an agent wants to determine if it should trust another agent or not, it looks into that agent's credentials. If the agent's credentials satisfy its policy, that agent can be trusted in its action. Otherwise, that agent should not be used. The most popular credentials system used in computer systems is the public/private keys system. In this way, when an agent wants to join a system, it has to create a pair of public key and private key in which the public key can be used to decrypt information encrypted by the private key and vice versa. Note that here, public key and private key are asymmetric keys. It means that it is impossible to regenerate public key from private key and vice versa. After keys are created, the public key is registered to a trusted party with the agent's information while the private key is kept secret at the agent as its identifier. When an agent wants to do business, it can sign the information with its private key. Since only the public key can be used to decrypt the encrypted information, and it has been registered to a trusted party, the credential of the agent can be verified by its partner. Because the keys are generated only once, this trust model cannot take into account past actions of an agent in trust evaluation. As a result, this model is probably suitable for a specific kind of systems: access control systems. For example, systems X.509 [162], PGP [352], PolicyMaker [51] and its successors, REFEREE [75] and KeyNote [50], are those applying this trust model.

7.2.2 Trust Model Based on Reputation

In many cases, we cannot always trust a person just by seeing his credential, as in the previous example: we cannot trust a person with the driving action just by seeing his drivers license. It is because a person may be good at the time of registration but he may become bad later. As a result, it is necessary to consider his past actions in trust verification.

The concept of reputation has been used widely in society, where each participant has a reputation score based on what he has done before. Common examples of trust management based on reputation systems are eBay [116] and Amazon Auctions [26]. These systems provide a feedback channel for users. After each transaction, both sellers and buyers can rate each other and the score is kept for references

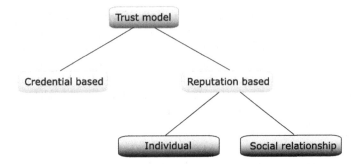

Fig. 7.1 Trust model taxonomy

later. As a result, from the reputation score of a person, people can decide if they can trust him or not (i.e., a person with many successful transactions is the one we can trust, while a person with all failed transactions should not be trusted at all). In general, the definition of reputation can be given as follows:

– Reputation: the perception of an agent x in the eyes of another agent y through past transactions of x. There are two kinds of reputation: local reputation is the impression that y has about x only from transactions between x and y. Global reputation is the overall reputation, that y gets from all past transactions of x with all agents in the system.

Using reputation to evaluate trust, we now give a new definition for trust, based on reputation.

– Trust: the belief of an agent y about another agent x in the success of a transaction function of x's reputation: If x's reputation is good, y trusts x. Otherwise, if x's reputation is bad, y should not trust x in the transaction.

Reputation based trust model can be further divided into two subcategories: one is only based on the individual reputation while the other also considers social relationships. By considering social relationships, reputation of an agent is based on not only individual aspect but also other aspects of the social network. Regret [277] and Node Ranking [261] are examples of systems belonging to this sub category while most P2P systems belong to the first category due to its simplicity [19, 83, 94, 113, 128, 171, 187, 191, 302, 303, 331, 332, 340, 350]. In general, the taxonomy of trust model can be depicted as in Fig. 7.1. In the next three sections, we introduce concrete systems applying these models.

7.3 Trust Systems Based on Credentials

7.3.1 PolicyMaker

PolicyMaker [51] is a trust management system based on credentials, developed at the AT&T Research Laboratories. The system provides a flexible framework using

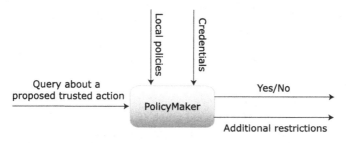

Fig. 7.2 PolicyMaker architecture

a "safe" programming language to uniformly describe policies, credentials, and trust relationships instead of treating them separately as other systems [162, 352]. In the system, each agent can take a decision in a flexible way: either locally or via a third party. Furthermore, PolicyMaker separates mechanism from policy, and hence makes applications independent from the infrastructure.

7.3.1.1 System Architecture

PolicyMaker operates like a database query engine, that can be either integrated into applications via a linked library or run as an independent service. It allows agents in the system to specify local policies and credentials as well as to raise queries about trust of actions. Depending on credentials and policies, the system may return "yes" for actions that are allowed, or "no" for actions that are forbidden. However, in some cases when the action cannot be justified, the system returns additional restrictions—a conditional acceptance. The acting agent is then considered trusted and allowed to proceed only upon the satisfaction of these additional requests. The system architecture of PolicyMaker is described in Fig. 7.2.

7.3.1.2 The PolicyMaker Language

PolicyMaker uses its own language for specifying local policies, credentials, and queries. Policies and credentials are described as assertions with the following syntax.

Source ASSERTS AuthorityStruct WHERE Filter

Here, *Source* specifies the source of policy that is either the local policy or the public key of a third party, *AuthorityStruct* represents public keys to whom the assertion is applied, and *Filter* describes actions that are trusted by the correspondent public keys at the assertion source.

When an agent wants to verify an action of another agent, it sends a query to the PolicyMaker. The query appears in the following form:

$key_1, key_2, \ldots, key_n$ *REQUESTS ActionString*

In which *ActionString* represents messages that describe a trusted action requested by a sequence of public keys.

7.3.1.3 Query Processing

Let us consider assertions as a directed graph G in which nodes are either policy
sources or keys, and edges are filters. For example, if we have an assertion whose
source is s, authority is a, and filter is f, they can be displayed by two nodes s
and a, and a directed edge labeled f from s to a: $s \rightarrow a$. In this way, for a query
containing keys $k_1, k_2, \ldots, k_n$ and action t, the process of finding an answer for a
trust query is just a process of finding a path in the graph from the source node s
that is a local policy, to the destination node d whose input is $k_1, k_2, \ldots, k_n$ and
containing action t.

Note that PolicyMaker does not verify the correctness of the credentials by
checking an agent's signature. This step is processed outside the system by applications themselves before submitting to the system. However, this weakness has
been solved in both REFEREE [75] and KeyNote [50] that are next generations of
PolicyMaker.

7.3.2 Trust-X

In a different approach, Trust-X [48] proposes a framework using an XML-based
language called X-TNL for specifying credentials and policies. Different from PolicyMaker, that does not verify correctness of credentials, Trust-X does. Additionally,
Trust-X improves the speed of trust verification by using trust ticket and caching:

— *Trust ticket:* is a special credential that can be issued by an agent to its partner
  after each successful transaction. Using trust tickets, the partner can speed up
  the negotiation process of resources related to the previous transaction. Each
  trust ticket has an expiration time, and it can only be used before that time.
— *Caching:* since two or more agents can ask for the same resource, and the negotiation process may be the same for all of them, caching can help to reduce
  the time of finding and setting up the negotiation process. It means that the sequence of operations pertaining to the negotiation process is cached for popular
  resources.

7.3.2.1 System Architecture

In the Trust-X framework, each entity has a profile of certificates, each of which can
be either a credential or a declaration. The negotiation process is processed through
four phases as follows:

- *Introductory:* in this phase, necessary conditions for establishing a transaction between two agents are checked blindly. Trust verification is not considered in this phase. For example, the client agent checks properties of the resource offered by the server agent while the server agent checks necessary conditions of the client agent to apply for the resource.
- *Sequence generation:* this is an important phase of the process where a sequence of certificates of both parties, required for taking resources in accordance with their policies, is determined. If the same transaction has been done before, and the trust sequence has been cached, it can be taken from the cache, to speed up this process. Furthermore, if an agent has a trust ticket, and if the trust ticket is still valid, the resource can be granted immediately and the whole process stops.
- *Certificate exchange:* once the trust sequence is generated and agreed between parties in the previous step, the certificate exchange starts: agents exchange required certificates. Once required certificates are checked and satisfied, the requested resource is granted.
- *Caching of trust sequence:* the final phase is to cache the trust sequence involved in the transaction such that it can be used to speed up the sequence generation later.

The negotiation process and its phases are described as in Fig. 7.3.

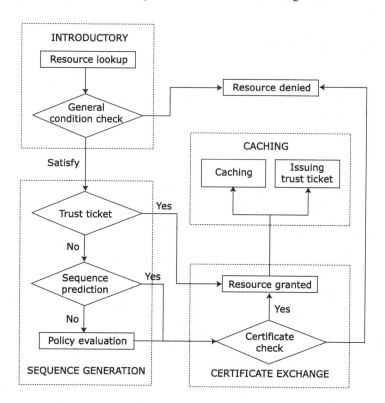

Fig. 7.3 Phases of a negotiation

7.4 Trust Systems Based on Individual Reputation

7.4.1 P2PRep

One of the biggest problems in Peer-to-Peer file sharing systems is that malicious peers may abuse the systems to distribute harmful content such as spyware or viruses. P2PRep [83] is a reputation based protocol used to identify malicious peers in such systems. This protocol is actually an extension of the Gnutella protocol [133] for trust management. The basic idea of P2PRep is that a peer looking for a resource should check the reputation of all peers that can provide such a resource before downloading. Reputation of a peer, that is either good or bad, can be determined by asking other peers, who have done transactions with that peer before. There are two versions of P2PRep: basic polling and enhanced polling. The only difference between these two versions is that the basic polling protocol treats all opinions from other peers about reputation of a peer equally while the enhanced polling protocol also considers credibility of peers' opinions. Note that to guarantee the correctness of message exchanges, P2PRep uses public/private keys for encryption/decryption of messages.

7.4.1.1 Basic Polling Protocol

The basic polling protocol is depicted in Fig. 7.4. It consists of five phases: resource searching, resource selection and vote polling, vote evaluation, best peer check, and resource downloading.

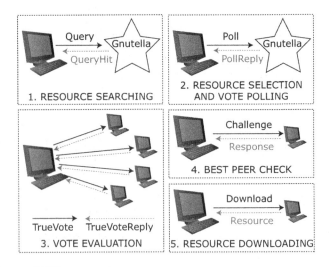

Fig. 7.4 Phases of P2PRep protocol

– *Resource searching:* this phase is processed in the same way as the search process in Gnutella. At first, the peer looking for the source sends a *Query* request to its neighbors, that in turn forward to other peers. Each query has a "Time to Live" used to control the number of steps in forwarding the query. When a peer receives a query request, if it contains the resources satisfying the search condition, it returns the result to the requester by a *QueryHit* message. The returned message contains the number of satisfied documents and information for downloading resources.

– *Resource selection and vote polling:* in this phase, the resource requester peer first selects the list of peers from returned results in the previous phase. After that, it broadcasts *Poll* messages to other peers in the system to ask for reputation of peers offering the resource. Peers receiving the *Pool* message check their knowledge about the asked peers, and send the feedback *PoolReply* to the requester.

– *Vote evaluation:* since malicious peers always try to interfere in the vote polling process, before evaluating votes, the requester has to analyze votes to identify suspicious votes for removing (i.e., votes coming from bad IPs). Additionally, the requester selects a number of voters to send messages *TrueVote* to check whether they are peers sending votes. True voters reply to this message with a *TrueVoteReply* message. Once the correctness of votes is verified, the requester can select the best reputation provider for downloading the wanted resource.

– *Best peer check:* before downloading the resource, the requester makes a final step of verification: checking the correctness of the selected resource provider. This verification is done by sending a *Challenge* message to the provider to ask for a confirmation of its identifier. If the requester receives a correct *Response* message from the provider, it can advance to the final step to download the needed resource. Otherwise, it comes back to the previous step to select another good resource provider.

– *Resource downloading:* the necessary resource is downloaded in this phase. After that, the requester updates its experience about the reputation of the peer providing the resource.

7.4.1.2 Enhanced Polling Protocol

As mentioned before, the basic polling protocol considers the opinions of all peers equally. As a result, it cannot reflect the importance in opinions of good and well-known peers compared to those of unknown or bad peers. This enhanced polling protocol improves the previous protocol by considering the credibility of peers in vote evaluation. To do that, each peer also maintains a credibility value of other peers in addition to their reputation. Similar to reputation management, the credibility of peers is accumulated after each transaction: if the result of the transaction is consistent with the opinion of a peer, its credibility is increased. Otherwise, its credibility is decreased. The enhanced polling protocol is actually similar to the basic protocol except for the vote evaluation process: the resource requester weights opinions of peers based on their credibility.

A disadvantage of P2PRep is that it incurs a high cost in the voting process because it needs to broadcast a message to ask all peers in the system about peers offering the resource. Additionally, the solution to check and remove suspicious votes from malicious peers seems to be unrealistic since it is not easy to identify malicious peers to remove their votes. The suggestion to identify malicious peers by simply checking their IPs does not always work. It is because malicious peers can deal with this solution by changing or hiding their IPs (actually, if it is able to identify malicious peers from their IPs, voting process may not be necessary because malicious peers can be identified directly when they offer the resource).

7.4.2 XRep

Even though malicious peers can be recognized through their reputation, as a result of their past behaviors, it is not easy to keep track of their identifiers because they can be frequently changed. As a result, XRep [94], a successor of P2PRep, suggests a method to keep track of the reputation of *resources*, in addition to the reputation of peers. In this way, each peer maintains two reputation repositories: one is for individual reputation, the other is for resource reputation. Since XRep is a variant of P2PRep, the protocol is similar to the P2PRep protocol. Just like there, XRep also contains five phases in the protocol: resource searching, resource selection and vote polling, vote evaluation, best peer check, and resource downloading. We will continue with describing only the differences between the two protocols.

– The first difference is in the second phase: "resource selection and vote polling": Instead of getting the top list of *peers* containing the searched query and asking for their reputation, XRep selects the top list of *resources* from returned results and asks other peers for reputation of both resources and peers offering the resources.
– As discussed above, the main difference between XRep and P2PRep is that XRep considers not only peer reputation but also resource reputation in the evaluation process. It means that from the opinions of other peers about resources and other peers offering resources, obtained in the previous phase, the requester selects the most suitable peer and resource for downloading. The criteria for selection here may be different depending on the preference of the requester. For instance, it may want either the best reputation resource amongst returned resources even if it comes from a peer with moderate reputation, or a moderate reputation resource from the best reputation peer.
– The final difference is in the last phase, "resource downloading": after the resource is downloaded, the requester updates its knowledge for both peer reputation and resource reputation depending on the quality of the downloaded material.

7.4.3 Cooperative Peer Groups in NICE

Cooperative Peer Groups [191] is a trust model system built on top of NICE [238], a platform for implementing *cooperative* applications over the Internet. The system identifies good peers to form cooperative groups and isolates malicious peers. By separating good peers from malicious peers, the security of the system is improved. Similar to other trust systems, in this system, after each transaction a peer rates its partner by the quality of the transaction. The score is kept in a *cookie*. However, different from other models, where scores are kept at either the peer issuing the trust assertion or the receiving peer, here scores are kept in both of them: positive scores are kept at receiving peers while negative scores are kept at issuing peers. Note that in order to keep a constant storage for cookies, old cookies are expired or discarded after a predefined time to reserve a place for new ones.

7.4.3.1 Trust Evaluation

In the system, trust evaluation is done via a directed graph called *trust graph* in which each directed edge between two nodes represents a relationship between two peers who have had successful transactions with each other. The source node is the one who issues the trust value, while the destination node is the receiving node mentioned in the previous paragraph. The weight of the edge implies how much the source node trusts the destination node. For example, after a successful transaction between peers A and B, if peer A sets a trust value 0.8 to B, we have a directed edge of weight 0.8 from A to B in the trust graph. Two strategies for calculating trust in the graph are suggested for the system: strongest path and weighted sum of strongest disjoint paths.

– *Strongest path:* in this strategy, a peer first finds the strongest path between itself and the destination node. The strongest path is determined as the path whose minimum valued edge along the path or the product of all edges along the path is the highest amongst all possible paths between two nodes. Once the strongest path is known, the trust value is the smallest weight among the edges in the path. For example, if we use the minimum valued edge function for finding the strongest path, the strongest path between A and F in Fig. 7.5 is $A \rightarrow C \rightarrow D \rightarrow F$. As a result, the trust value of F inferred by A is 0.65.

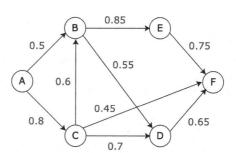

Fig. 7.5 NICE trust graph

– *Weighted sum of strongest disjoin path:* in this strategy, the trust value is computed by the weighted sum of the strengths of all of the strongest edge-disjoint paths. As exemplified in Fig. 7.5, there is another path between A and F: $A \rightarrow B \rightarrow E \rightarrow F$. Since the strength of this path is 0.5 while the strength of the previous edge-disjoint path is 0.65, the trust value of F is $\frac{0.5 \cdot 0.5 + 0.8 \cdot 0.65}{0.5 + 0.8} = 0.59$.

7.4.3.2 Finding Paths Between Two Nodes in the Trust Graph

We need to notice first that the trust graph is formed virtually and no peers know the entire graph. The good news is that in order to evaluate the trustworthiness of another peer, one does not need to know the entire graph. It only needs to know all paths from its position to that peer. These paths can be found when a peer looks up the trust value for another peer. In particular, when a peer wants to find a path to another peer, it sends a search request to all nodes that it trusts, by looking them up in the list of trust cookies it has. These nodes, at their turn, if they do not keep a cookie of the sought peer itself, forward the request to other trusted nodes. If they do keep the cookie of the requested peer, they return it to the requester. The rationale behind using the path connecting two nodes A and C is that if A is trusted by B, and B is trusted by C, A should be trusted by C.

It is interesting to note that the approach of trust verification proposed in this system is different from other systems because in other systems, resource owners are the ones to verify the trustworthiness of the requester. However, here, requesters take the responsibility to show evidence to resource owners that they can be trusted. Additionally, each node is required to keep a preference list containing potentially good nodes (i.e., nodes having high trust values). These good nodes can be found during the process of identifying paths. In this way, the system increases the ability of good peers to form groups together, and consequently, malicious peers can be isolated. The weakness of this system, however, is that it incurs a high cost in searching the trust path between the requester and the resource owner if either the requester or the resource owner is a node not having many transactions with other nodes before (e.g., the requester or the resource owner is a new node of the system).

7.4.4 PeerTrust

PeerTrust [340] analyzes the reputation of a peer in more details. It points out that if the reputation of a peer is simply based on the number of successful transactions, it may not be enough to eliminate malicious peers. As a result, PeerTrust suggests five important factors that should be used to form reputation of a peer. They are presented as follows:

– *Amount of satisfactory transactions:* a basic idea would be to trust a peer if it has a big number of good transactions with other peers.

- *Number of transactions:* a problem with the above criteria is that malicious peers only need to have a sufficient amount of good transactions to get a good record. After that they can always do bad transactions without losing their reputation. As a result, it is necessary to consider also the total number of transactions to determine the reputation of a peer.
- *Credibility of feedback:* the idea behind this factor is that if a peer is malicious, we should trust neither the peer, nor its feedback about other peers. Otherwise, malicious peers can cooperate to give high scores for each others to increase their reputation scores.
- *Transaction context:* if we do not consider the transaction context, malicious peers can be very good in many small transactions but be bad in some big transactions to earn benefit. In this scenario, if the context is not taken into account, they can still have a good reputation because the number of good (but small) transactions is greater than the number of bad (but big) transactions.
- *Community context:* sometimes, it is necessary to also consider community contexts in trust evaluation. For example, agents may be lazy in providing feedback for their transactions. As a result, giving some points for those who give feedback, may encourage them to actively provide such information, and hence increase the system's knowledge. Another example is to assign a higher weight in the process of calculating the reputation, to the opinions of some old, well-known or apriorically trusted peers.

7.4.4.1 General Trust Metric

From the above criterion, a general trust metric is proposed as follows:

$$T(u) = \alpha \cdot \sum_{i=1}^{I(u)} S(u,i) \cdot Cr\big(p(u,i)\big) \cdot TF(u,i) + \beta \cdot CF(u).$$

Here, $I(u)$ denotes the total number of transactions peer u has with other peers in the system; i represents the ith transaction of u; $S(u,i)$ is the level of satisfaction of u's partner in the ith transaction; $Cr(p(u,i))$ is the credibility of the feedback of its partner p about the ith transaction; $TF(u,i)$ is the adaptive transaction contact factor in the ith transaction; $CF(u)$ is the adaptive community context factor for peer u. The coefficients α and β are the normalized weight factors for the collective evaluation and the community context factor. These coefficients are adjustable depending on situations. For example, α and β can be given values such that, if a peer has enough transactions to evaluate, the system can be simply based on feedback information. Otherwise, if the evaluated peer is a new peer with only a small amount of transactions, the system may prefer to use default values.

7.5 Trust Systems Based on Both Individual Reputation and Social Relationship

7.5.1 Regret

Similar to previous works [83, 94, 191, 340], Regret [277] is also based on reputation for trust evaluation. However, different from the above systems, Regret also considers social relationships in the evaluation of trust. In particular, Regret takes into account three aspects of reputation: individual, social, and ontological.

7.5.1.1 Individual Dimension

The individual reputation of a peer j in the eyes of peer i on a subject s reflects only the direct experience (or individual ideas) of peer i about peer j from their past transactions and is defined as follows:

$$R_{i \to j}(s).$$

7.5.1.2 Social Dimension

It is important to realize that when an individual belongs to a society, its behavior is influenced by behaviors of others in that society. In other words, individuals in the same society have a tendency to behave in the same way, and the society's behavior is affected by every individual's behaviors. In the opposite way, the reputation of an individual is affected by the reputation of the society it belongs to. As a result, it is necessary to consider social reputation in addition to individual reputation. In particular, the social reputation value of a peer j in the eyes of peer i, $SR_{i \to j}(s)$, takes into account four factors. The first two factors are individual ideas of i about the individual reputation of j: $R_{i \to j}(s)$, and group reputation of J: $R_{i \to J}(s)$, the group j belongs to. The last two factors are group ideas of I, the group i belongs to, about individual reputation of j: $R_{I \to j}(s)$, and group reputation of J: $R_{I \to J}(s)$:

$$SR_{i \to j}(s) = \xi_{ij} \cdot R_{i \to j}(s) + \xi_{iJ} \cdot R_{i \to J}(s) + \xi_{Ij} \cdot R_{I \to j}(s) + \xi_{IJ} \cdot R_{I \to J}(s),$$

where $\xi_{ij}, \xi_{Ij}, \xi_{iJ}$, and ξ_{IJ} are coefficients that reflect the importance of each component in the calculation; $\xi_{ij} + \xi_{Ij} + \xi_{iJ} + \xi_{IJ} = 1$. These coefficients are adjustable depending on situations. The formula is illustrated in Fig. 7.6.

7.5.1.3 Ontology Dimension

There are usually many properties that may contribute to the reputation of an agent. For example, when we want to book a hotel for our holiday, we may consider its

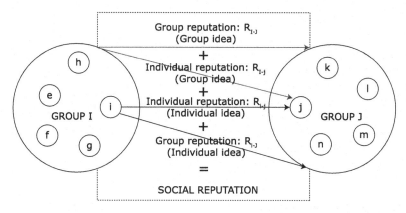

Fig. 7.6 Social reputation

reputation as a composition of reputations on its price, its location, and its services. By combining all aspects of reputation into one, we form an ontology on reputation. In Regret, the ontology reputation value of a peer j in the eyes of a peer i is computed by the following formula:

$$OR_{i \to j}(s) = \sum_{k \in \text{children}(s)} w_{sk} \cdot OR_{i \to j}(k).$$

Here, $OR_{i \to j}(k) = SR_{i \to j}(k)$ if k is an atomic feature; w_{sk} represents some weights in the calculation, normalized such that $\sum_{k \in \text{children}(s)} w_{sk} = 1$. The existence of these weights is necessary because different agents may have different points of view on properties in the formula. Furthermore, these weights at each peer are not fixed. They may change over time, depending on necessities. Figure 7.7 shows an example of an ontology for the reputation of a hotel, consisting of price, service, and location.

While the idea of using both individual reputation and social relationship in trust evaluation is interesting, the cost of building and maintaining societies, computing reputation of societies and determine to which society a node belongs to, is high. Furthermore, there are always holes that malicious peers can exploit and use to get benefits from society reputation once they know the way societies are formed.

Fig. 7.7 Ontology

7.5.2 NodeRanking

Similar to Regret [277], NodeRanking [261] also considers social relationship in trust evaluation. However, different from Regret, NodeRanking takes a very different approach in reputation calculation. The basic idea of NodeRanking is that in a society, a good agent always has relationships with many agents while a bad agent usually stands alone since no one wants to make a relationship with it. As a result, if in some ways we can have an overview structure of social network, we can infer reputation of each agent inside it. The advantage of this method is that it does not require agents to provide feedback for every transaction as other methods.

7.5.2.1 Social Network Construction

Social network can be built from many sources of information such as links in personal web pages, email traffic, collaboration of agents in transactions, etc. For example, a simple formula for constructing relationship between two agents i and j in the system via information retrieved from personal web pages is as follows:

$$w(i \to j) = w_{\text{email}}(i \to j) + w_{\text{link}}(i \to j).$$

Here, $w_{\text{email}}(i \to j) = 1$ if there exists an email address of j in the web page of i. Otherwise, $w_{\text{email}}(i \to j) = 0$. Similarity, $w_{\text{link}}(i \to j)$ is 1 if there exists a link to the web page of j in the web page of i, and 0 otherwise.

We may think of data mining techniques to retrieve this kind of information. From the retrieved knowledge, a social network is constructed as a directed graph in which the direction of a node to another node reflects the influence of that node on the other.

7.5.2.2 Reputation Evaluation

The reputation value of an agent in a society can be evaluated by the references other agents have given it: The higher the number of references, the higher the reputation of an agent. Since the social network is represented as a graph, the reputation of an agent is simply measured as the incoming degree of the correspondent node in the graph. If a node is not referenced by any node, it is assigned a default reputation value. Note that when the system is first initialized, the same reputation value is assigned to all nodes. For example, in Fig. 7.8, nodes C, G, and H are good nodes since each of them has at least three references from other nodes, while node F may not be a good node because no one makes a reference to it.

7.5.2.3 NodeRanking Algorithm

Since the reputation of a node i is calculated from referring nodes, while reputation of other nodes, to which i references, is calculated from i's reputation, if there is a

Fig. 7.8 Social network

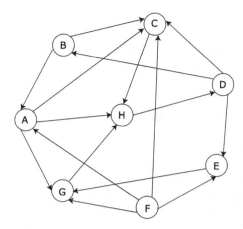

circular reference, the calculation process may be infinite. As a result, it is necessary for the NodeRanking algorithm to consider and prevent this problem. The suggested NodeRanking algorithm is adopted from the random walk strategy: It starts from an arbitrary node and follows outgoing references to other nodes. The algorithm stops when the reputation values converge.

7.6 Trust Management

So far, we have discussed trust models and concrete systems using them. Recall that there are two trust models: credential based model and reputation based model. The latter model can be further divided into two submodels: one only considers reputation of individuals while the other also takes into account social relationships. Since all of these models require a global knowledge to evaluate trust, and such a knowledge does not exist at any individual peer, this section discusses the way trust is evaluated in a distributed manner. In particular, we focus our discussion on the way peers manage and exchange their knowledge about reputation of others in order to get a global view of the Peer-to-Peer system. Solutions for this problem have been partly discussed in concrete systems presented in the above sections. However, we want to emphasize and organize them into categories and discuss them in more details here. In general, there are three methods for trust management in Peer-to-Peer systems, as follows.

7.6.0.1 Server Based Trust Management

This is the simplest way, where servers are used to maintain the reputation of peers. In this way, after a transaction, each participant peer only needs to send its opinion about its partner to a server. The server takes the responsibility to manage the reputation of these peers and answers queries about them later. This way is suitable for structured Peer-to-Peer systems based on servers because they can utilize the existing structure for trust management. However, since this method bases on servers, it suffers the problems of server based systems such as bottleneck, single point of failure, and lack of scalability.

7.6.0.2 Gossiping Based Trust Management

Without servers, there are two methods to manage global trust. The first one uses a gossiping algorithm for exchanging knowledge among peers in the system. As a result, after enough exchange steps, a peer may have a global view of the system. In particular, after each transaction or after a time interval, peers report the score of their partners in latest transactions to all nodes in the system by using a gossiping algorithm. At first, the peers send the score to all peers they know, which in turn forward it to others. Step by step, the score is updated at all peers. This naive method is very expensive since it requires to keep global knowledge of all peers in the system at every peer even though most of times, a peer only does transactions with a small number of peers in the system. Alternatively, most systems suggest that only local reputation of other peers that have done transactions with a peer should be maintained. Whenever a peer wants to retrieve the reputation of an unknown peer, it can use the gossiping algorithm to ask for that peer's reputation from its neighbors, neighbors of its neighbors, and so on. Combining feedback results with its local knowledge, it can determine the trust value of that peer. Note that this method is cheaper than the above naive one because it may not be necessary to ask all nodes in the system for the reputation of a peer. The correct value may converge just after some steps of propagating the reputation query.

7.6.0.3 Structured P2P Based Trust Management

The previous method, based on gossiping methods, is expensive because the reputation of a peer or a query has to be broadcasted to either all or a majority of peers in the system. However, without doing this, the query's result about reputation of a peer may not be correct. Alternately, the third method proposes that a structured Peer-to-Peer network itself can be used to manage reputation of peers in the system.

The basic idea is that for each peer in the network, its identifier is considered as a key, and its reputation is indexed together with the identifier key into the network. When a peer wants to retrieve the reputation of another peer, it simply issues a query with the identifier of that peer as the search key. A potential problem is that a peer may keep reputation of itself if it is in charge of the range of values containing its identifier, and hence it is possible that it may change the value of its reputation if it is a malicious peer. To avoid this problem, instead of keeping the reputation of a peer at one place, the system replicates the reputation of a peer to several places. However, if there are many malicious peers, and if they cooperate with each other, it is still possible for them to provide false scores for some peers. The solution to

Fig. 7.9 Trust management taxonomy

this problem is asking a peer to evaluate the reputation of referenced peers too. This may lead to a circular check for all peers in the system, which is costly, but in many cases, the system can decide the correctness of reputation values just after a few steps. This method can be applied in any structured Peer-to-Peer systems such as P-Grid [17], CAN [266], or CHORD [173].

In conclusion, the taxonomy of trust management methods can be displayed as in Fig. 7.9. It is interesting to realize that the taxonomy of trust management is similar to the taxonomy of Peer-to-Peer networks: the first model can be considered as the unstructured, server based Peer-to-Peer model, the second model using gossiping can be considered as the unstructured, pure Peer-to-Peer model, and the last one as the structured Peer-to-Peer model. In the following parts of this section, we introduce three systems that are representatives of these models. They are XenoTrust [113], using server based trust management model, EigenRep [171], employing gossiping based trust management model, and the work of Ge, Luo, and Xu [19], using P-Grid for trust management.

7.6.1 XenoTrust

XenoTrust [113] is a trust management system used in the XenoServer Open Platform [150, 267], an open and public infrastructure, in which servers can lease their resources to clients for deploying applications. The XenoServer Open Platform contains five entities:

- *XenoServer:* provides hosting services for clients. Any server can join the platform by registering itself with the XenoCorp first. Then it needs to advertise its services to the XenoServer Information Service (XIS). Additionally, it has to notify XIS periodically about its status (services). When a client is going to purchase its resources, the server can ask the XenoCorp to validate and charge the purchase order.
- *XenoCorp:* works as a trusted party for payment processing. It takes the responsibility for authentication of both XenoServers and clients in the platform, and guarantees the correctness of payments.
- *XenoServer information service (XIS):* is in charge of maintaining the status and the list of services of XenoServers. This information can be queried by either clients or by the Resource Discovery System.

— *Resource discovery system:* is used to help clients find the corresponding XenoServers they want.
— *Client:* rents resources from XenoServers. Just like XenoServers, to participate in the system, a client has to register itself through XenoCorp first. After that, it can find a suitable XenosServer either through the Resource Discovery System or by itself thought XIS. The client can further check the server's services by querying them directly. For renting resources, the client needs to purchase order from XenoCorp. Finally, it can create sessions at the servers and deploy its tasks.

The framework of the XenoServer Open Platform can be seen in the top part of Fig. 7.10. Although the platform has a component, XenoCorp, that can provide a trusted payment service for its clients, it cannot let them know the reputation of each other (i.e., if they are good or bad servers/clients). Since servers and clients are autonomous, it is necessary to provide users (both servers and clients) a mechanism for evaluating the reputation of each other. XenoTrust is dedicated for this purpose.

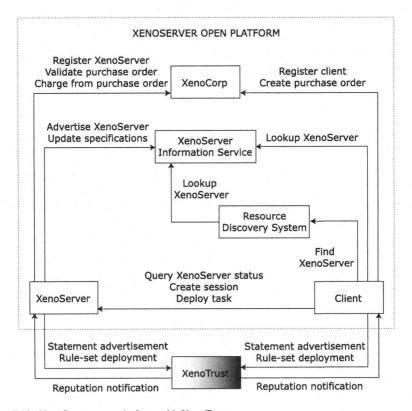

Fig. 7.10 XenoServer open platform with XenoTrust

7.6.1.1 Architecture

XenoTrust is an event-based trust management component that allows participants in the XenoServer Open Platform to find, as well as to distribute, the reputation of others in the system. The new component adds a new level of trust: reputation-based trust on top of the existing trust level: authoritative trust. This is the process of verifying an agent's credentials from registrations at XenoCorp. XenoTrust is based on servers for managing trust. Clients can contribute to the reputation of the servers after each transaction by informing XenoCorp. They can also ask it for information about the reputation of servers they are about to work with via the following two methods:

— *Statement advertisement:* is used when a peer wants to make a report about the reputation of another peer. A statement is in the form of *(advertiser, subject, token, value(s), timestamp)*, in which *advertiser* and *subject* are identifiers of the reputation's evaluator and receiver, *token* is the aspect of evaluation, *value(s)* denote reputation score(s), and *timestamp* sets the validity time of the claim.
— *Rule-set deployment:* is used to query about the reputation of a peer. It has a format of *(principal, property, advertiser, function, [trigger])*, in which *principal* is the identifier of the peer whose reputation is looked up, *property* is the aspect of reputation, *advertiser* is a nonempty set of advertisers considered during evaluation, *function* gives the method to calculate the reputation (e.g., min, max, or average) and *trigger* sets the threshold of change in values when a notification should be sent to the client.

In general, the reputation of a peer is inserted/updated in the system by advertisement statements. The rule-set can be deployed in two modes: event-based mode or query mode. In event-based mode, after setting, a notification will be sent to the peer whenever there is a significant change in the reputation of the queried peer, according to the trigger condition. In query mode, XenoTrust simply returns the result to the requester. The structure of XenoTrust is shown in the bottom part of Fig. 7.10.

As discussed in the first part of this section, by employing servers in trust management, XenoTrust has to suffer several problems of server based systems such as bottleneck, single point of failure, and lack of scalability.

7.6.2 EigenRep

EigenRep [171] is also a trust management system based on the individual reputation of peers. Here, each peer maintains a list of reputations of peers with which it has previously had transactions. The global reputation of peers is aggregated via a gossiping algorithm.

7.6.2.1 Local Reputation

The local reputation of peer j in the eyes of peer i is

$$s_{ij} = sat(i, j) - unsat(i, j)$$

where $sat(i, j)$ is the number of satisfactory transactions i has done with j and $unsat(i, j)$ is the number of unsatisfactory transactions i has done with j. For example, when peer i downloads a file from peer j in a file-sharing network, if the file is good, the transaction is considered satisfactory and hence it increases $sat(i, j)$ by 1. However, if the file is bad or i cannot finish its download, the transaction may be considered unsatisfactory, and hence it increases $unsat(i, j)$ by 1.

7.6.2.2 Global Reputation

Using only local reputation maintained at a peer is not enough for determining trust values, especially if the peer has to evaluate an unknown peer with which it has no prior experience. As a result, a peer has to look for the opinions of other peers in the system. In other words, it has to calculate a global reputation for the peer of interest in order to evaluate the trust value it can assign to it. Intuitively, the global reputation of a peer should be calculated by aggregating local reputations. However, it is not that simple. If there are many malicious peers, and if they collaborate, it is possible that they give each other high local reputation values while giving remaining peers low local reputation values. As a result, they can corrupt the trust system. To avoid this problem, the local reputation has to be normalized before aggregation, as follows:

$$c_{ij} = \frac{max(s_{ij}, 0)}{\sum_j max(s_{ij}, 0)}.$$

This formula guarantees that the normalized local reputation is neither high nor low. It is always between 0 and 1. However, if a peer has no reputation values for any peers (as it would happen if it had just joined the network), then $\sum_j max(s_{ij}, 0) = 0$. As a result, c_{ij} is undefined. The solution for this problem is to have a set of trusted peers that are globally known (e.g., network access points). Therefore, the above formula is revised to

$$c_{ij} = \begin{cases} \frac{max(s_{ij}, 0)}{\sum_j max(s_{ij}, 0)} & \text{if } \sum_j max(s_{ij}, 0) \neq 0, \\ p_j & \text{otherwise} \end{cases}$$

where $p_j = 1/|P|$ is a predefined reputation value of a well-known peer j amongst P, well-known or pre-trusted peers. Normalized local reputation values, once calculated, are stored in a vector called the *normalized local reputation vector* on the local peer: $\vec{c}_i = (c_{i_1}, c_{i_2}, \ldots, c_{i_n})^T$. Since a peer has different trust levels on other peers, the formula has to consider it by adding the local reputation values of

---

Algorithm 16 : Distributed_Algorithm()

1: **for** each peer i **do**
2:     Query all peers $j \in A_i$ for $t_i^{(0)} = p_j$ (*)
3:     **repeat**
4:         Compute $t_i^{(k+1)} = (c_{1i} \cdot t_1^{(k)} + c_{2i} \cdot t_2^{(k)} + \cdots + c_{ni} \cdot t_n^{(k)})$
5:         $c_{ij}, t_i^{(k+1)}$ to all peers $j \in B_i$
6:         Compute $\delta = |t_i^{(k+1)} - t_i^{(k)}|$
7:         Wait for all peers $j \in A_i$ to return c_{ji}
8:     **until** $(\delta < \epsilon)$
9: **end for**

---

its neighbors as coefficients in calculating the global reputation value of a peer. As a result, the global reputation value of peer j in the eyes of peer i is calculated as follows:

$$t_{ij} = \sum_k c_{ik} \cdot c_{kj}.$$

If we combine all global reputation values of peers in the system into a global reputation vector $\vec{t}_i$, and let C be the matrix $[c_{ij}]$, then $\vec{t}_i = C^{\mathrm{T}} \cdot \vec{c}_i$

$$\begin{pmatrix} t_{i1} \\ t_{i2} \\ \cdots \\ t_{iN} \end{pmatrix} = \begin{pmatrix} c_{11} & c_{21} & \cdots & c_{N1} \\ c_{12} & c_{22} & \cdots & c_{N2} \\ \cdots & \cdots & \cdots & \cdots \\ c_{1N} & c_{2N} & \cdots & c_{NN} \end{pmatrix} \cdot \begin{pmatrix} c_{i1} \\ c_{i2} \\ \cdots \\ c_{iN} \end{pmatrix}.$$

The above formula reflects the experience of the peer and its neighbors. However, if neither the peer nor its neighbors have experience about an unknown peer, the peer should continue to consult its neighbors's neighbors. In this way, the above formula is changed to $\vec{t}_i^{(2)} = (C^{\mathrm{T}})^2 \cdot \vec{c}_i$. Continuously, the overall knowledge of the system can be determined after n steps, for large enough values of n: $\vec{t}(n)_i = (C^{\mathrm{T}}) \cdot t_i^{(n-1)} = (C^{\mathrm{T}})^n \cdot \vec{c}_i$.

Following the above discussion, the distributed algorithm is designed as in Algorithm 16, in which A and B are, respectively, a set of peers that have downloaded files from peer i and a set of peers from which peer i has downloaded files. The process of calculating $t_i^{(k+1)}$ can be illustrated in Fig. 7.11.

Note that in the distributed algorithm, on line 3, $t_i^{(0)}$ can be initialized with either uniform probability distribution values over all peers in the system or predefined trust values of pre-trusted peers. Since the second method makes the convergence process faster, it is generally selected for this algorithm.

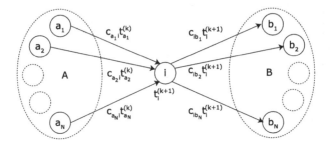

Fig. 7.11 Distributed algorithm

7.6.3 Trust Management with P-Grid

Both of the previous trust management models do not scale well with the network size because they are either based on servers, or use gossiping algorithms for broadcasting reputation amongst peers in the system. On the other hand, one of the outstanding properties of Peer-to-Peer systems is scalability. As a result, why not use the structure of Peer-to-Peer systems themselves to manage trust for Peer-to-Peer networks? The question is answered in the work of Ge, Luo, and Xu [19], where a structured Peer-to-Peer system, P-Grid [17] is used to deploy a trust management system.

7.6.3.1 Trust Evaluation

In this system, the reputation of a peer is based on the number of claims made by other peers and the number of claims it makes about others. Although counting the claims a peer makes about others in its evaluation of reputation may seem like an overhead, it helps to identify malicious peers faster. The reason is that if a peer is malicious, it always makes a claim about its partner(s), since it knows that its partner does the same thing. Therefore, malicious peers not only receive many claims from others but also make a lot of claims about others. Adding them up, malicious peers should have a very high number of claims compared to others, and hence they are easier to identify. In general, let P denote the set of all peers and $c(p, q)$ denote a claim made by p about q. Then the reputation of a peer is defined by the following formula:

$$T(p) = \left| \{c(p, q) \mid q \in P\} \right| \times \left| \{c(q, p) \mid q \in P\} \right|.$$

7.6.3.2 P-Grid Based Trust Management

In the P-Grid structure, each peer is associated with one path of a binary search tree, and is responsible for all data that contains the search path as its prefix identifier. As a result, it can be used to store complains of peers in the system by using peers' identifiers as the keys. An example is shown in Fig. 7.12. There are a total of six

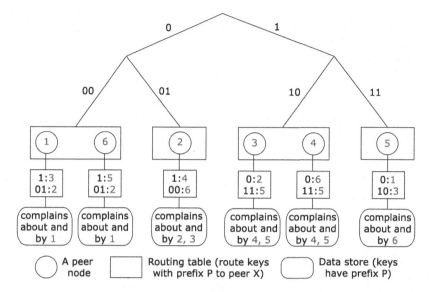

Fig. 7.12 P-Grid based trust management system

peers in the shown system, arranged in a binary search tree of depth 2. If we use three bits for encoding the peers' identifiers, complaints about and by 1 are stored in both peer 1 and peer 6 because the binary search path leading to peers 1 and 6, 00 is the prefix of peer 1's identifier, 001. Similarly, peer 2 stores complaints about peers 2 and 3, whose identifier's prefix is 01; peers 3 and 4 store complaints about peers 4 and 5, whose identifier's prefix is 10; peer 5 stores complaints about peer 6, whose identifier's prefix is 11.

Using the P-Grid structure, complaints are inserted and queried following the routing links maintained at peers. For example, if peer 2 has just done a transaction with peer 6, and wants to issue a complaint about peer 6, it creates a request for complaint insertion with key 110. By checking its routing links, peer 2 sends the request to peer 3. In turn, peer 3 forwards the request to peer 5, the one keeping complains about peer 6. A similar process is done for search. In particular, insert and search requests are defined in the following formula:

- $insert(t, k, v)$: in which t is the target of the complaint; k is the key or identifier of t; and v is the complaint value.
- $query(t, k)$: in which t is the target whose reputation is investigated; k is the key or identifier of t.

One thing that the keen reader will observe in Fig. 7.12, is that node 1 keeps the complains about itself. If node 1 is a malicious peer, it may change the result. Therefore, it is suggested that complaints should be indexed at several places instead of only one place, by using a replication technique, as discussed in Chap. 5. This way, the query's results can be double-checked. Additionally, it is also suggested that the reputation of peers giving the result should also be checked, to avoid the

---

Algorithm 17 : Trust_Evaluation(n)

1: Retrieve complains of n
2: **if** retrieved results are inconsistent **then**
3:      **for** each node n' providing the result **do**
4:          value = Trust_Evaluation(n')
5:          **if** value = "un-trusted" **then**
6:              Remove the returned result from n'
7:          **end if**
8:      **end for**
9: **end if**
10: Aggregate search complaints to generate final result
11: **return** final result

---

problem of a group of malicious peers cooperating to give false results. Even though this may lead to circular checks in the entire system, this rarely happens because the process should stop after a few steps, when the received results are consistent. Algorithm 17 shows the overall algorithm to evaluate the trust of a node.

7.7 Summary

In this chapter, we have provided an in-depth look inside trust and trust management in Peer-to-Peer systems. Trust can be defined as "a belief or confidence in the honesty, goodness, skill, or safety of a person, organization, or thing". However, this definition is not unique, and different points of view may give rise to different definitions.

Trust models can be classified into two main categories: credentials based and reputation based. In the credentials based model, if an agent has a credential satisfying our policies, we trust it. Since this model is too simple to deal with complex situations, it can only be used in access control systems. On the other hand, in the reputation based model, reputation, created through past actions, is used to determine the trust of an agent. In general, after every transaction, each participant gives a comment/score/complaint about the other, indicating that its partner was good or bad in the transaction. If an agent has done several successful transactions, it should have a good reputation, and hence we should trust it. This model can be further divided into two submodels: one only considers individual reputation while the other also considers social relationships among agents. Several concrete systems have been described to illustrate these models.

Trust management is not easy in Peer-to-Peer systems because a peer does not know all the other peers in the system. As a result, an efficient trust management model is needed to manage and distribute the reputation of peers in the system. It is interesting to realize that there are exactly three main methods for trust management, following the taxonomy of Peer-to-Peer systems: The first method is based on servers and is similar to server based, unstructured Peer-to-Peer systems. In this method, the reputation scores of peers are managed at servers. Since servers are used for trust management, this method suffers the same problem as the server based unstructured Peer-to-Peer systems: bottleneck, single point of failure, and lack of scalability. Conversely, the second method is based on gossiping algorithms to distribute reputation values. This method is similar to pure, unstructured Peer-to-Peer systems. The problem of this method is that gossiping algorithms usually incur a high cost in term of message passing. Furthermore, the results may not always be correct. The last method employs the structured Peer-to-Peer systems themselves. Peer identifiers are used as keys for inserting reputation values into the network. As a result, this method can avoid the problems of the above two methods. This is the most prominent method for trust management in Peer-to-Peer systems in terms of research interest.

Finally, before ending this chapter, we summarize the features of P2P systems that have been presented through the chapter as examples of trust models and management methods, in Table 7.1.

Table 7.1 Summary of representative P2P systems discussed through the chapter

System	Trust Model	Trust Management
PolicyMaker	*Credential based*: Trust is determined by checking policies issued by applications and credentials of requesters.	*Distributed control*: Application policies and credentials are managed locally at nodes in the system.
Trust-X	*Credential based*: Trust is determined by checking policies issued by applications and credentials of requesters. In addition, a trust ticket is proposed to speed up checking process.	*Distributed control*: Application policies, credentials, and trust tickets are managed by entities that are locally stored at nodes in the system.
P2PRep	*Individual reputation based*: Trust is determined by a voting process from existing nodes in the system that have done transactions with the node in the past.	*Distributed control*: The reputation of a node is maintained locally at nodes that have done transactions with the node in the past. Voting is done by gossiping.
XRep	*XRep is similar to P2PRep except that it considers reputation of not only the peer but also its resources in the voting process.*	
NICE	*Individual reputation based*: Trust is determined by finding the strongest path in the trust graph that is formed by trust relationships of nodes that have had successful transactions with each other.	*Distributed control*: The reputation of a node is maintained locally at nodes that have done transactions with the node in the past, in the form of a cookie. A gossiping algorithm is used to find the strongest path.

Table 7.1 (continued)

System	Trust Model	Trust Management
PeerTrust	*Individual reputation based*: Trust is determined by reputation of a node in previous transactions from different aspects of the transactions.	*Distributed control*: Reputation of nodes from previous transactions is managed by P-Grid, a P2P system.
Regret	*Individual reputation based and social relationship*: Trust is determined by individual reputation of a node and reputation of the society the node belongs to. Different aspects of node properties are considered in the reputation evaluation process.	*Centralized control*: Reputation of nodes from previous transactions and social relationships are managed by servers.
Node Ranking	*Individual reputation based and social relationship*: Trust is determined by calculating the number of relationship a node has with other nodes. The higher the number of relationships a node has, the higher the rank of the node in the society is (higher trust value).	*Distributed control*: Relationships of nodes in the system are constructed locally at nodes. A gossiping algorithm is used to explore and rank nodes in the system.
XenoTrust	*Individual reputation based*: Trust is determined by reputation of services provided by the node in the past.	*Centralized control*: Reputation of nodes from previous transactions is managed by XenoTrust servers.
EigenRep	*Individual reputation based*: Trust is determined by individual reputation of a node in previous transactions.	*Distributed control*: Local reputation of a node is maintained locally at nodes that have done transactions with the node in the past. Global reputation of a node is aggregated through a gossiping algorithm.
P-Grid	*Individual reputation based*: Trust is determined by individual reputation of a node in previous transactions.	*Distributed control*: Reputation of nodes from previous transactions is managed by P-Grid, a P2P system.

Chapter 8
P2P Programming Tools

In the previous chapters, we presented architectures, routing methods, and several other issues pertaining to peer-to-peer networks. All of them are important theoretical aspects that define the concept of such networks. But how does one implement a peer-to-peer network?

The first answer that comes to mind is to use existing network protocols and the corresponding APIs defined in many popular programming languages. Sockets, for instance, can be used to connect two machines and then the entire peer-to-peer application can be built on top of that. At a higher level, web standards could be used to connect peers and the resulting systems would bear striking resemblance with web services. Without going into many details, we discuss these approaches in Sect. 8.1.

The difficulty in developing and deploying peer-to-peer applications from scratch has resulted in the appearance of several systems that introduce specific libraries, or, even more, specific languages, to help the user implement a particular architecture, or a service on top of an existing architecture. Ideas in this direction have appeared almost immediately after structured peer-to-peer networks became popular (at least in the academic environment), around 2002: Teaq [117], P3 [244], P2P-RPC [109, 110], or JXTA [317] are some of the systems that were proposed. However, among the above, only JXTA managed to be fully developed into a usable system, mainly because of the continuous support of Sun Microsystems. Now, after five more years of experience in the research community, new such systems have been introduced. We present the most significant of them in Sect. 8.2.

Having implemented a network, either from scratch or using some particular library or programming language, it needs to be tested and eventually deployed. Section 8.3 shows three such deployment and testing environments: PlanetLab, Emulab, and Amazon's Elastic Computing Cloud.

8.1 Low Level P2P Programming

Fundamentally, all P2P networks rely on the internet protocols suite to provide the necessary connectivity functionality. More recently, other communication protocols have become present, such as Bluetooth.

8.1.1 Sockets

The original RFC147 that introduced network sockets defined one as *"the unique identification to or from which information is transmitted in the network"*. In the context of an Internet-connected PC, a socket is defined by an IP address, a port number and a protocol (TCP, UDP, or raw). To establish communication, one of the two hosts must first open a listening socket and wait for an incoming connection. The second host, which by some unspecified means must know the IP address, port number and required protocol of the first host, can then complete the link by sending a message specifying its own IP address and port number.

The study of network programming using sockets is well documented ever since the ARPANet, the predecessor of the Internet, was created. Currently, *Unix Network Programming* [304] is probably the most referenced book in the field. Its third edition, released in 2003, is updated to also include the new IPv6 protocol, the proposed new addressing space for the Internet.

8.1.2 Remote Procedure Call

Remote procedure call (RPC) is a technique to trigger computations on another machine, generally in order to perform tasks that are too costly on the local machine. While one could easily imagine a way to do this using sockets (client sends a message with parameters and the method name; server receives message and somehow locates the correct method to apply; server sends result back to client), the RPC standard provides a layer on top of that, which makes the procedure of sending the message, identifying the correct method, and returning the results much easier.

Probably the best known RPC implementations are that of Sun Microsystems (ONC RPC), the Open Software Foundation (DCE RPC), and possibly XML-RPC (which is no longer an active project, but has been included into SOAP[1] [325]). The technique is widely used in distributed computing, as proven for instance by its incorporation in the Google Web Toolkit [136] or its use in Facebook to run the embedded applications (the Thrift software stack [299]). However, these applications generally assume that the distributed environment is stable and failures are rare. This is not the frame of mind in which peer-to-peer systems operate, so there have been proposals to make RPC more fault tolerant [109, 110].

To alleviate the need for the client to handle possible failures of the other peers, as it would be the case normally in RPC, Djilali introduces a *coordinator* that manages the distribution of jobs [109]. Later, in a follow-up article [110], the coordinator is redesigned from being a single machine to being a service provided by several machines, further increasing the fault tolerance, but adding complexity to the system (see Fig. 8.1). For instance, the nodes that are part of the Coordinator must replicate

---

[1]Simple Object Access Protocol.

Fig. 8.1 P2P-RPC uses a
coordinator service to
maintain fault tolerance

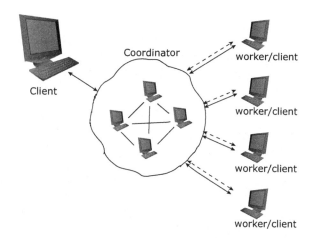

among themselves information pertaining to a particular job and they must keep
track of the status of each other using ping messages. Still, for the user, the advantage is that all of this is transparent, and the RPC interface is similar to what one is
used from ONC RPC or DCE RPC.

8.1.3 Web Services

Web services add another layer of abstraction on top of RPC. Though they represent a complex application development environment [254], we include them in this
chapter because they are not specifically designed to handle peer-to-peer interaction.
However, as P2P, web services handle decentralized computing.

According to the World Wide Web Consortium (W3C, Feb. 2004), the definition
of a web service (WS) is as follows: "*a web service is a software system designed
to support interoperable machine-to-machine interaction over a network. It has an
interface described in a machine-processable format (specifically WSDL). Other
systems interact with the web service in a manner prescribed by its description
using SOAP messages, typically conveyed using HTTP with an XML serialization in
conjunction with other web-related standards*".

Web services use a centralized index (UDDI) to search for, and bind to different
services. Though not specifically described in the documentation, there does not
appear to be a reason for which a web service should not be allowed to connect
directly to another web service, provided there exists a mechanism to locate such a
web service. It is here that P2P architectures and methods can be applied.

8.2 High Level P2P Programming

Building a new peer-to-peer system from scratch is very difficult. Like for so many
other applications, there is a need for libraries and tools to make it easier for the

developers to sketch up a system and then build on top whatever specific services are needed in a particular context. Even more, the flexibility requirements of the network may require the same system to be able to adapt its entire structure according to medium term conditions in the network.

For many peer-to-peer networks that came out of the academia, the research groups that developed them make the source codes available under some form of public licensing. One could, for instance, download the source codes of Chord [173] (http://pdos.csail.mit.edu/chord/) or of Pastry [275] (http://freepastry.rice.edu/), apply any modifications that might be needed, and deploy the new peer-to-peer network.

Still, learning the API of a big application such as Chord or Pastry may seem daunting, especially considering that it will be hard afterwards to move the same application to another peer-to-peer structure. Consequently, more flexible solutions have been suggested and we will discuss these in the current section.

8.2.1 JXTA

As stated on its website, JXTA is "*a set of open, generalized peer-to-peer (P2P) protocols that allow any networked device sensors, cell phones, PDAs, laptops, workstations, servers, and supercomputers to communicate and collaborate mutually as peers*".

JXTA defines a set of concepts, at the core of which lies, naturally, that of a *peer* and of *peer services*. A peer may be any type of device, ranging from the smallest smart-card to a fully blown server. Function of its capabilities, a peer can provide more or less services for other peers. Figure 8.2 illustrates the hierarchy of services and specific denominations given to the peers implementing only subsets of these services. In this figure, it is worth pointing out the existence of *super-peers* which are peers that help other peers to communicate with the network by translating some particular communication protocol into the general TCP/IP stack, or act as meeting points between peers. They implement all or a subset of the Relay, Rendezvous and Proxy protocols.

On top of the concept of peer, JXTA defines that of *peer group* and, respectively, *group service*. A peer group is a subset of all the nodes in the network that either

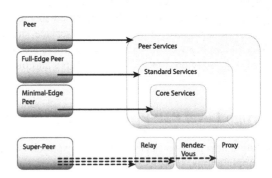

Fig. 8.2 Peers and services in JXTA

provide a collaborative service, or have a common interest. Groups may also serve as an additional layer of security, as they can impose strict authentication procedures and encryption protocols to their members.

All types of services, be they peer or group services, are published in the network through *advertisements*—specific XML messages sent between peers and/or super-peers. Advertisements, along with other types of messages (e.g., service specific or simply data transfer messages) are transferred through *sockets* and *pipes*.

8.2.1.1 Implementations

Currently, Sun Microsystems, the main promoter of JXTA, provides two implementations:

JXSE: implementation of the JXTA standards for Java 5.0 Standard or Enterprise Edition.
JXME: implementation of the JXTA standards for Java Micro Edition.

Apart from these standard implementations provided by Sun Microsystems, several other implementations exist, for different programming languages (e.g., jxta-c[2] for C, C++, C#) or for different platforms (e.g., symbianjxta[3] for the Symbian operating system).

8.2.1.2 Protocols

Peer Resolver Protocol (PRP)—the most low-level protocol in the stack, used to send any kind of queries.

Peer Discovery Protocol (PDP)—in JXSE, it relies on multicast or on super-peers. PDP locates published peer resources, represented as advertisements and is the default method for finding resources in any group, though each group may define one that is appropriate for its needs. PDP does not guarantee a reply.

Peer Information Protocol (PIP)—used to enquire about a peer's status, in terms of alive-time or network traffic statistics. A ping message is sent to determine this information and a reply can either be a simple acknowledgment to indicate that the peer is still alive, or a more complete set of data, structured into an advertisement.

Pipe Binding Protocol (PBP)—is used to create an actual link between two or more peers via pipe advertisements. A peer initiates a connection by sending a PBP query indicating the pipe it needs to connect to. The query will identify one or more other peers that already have connection to the opposite endpoint of the same pipe, such that actual connections can be established using some physical network transport protocols, such as TCP/IP, for instance.

---

[2]https://jxta-c.dev.java.net/.

[3]https://symbianjxta.dev.java.net/.

Fig. 8.3 Overview of interactions between JXTA protocols

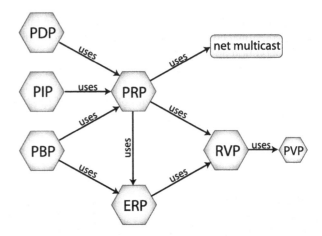

Endpoint Routing Protocol (ERP)—provides capability to send messages via intermediaries, or relay nodes.

Rendezvous Protocol (RVP)—message propagation within a peer group. Rendezvous nodes use a PeerView Protocol (PVP) to organize themselves, protocol that may define a structured peer-to-peer network.

Figure 8.3 gives a high level overview of the interactions between these protocols.

8.2.1.3 Adding Value to the Network

The existing infrastructure of JXTA provides the user (i.e., developer) with sufficient tools to deploy a super-peer based peer-to-peer network. Customized services can be deployed in two steps:

1. Implement the new functionality in some library.
2. Install on a set of peers.
3. Publish advertisements for this new functionality.

The first step is abstracted away from the JXTA infrastructure, that is visible only in the second and third step. Here, three types of advertisements are used to publish any module: *ModuleClassAdvertisement*, *ModuleSpecAdvertisement*, and *ModuleImplAdvertisement*. The idea is that a subsequent discovery process may have more or less specific requirements regarding the type of service needed. Commonly, a client of a service will look for the module through its specification (i.e., searching for *ModuleSpecAdvertisements*). This specification includes a *PipeAdvertisement* containing the necessary information for creating a direct link between the service requester and the service provider.

8.2.1.4 Other Considerations

JXTA defines an unstructured peer-to-peer network, using a super-peer approach. Though the discovery and routing protocols can be redefined, this is much more difficult to do than simply adding a new services and letting the existing routing process make it available to the rest of the network.[4]

8.2.2 BOINC

Keeping in line with the inclusion of Seti@Home in the category of peer-to-peer applications, we present here BOINC (Berkeley Open Infrastructure for Network Computing)—an open-source platform for *volunteer computing* developed at the University of California at Berkeley.

As Seti@Home, its direct predecessor, BOINC does not require users to communicate between themselves, and, consequently, does not need any routing protocols: the only communication possible is between one central server and a cluster of peers that process data (Fig. 8.4).

As a client, the user needs only to download the software from the BOINC website and register to one of the existing projects. Data will be automatically sent to this new participant and it will be processed whenever the client has CPU cycles t spare.

It is more interesting however to create and start a new BOINC project. For this, a user needs only a medium to high-power Unix/Linux server, for which the hardware requirements are similar to those of a web-server: reliable internet connection, static IP address, firewalled and overall secured. In terms of software, the server requires a set of software packages that are not normally installed by default: a database management application (MySQL), a web server (Apache) and PHP5—a server-side web programming language. Once all the prerequisites have been satisfied, the source codes of the BOINC project can be downloaded from http://boinc.berkeley.edu/trac/wiki/SourceCode.

To create and start a BOINC project on the newly installed BOINC server, several scripts must be executed:

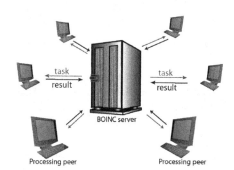

Fig. 8.4 The architecture of the BOINC volunteer computing framework

---

[4]A project in this direction has been described in [177] and is available online at https://gisp.dev.java.net/.

make_project: creates the server components of a BOINC project.

xadd: reads platform and application records from the project.xml file in the
    project's root directory.

update_versions: traverses the project's folder, identifies new versions and
    creates database entries for each of them.

start: starts the project.

These scripts manage different versions of the data processing functions, as there
need to be different implementations for each hardware/software environment that
these functions will be operating on.

Finally, to create utility for the project, three back-end components must be implemented to generate data packets and to receive, validate and integrate the results:

work generator—input/output specifications, together with a program or a script
    to submit the jobs.

validator—a daemon program that compares redundant results and decides which
    one is correct and assigns credit to every correct result.

assimilator—a method that is able to handle both correct and incorrect results, to
    apply further processing on the result and/or to write messages in the process
    logs.

8.2.3 P2

JXTA and BOINC are popular systems, mainly because they are the result of years
of experience. At the time when they were started, structured peer-to-peer networks
were in their infancy. This is possibly why there are no popular *structured* peer-to-
peer frameworks. However, as the research in this direction matures, we will be able
to observe the emergence of systems that allow different structured routing protocols
to be implemented easily. One such proposed system is P2 [198]. It allows a network
routing protocol to be specified in a version of a Datalog language [67], which, in
turns, is a version of Prolog [185].

8.2.3.1 The Specification Language: NDlog

The specification language used by P2, like Datalog, generates programs that are a
set of declarative rules and an optional query. A rule $y : -x_1, x_2, \ldots, x_n$ consists of
a head (y) and a body (the set of literals $x_1, x_2, \ldots, x_n$) with the usual meaning that
"*if x_1 AND x_2 AND $\ldots x_n$ are true (exist), then y is also true (assert y)*". A query
is just one literal.

The idea behind this kind of definition for a network routing specification is
something like "*if the message's destination fits ¡this¿ pattern and there is a link to
¡this¿ node then move message to ¡this¿ node*". As such, the language defines recursive programs, with the difference that every iteration of the recurrence is executed
at a possibly different node.

8.2.3.2 The Execution Framework

The specification programs written in NDlog are implemented and executed automatically by the P2 system. To interpret the rules, P2 uses variants of the *seminaive* interpretation method of Datalog programs [36]. The idea is to identify what changes are triggered by a rule in the routing tables or data indices (all stored as relational database entities) and apply them locally. At the same time, if the rule refers to different nodes, create the necessary forwarding messages.

8.2.4 Mace

Mace[5] [184] is an overlay development tool designed and implemented at the University of California at San Diego. It is a continuation of the ideas of MACEDON [272] that had been proposed 3 years earlier by more or less the same researchers, in a collaboration between UCSD and Duke University.

The aim of Mace is to provide a tool that allows developers to implement efficient overlays that can also be formally analyzed. In this sense, it is a midway between the finite state automata-based models of distributed systems, that allow extensive analysis but too little flexibility to be used in practice, and practical implementations using a common programming language (Java, C++, etc.) that work in practice but are hard to reason about.

Mace achieves its goal by defining a layered architecture and, more precisely, the tools for specifying each layer (i.e., service objects), and the interaction between layers (i.e., events). To further ease the job of the developer, Mace defines *aspects* to monitor network conditions and perform certain actions when a set of conditions are satisfied (e.g., trigger load rebalancing).

8.2.5 OverlayWeaver

OverlayWeaver[6] [294] is a new project, currently under development at the Japanese National Institute of Advanced Industrial Science and Technology. Though still under development at the moment of writing this book, it has the potential to become the first system to provide the means of development of true peer-to-peer networks with only a relatively small number of lines of code, due to its high modularity.

The authors allow the user to work at a very high level, to develop services on top of already defined overlays (and they provide sample implementations for Chord, Pasty, Tapestry, and Kademlia), as well as at a low level, to define their own routing algorithms.

---

[5]http://mace.ucsd.edu.

[6]http://overlayweaver.sourceforge.net/.

8.2.6 Microsoft's Peer-to-Peer Framework

Ever since its Service Pack 2 for Windows XP, but more manifestly since the release of the Vista operating system, Microsoft has provided a Peer Name Resolution Protocol (PNRP) [221] and an API to allow developers to take advantage of this protocol.

For instance, the PNRP Software Development Kit defines the following functions:

PeerPNRPStartUp() start the peer name resolution service
PeerPNRPShutdown() terminate the peer's participation in the network
PeerPNRPRegister() register a name for the current peer in the network
PeerPNRPResolve() identify the IP address[7] of a peer with a specific name

Essential to PNRP is, naturally, the peer identifier. Here, a PNRP ID is a 256 bits long string, composed of 128 bits representing the peer itself and another 128 with location information. Figure 8.5 illustrates this.

Because a name can represent any type of service that can be shared over the network, the name resolution process works in two phases:

1. identify the IP of the machine that published the name.
2. identify the service on that machine that corresponds to the given name.

The first phase works similarly to any other DHT-based overlay: a name is resolved by sending it to the neighbor that, in the routing table of the current peer, has

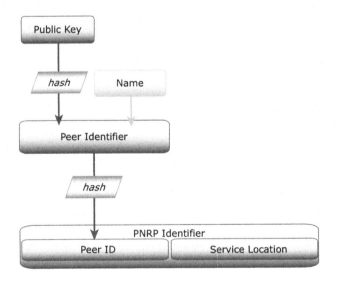

Fig. 8.5 Composition of a PNRP identifier

---

[7]PNRP uses IPv6.

an associated name that is closest to the requested name. Upon identification of the IP of the node holding the name, the protocol specifies a sequence of messages to determine the exact service to be executed.

8.3 Deployment and Testing Environments

After having implemented your peer-to-peer network, either from scratch using low-level programming tools described in Sect. 8.1, or some existing libraries and tools such as those presented in Sect. 8.2, one must be able to test it before releasing it to the public or to the corporate client. Simulations on a single machine are limited by the resources of the machine, as well as by the difficulty of implementing realistic scenarios. To fully test a peer-to-peer network, one needs many computers, preferably widely distributed both in terms of resources as well as geographically. We present here three such systems. The first, PlanetLab is a research cooperation between the academia and industry players and represents the largest, open, distributed environment. The other two are emulators, meaning that the machines that compose them are generally located at the same site or in close proximity. One of them is open for research, the other one is a commercial system.

8.3.1 PlanetLab

PlanetLab [76] can be most easily described as a set of machines distributed across the internet and the world. However, it is much more than that, mainly because all participants can request, and obtain, access to any other machine in PlanetLab. As such, PlanetLab is also a software package that manages this collection of computing resources across the internet.

The PlanetLab Consortium is a set of academic, industrial, and governmental institutions that collaborate and fund the PlanetLab network, whose main objective is *"to understand how the Internet can be architected to better support overlays"*. Currently, the network consists of over 850 nodes at over 400 sites in over 35 countries and is in the process of moving from a centralized administration system to a federated one, to further extend its scaling capacity.

8.3.1.1 Participating in PlanetLab

As a consortium dedicated to academic research, PlanetLab cannot be used by individual members of the public. Instead, a researcher gains access to the network via one of the participating institutions.

Apart from the legal proceedings of participating in the consortium, an academic institution must make available two or more server-class machines that will serve as PlanetLab nodes. Another significant requirement is that the nodes be given static

IP addresses and be located outside the institution's firewall, to allow for maximum reachability. The PlanetLab software package must be installed on these machines and, as such, they will be completely dedicated to the system, without the possibility of running anything outside the PlanetLab framework.

After becoming part of the PlanetLab consortium, an institution will be able to create user accounts and allocate "*slices*". The concept of slice is central to the PlanetLab framework: it provides the necessary allocation of resources for a distributed application, as well as the insulation between different applications. Once a user has a PlanetLab account and has been assigned a slice by a participating institution, he or she is able to create and deploy applications across all the nodes in the network.

8.3.1.2 Application Deployment on PlanetLab

Once a user has a site and a slice, the only step left is the addition of nodes to the slice. On each node that is added, resources will be allocated for that slice. The simplest way to add nodes is through the web interface at www.planet-lab.org, but nodes may also be added automatically through the PlanetLab Shell (plcsh) or through the Python scripting language.

After being added to the slice, the nodes appear to the user as individual systems made entirely available for the new application. Several scripting tools are available for working executing commands in parallel on different UNIX-like machines, but the PlanetLab recommends using CoDeploy (http://codeen.cs.princeton.edu/codeploy) to deploy the application and execute it concurrently on all nodes. CoDeploy helps alleviate the risk of overloading common repositories, especially during the deployment phase.

8.3.2 Emulab

Emulab [1] is a hardware installation as well as a software package maintained by the Flux Group at the University of Utah. As PlanetLab, Emulab is made available to the research community free of charge, even without the requirements of participating with resources in the project. However, as opposed to PlanetLab, Emulab systems (there are several at different universities) use servers that are collocated. Each system is firewalled, and the addressing space of the nodes participating in the system is local. This is why the Emulab software provides means of specifying artificial network delays in the system, to better simulate realistic network conditions.

Running experiments on Emulab involves three major steps: obtaining an account requires a senior researcher to specify a project and obtain authorization from the Emulab Approval Committee. Subsequently, an experiment can be initiated by designing a network topology. For this, Emulab uses a language very similar to the one used by the Network Simulator [15]: a scripting language used to define nodes, nodes properties (e.g., operating system), network links, as well as commands for running the experiment and for stopping it. Finally, after the experiment has been set up (i.e., the network topology has been instantiated), the user has full access to all the participating nodes.

8.3.2.1 Interfacing Emulab and PlanetLab

Emulab provides an interface to PlanetLab, via which a user can create a slice and add PlanetLab nodes to an existing Emulab experiment.

8.3.3 Amazon.com

Emulab and PlanetLab are both dedicated to academic research and it is very hard, or very costly, for a commercial entity to use their resources. For a start-up, small or mid-size company, it would be difficult to pay its way into these projects. Instead, such a company would prefer a pay-per-CPU cycle scheme. Amazon.com Inc., the online bookseller, has opened its large hardware infrastructure and sells computing cycles through its Elastic Compute Cloud (EC2) framework.

The Amazon EC2 provides a web service interface via which a user can request computing resources. The building block of EC2 is an Amazon Machine Image (AMI)—a software bundle that includes the operating system and all the libraries that a user might need. An AMI, either created from scratch by the user, or a predefined one, is first stored on Amazon's storage service (Amazon S3—Simple Storage Service), from where it can be instantiated in EC2.

Though the EC2 framework provides the conceptual prerequisites of geographically distributed computing, in the form of *Regions* and *Availability Zones*, it currently makes available only one Region. Availability Zones, several of which make a Region, are insulated from each other both physically and logically. They provide low bandwidth communications between those that belong to the same Region. Unlike Emulab, Amazon EC2 does not provide the tools to artificially delay communications, or simulate link failures—because that is not the purpose of this system. In this case, the user who needs to test more severe network conditions has to implement his own simulator.

The Amazon Elastic Compute Cloud, together with the Amazon SimpleDB, the Amazon Simple Storage Service and the Amazon Simple Queue Service, though not designed specifically for peer-to-peer networks, provide sufficient flexibility to the user who does not have access to academic network research facilities such as those described in previous sections of this chapter.

8.4 Summary

There are many ways through which one could implement a peer-to-peer architecture: either by working directly with the network protocol stack, through custom web services, or by using existing libraries that implement unstructured, semi-structured, or DHT-based overlays. However, a peer-to-peer system is, by definition almost, a complex system and, at this time at least, there is no easy way to define a peer-to-peer network that satisfies specific user requirements.

After implementing such a complex system, and before deploying it into the real world, several hardware and software environments provide the necessary scale to test the performance of the system, as well as its conformity to the requirements. Some of these platforms are nonprofit, dedicated to academic research, like PlanetLab and Emulab, others are commercial computing platforms, like that of Amazon.com Inc.

Chapter 9
Systems and Applications

In the earlier chapters, we have examined the enabling technologies for peer-to-peer computing. This chapter will look at several existing systems/applications that have employed P2P technologies. We shall look at (a) file sharing systems; (b) backup systems; (c) data management systems; (d) caching systems; and (e) mobile systems in the following sections. For each of these applications, we shall look at representative systems in the literature.

9.1 Classic File Sharing Systems

9.1.1 Napster

It is partly thanks to Napster, for having caught the attention of more than 38 million Internet users, that P2P has opened up a new research area in networking and distributed computing [12, 291]. In Chap. 2, this file sharing system has been presented, from the architectural point of view, as an example of centralized P2P systems. In this chapter, we will dedicate this subsection to describe this system from other viewpoints. First, we will present an overview, including the motivation of its development, roles of different nodes and basic functions. Second, we will describe its working procedure. Then we will detail the sharing protocol and, finally, touch on the intellectual property rights discussion that it has aroused.

9.1.1.1 Overview

The development of Napster was motivated by the demand to efficiently and conveniently search music across the ever increasing number of individual users of the Internet. Several years before, music fans were able to download music files of certain digital formats off the Internet. They found that, compared to the traditional manner of buying hard copies, it was more convenient and efficient to obtain (i.e.,

Q.H. Vu et al., *Peer-to-Peer Computing*,
DOI 10.1007/978-3-642-03514-2_9, © Springer-Verlag Berlin Heidelberg 2010

download) the music from the network. Furthermore, any user on the Internet was able to get any number of copies of these files easily and, in some cases, cost-free. However, this searching style inherently has the limitations of the client-server architecture. First, servers are usually powerful computers, resulting in expensive cost of infrastructure purchase, maintenance and administration. This means that only large companies could afford them, and consequently, all the data that is stored at individual users, even if they have an internet connection, remains under-used. Second, with the requests from users increasing, the performance of servers degrades dramatically. Even worse, once servers breakdown, none of the users are able to download any music files. In early 1999, Shawn Fanning (like some other successful IT business people, a college dropout), having himself faced the problem above, came up with the idea to develop a special utility to satisfy some basic requirements:

- Searching: users should be able to efficiently seek mp3 files in the network;
- Sharing: users should be able to share their mp3 files as they like, directly from their machines;
- Chatting: any user can find out and chat with others who are currently online.

After several months of hard work, Fanning had finished the development of this special program with the above features, and named it *Napster*, his nickname when he was in high school. This is the amazing story of the birth of Napster. At that time, it was hard to realize that "Napster" would become one of the P2P precursors and that it would have aroused a wave of research and development in P2P computing.

Just as pointed out in Chap. 2, Naspter is a centralized P2P system, where there are two kinds of nodes in the system, i.e., one or several servers and thousands or even millions of peers. The servers of Napster maintain the metadata of all currently available peers and locate the queried objects. Note that the servers themselves do not contribute any sharable files. However, the peers, whose population had sometimes been larger than 38 million, are really the active heroes of the system, since it is the peers that really maintain and trade these sharable music files. Furthermore, through their peers, users cannot only contribute but also obtain their desired MP3 files. In addition, the chat functionality further helps users to enjoy the community experience.

Even though Napster, as a public software utility, no longer exists, in what follows, we will continue to refer to its protocols and functionality in the present tense, because the ideas and protocols remain, even if they are not currently used.

9.1.1.2 How Napster Works

The working mechanism of Napster includes many specific phases, which can be described, from a high level, in two phases.

(i) *Joining the network.* To share and trade mp3 files, peers should first join into the centralized P2P network. This implies the installation of the Napster utility on the user's machine and, possibly, the sharing of some files.

(ii) *MP3 trading*. Once a user wants to search any music file in Napster, he or she performs the following operations:

- Runs the peer utility installed on his (or her) computer;
    - The utility software checks whether a network connection is built;
- Logs onto the central server;
- Sends a request to the server, and the server identifies the locations of the desired files in network, i.e., the IP address of the peers providing the answer;
    - Once the search is completed, the server returns the requestor with a list of contributors of the desired objects. By now, the server has accomplished all its processing in this transaction of file trading;
- Chooses one of contributors to download the music files as he (or she) likes, while the utility establishes a direct connection between the requestor and the selected contributor;
    - The requested files are transferred directly from the contributor to the requestor. After transferring, the contributor breaks down the connection immediately.

9.1.1.3 Protocol

The discussion on Napster's protocols [13] covers four aspects, i.e., peer-server protocol, message, peer-to-peer protocol, and peer-to-peer browsing, which will be described as follows.

Peer-Server Protocol. In Napster, the communication between a server and a peer uses the Transport Control Protocol (TCP). Basically, each message sent to or received from a server is in the form of $< length > < type > < data >$. Where both the segments of $< length >$ and $< type >$ are of 2 bytes, respectively. Further, the $< length >$ denotes the length of the $< data >$ portion in the message, that is, it precisely tells the amount of the data being transferred. In addition, $< length >$ and $< type >$ should be in the "little-endian" format (least significant byte goes first). The $< data >$ portion in the message is a string of plain ASCII. In many cases, the strings are transported as double-quoted entries.

Message. The $< data >$ segment specifies all the operations and messages in Napster, such as: error messages, users' logins, download requests, and so on. Indeed, there are more than 900 types of operations and messages all together, and a certain $< data >$ field represents each of them. To note that any combination of the $< type >$ and $< data >$ segments represents one certain message. Specifically, the $< type >$ specifies the message's id, while the $< data >$ tells its content. The format of the $< data >$ field should be under some criterion, so that it can be recognized by all the servers and peers.

Table 9.1 exemplifies a combination of $< type >$ and $< data >$ segments, representing the peer's request for removing a file from the shared library.

Peer-to-Peer Protocol. In Napster, the file transfer is undertaken directly between two peers. There are two pairs of cases, based on whether or not there is a firewall in between the two peers, which will be discussed in the following table.

Table 9.1 Example of a message

< type >	< data >	Specification
102(0x66)	< filename >	Client's requests to remove file from the shared library

    — *No firewall.* In a normal instance, a peer seeking a music file (requestor) manages to make a TCP connection to another one, who possesses the desired file (contributor). Upon the connection being built, the desired file is transferred from the contributor to the requestor. In addition, at the beginning of each transfer, the requestor sends a message to the server for a notification, and when the transfer is completed, it will send another message to the server. For example, the 218/219 message pair is used for the initiated/completed notifications, respectively. If the requestor downloads multiple files, the pair of message will be sent for each transfer, which informs the server on how many transfers are going on. Likewise, the contributor should send another pair of messages for the case of upload (the 220/221 message pair).

    — *Firewalled.* When the peer sharing data (the contributor) is behind a firewall, and hence the peer wanting data (the downloader) cannot establish a direct TCP connection to the contributor to download data, it is necessary for the contributor to "push" the data by making a TCP connection to the downloader's data port [13] (note that if this alternative connection cannot be setup because the downloader is also behind a firewall, file transfer cannot take place). Once a music file should be "pushed", the requestor sends a message, 500, to the server immediately, and then, the response message, such as 501, will be sent to the contributor, i.e., the peer sharing the file. After the contributor receives the response message from the server, a TCP connection will be built between these two peers, while the port of the requestor is determined according to the response message. Upon this TCP connection, the desired file is going to be transferred. In addition, the peers should also tell the server that they are downloading or uploading with different message pairs, as described above.

Peer-to-Peer Browsing. In the latest version of Napster, any peer is allowed to browse files in another peer, with the condition that only objects which have been previously shared by their owner are displayed. To browse shared file of another peer, a TCP connection should be first built between the two peers. Figure 9.1 illustrates how this connection is built.

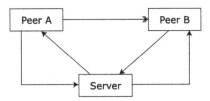

Fig. 9.1 TCP connection in
the browsing case

In the figure, peer A wants to browse the shared files of peer B. The TCP connection between them is created as follows:

(1) A sends the message 640 $< A'sname >$ to the server;
(2) The server then sends command 640 $< A'sname >$ to peer B to inform B that A would like to browse the shared files of B;
(3) If B allows A to browse its files, it will return the command 641 $< A'sname >$ to the server;
(4) After receiving B's permission, the server forwards the message 641 $< A'sname > < B'sIPaddress > < port >$ to A;
(5) Peer A makes a TCP connection to B's data port given by the server.

Finally, the connection is built. By sending the command GETLIST, peer A can browse all the shared files of B.

If B is behind a firewall, B will make a TCP connection to peer A, and will let the list of shared files be pushed to A.

9.1.1.4 Litigation: an Issue Beyond Technology

Thanks to the advantages of P2P computing, Napster harnessed the resources at the edges of the Internet, and in particular it facilitated the free trade of music files. As a consequence, it became more and more popular since its birth, especially on the university campuses in the United States. And indeed, it had more than 38 million users before November of year 2000 [161]. However, the free trade among the users of Napster had arguably hurt the profits of the music recording industry, since users in such communities could obtain what they desired without paying. In December 1999, the Recording Industry Association of America (RIAA) filed a suit against Napster, alleging "contributory and vicarious" copyright infringement. Eventually, Napster was forced to interrupt its services. From then, the discussion on the *Property Right Issues* has been a hot topic around Napster and other P2P-based file sharing systems.

9.1.2 Gnutella

In Chap. 2, we have described the architecture of Gnutella, one of the pioneers of fully distributed P2P systems. In this section, we will first introduce an overview of the system. Then we will provide more details on its protocol and working mechanism. Finally, we will summarize its advantages and challenges.

9.1.2.1 Overview of Gnutella

Gnutella [7, 172] is one of the pioneers of fully distributed P2P systems, whose history began in early March 2000. The system was invented by Justin Frankel and

Tom Pepper, two former employees of a division of America Online called Nullsoft. The name is the combination of GNU and Nutella, which implies its innovation and impact on the computing field as well. The system was primarily started to share recipes by the Nullsoft division. Theatrically, just after its birth, America Online cut off its support, since the project headers were aware of its potentially causing copyright infringement. However, Brian Mayland, a programmer, reverse-engineered the protocol and started a new project to develop clients. Consequently, Gnutella has become an open source project with clients registered under the GNU License [248]. In fact, Gnutella is a file sharing protocol rather than a brand new software. As long as the nodes comply with the Gnutella protocol, they form a Gnutella network and each node can search and download files from the other peers. Among the most famous citizens of large-scale and fully decentralized P2P systems, Gnutella has attracted a wide interest. In general, Gnutella has the following features:

- *Elegance and generality.* Gnutella is elegant by its simplicity. Its minimalist requirements can be mastered even by a programming apprentice. Furthermore, the Gnutella protocol is so generic that it has been implemented in a large number of P2P systems, such as Gnotella [6] and Furi [4] and usually serves as a primary "benchmark" in academic community;
- *Transparency and user-friendliness.* Instead of defining a set of complicated symbols as the Internet's protocols, most of Guntella-compatible systems take keyword as their inputs and reply requesters with matching files. Moreover, the underlying structure of the Internet where such systems survive is almost transparent to their users, especially in the context of recent implementations;
- *Dynamicity and self-organization.* As known, the traditional Internet applications, including the Web and FTP, are directly implemented upon the Internet and the roles of server, client and router are pre-defined and static. However, Gnutella (including other fully decentralized P2P systems) creates an overlay of dynamic and self-organizing peers, where participants are equal and work as servers, clients and routers at the same time. Furthermore, the infrastructure itself is dynamic and ad-hoc, since each peer can join and leave the community at any time;
- *Full decentralization.* Compared to previous systems, one of the predominant features of Gnutella is its total decentralization. In Gnutella, there exists no centralized mechanism.

From the above description, we can see that Gnutella has eliminated one of limitations of previous architectures: single points of failure. Gnutella brings out an ideology of full decentralization, dynamics, ad-hoc, and self-organization. Therefore, Gnutella was regarded as a way to reshape the Internet and also inspire us to rethink our concept of the network-based applications. It had greatly attracted the interests both from the academic community and the IT industry, especially when Napster had been entangled in litigation.

9.1.2.2 Protocol

To be precise, it is more appropriate to define Gnutella as a set of generic P2P protocols, rather than a P2P system. Therefore, we should not be surprised to find out that there are many Gnutella-compatible systems, such as Gnotella [6], Furi [4], and Gnewtella [5], which are running upon various operating systems. Moreover, the Guntella protocol usually serves as an underlying overlay upon which some sophisticated schemes, such as Routing indices [89] and Directed Search [342], are implemented to improve the efficiency and effectiveness of searching in the context of this computing paradigm. In the following, we summarize the kernel of the Gnutella protocol, while for its details, we refer the reader to [8].

Gnutella adopts the HTTP-based protocol, which defines the way peers communicate with each other over the network. A Gnutella message transported over the TCP protocol has a header, which is fixed to 23 bytes and contains five fields: Identifier, Function (or Payload Descriptor), TTL(Time To Live), Hops and Payload Length. The "Identifier" field having a length of 16 bytes stores the identifier of the message, which is generated by the peer initiating the message and is used to identify the message. The "Function" field having a length of 1 byte describes what action a peer should take when it receives the message. The "TTL" field having a length of 1 byte defines the number of hops the message can be (further) forwarded from now on. The "Hops" field having a length of 1 byte defines the number of hops the message had already passed until now. The "Payload Length" field having a length of 4 bytes specifies how many bytes the next message header is from this message header. Depending on the function of the message, certain rules must be followed. This means that the Gnutella protocol is made up of two parts: (i) a set of specific messages employed for transmitting data between peers, and (ii) a set of rules managing how messages are processed at peers. Generally, the routing of Gnutella messages on the network can be classified into three categories:

— *Group Membership Messages (Ping and Pong)*. A peer who wants to join the network initiates a *Ping* message in broadcast-based manner to declare its presence. Those that receive the Ping message forward the message to their neighbors and respond with a Pong message. The Pong message also has information regarding its own initiator, such as its IP address and the number and size of shared files.
— *Search Messages (Query and QueryHit)*. Query messages contain a search string specified by the user, employed by the receiving peers to determine whether they maintain good enough answers locally. Query messages are also distributed in a broadcast style. "QueryHit" is the response to Query and includes information necessary to download related files.
— *File Transfer Messages (Get and Push)*. When the requester receives the Query-Hit Messages, it is prepared for the data exchange with the file providers. Ordinarily, the requester only needs to contact the providers with a Get message, and then directly downloads the desired files from them by standard HTTP protocol, if the providers agree to the download request. Unfortunately, many computers in the Internet are separated by firewalls for security and privacy reasons. That

Table 9.2 Message managing rule

Message	Managing rule
Ping	This kind of messages is employed by Gnutella peers to probe the activity of others in the network. On receiving a Ping message, a peer should reply with a Pong message.
Pong	Pong messages are the response to an incoming Ping message. It packages the address of the pong message sender and information indicating the amount of data currently available to other peers in the network.
Query	This sort of messages is sent to create the primary mechanism of Gnutella, i.e., searching digital objects on the network. A peer who receives a Query message will respond with a QueryHit if it finds one or several matches in its local data store.
QueryHit	QueryHit messages are the replies of an incoming Query message. A peer should reply a Query with a QueryHit if it contains data strictly based on the query processing criteria.
Get	Get messages are used to download the files indicated in a QueryHit message.
Push	A peer can send a Push message if it receives a QueryHit message from an answer contributor that doesn't support incoming connections. Push is a mechanism that helps peers behind a firewall to contribute file-based data to requestors.

is to say, the HTTP Get method does not work, if the provider is behind a firewall. In order to solve this problem, a Push method is employed. If the requester cannot build a direct connection with the provider, it then tries to send a Push message to the provider. As long as the provider receives the Push message, it initiates itself a direct connection with the requester.

For clarity, we summarize the messages and their respective managing rule in Table 9.2.

9.1.2.3 Challenges

While Gnutella enjoys many desirable characteristics, and is regarded as one of the pioneers to reshape the Internet, as well as our concepts of network-based applications, it is confronted with many challenges, which have been briefly discussed in Chap. 2. Here, we just highlight the two most urgent ones, to maybe inspire the reader to pay attention to the topic.

- *Scalability*. Gnutella has indeed eliminated the problems resulting from centralized servers, but it still lacks scalability due to its broadcast-based message routing scheme. First, to probe the activity of others, a peer periodically produces a ping message and broadcasts the message to all of its neighbors, who in turn perform the same operation until the TTL of the ping message reaches zero. This processing results in exponential messages in the network. Moreover, each pinged node will reply with a pong message, which also generates the same volume of messages as "ping". This is even worse if we remember that it is necessary for a peer to ping its neighbors when it joins the network, ant that one of the predominant characters of P2P systems (including Gnutella) is dynamic and ad-hoc, which indicates there are continual peers joining the network. Finally, peers in the network definitely need to search their desired digital objects, which also results in an exponential number of messages. As a consequence, Gnutella is inevitably flooded by the messages running on the network.

- *Security*. Gnutella provides no security guarantees, since all messages are routed in the form of plain text, which can be parsed and even modified by every peer. Specifically, since every peer through which a message passes is able to read the full contents of the message, the system is highly vulnerable to malicious attacks.

To overcome these two challenges is urgent, since they greatly hinder the further development.

9.1.3 Freenet

Freenet [3, 78, 189] is a fully decentralized and adaptive peer-to-peer system to facilitate users to publish anonymously, replicate, and retrieve key-identified digital files. This system has specific features to differentiate itself from other existing P2P systems, as summarized in Table 9.3.

The first version of Freenet software was released in March 2000, when Napster was facing its darkest day of censorship. Indeed, the development of Freenet can be retrospected to 1997, when Ian had his paper "Distributed Address Lookup System" published, which implicitly declared the philosophy of Freenet: Information Freedom. When Ian accomplished his thesis "A Distributed Decentralized Information Storage and Retrieval System" in 1999, the development basis of Freenet was set up. Ian and his colleagues further clarified their designing goal [78]:

- Protecting the privacy of information producers, maintainers, and consumers;
- Resisting to any information censorship;
- Realizing high information availability and system reliability through decentralization;

Table 9.3 Distinguished features of Freenet

Compared system	Distinct feature
Centralized P2P systems (e.g., Napster)	Freenet has no centralized mechanism.
Structured P2P systems (e.g., Pastry)	Freenet adopts a location-independent key to identify corresponding data, and there is no mapping between the data and its location.
Unstructured P2P systems (e.g., Gnutella)	Freenet does not employ broadcast search.

– Enjoying efficiency, scalability, and adaptability of information storage and message routing.

Based on the above description, we can conclude that the most important policy of Freenet is anonymity or protecting the user's privacy, while the main functions are publication, replication, and retrieval. In the rest of this subsection, we focus on the discussion of this P2P system's working mechanisms, protocol, and its advantages and disadvantages.

9.1.3.1 Freenet Working Mechanisms

In this part, we discuss the working mechanism of Freenet, including its key-based file identification, query and storage methods, and how a new peer joins into the network.

Foundation mechanism: key-based file identification strategies. All shared files in the Freenet are identified by certain kinds of location-independent keys. Specifically, Freenet has adopted three types of keys to name the files in the network, i.e., keyword-signed key, signed-subspace key, and content-hash key. In the following, we will describe their generation, function, as well as their limitation.

– *Keyword-signed key (Abbr. KSK).* This simplest type of key (in Freenet) is constructed from a short text string, which is given by its contributor (the user inserting the file into system) and is descriptive enough to denote the file. For instance, when a user inserts a disquisition on how human cloning impacts ethics, one could use *"text/philosoph/ethic/human−clone"* to describe the file. Such a string is used to deterministically produce a public, private key pair. The public component is used to generate the file's keyword-signed key (KSK) while the latter serves as the signature of the file being inserted. This signature can just provide minimal integrity check of the retrieved file that matches the KSK. To retrieve the file, any user (either the contributor or other participants) just needs to input the descriptive string published by its contributor, instead of inputting the KSK itself. However, this sort of key mechanism obviously suffers from two problems. First, since malicious attackers can employ a dictionary to compile a list of descriptive strings to assault against the signature, the proved integrity check is really minimal and even takes no effect. Second, since there is no global coordination and users are also hardly able to have enough knowledge of the whole system, it is possible for two users to independently use the same description to denote different files.

– *Signed-subspace key (Abbr. SSK).* This sort of key integrates the personal namespaces of Freenet users. To generate an SSK for a file, the following procedure is indispensable:

   (i) A user randomly creates a namespace in form of public key, private key pair;

(ii) The user appoints a descriptive text string to the file to store into the system (as in KSK);

(iii) Both the user's public namespace key and that of the file's descriptive string are hashed independently;

(iv) Both the hash values of (iii) are joined through a XOR operation;

(v) The results of (iv) are hashed to produce the SSK of the file to be storing.

In order to let other citizens of the community to retrieve a file identified by an SSK, the contributor should publish the descriptive string of the file and the public key of his/her namespace. On the other hand, storing a file also requires the private key of the namespace, so that only its owner can modify it. In addition, users have access to manage their own namespace, which enables them to find smarter schemes to improve file retrieval.

From the above description, we can observe that the SSK strategy is more sophisticated than that of KSK and able to conquer both problems KSK faces. As mentioned above, the namespace of a user is randomly generated, so it is hard for different users to obtain the identical namespace. Therefore, it is virtually impossible for two different users independently to identify two different files with a same key. Furthermore, since the signature of the file identified by the SSK is the private part corresponding to its user's namespace, which is randomly produced, it is more secure than that of a KSK.

— *Content-hash key (Abbr. CHK).* This sort of key is produced by directly hashing the contents of the file being inserted. Furthermore, a randomly generated encryption key is also used to encrypt the file. In order to allow it to be retrieved by other users, both the CHK and the decryption of the file should be published by the contributor.

The greatest merit of CHK is that it helps users to update and split their files. Users can update their files by employing CHK together with the SSK strategy. When a file, for which we want to let it be updated later, is to be inserted, it is first stored under its CHK. Then an indirect file pointer is inserted under an SSK whose contents are the CHK of the file. To update the file, its new version is first inserted under its new CHK. Then a new indirect file pointer of the new version is inserted under its original SSK pointing to the new version. When the insert arrives at a peer maintaining the old version, it triggers a key collision. The peer verifies the validity and timestamp and finally accomplishes the updating.

File splitting is also useful in the context of networking computing. With the application of CHK, the file splitting is very easy to achieve in Freenet. First, the file being inserted is split into several parts based on certain metrics. For example, each part is given a fixed size, function of the total size of the file. Each part is separately inserted into Freenet under its own CHK. Finally, an indirect file pointer is created, which points to all of the separate parts.

Briefly speaking, the key mechanism, the working foundation of Freenet, is sophisticated enough to cater to many utilization demands. However, all three strategies are confronted with the challenge of finding the keys in the first place.

Query processing: how to retrieve a file in Freenet. To retrieve a desired file from Freenet, a user should first initiate a request message through his own peer to express the target with a file key, which is determined beforehand. Further, he must specify the message's *hops-to-live*, whose function is equivalent to that of the TTL in a Gnutella message. By now, what the user needs to do is just waiting for the result. When receiving a retrieval request, a peer will first lookup against its own repository and if it finds the answer, it declares itself as the data source and returns the answer along the same path as it came. Furthermore, all peers along the path, independently, cache the file in their local repository, and create a new entry in their routing table to store the actual source as well. Obviously, subsequent requests containing the same key can be efficiently resolved from the cached results. Otherwise, if the peer cannot find the answer locally, it will select a key in its routing table that is nearest to the one contained in the request and route the request to the corresponding peer. If the current peer cannot forward the request to its downstream neighbor associated to the nearest key, either because the operation results in a loop or because that neighbor is currently down, then the current peer will try the second nearest, then the third, and so on. Further, if the peer cannot route the request downstream after all possible attempts, it will return a failure to its upstream peer and the latter will try its second nearest and so on. If the request's hops-to-live limit is reached, a failure message is returned to the original peer without any more peer trying.

File storing: inserting files into Freenet. To store a file into Freenet, the process is to insert the file into the P2P network, which "reuses" the scheme of query processing adopted by the network and includes three sequential processing procedures:

- file key deciding;
- insert message propagating;
- file inserting.

To store a file, a user should first decide which key strategy to use and declare or obtain the corresponding file key. Then the user should initiate an inserted message through his own peer and specify the file key and the message's hops-to-live, which determine how many copies of the file will be stored in the network. An insert message is propagated in the same style as a request message described above. Specifically, when receiving an insert message, a peer first verifies whether or not its routing table has already seen the file key and perform following two processes, respectively. (i) If it has seen the file key before, the peer will return a message to inform the user that there already exists a file named by the key, so that the user learns about the key collision and makes a second try with another key. Note that along with the key collision returning to the original inserting peer, the existing file is cached along the same path, which equals to retrieving the file by the original file key. (ii) Otherwise, the peer will try to forward the inserted message to its neighbor maintaining the nearest key to the inserted one in its routing table. If it cannot, due to the downstream neighbor being down or creating a loop, it will try to route the inserted message to the neighbor corresponding to the second nearest key in the routing table, and so on. If the message runs out its hops-to-live without a key collision, a "clear" result message will be returned to the original inserting peer. Finally, the inserting file will be stored in each peer along the way of the inserted message routing. Note, just as a query processing, an inserting processing also has the effect of file key clustering.

File managing. This is the mechanism by which a peer deals with the conflict between a limited storage capacity and a continuous stream of files to be stored. In Freenet, each peer adopts the policy to first delete the least recently used, which is similar to the LRU (Least Recently Used) cache policy proposed in [309]. That is to say, when inserting a new file while not having enough sharable storage space, a peer will first delete the least recently requested files until there is enough space to cater for the new insertion.

Peer joining. The mechanism defining new peer joins has been proposed based on two considerations: efficient routing and anonymity preservation. Indeed, they are, to a certain extent, two conflicting demands. Freenet caters to them simultaneously by adopting a cryptographic protocol. Before joining the network, a new peer should obtain the address of one or several existing peers, so that it can propagate its message through the existing nodes, to announce its presence. First, the newcomer chooses a random sequence (called "seed") and informs the veteran peers via a message including its address and the hash value of the random seed. On receiving such an announcement, a veteran chooses itself a random seed, further XORs the seed chosen by itself with the hash value in the announcement and hashes the result again. Furthermore, the peer routes the most recent hash to a randomly selected neighbor (based on its routing table). Similarly to query and storing processing, the processing is terminated when the hops-to-live of the message arrives at its lower bound. All peers in the path of the announcement routing can discover and verify the key of the newcomer and create an entry in their routing table for the newcomer.

9.1.3.2 Freenet Protocol

Freenet adopts a packet-oriented protocol while the kernel is self-contained messages. Each message is embedded a transaction ID to enable the currently processing peer to decide the status of either insert or request messages. Further, Freenet has the flexibility of employing different message transport mechanisms, such as TCP, UPD, even radio package and so on. Indeed, it adopts TCP in most cases and the addresses of a peer consists of its IP address and the employed port number. In addition, the P2P system exploits the scheme of virtual addresses to overcome the challenge resulting from the frequent change of some peers' addresses. All messages include a 64-bit transaction ID, a hops-to-live, a depth and even a key in some cases. The ID is randomly generated and the probability that two different messages share the same ID is extremely low. Hops-to-live, deciding how far the message will be routed, is given by the message initiator and is decremented at each hop. However, a message will not be terminated at once after its hops-to-live reaches 1, but is still routed further with a finite probability with the consideration of security. Conversely, the depth of a message is incremented at each hop and serves as the basis for the current peer to set the hops-to-live of the replying message.

Connection building up. To carry out a transaction, the initiator should initiate a *Request.Handshake* message, which is routed in the same manner as the request described previously. If the remote peer corresponding to the request is active, it replies with a *Reply.Handshake* indicating the version of the protocol that it can understand. Since a handshake can be "remembered" for some time, the subsequent transaction between the same peers can omit the processing during the period.

Query processing. In order to retrieve a desired file, the initiator should initiate a *Request.Data* message containing a transaction ID, the hops-to-live counter, the depth and the search key. The request message is routed in the network as discussed previously. Further, based on the chosen hops-to-live, the initiator starts a timer and assumes failure after the period. However, the remote currently processing peer can periodically send back *Reply.Restart* messages to extend the timer. If the query is successful, the answer contributor replies with a *Send.Data* message carrying the desired file and the source address (possible faked). If the message runs out its hops-to-live without finding the answer, the peer will reply the initiator with a *Reply.NotFound* message. During the replying procedure, the sending peer decrements the hops-to-live of the *Send.Data* (or *Reply.NotFound*) and forwards the message upstream until it reaches the actual requestor. If a peer cannot forward the message downstream while there are still hops-to-live, it will reply its upstream neighbor with a *Request.Continue* message specifying the left hops-to-live. On receiving a *Request.Continue* message, the peer tries to contact the next most likely peer and returns a *Reply.Restart* message upstream.

Storing processing. To store a file into Freenet, the initiator sends a Request.Insert message containing a transaction ID, an initial hops-to-live counter, depth, and the proposed key. The message is routed in Freenet as discussed previously. The timers and *Reply.Restart* messages are performed in the same manner as they are in the query processing. If the insert induces a key collision, the peer replies with a *Sent.Data* message containing the existing file or a *Reply.NotFound* message (if the file is not found while there is a corresponding entry in the routing table). If the insert has not confronted a collision and traverses all possible peers and there are still hops-to-live, the peer replies with a *Request.Continue* indicating a failure in this context. If the hops-to-live counter reaches zero without facing a key collision, the peer will reply with a *Reply.Insert*, which is routed upstream to the initiator. All peers along the path are waiting for their upstream neighbor's *Send.Insert* message containing the file (to store). When receiving it, they store the file locally while forwarding the *Send.Insert* message downstream until the initiator of the corresponding *Reply.Insert*.

9.1.3.3 Merits and Limitations

As one of the pioneers of P2P systems, Freenet has many merits and several limitations as well. In this part, we first present the merits that Freenet enjoys and then discuss the limitations it is confronted with.

− *Merits*

   (1) Freenet has eliminated many problems of centralized architectures, including single points of technical failure and censorship, and lack of scalability.
   (2) Freenet has gotten rid of the common problem of conventional network-based application, i.e., the slashdot effect (popular data becoming less available with the increase in request).
   (3) Freenet is one of the most successful P2P systems which protect the privacy of their users and have high security.
   (4) The search strategy of Freenet has the effect of clustering similar identifier of files together, and thus is beneficial for peers to answer similar queries efficiently according to the previous search experience.

− *Limitations*

   (1) Not providing permanent file storing: Although Freenet has eliminated some limitations resulting from centralized architecture and improved the information availability and system reliability, it indeed does not provide permanent storing. Therefore, some files that are seldom requested may be removed from the system.
   (2) Inefficient searching: Although the Freenet's working mechanisms and protocol are much more sophisticated, e.g., key clustering and caching, it is not sufficiently efficient to be a search engine as present. Indeed, many users complain that the period from their request submission to the answer arriving is usually too long. This makes the system hardly practicable.
   (3) Disputable philosophy. Information freedom is the main policy and the philosophy of Freenet. Commonly, information freedom is desirable in the digital age, especially with the growth of censorship and erosion of privacy increasing in the Internet. However, a level of control is desired in most civilized societies.

9.2 Peer-to-Peer Backup

Today's PCs typically come with large storage capacities that have outgrown the needs of many users. To utilize the unused storage space, these PCs can be "connected" in a peer-to-peer (P2P) network to backup each other's data. Designing such a P2P backup system is challenging: the P2P network is inherently dynamic (nodes join and leave anytime), fairness must be enforced to prevent free-riding, the maintenance traffic has to be kept at an acceptable level, heterogeneous needs and capacities of nodes have to be considered, and the number of *replicas* must be controlled, and duplicates have to be eliminated. (Note that we follow the terminology presented in [55]—*replicas* refer to copies generated by a backup system to enhance reliability, while *duplicates* refers to logically distinct blocks with identical content.)

Existing works have focused on two directions. On one hand, there exist distributed storage systems (e.g., PAST [114], OceanStore [186], and Farsite [55]) that pool together the storage resources of the peers in the P2P network for sharing, archiving, and/or providing a distributed file system. However, these systems provide little or no data backup semantics, such as incremental updates and versioning. On the other hand, we have P2P systems that offer backup solutions, e.g., pStore [38], Pastiche [84], and the Cooperative Internet Backup Scheme [195].

This section will introduce four Peer-to-Peer backup systems in detail and give a short overview of other related work.

9.2.1 pStore

The pStore system [38] separates backup and underlying Peer-to-Peer functionality. pStore completely surrenders all Peer-to-Peer tasks to Chord [173], a distributed hash table (DHT) implementation, concentrating on the implementation of backup semantics on top of it. When creating a new backup, pStore splits each individual file of the backup set into a number of equal-size blocks (except the last block, which may be smaller) and creates a metadata record, which are then stored inside the hash table (Fig. 9.2). The mapping of data blocks to nodes inside the Peer-to-Peer overlay is managed by Chord.

Before being inserted into the network, each file block (FB) is encrypted using *convergent encryption* [55]. In this scheme, each block is encrypted with a sym-

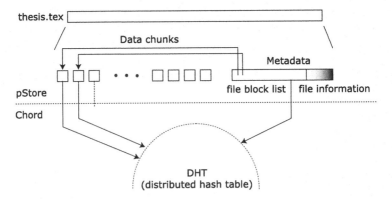

Fig. 9.2 Overview of pStore

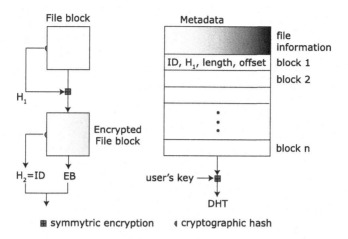

Fig. 9.3 Block creation process in pStore

metric cipher using a cryptographic hash value of the block, H_1, as the key. The encrypted block (EB) is run through the hash function once more to obtain a hash value H_2, which serves as the identifier (ID) of that block. After that, the tuple (H_2, EB) is inserted into the distributed hash table (DHT). Both H_1 and H_2 and general information on the block are added to the metadata descriptor (called file block list, FBL). Finally, the FBL is inserted into the hash table as well. Since it contains keys for all files blocks, it is encrypted using the symmetric key of the user, which can be derived from a password. The block creation process is illustrated in Fig. 9.3.

Data Sharing By employing convergent encryption, pStore ensures that all peers that back up the same file produce the same set of encrypted blocks. This guarantees that all storage requests for identical blocks will be routed to the same host in the DHT. If a host receives a duplicate request, asking it to store a block which is already present in its block store, it will silently ignore it and return a "success" response. The scheme ensures that only a single copy of each block is stored in the system and common blocks are shared. Each host stores an owner tag list (OTL) with each block stored to indicate all the peers that send a storage request for this particular block. Figure 9.4 illustrates the block sharing in pStore.

To further decrease the storage requirements, pStore incorporates an incremental backup scheme. Exploiting the observation that files in consecutive backup snapshots often show only minor differences, pStore tries to match previously stored file blocks with the new version of a file using a modified rsync algorithm [319]. The original rsync algorithm is designed for fixed-size blocks, pStore extends it to support matching blocks of different sizes. The matching process is illustrated in Fig. 9.5. When backing up a new version of a file, pStore updates the existing metadata record(i.e., the FBL) by appending a new list of file block identifiers. As shown in Fig. 9.6, the new list contains references to matching old blocks as well as a small number of newly created blocks. Under this scheme, the frequent backups of a file with small changes should only demand moderate resources.

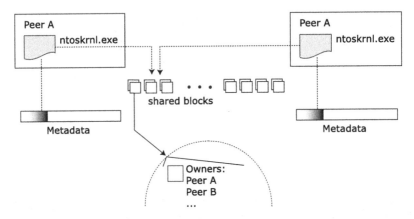

Fig. 9.4 Block sharing in pStore

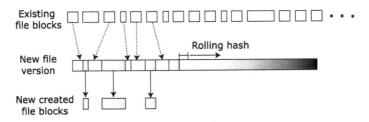

Fig. 9.5 Block matching in pStore

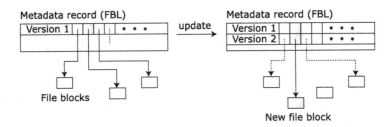

Fig. 9.6 Adding version to file in pStore

By employing these techniques, significant savings on the global storage requirements can be achieved. The authors of pStore claim a reduction of between 3 and 60 percent in total storage requirements. However, savings depend heavily on the data inserted into the backup system and scale directly with the degree of overlap between hosts. (A study conducted as part of the Farsite project [55] found up to 50% overlap between the computers of Microsoft employees.)

Replication As discussed in Chap. 5, replication is needed in order to make data storage robust against host failure. pStore places multiple copies of blocks under different keys inside the hash table, it accomplishes this by hashing the block identifier together with a salt value. pStore uses a collection of well-known salt values for different replicas. To create the identifier of the ith replica of a block, the client simply appends the salt value for replica i to the block identifier, H_2, and calculates the hash value of this concatenation. Using the obtained hash value as the key, the client then proceeds to insert the replica into the system. In this way, clients can create any number of replicas they want.

Fairness pStore offers no dedicated mechanism to fairness. Nothing prevents peers from overloading the system with too much data and nothing prevents clients from free-riding, storing data inside the system without providing storage themselves.

9.2.2 A Cooperative Internet Backup Scheme

"A Cooperative Internet Backup Scheme" [195] tries to address the Peer-to-Peer backup problems in an entirely different manner. This system focuses on providing a virtual replicated "disk", leaving the actual implementation of the actual backup to clients. The system emphasizes a lot on fairness, at the cost of losing a few other desirable properties.

The main idea of this scheme is: Peers exchange disk space in a symmetric manner. When forming a trading partnership, both peers agree on terms like the exchange quantity, the time-frame of the exchange and certain availability of each peer. Of course, it is rare for two peers to find exact matches in exchanging quantities, so trade ratio might be used. Once both peers have agreed to the deal, they can begin storing data on each other's hard disk.

Replication Peers are assumed to build a virtual "disk" using erasure-coded stripes in the manner of a RAID disk array (Fig. 9.7). Erasure codes [333] are a special variant of error-correcting codes that only deal with *erasure* (lost blocks) instead of general single- or multiple-bit errors. In general, the space efficiency of erasure codes increases with the number of fragments being used. On the one hand, this

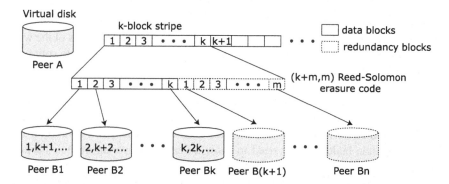

Fig. 9.7 Virtual disk using erasure code

means a peer can increase system efficiency by trading with many partners, which keeps the storage overhead low. On the other hand, bandwidth consumption and latency increases with each partner added because more fragments must be retrieved to reconstruct data, leading to decreased system efficiency. Selecting the right number of fragments is a trade-off between space efficiency and network overhead.

Finding Partner Cooperative Internet Backup suggests a *central server* acting as a matchmaker in order to facilitate finding trade partners among peers. A peer that is willing to trade (to backup data) contacts the server with the description of the partner it is looking for. The server keeps all this information in a database and will return to the requesting peer a list of potential candidate partners. The requesting peer will contact these candidate partners to establish suitable trades.

There is one problem with the approach in this system: a peer must remember the list of peers it has traded with, i.e., its partners.

Fairness Fairness is the focus point of Cooperative Backup Scheme. Building on the base of symmetric trading, there are a number of mechanisms dealing with free-riding and malicious peers.

Replacing a bad partner is the first step. If a partner loses data or does not keep its uptime promises, a peer will drop the partner and prefer to look for a new partner. The misbehaved partner will be kept in a black list so as to avoid adding these partners in the future. Of course, a peer does not drop its partner on its first failure, since the partner may be temporarily experiencing downtime or crashing, in order to take this into account, peers will wait for a time interval before deciding that the partner is "bad".

In order to locate bad partners, a peer needs to check their partners periodically whether they are still holding the required backup data and whether they are still in their up time as they agreed. The peer will request *random* blocks now and then to make sure the partner is doing well.

9.2.3 Pastiche

Pastiche [84] combines the features of the previous systems, though itself has no direct connection with either of them. Pastiche resembles pStore in terms of the way backup data is managed and overlap is exploited. Files to be backed up are split into blocks which are encrypted using convergent encryption to support sharing of blocks between peers. Metadata is considered a special block which will never be split. However, during the process of distributing the data blocks, Pastiche is more similar to the Internet Cooperative Backup Scheme. Pastiche uses DHT routing to discover backup "buddies", which will store data for each other. There is a restriction for peers to become buddies: they need to show a very high overlap in their backup data, so that this enables them to create a complete backup for each other by only exchanging a small set of blocks not present at the partner. In this way, symmetric trading is formed, with each partner storing data for the other.

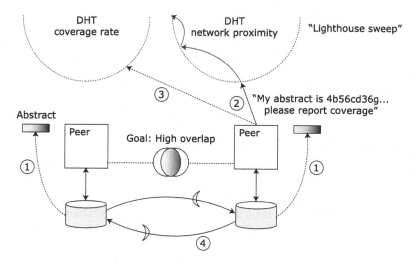

Fig. 9.8 Buddy searching process in pastiche

Discovering Buddies During the process of finding the partner, one important criteria is the overlapping data in backup sets. The reason is that the higher the overlap
between buddies the less data they need to exchange. Discovering matching peers is
done in a distributed scheme with the help of a *central server* which is also used by
Cooperative Internet Backup Scheme.

Each peer joins two Distributed Hash Tables (DHT). The first DTH is organized
by network proximity and the second DHT is organized by coverage rate, based on
an estimate of overlap between peers. The second DHT is used only when discovering partners in the first DHT fails.

The process of partner discovery works as following (Fig. 9.8):

1. A host first calculates an *abstract* of its file system. The abstract consists of
   checksums of a small randomly chosen set of files which is used as a fingerprint
   of the host's data.
2. With the abstract obtained, the host initiates a search in the network proximity
   DHT (i.e., the first DHT) by doing a *lighthouse sweep.*
3. If the lighthouse sweep fails, a search in the coverage DHT (i.e., second DHT)
   is used as a backup. Inside the coverage DHT, instead of using the lighthouse
   sweep, the request is forwarded towards hosts with higher coverage at each hop
   during a single search.
4. Finally, when a high-overlapped partner has been found, the set of different data
   blocks are exchange between the established partners.

Data Sharing and Replication All peers need to split their data so as to produce
similar sets of blocks for files with minor differences. In Pastiche, instead of splitting
a file at regular intervals, *content-based indexing* is used to split the file every time
a "magic" pattern is encountered. The pattern is called *anchor* [214]. By relying

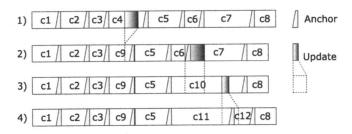

Fig. 9.9 Robustness of anchors during file modification

on patterns to discover block boundaries, only directly affected blocks are changed during an update process of the file, while the rest blocks are undisturbed (Fig. 9.9).

Security and Fairness The security of Pastiche is same as pStore: blocks are encrypted with convergent encryption, an owner list for each block is kept and keys are stored in its metadata structure. Pastiche offers a periodic-challenge model with *probabilistic punishment*, to ensure safekeeping of the backup data at partners, which is an improvement in terms of fairness. Further improvements for fairness enforcements are proposed by Samsara [85].

9.2.4 Samsara—Fairness for Pastiche

Samsara is an improved system for Pastiche, which enforces users to contribute storage to the system, proportionaly according to their consumption of the system resource. The main aim of Samsara is to convert asymmetric trades that have been established by different pairs of partners into symmetric ones, with the usage of *Storage Claim*.

A storage claim is a place-holder to indicate the unused storage space. When a host requests storage from peers, it must store a storage claim of the same size in return, which means reserving the same amount of space for future use by partner. In the situation when a peer has no data to store at a trade partner at the time of establishing trade, it issues a storage claim, saving the storage for later use. It is also possible that in the end the partner never has any data to store for his storage claim, if this happens, storage claims will not be removed from the system which leads to reduced available storage, instead, Samsara incorporates the idea of *forwarding* storage claims. During a trade, a peer may forward a foreign storage claim (claims are supposed to be of equal size) or to replace one of his previously issued storage claims by a foreign one later on. These scenarios are depicted in Fig. 9.10.

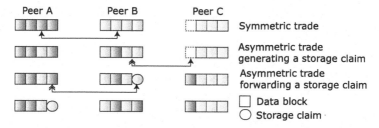

Fig. 9.10 Generation and forwarding of storage claims in samsara

9.2.5 Other Systems

There are a number of other Peer-to-Peer backup systems which are similar in one or another way to the above four systems. Here is a brief description for each of them:

— *PeerStore* [188] is a peer-based backup system that decouples the management of metadata and backup data. This separation allows different mechanisms to be exploited to optimize the design of the system. For the metadata, a DHT structure is employed to efficiently detect duplicates and track backup locations. Using DHT also enables aggressive maintenance of the metadata accuracy at a low overhead. For the actual data backup, a symmetric trading scheme in an unstructured network is adopted to preserve fairness among peers. The reported experimental study showed that PeerStore realizes fairness without excessive maintenance overhead.

— *SwarmBackup* [157] is a commercial Peer-to-Peer backup system. The system is based on a distributed hash table implementation similar to Kademlia [218]. The system employs small-scale broadcast queries (trying a routed query first) to increase flexibility in data placement inside the DHT. A kind of error coding, most likely erasure coding, is used to provide replication. Data is encrypted using convergent encryption.

 The system is to be deployed into a corporate environment, which has special monitoring and administration hosts that can affect how much data is stored at each peer. This implies that SwarmBackup has no explicit mechanism against free-riding, which make it unsuitable for use in a large open network such as Internet.

— *Venti-DHash* [296] is a system built on top of DHash, a replication-enabled distributed hash table proposed in [65]. Venti implements snapshot-based backup at the disk-block level. The DHash back-end stores data blocks created by the Venti system in a modified Chord DHT [173]. Convergent encryption is also used to ensure security. It uses erasure code to store replicas at consecutive hosts in the identifier space. However, it offers no fairness mechanism, which makes it improper for the use in an environment without trusted peers.

— *Distributed Internet Backup System* [217] is a small-scale Peer-to-Peer backup system relying on trusted peers. However, the system requires manual configuration for the relationships of the peers. The design of the system does not include mechanisms for peer discovery, metadata management and fairness, which limits its applicability.

— *MagicMirror Backup* [107] is a system that simply enables copying files to remote machines, which the user has to select manually. In exchange, these machines may copy their data to the host. There is no specific encryption techniques and no fairness mechanism to be employed.

— *Dynamo* [101] is a commercial key-value storage system that some services of Amazon [25] deploy on. The system partitions and replicates data by consistent hashing to achieve scalability and availability. The consistency of replicas are maintained by data versioning.

9.2.6 Analysis of Existing Systems

Here, we shall discuss the suitability of three existing Peer-to-Peer backup systems: pStore, Cooperative Internet Backup Scheme, and Pastiche in terms of their advantages and disadvantages when used in a *global scenario*: A world-wide Peer-to-Peer backup network of anonymous users, cooperating in a way similar to current Peer-to-Peer file-sharing systems. Any interested user can join the Peer-to-Peer network and distribute her backups on arbitrary peers.

In the *global scenario*, there are a number of problems that need to be taken care of: First, a fairness mechanism is needed to ensure safekeeping and fair contribution to avoid a breakdown of the service due to malicious and free-riding peers; Second, duplicate removal is also important in order to reduce the resource consumption in the global environment in networks with a high degree of overlap; Lastly, support for peer heterogeneity is also important since in the global environment peers with different free space and different network bandwidth can join at any time.

pStore With Distributed Hash Table (DHT), pStore can detect blocks already existing in the system efficiently. DHT also offers a nice mechanism for data distribution. However, fairness and node heterogeneity, which are two important criterions in judging a Peer-to-Peer backup system, is not supported explicitly by pStore. The reason lying behind is because pStore chooses to store *actual* data blocks inside the DHT. This decision restricts a peer from selecting peers to store replicas freely because this design binds a block's storage location to the block identifier. As a result, every peer has the same chance of being selected to store a block, leading to its inability to deal with heterogeneity. Fairness is also hard to implement in this restricted design as there is no way for a peer to punish a misbehaving partner by dropping its data. The other main problem of pStore is the high maintenance cost generated by DHT in an unstable network. Peers join and leave the network frequently in the network and thus cause two types of maintenance cost: update traffic of routing tables of the DHT and data migration between peers. The latter has not received much attention from the recent research works in Peer-to-Peer backup.

So far most research works focused on the *routing-maintenance cost*, which is the traffic needed to keep the routing tables of peers up-to-date. However, when

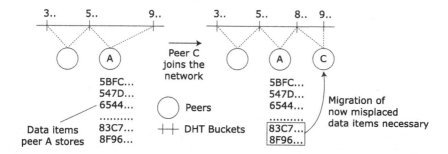

Fig. 9.11 Data migration in distributed hash table

DHT is used to store data items indexed by keys, additional maintenance cost, and probably the more dominant cost, will rise: data migration cost. Whenever a peer joins or leaves the network, it forces a reorganization of the key mapping in DHT which causes data items to become misplaced. As a result, a number of data items will be stored at a peer that is no longer responsible for them. In order to ensure correct retrieval of these misplaced data items, they need to be moved to the peer that is now responsible for them. As depicted in Fig. 9.11, without this process, more and more data items in the DHT would not be retrievable as queries for them will eventually reach the wrong responsible peer.

In order to show the dominance of the *data migration cost* comparing to the *routing-maintenance cost*, we carried out an experiment over a 50 PCs network, which is explained in details in Chap. 5. From the results obtained, we were able to conclude that storing large amounts of data in a DHT causes high maintenance cost the majority of which comes from the *data migration cost*. Especially, as the amount of data in the DHT grows, data migration will become more and more dominant. As a conclusion from the experiment, to achieve good performance in unstable networks, a Peer-to-Peer system should aim to minimize the amount of data stored in the DHT.

Cooperative Internet Backup Scheme Regarding the suitability for global scenario defined at the beginning of this section, the Cooperative Internet Backup Scheme does not look like a good choice. There are two major problems with this system: the centralized server and the high maintenance cost when enlarging the set of partners of a peer.

The advantage and probably the property that we can utilize in the proposed system is the symmetric-trading scheme. It is a good way to enforce both safekeeping and fair contribution, which are two important aspects of the fairness of a Peer-to-Peer backup system. However, when adding new backup partners, its strict rules for replica replacement will cause problems and make the system unsuitable for large dynamic unstable networks, resulting in a high maintenance cost. The other disadvantage is that it does not provide any mechanisms for duplicate checking and removal, which pStore does. This may consume too much bandwidth in a network that contains highly overlapped backup data.

In conclusion, the symmetric-trading mechanism can be one useful idea that we can apply into the new system that we will be working on.

Pastiche with Samsara Pastiche's buddy system has the nice property for supporting peer heterogeneity, that allows peers with different resources (hard disk free space, network connection bandwidth, etc.) to participate in the system accordingly. Since the backup buddies need to have large overlaps between their backup data, this effectively serves as a mechanism for duplicate removal for both backup partners, which largely saves the network traffic and lowers the resource consumption. The periodical challenges, together with the probabilistic punishment model enforces the safekeeping of partner's backup data. The storage claim is another elegant aspect of the system which makes the whole system more fair in terms of peer contribution.

Disadvantages of Pastiche just come from its advantage: In order to make a trade, peers need to have a high degree of overlap in their data, which may be rare in most of the cases. Storage claim can possibly reduce the availability of blocks if a block is part of a forwarding chain and might wrongly punish a peer.

In conclusion, Pastiche has several nice features in terms of fairness and suitability for large unstable networks, but the way these features are provided has internal problems which need to be taken care of.

9.3 Data Management

Supporting data management features, such as high-level complex query processing, meta-data management, and user management in P2P systems is a natural extension to file sharing systems. In this section, we first discuss two architectures for database sharing applications. After that, two specific data management tasks on top of overlay networks, i.e., XML data routing and continuous query answering, are introduced separately.

9.3.1 Architectures for P2P Data Management Systems

9.3.1.1 PIER

The problem of query processing in P2P systems is firstly presented in [153], in which the authors argue that query processing should be studied first, before other P2P database issues are addressed. Furthermore, a framework based on distributed hash table (DHT), for answering complex queries, is introduced. The framework suggests to use an enhanced DHT layer over data storage to support query processing. The tables, tuples, and fields are suggested to be organized in hierarchical namespaces on top of the flat identifier space provided by DHTs. The PIER system, which is developed according to the framework, tends to provide traditional relational database operators under the communication expensive, parallel, and online themes. In [159], the framework is presented as shown in Fig. 9.12.

In PIER, the Content Addressable Network (CAN) [266] is employed as the DHT layer for providing routing and storage functions in *Overlay Routing* and *Storage*

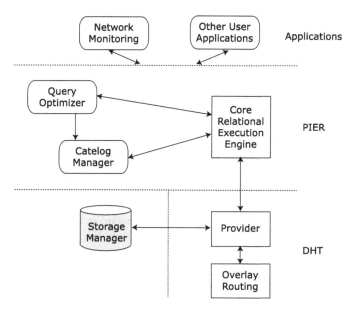

Fig. 9.12 PIER architecture

Manager modules. The namespace, resourceID, and instanceID are used to uniquely identify an object, and the namespace and resourceID are used to calculate the DHT key [159]. In implementation, namespaces are relation names, while resourceIDs are by default the values of primary keys, and instanceIDs are used to separate objects with the same namespace and resourceID. This CAN-based DHT layer is enhanced to provide following operators in *Provider* module:

- *Item←get(namespace, resourceID)* It retrieves objects based on their namespaces and resourceIDs.
- *Put(namespace, resourceID, instanceID, item, lifetime)* It locates the site based on an object's namespace and resourceID, and puts the object to this site. It should be noted that this operator accepts a parameter *lifetime*, which means the low bound of the period of time the object should be stored.
- *Bool←renew(namespace, resourceID, instanceID, item, lifetime)* It informs the site storing an object to keep the object for another period of time, as it is denoted in the lifetime parameter.
- *Multicast(namespace, resourceID, item)* It multicasts to neighboring peers for contacting the peers holding data in the namespace.
- *Iterator←lscan(namespace)* It provides scan access to all data in the namespace through the iterator.
- *Item←newData(namespace)* It informs the application when a new data object is inserted into the namespace.

The *Query Processor* module is implemented in a "boxes-and-arrows" style [159]. A push-and-pull model is employed. The results are produced by an operator and enqueued by *push*. The data can be retrieved for the next operator by *pull*. In the design of PIER, the queue is in charge of the networking issues. Furthermore, it is reported that system catalogs, an extensible operator interface, and declarative query parsing and optimization will be added to the Query Processor module as future work [159].

9.3.1.2 BestPeer

While PIER focuses most on complex queries over structured P2P networks, a more recent system, *BestPeer v2.0*[1] advocates a practice-oriented peer data management system. In [99], the authors present the vision, implementation, and test results for a practical PDMS.

One of the scenarios that BestPeer v2.0 starts from, is that of a Supply Chain Management application, where different participants (i.e., peers) need to share data for mutual advantage (Fig. 9.13). Consequently, apart from the "traditional" PDMS areas of interest (query processing, index management), BestPeer v2.0 also addresses issues of access control and data synchronization (Fig. 9.14) in order to protect each participant's private data stored, for instance, in an internal ERP[2] system.

Fig. 9.13 Vision for a corporate PDMS

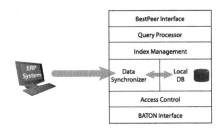

Fig. 9.14 Layered structure of the Bestpeer v2.0 PDMS

---

[1]http://www.bestpeer.com.

[2]Enterprise Resource Planning.

Table 9.4 Index types for BestPeer v2.0

Type	Key	Indexed Value
Table index	Table name	Peer list
Column index	Column name	Peer list
Data Index	Data Value	(Column Bitmap & Peer IP) list

BestPeer v2.0 relies on a global schema, to which all participants must adhere. That does not mean that each enterprise needs to change its internal data storage, but simply that they must provide a mapping from their own data schema to the global schema. In what follows, we will in general refer to this global schema when mentioning tables or columns, unless otherwise specified.

The underlying structure of this system is BATON [166]. As in PIER, one of the most important things to consider when choosing the underlying structure is whether or not it can support efficient range queries. It is definitely the case of BATON and, in addition, it also comes with a native load balancing mechanism.

To speed up query processing, be they range or otherwise, BestPeer v2.0 uses three types of indices: table index, column index, and data index. Table 9.4 shows their formats. The first two types (table and column) are rather straightforward: they maintain a list of peers that store that particular table or column. For the data index, the idea used by this system is to assign an ID to every column and to map this ID to a position in a bitmap. Then, when indexing a particular data value, the generated bitmap contains values of 1 only where the data appears as a value in the corresponding column.

Maintaining three types of indices would seem like an overhead, but it is just a design choice, balancing index management with query processing times. However, in the case of the data index, it may result in a particularly high management cost, since the data space is potentially unbounded (e.g., if we consider product codes—there are limitless possibilities in data values). BestPeer v2.0 indexes data values only upon request of the user (a similar strategy to that of centralized DBMS).

Using these three types of indices, the system's query processor takes responsibility for collecting statistics, generating a query plan, and executing it. A simple query may involve only one table, and in that case, the query processor first identifies the peers that have data for that table, sends them individual requests, and then collects and merges the answers. It is more interesting when a query involves joining operations between tables on different peers. In this case, the query processor rewrites the query into some subqueries, where each subquery can be processed by a peer individually. The processed result is stored in the local DBMS of the peer as a temporary table. Then a bloom filter join algorithm is used: all peers that store one of the two tables compute a bloom filter and send it to all peers that contain the other table. These latter ones compute the join and send the data back to the peers storing the first table, where the actual final result is computed.

In [99], the authors compare the performance of the BestPeer v2.0 system and a centralized DBMS in terms of response time, throughput, maintenance costs, and scalability. Because of its distributed nature, BestPeer v2.0 is able to outperform the centralized system in terms of response time, throughput and even index maintenance costs, as well as scale smoothly as the number of participants increases. The disadvantages of the system include an increase in the bandwidth overhead. This is to be expected, since join operations have to send data across the network.

BestPeer v2.0 seems to be the first attempt at a truly practical, comprehensive, peer data management system. Though bandwidth consumption is increased overall, this is something that can be easier to share among participants, compared to the costs of a centralized server.

9.3.2 XML Content Routing Network

The idea of an XML routing network is first presented in [300], driven by the motivation of data distribution technologies to deliver information to data consumers. XML routing networks are proposed to be useful in many real-life applications, such as real-time trading systems, or live media transmitting.

In an XML-routing network, data is organized into *XML packets*, each of which is a single XML document, maybe with corresponding DTD. A sequence of XML packets forms an *XML stream*. The XML streams are transferred from peers to peers. There are different roles that a peer may take: As a *root router*, a peer produces XML packets, and sends them to downstream peers. An *internal router* is a peer receiving XML packets from upstream peers, and it forwards them to one or more downstream peers after a set of operations on each packet. The forwarding is stopped when the XML packets arrive at the *client*, who consumes the XML data without further distribution.

Two different configuration schemes exist in XML content routing networks. A *static configuration* requires that each internal router forwards the XML packets without modification or elimination, while a *dynamic configuration* allows internal routers to forward only the packets needed by downstream peers. Static configuration may cause wasted bandwidth cost, a problem which is especially serious when downstream peers are interested in very specific packets. However, dynamic configuration also has its own disadvantages in that it adds additional burden to internal routers, which should store the queries from the downstream peers, and judge if a packet is useful for a specific downstream peer. Furthermore, when a new client comes, the needed packets may be temporarily unavailable in dynamic configuration scheme. The problem can be solved by reconstruction of the network.

Several techniques are developed for enabling the processing on the routers.

9.3.2.1 Mesh-based Content Routing

Mesh-based content routing is proposed for establishing and maintenance of the XML content routing network [300]. The approach is based on diversity control protocol (DSP), which is at the same level of the internet protocols stack as TCP. DSP ensures the global ordering of the packets from the same original stream from a root router. Thus, a router may reassemble a stream even if the packets are sent from two or more different internal routers. Each router has three primitives [300]:

- *Join(Q)* The current peer adds a down-stream peer with query Q.
- *Children(Q)* The current peer returns all its down-stream peers whose query is a subset of Q.
- *Parents* The current peer returns all of its up-stream peers.

Thus, when a new peer comes, it initializes its queries and finds the root routers. Then the peer sends `Join(Q)` requests to the root routers. If a request is approved, the router is added as an upstream peer. Otherwise, the children of the root router are queried by `Children(Q)`, and the `Join(Q)` request is sent to these children. The newly arrived peer iteratively requests to be the downstream peer of the subsequently downstream internal routers as long as the request is not approved, or the number of parents threshold is reached. Furthermore, each peer remembers its level when it joins the network, which is the maximum level number of its upstream peers plus one.

When a peer finds that one of its upstream peers has failed, it finds another upstream peer to take the place of the failed one using the same method as joining the network, except that only routers with smaller level numbers are considered. If such substitutive upstream peers cannot be found, the peer must disconnect all its downstream peers, and rejoin the network. Therefore, the overlay network established by the above method is resilient, in the sense that neither peer nor connection failure may cause the entire network to be reconfigured.

9.3.2.2 View Selection

In an XML content routing network, a router needs to evaluate the queries of downstream peers, such that which packets should be sent to which downstream peers can be determined. However, evaluating the queries over XML documents, e.g., XPath, is a time consuming process. Gupta et al. propose to employ views as headers of XML packets to accelerate the evaluation process [142, 144].

A *view* is an XPath expression. The value of the view given to an XML document is the offset of the first byte of the fragment satisfying the XPath expression, or NULL, if no such fragment exists. A *view collection* is an ordered set of views, and its value is an ordered set of offsets, respectively. Intuitively, a good view configuration is one that maximizes the throughput given the header size, or minimizes the header size given the throughput. The problem for finding such view configurations is denoted as *view selection* in [142, 144].

The views can be selected online or offline [142]. In offline mode, the workloads are assumed to be known by a centralized server. The view selection is done by the centralized server, and root routers generate the views according to the view configuration. In online mode, each root router generates a view configuration according to the feedback of the downstream peers. Currently, only the method for offline view selection is reported in [142, 144], while the online view selection remains an open problem.

In fact, the online view selection problem is proved to be NP-complete [142, 144], and greedy algorithms are suggested for determining the view configuration.

9.3.2.3 XML Data Filtering

On each router, the XML packages should be parsed and evaluated according to the workload, so that the router knows where the package should be forwarded to. Several techniques are developed for such XML stream processing systems [24, 68, 106, 137, 143].

Altinel and Franklin proposed that an XPath expression be represented as a finite state machine (FSM). They employ a hash index to navigate the matching between the query and the XML document [24]. Chan et al. [68] proposed to index substrings of path expressions that only contain parent-child operators. This way they can share the processing of these common substrings for different queries. Diao et al. developed YFilter [106] which converts the entire workload into a lazy deterministic finite state automaton (DFA). Green et al. [137] prove that the problem can be resolve by DFA. Another alternative is XPush [143], which precomputes the entire workload and converts it into a pushdown machine. All these methods can judge if an XML document can satisfy a given query. They can be used in the routers to determine the downstream peers.

9.3.3 Continuous Query Processing

Continuous queries, or *continual queries*, are long-running queries that are used to monitor specific data semantics. Usually, continuous queries need to be evaluated on data streams. Driven by the applications of information monitoring, much work has went into building systems for continuous query answering. Existing such systems include OpenCQ [197], CACQ [211], Aurora [62], AdaptiveCQ [316], NiagaraCQ [71], TriggerMan [151], and TelegraphCQ [69].

Some applications involve nodes spread in a large-scale distributed environment, or even Internet. In such applications, a large portion of nodes may generate data, while each node may issue (continuous) queries. Usually, a query is to monitor the data satisfying a specific condition. The data to be queried in most cases reside on nodes other than the querying one. Each query needs to be evaluated for a long period of time. Furthermore, in some of such applications, e.g., routing networks monitoring and Web server log monitoring, data are generated fast, so that they should be treated as data streams, which means their volume is large, and it is impossible to store the whole data set.

Three prototype systems are reported for evaluation of continuous queries under such circumstances. They are PeerCQ [129], CQ-Buddy [233], and Medusa [73].

These systems aim at low-degree duplication of data transmitting, high-speed response of event reporting, and heterogeneous-aware scheduling for workload balancing.

9.3.3.1 PeerCQ

PeerCQ [129] is a prototype system developed for fully decentralized information monitoring. The system is developed in a two-tier architecture. The *PeerCQ Protocol Layer* extends the traditional DHT functions of overlay networks, in which the peers are organized in an identifier circle. First, the number of identifiers assigned to one node (peer) is consistent with the volume of resource the peer shares. Second, to map a continuous query to a specific identifier, the data to be monitored is mapped to the first part of the identifier, while the peer's properties, such as IP address, are mapped to the second part. Gedik and Liu make the assumption that the number of queries is usually larger than the number of peers [129]. Thus, *similar* queries have large probabilities to be mapped to the same peer. By *similar queries*, we understand queries with the same interests in data, i.e., same data sources and same monitored data items. Last, a query may be assigned to a peer without the mapped identifier in its identifier list. However, that peer should satisfy a heuristics-based condition according to its cached data, its connection to the peer corresponding to the mapped identifier, and its current workload burden. Thus, no peer in the system would be overloaded. The *Information Monitoring Layber* is application-dependent. It provides functions for further processing of monitored events.

The advantage of PeerCQ is that it can ensure the workload balancing. Furthermore, the extended DHT functions improve the probability that similar queries find the same useful peer, such that duplicated processing can be eliminated. In PeerCQ, only queries with same querying objects, i.e., data sources and data items, are considered as similar. Last but not least, the workload balancing scheme in PeerCQ considers the heterogeneous nature of peers. However, in real applications with complex queries, the result of one query may be useful for another query's evaluation. Currently, PeerCQ does not support these kinds of processing sharing. In other words, PeerCQ supports intrapeer process sharing but no interpeer processing sharing.

9.3.3.2 CQ-Buddy

CQ-Buddy [233] is another continuous query processing prototype system designed for P2P-based environments. Similar to PeerCQ, it aims at duplicated processing elimination and workload balancing. However, it uses a different scheme which enables both intrapeer and interpeer sharing of processing.

First, CQ-Buddy uses a different definition of similar queries. The similar queries are defined based on the similarity of selective predicates. Two selective predicates are similar if and only if they share the same interest attribute and operation (one of $\leq, \geq, \neq, =$). Second, a query can be partitioned into subqueries. The subqueries can be assigned to intermediate peers. Thus, a peer can use answer queries by itself, or ask intermediate peers to help to answer the queries. Last but not least, a new arriving query may choose to evaluate the query by the peer itself, or assign the task to a peer with similar queries, or simply ask other peers to help evaluate the query. Thus, CQ-Buddy provides different granularities of processing sharing.

9.3.3.3 Medusa

Medusa [73] is designed to be a distributed infrastructure for service delivery among autonomous nodes, which is an extension to Aurora [62] for inter-participant federated operation. Aurora is a centralized stream processing engine using a *boxes-and-arrows* model, in which the operators are implemented as boxes accepting and producing data streams as input and output. A Medusa node (peer) can be a device running Aurora, a PC or PDA consuming the result, or sensor networks generating data streams. Peers in Medusa run according to economic principles. Each stream is organized in messages. A positive value is attached to each message. The receiver of the message should pay the sender according to the value of the message. If a stream is processed by a box, the value is increased, and the message can be sold to other peers.

Similar to PeerCQ, Medusa is built upon a structured overlay network using DHT. However, for workload balancing, the boxes in the processing workflow can be *slided* from one peer to another or be *splitted*. Three different kinds of contracts exist, which are used to determine the upstream and downstream relationships among peers. A *content contract* determines the specific stream to be transmitted from a sending peer to a receiving peer, its quality, and the cost. A *suggested contract* provides an alternative stream that can supply same content to the stream of the suggesting sending peer. The suggested contract may be ignored by the receiving peer. Finally, a *movement contract* provides functions of box sliding, for workload balancing. However, whether a movement contract is accepted should be decided by an *oracle* on each side of the contract.

9.4 Peer-to-Peer-Based Web Caching

As mentioned previously, P2P computing enjoys many desirable characteristics that can be employed to cater to many newly emerging demands. Recently, this computing paradigm has been successfully deployed in the application of Web caches. In this section, we will first introduce the background of Web caching. Next, we will present two P2P-based web caching systems, i.e., Squirrel and BuddyWeb.

9.4.1 Background of Web Caching

Web caching is a popular technique implemented at the boundary of an intranet or Internet service provider. It can reduce the bandwidth consumption of the Internet, alleviate the workload on web servers on the Internet, and eventually improve the response time for the web browser [60, 239, 328]. To obtain an Internet object (e.g., an HTML page), a web browser usually fires an HTTP GET request to the local browser cache, web cache or the original web server. On receiving such a request, the local browser cache or the web cache will first determine the exact situation: (i) the target is uncacheable; (ii) the cache is lost; or (iii) the target is cached. If the target is uncacheable or the cache is lost, the request is routed to the next level of cache towards the original web server. If the target is cached, the cache is returned as the answer to the request if it is verified to be fresh. If it is not considered to be fresh, a conditional GET (Abbr. cGET) corresponding to the request is forwarded as the first two cases. The cGET is answered (by a further cache or the original server) with either an entire fresh object or an "unmodified" message if the cached object has not been updated. Note that the freshness of an object is determined by the expiration policy of the web cache.

Traditionally, web caching is based on a centralized architecture, where it is commonly deployed on one or several dedicated powerful machines. This can be expensive, function of to the cost of infrastructure purchase, maintenance and administration. Furthermore, this architecture invariably suffers from a single point of failure, bottleneck of scalability, slashdot, and other limitations. On the contrary, in a P2P-based caching application, such as Squirrel [163] and BuddyWeb [330], the (computing, bandwidth and cache) resources within an intranet can be exploited to achieve the same functionality and performance as the centralized one. More inspiringly, it can overcome the inherent limitations of the centralized architecture. In the following, we will introduce two pioneers of this sort of novel application, i.e., Squirrel and BuddyWeb.

9.4.2 Squirrel

Squirrel is a P2P-based caching utility that enables the browsers of PCs in an intranet to export their cache objects to each other. As a result, a large virtual web cache is naturally formed. Each peer (i.e. a PC with the Squirrel software installed), can act as a web browser and a web cache at the same time. In the system, each peer runs a Squirrel instance employed as local proxy cache, and adopts a standard expiration policy. This application has inherited many desirable features from its supporting infrastructure Pastry [275], such as lack of administration, resilience to node failures and reliability. Moreover, Squirrel enjoys the performance comparable to a centralized web cache in term of response time, hit ratio and external bandwidth consumption, i.e., armed with the Squirrel, the intranet can collectively reuse a larger set of already retrieved pages and will re-fetch a smaller number of objects from outside. In the following two subsections, we will discuss its supporting infrastructure and working mechanism.

9.4.2.1 Pastry: The Supporting P2P Infrastructure

Pastry is a self-organizing, fully decentralized P2P system that provides functionalities of routing, locating and storing. Armed with a scalable distributed hash-table (DHT), it maps any given key of digital object to the location of an active peer in the network, based on the numeric closeness of hash values of both identifiers (or keys). According to [275], Pastry has many desirable characteristics:

(1) The routing cost is bounded by $O([\log_2 b^N])$ hops. When inserting or searching for an object, the message can be routed to the target peer within an expected $[\log_2 b^N]$ hops, where N is the total number of peers in the system;
(2) It is resilient to concurrent node failures. A message can still be routed to its target even if $[l/2]$ adjacent neighbors failing, where l is typically of $8*\log_{16} N$;
(3) It provides a "leaf" set (consisting of l peers of numerically nearest identifier centering around the local peer), which determines the status of neighbors and replicate objects among them.

Here, we have just briefly introduce some important characteristics of Pastry to help readers to obtain a high level concept of the infrastructure of Squirrel. For detailed information of Pastry, please refer back to Sect. 3.3.3 or to [275].

9.4.2.2 How Squirrel Works

When searching an object, a web browser initiates a request to the locally embedded Squirrel proxy, which will first decide whether the object is cacheable in the intranet or not. If not, it will route the request out of the intranet to the original web server. Otherwise, the peer will try to obtain the fresh answer locally or from other peers within the same organization. To obtain an answer from other peers, a peer should first calculate the SHA-1 [16] hash value of the answer's key (URL) and use it to decide which peer maintains the answer (home-store, defined later) or has the knowledge of the location of the answer (Directory, also defined later). To facilitate the description, we shall introduce three important definitions firstly.

(1) *Home peer*. If the identifier of peer P is numerically closest to (a 128-bit) hash value of a caching object O, then P is defined as the *home peer* of object O;
(2) *Home-store*. If object O is really maintained by its home peer, then the management scheme is defined as *home-store*; and
(3) *Directory*. If the home peer of object O just maintains an index on the set of peers storing the object, then the management scheme is defined as *directory*.

In the following, we will discuss how Squirrel works on the two different management schemes:

Home-Store. In the first scheme, internet objects are stored at both common peers and their home peers. When searching a given object, if the current peer cannot find the fresh object locally (due to either having a stale copy or having none at all), it sends a request to the object's home peer. The latter will in turn reply with a fresh object or a "not-modified" message, if it has the fresh copy. Otherwise, if the home peer also has just a stale copy or no copy at all, it will fire a cGET or GET request to the original web server. If the home peer receives a cacheable object from the server (or a "not-modified" message), it will update its local cache (or freshness information) and answer the requestor accordingly. If the object is uncacheable, the original server just replies the requestor directly away from the home peer. Note that, since all external requests are touted outside through the corresponding home peers, the home peers maintain the most up-to-date copy in most cases.

Directory. The rationale of "directory" is that a peer having recently queried an object can be employed to satisfy the same request from other peers. Managed with this scheme, the home peer of an object manages a small index of up to (system-widely predefined) k pointers to the object's delegates, i.e., those peers that have most recently requested the object. Consequently, an object might be stored at than one (or even k) delegates. However, these copies (of the same object) are of the same version and go stale independently and simultaneously. As for the directory, it manages the necessary metadata of the homed objects, including the ETag, fetch time, last modified time, TTL and cache-control information.

Let us now go on to present the procedure of how a HTTP request is satisfied in Squirrel. When looking for an object, a peer will first try its local cache and forward a corresponding cGET or a GET request to the home peer of the object, which is the same as the processing in the home-store scheme. When receiving such a cGET or GET message, the home peer will take different decisions and take different corresponding actions based on the situation:

- Never met the object before. If the home peer has never met the requested target before, it has not created a directory for the object. It creates a new one for the object with unknown Etag and metadata (as discussed above) and informs the requestor of its actions with a message. The requestor will fetch the object from the original sever and fire a message (containing the metadata) to the home peer and the home peer accordingly updates the directory. However, if the object is uncacheable, the home peer deletes the directory.
- Directory pointing to fresh copies. The home peer has already stored a directory pointing to several delegates containing fresh copies. When receiving a cGET message from the requestor and finding the ETag matched, the home peer replies the requestor with a "not-modified" message to the requestor. Otherwise, the home peer randomly forwards the request to one of the delegates and updates the delegate set with the requestor.
- Directory pointing to old copies. When receiving a cGET request, the home peer informs the requestor to fetch the object from the original sever. After fetching the target, requestor will help the home peer to update the directory. If receiving a GET message, the home peer randomly forwards the request to one of the delegates, who in turn fetches the object from the original server. Then the delegate will send the object directly to the requestor and helps the home peer to update the directory.

According to [163], both schemes perform equally well; furthermore, they are shown to be comparable to the centralized approach. Indeed, it is hard to explicitly claim which one is better than the other, since "home-store" is simpler and more elegant, while the "directory" can theoretically offer better workload balance in the network.

9.4.3 BuddyWeb: A P2P-based Collaborative Web Caching System

By early 2002, BuddyWeb, a P2P-based Collaborative Web Caching System [330] has been implemented through the collaborative efforts of the Fudan University in China and the National University of Singapore. This system does not only improve the performance of web search and the reliability of intranets, but also saves on the expenditure of enterprises. Unlike existing web caching techniques that typically are managed by the proxies, BuddyWeb exploits local caches of nodes (i.e., the browser of PCs) within an enterprise network to satisfy repeated searches. Note that one of the major difference between enterprise-based P2P systems and Internet-wide systems is that the former is not as exposed to security threats as the latter as peers within an intranet are protected by a firewall. In addition, the intranets are well manageable and controllable. To illustrate the situation, consider the campus network at the Fudan University, where there are thousands of PCs, each with a web browser installed. Here, the network is shielded from the "outside world" by its firewall, where any incoming and outgoing requests must go through its central proxy. Furthermore, there is a quota policy (in Fudan University) to restrict the amount of bandwidth each member of the university community can utilize, and every bit of external data transferred will be charged! In the current web browser architecture, since there is no cache sharing among different browsers, any request must be sent out of the intranet to fetch its answer, even if the requested information has already been available in nodes within the campus network, which results in long response time and supererogatory cost as well. BuddyWeb, the novel P2P-based application, which can facilitate the sharing of local caches among browsers within the same Intranet, can solve the problems described above very well.

Compared to the existing Peer-to-Peer systems, BuddyWeb enjoys many distinguished characteristics, summarized as follows:

— Peers in the BuddyWeb network can dynamically reconfigure their neighborhood based on the similarity of interests. In other words, as time goes on, it could be expected to naturally generate communities of interests (e.g., community with interest in database studies, community with interest in bioinformatics studies etc.);

— A novel routing strategy that is based on the similarity of peers' contents is employed in BuddyWeb. Therefore, queries will be routed from a peer to its neighbor that has the highest similarity of content, so that their answers can be obtained in a small scope and query fewer peers;

— BuddyWeb has adopted a self-adaptive multi-hop strategy, in which the TTL
(Time-To-Live) of a query message is automatically adjusted to maximize the
positive search results while minimizing the consumed bandwidth.

In the remaining subsections, we will discuss the architecture of BuddyWeb
and its novel mechanisms, i.e., similarity-based reconfiguration and similarity-
based routing and self-adaptive hopping. Note that since BuddyWeb is implemented upon BestPeer, its protocol is inherited from the platform (i.e., BestPeer)
described in Chap. 2.

9.4.3.1 Architecture of BuddyWeb

The architecture of BuddyWeb is presented in Fig. 9.15. The figure on the left depicts the architecture of an autonomous peer in BuddyWeb.

The web browser serves as the front-end interface to the user. Thanks to its
transparency, users are not aware of any difference between the BuddyWeb-enabled
browser and the common one. In the BuddyWeb enabled browser, there is a personal
proxy that works with the local cache and a HTTP daemon to support HTTP requests. The cache, in collaboration with the BestPeer platform [234], is responsible
for sharing cached data with other peers in the BuddyWeb network. The low level
communication between peers is managed by the BestPeer platform. Whenever the
web browser submits an URL query, the local proxy will receive and rewrite the
query into the input format of the BestPeer platform. The query will then be passed
to the BestPeer platform. Based on the requirement, BestPeer generates several mobile agents and dispatches them to the BuddyWeb network to search for matching
documents. Upon receiving a match, BestPeer returns the information, i.e., document location, back to the personal proxy. In this way, the personal proxy will issue
HTTP daemon directly to the peer that has the desired documents. The answer contributor, upon receiving the HTTP request, will process it by the HTTP daemon and
send the requested documents to the requester.

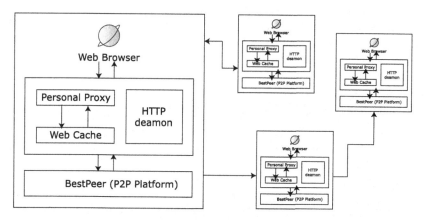

Fig. 9.15 The Architecture of BuddyWeb

9.4.3.2 Similarity-Based Reconfiguration

Instead of directly inheriting the default reconfiguration strategies (i.e., *Maxcounts* and *Minhops*) from BestPeer [234], BuddyWeb makes good use of its *LIGLO*s to facilitate the processing. Each registered peer is responsible for sending its supervising *LIGLO* (LIGLO is a super-peer that manages meta-data of peers) its IP address and extra surfing information. Indeed, such surfing information will reasonably reflect the peer's *interests tendency*, which will be defined later.

To determine the interest tendency of a peer, the pages that it has browsed are examined. Different schemes from the IR field can be adapted here. With the consideration of performance and storage consumption, the extracted information from the browsed pages must be representative as well as brief. One simple strategy is to send some useful metadata (say, <TITLE> </TITLE>) of the surfed pages to the peer's associated *LIGLO*. Alternatively, an user can provide feedback in the form of highlighting some keywords in the browsed pages.

The peers' interest tendencies can be represented as word lists maintained in their *LIGLO*. Dynamic reconfiguration could be facilitated on the basis of those word lists, which are referred to as *Peer-Tendency*. Keeping reconfiguration in mind, we could view all the words in Peer-Tendencies as a word bag, which could be used to construct a vector space. Each Peer-Tendency will be transformed to a corresponding vector in such a vector space according to some weighting schemes. Note that each *LIGLO* only holds information of the peers registering to it. Thus, a negotiation must be held among all the *LIGLO*s to determine which *LIGLO* receive the Peer-Tendencies of all the peers. An alternative approach to address this problem is to use a hash method, which could avoid vector computation in a single server. However, in the BuddyWeb network there are relatively fewer *LIGLO* severs. Besides, the Peer-Tendencies are rather "light-weight" files. Therefore, the former scheme, i.e., the Vector Space Model-based (*Abbre., VSM-based*) strategy has been adopted.

A proper similarity function, e.g., cosine function, could be defined using Vector Space Model (*VSM*). To keep most beneficial peers as its neighbors, each peer should maintain those peers with which it shares the highest similarity value. However, the computation of all pairwise peers is a time-consuming task, especially where there are a large number of peers in the network. A simple alternative way to solve this problem is to distribute the similarity computation to every peer, while the responsible *LIGLO* computes only all the vectors in VSM. After peers finishing their processing, those vectors will be sent to their *LIGLO* server, respectively.

In summary, the reconfiguration procedure is as follows:

- After a certain period (say, every midnight), the *LIGLO*s will negotiate with one other to decide which one is responsible for computing the vectors of all the peers. After the processing, each of them will hold the computed vectors of all the peers.
- When a peer logs in to the network, it will communicate with its registering *LIGLO*, and send its current IP address. It will also request all the other peers' vectors. Similarities with all the other peers will be computed by the peer locally.

— The k peers with the highest value of similarity will be kept as the directly connected neighbors, where k is a system parameter that can be adjusted by individual participants according to their capacity and current workload status.

It is necessary to point out that effective clustering algorithms could be easily deployed to group peers sharing common interests into clusters. This gives us a way to discover the peer communities appearing in the BuddyWeb network.

9.4.3.3 Similarity-based Routing and Self-adaptive Hopping

In BuddyWeb, the dynamic reconfiguration is facilitated by the use of a similarity computation, which provides a reasonable measurement of the relationships between peers. Consider, for instance, the situation in which a query has to be forwarded to one of the neighbors to which the current peer is directly connected, and that this peer maintains similarity values with its neighbors. Instead of forwarding the query to all direct neighbors, the peer could select the neighbor with the highest similarity value. Note that the query from the initial node will be propagated to all directly connected neighbors and that the similarity-based routing policy will only adopted when further forwarding.

Another benefit of using a similarity metric is that query agents could determine themselves the number of hops they need to take. Previous P2P systems have to pre-determine the number of hops of queries (i.e., TTL). If the number of hops is set too low, the process of search will be confined within a small scope. On the other hand, if it is set too high, the traffic over the peer network will be rather heavy. An appropriate tradeoff is hard to be achieved because the TTL value of queries are set to one-size for all.

The self-adaptive hopping strategy works as follows:

— A peer initiates a query agent with a parameter s instead of a *TTL* value, where s is predefined by the P2P network. The diameter of the peer network is denoted by D, which will be obtained in the process of facilitating the dynamic reconfiguration.
— When a query agent is forwarded to the directly connected neighbor by a peer, it "*remembers*" the distance value between the peer and its neighbor. The value is summed with the previous remembered distance values along the routing path.
— If the sum value exceeds the value of $s \bullet D$, the hopping will stop. Otherwise, the peer will forward the query agent to its neighbor further.

As such, the system does not need to have a fixed hop number for all the queries. With the parameter s given by the system, the number of hops of each query will be self-determined according to its searching scope in the concept space. The parameter s reflects the extent of scope the system likes its peers to search in, and thereby enables BuddyWeb to find a proper tradeoff between network traffic and search completeness in a dynamic way.

9.5 Communication and Collaboration

As peer-to-peer can arguably be defined as a technological parallel to day-to-day human interaction, the communication and collaboration platforms are possibly one of the most obvious applications. Still, even in this case, the number of applications is limited. We will describe a few in what follows.

9.5.1 Instant Messaging

In general, instant messaging is not considered as a vital application. Thus, even with the stigma of "unreliability", peer-to-peer technology has been able to successfully penetrate this market. Even more, with voice and video now a common feature in instant messaging applications, the increased bandwidth needed to pass along multimedia, has encouraged application developers to move to a peer-to-peer architecture.

9.5.2 Jabber

Jabber is the original IM service that eventually resulted in the open standard XMPP[3] (eXtensible Messaging and Presence Protocol), and at the same time, it's main user. The protocol was invented by Jeremie Miller as Jabber in 1998 and the first server, clients and libraries were available on year later, followed by many more open source and commercial extensions since then.

The official standardization came under the IETF (Internet Engineering Task Force) between 2002 and 2004 as a series of RFCs (most notably of which: RFC3920[4]). As a consequence of this standardization, many software producers have created or adapted their products to this new standard (among them, big names such as Apple, Google, Nokia, or Cisco).

The idea at the core of XMPP is to provide a standard way in which applications can communicate simple messages with each other and inform each other of their status. It is based on XML and has two main components: XML Streams (the communication channels) and XML Stanzas (the communicated informations). As such, XMPP is not in itself a peer-to-peer protocol (it actually defines itself as a client-server protocol), but, because it is quite flexible, there are already a number of extensions that allow it to provide peer-to-peer communication.

---

[3]http://xmpp.org.

[4]http://tools.ietf.org/html/rfc3920.

9.5.2.1 Jingle

Jingle is an extension protocol under review by the XMPP Standards Foundation as XEP-0166 [203] and it addresses the fact that XMPP was not originally designed to support data streams. In fact, Jingle defines the set of messages that two parties need to exchange to set up a direct connection between them. What is transfered on this connection is irrelevant for the protocol itself.

9.5.2.2 Serverless Communication

Serverless communication allows XMPP clients to contact each other directly without going through the standards authentication mechanism via a server. Like Jingle, it is also defined as an XMPP Extension protocol [282].

Without using servers, the client needs to advertise its presence and discover the presence of others. It does so using DNS-based Service Discovery (DNS-SD [74]) and Multicast DNS (mDNS citemdns). As such, this advertisement only works on the local network and communication can only take place within this local network. This may be a limitation, but it is a security feature as well.

9.5.3 Skype

The widely popular communication service is probably the most visible success story of a peer-to-peer application. With millions of users online 24 hours a day and 365 days a year, it has been the focus of attention for international media throughout its 6 year history. It has also been a success story for its creators, when eBay acquired it only after little more than 2 years from its original release, in September 2005, paying for it no less than $2.6 billions.

The Skype protocol is not opened and little more than a one page description on their website is available to the world to understand how it works. However, in 2006 three researchers from Cornell University and Google Inc. have published an experimental study that tried to, in a way, reverse-engineer the architecture of the Skype service from connection and traffic logs monitored over a period of 4.5 months [140].

Considering that the Skype was founded by the same people that founded Kazaa and their initial staff overlapped to a large extent, one can easily take as an initial assumption the fact that Skype must be using a hybrid approach, where a set of super-peers have more responsibilities than the vast majority of the other peers. In fact, Skype briefly mentions this on their website, when describing their decentralized user directory.[5]

---

[5]http://www.skype.com/intl/en/help/guides/p2pexplained/.

One of the most interesting observations that Guha and his colleagues made in their experimental study is that Skype differs significantly from file-sharing networks in terms of predictability of peer behavior. In fact, with Skype, most clients will be available during the daytime and off at night. With a worldwide coverage, that results in a relatively constant and predictable number of users present in the network at all times. It may be that this is what gave the network the extra push to become the most successful P2P application to date.

9.5.4 Distributed Collaboration

A step forward from instant messaging, in terms of business applications, is collaboration. In many situations nowadays, documents within one organization need to circulate, be edited or approved by employees located at more or less great distances from each other. This can obviously be done in a centralized fashion, where an enterprise server collects and distributes all information. However, in this scenario, of enterprise collaboration, peer-to-peer has a distinct advantage: the peers are reliable and their action predictable (i.e., regulated by office hours). There is little point in having a central server to mediate communication if you know that after 5pm there will be no one to talk to. A peer-to-peer system will then be able to provide all the services that a centralized approach would (notably reliability and robustness), without the costs associated with the maintenance of an enterprise server and of upgrading it together with the entire IT infrastructure of the company.

We chose three examples to showcase this idea: JBuilder is a software development tool, MS Groove is the descended of Groove Networks, after it was acquired by Microsoft and Collanos Workplace is a peer-to-peer collaboration tool developed by an innovative start-up company.

9.5.4.1 JBuilder

Since its 2006 version, JBuilder, a software development tool, has included a peer-to-peer collaboration to enhance its development environment and increase the performance of widely spread teams of software engineers. This kind of collaboration is more than communication or versioning. The idea is to allow two programmers to work in real time over the same piece of code. In this sense, though details on the precise architecture are not released, JBuilder is peer-to-peer in the sense that pairs of users can collaborate directly without going through a server, but it is unlikely that this communication travels over many hops in a structured P2P network, or, even less likely, an unstructured P2P network.

9.5.4.2 MS Groove

Groove Networks started from the vision of its founder, Ray Ozzie, inventor of Lotus Notes, but never quite reached a successful business until it was bought over by

Microsoft in 2005 and incorporated into its Office suite in 2007. Somewhat similar to the JBuilder P2P approach, a client in Groove will first contact a known server and then, if the destination party is also online, it will instantiate a direct communication channel between the two.

In this environment, emphasis is placed on collaboration on documents, synchronization of work done while offline and less on instant communication or simultaneous editing.

9.5.4.3 Collanos Workspace

Collanos workspace is similar to MS Groove, but it is worth mentioning here because it is a very interesting example of different open source technologies put together towards a [potentially successful] collaboration tool. For its peer-to-peer technology it relies on JXTA (see Chap. 8), while for the rest it is based mainly on an innovative way to use the Eclipse software development platform as a collaboration platform.

9.6 Mobile Applications

As the handheld devices become more and more powerful and connected, we begin to see a trend of moving applications from PCs to PDAs and cellphones. We see this for email, office documents, web browsing, etc. It is not hard to imagine then, that peer-to-peer applications will also make their way towards smaller, portable devices. In this section, we will present two types of applications for mobile devices: *file sharing* and *text messaging and voice communication*. We begin in chronological order, with the latter ones.

9.6.1 Communication Applications

Peer-to-peer applications that aim to by-pass mobile services providers have appeared as far back as 2002 [347]. More recently, the Swedish company TerraNet (www.terranet.se) has proposed a system to provide multi-hop wireless voice communication for areas where the mobile operators do not have cellular towers. They planned to commercialize it in 2008, but in June 2009 there was still no update on the outcome of the venture.

Such applications, despite their apparent utility, have a hard time imposing themselves onto the users for two reasons:

1. Given that mobile communications provided by mobile operators are relatively cheap and generally of high quality, it is hard to motivate a user to use an unreliable connection that will most likely drain the power of the cellphone as it acts as an intermediary for other users' communications.

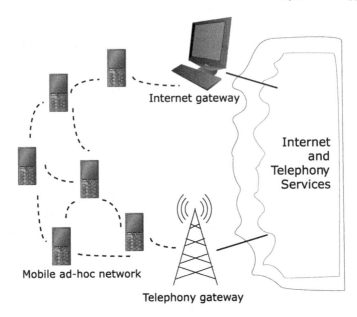

Internet gateway

Internet
and
Telephony
Services

Mobile ad-hoc network

Telephony gateway

Fig. 9.16 Communication via ad-hoc network and proxies to Internet and other telephony services

2. The mobile networks operators are even more reticent of such applications, even
   if the claim is that it will be used only in areas where they are not present: if the
   application works, there is no reason for which a user will not use it even in areas
   where there is network coverage, thus chipping away the profits of the operators.

As shown in Fig. 9.16, the mobile devices create an ad-hoc network and then
use a dedicated gateway to connect to the Internet or to a regular telephony services
provider. To be practical, the mobile devices must be able to connect directly at distances far greater than the current Bluetooth standards (at most 100 m). TerraNet's
claim is that their devices can communicate directly at 1000 m, and we can only
assume that they use something else than Bluetooth or Wi-Fi.

9.6.2 File Sharing Applications

File sharing applications have appeared later on mobile devices, mainly because
until only a few years ago, there was not enough storage on a handheld to keep
enough information to be worth creating a peer-to-peer network for. Nowadays,
with phones frequently acting as entertainment devices, holding music, photos, and
videos, the idea of peer-to-peer file-sharing that was at the base of Napster 8 years
ago has a new development ground.

There are two trends that seem to have appeared recently: first, commercial applications that advocate file sharing through a social network, peer-to-peer in spirit
but not in implementation, as they use a central server to manage content. Second,

research systems that are fully peer-to-peer and attempt to solve the unique issues that occur in a mobile environment.

9.6.2.1 Peer-to-Peer in Spirit

We identified three applications that offer their customers the possibility to share files from their handheld devices. All of them have a social network component, whereby a user can specify a list of friends to share the files with. Also, all of them use the network operator's internet services, or a Wi-Fi connection if one is available, but do not link directly between two devices.

CloudTrade[6] allows a user to store up to 1 Gb on their servers, and each file can be either private, shared with friends or public. The other users can freely download any file that is available to them, without any charge, as the system is supported by advertisements.

Nareos's *peerboxmobile*[7] is fairly similar, except it does not impose a limit on the size of the data that can be uploaded and also does not allow a user to store private files, as everything is made available to all the users as soon as it is uploaded.

Melodeo's *nuTsie*[8] is a program to share and listen to one's iTunes library via the mobile phone. It extends iTunes's music sharing, which only works on a LAN, to the entire Internet and makes it available on mobile phones. As in iTunes, the user can see and listen to other songs, but he or she cannot save them for later use. Instead, the user is redirected to a web store from where the song can be acquired.

None of these applications allow files to be shared freely, as a consequence of the lessons learned from Napster: because they use central servers to manage the data, they are vulnerable to legal action from copyright owners.

9.6.2.2 Peer-to-Peer in Implementation

Contrary to the commercial trends described above, the research environment has been looking more at truly integrating the mobile device into the peer-to-peer network, at a deeper level than just conceptually. There are three trends that one can observe in this sense:

1. *Integrate the mobile device into an already existing peer-to-peer network.* Examples of such systems are Symella[9] or Symtorrent[10] which connect to Gnutella and to BitTorrent, respectively. These applications are implementations for the Symbian mobile platform of the usual peer-to-peer client software. As such, they

---

[6]http://www.cloudtrade.com.

[7]http://www.peerboxmobile.com.

[8]http://www.nutsie.com.

[9]http://symella.aut.bme.hu.

[10]http://symtorrent.aut.bme.hu.

appear to the network as regular nodes, without any distinction for the other nodes that reside on PCs.

2. *Create an ad-hoc, single-use, peer-to-peer network for devices that are temporarily collocated.* It is not hard to imagine how people would have to spend relatively long amounts of time collocated, on public transport, in the office, at conferences, etc. It is then useful to design a multi-hop connectivity framework to allow them to share useful data without going through the Internet to do so. Hyper-M [205] is such a system, whereby peers use bluetooth communication to create a structured peer-to-peer overlay.

   When creating such a network, one must keep in mind that its existence is limited in time, as such communities do not last together for more than a few hours. It is then imperative to be able to share data fast, while still allowing it to be retrieved accurately, without querying all the peers. Hyper-M achieves this for multi-dimensional data (images, sounds) by applying a combination of discrete wavelet transform (DWT [98]) and clustering.

3. *Use the mobile devices as physical carriers of content.* The idea of having the mobile devices act as physical transporters of information has appeared recently and has been promoted by some of the handphone manufacturers [34]. However, as long as there is no consensus among all phone manufacturers, it is unlikely that such a system would gain enough mass to provide real utility to the users. For this, there is a need for standards and one direction that research should look into is Delay Tolerant Networks [66] protocols currently under discussion at the IETF. DTN has been proposed in response to the advances of space exploration [57]. In that context, communication delays are caused by astronomical distances and temporary communication obscurity due to interposing cosmic bodies. The same protocols can be applied in a mobile environment, where delays are caused by devices being out of reach of each other. There is already an existing project in this sense, an implementation of the protocols for Symbian-operated phones [249, 256], available at the Networking Laboratory of the Helsinki University of Technology.[11]

9.7 Summary

The broad definition of peer-to-peer leaves ample room for applications to be categorized as "P2P applications". In this chapter, we, more or less, described applications that identify themselves as using a peer-to-peer infrastructure. There is a clear preference for everything that involves sharing disk resources. Such applications range from simple file sharing tools, to storage sharing and to data sharing. One type of applications that does not fit into this category is the new, emerging, mobile applications. Here, even though storage is shared to some extent, what is more important is the sharing of connectivity. When using an intermediary mobile device to

---

[11] http://www.netlab.tkk.fi/~jo/dtn/.

temporarily store a file and relay it later when within reach of the destination node or another node closer to the destination, you are not actually sharing storage, but connectivity. In this case, storage is just a side-effect, a tool to be used.

There are probably many other applications out there that would fit into the peer-to-peer paradigm. Some even in the commercial world. It is hard to identify those because companies generally do not release the inner workings of their software systems, nor do they advertise them as being "peer-to-peer". This is an interesting point: the term *p2p* has accumulated so much "bad karma" from the endless file-sharing legal problems, that, to some extent, it became taboo in the corporate environment. Even though there is nothing inherently illegal about the technology, companies seem to shy away from mentioning this in their business meetings.

Chapter 10
Conclusions

In this book, we covered the concepts and principles of P2P computing in the context of data sharing and processing. This chapter summarizes the main issues and approaches that have enabled P2P computing. There are many interesting problems that remain open and worthy of further investigation from both theoretical and application viewpoints. We shall examine some of these problems and applications in this final chapter.

10.1 Summary

In this book, we have looked at the issues and solutions of P2P computing. Most of these mechanisms have been designed to make P2P computing a practical and useful technology.

10.1.1 Architecture

In general, architectures of P2P systems can be classified into three categories: centralized, decentralized, and hybrid P2P systems.

- Centralized P2P systems: P2P systems belonging to this type of architecture employ the traditional client-server architecture where a set of servers are in charge of managing basic operations such as data indexing and query processing in the systems. In particular, when a client peer wants to share a resource such as a file, it sends an insert request to its correspondent server. That server then indexes the shared resource. When a peer wants to search a resource, it sends a search request to its server. The server looks up indices and returns the result to the requester peer. The difference between centralized P2P architecture and client-server architecture, however, is that the servers in centralized P2P systems are just brokers for client peers. When client peers agree on a transaction, they execute the transaction independently from the servers.

Q.H. Vu et al., *Peer-to-Peer Computing*,
DOI 10.1007/978-3-642-03514-2_10, © Springer-Verlag Berlin Heidelberg 2010

- Decentralized P2P systems: unlike centralized P2P systems, no servers are used in this type of architecture. Peers in a decentralized system are organized either arbitrarly (unstructured P2P systems) or accordingly to some topologies (structured P2P systems) in a flat form (single-tier) or a hierarchical form (multi-tier). In unstructured P2P systems, it is often that no data is indexed and heuristic algorithms are utilized to broadcast queries to nodes in the systems for processing. However, in some cases, data is partially indexed to speed up query processing. On the other hand, in structured P2P systems, data is completely indexed to facilitate query processing. The difference between a flat form and a hierarchical form is that in a flat form, peers should have the same load and functionality while in a hierarchical form, peers are arranged at different tiers each of which may have different load and functionality.
- Hybrid P2P systems: this is a mix architecture between centralized and decentralized architectures. On the one hand, this architecture is similar to the centralized architecture because it has some nodes holding the role of servers serving other client nodes. On the other hand, these server nodes do not manage all data indices. They are organized in a decentralized architecture. In this way, the hybrid architecture inherits the advantages of both centralized and decentralized architectures.

10.1.2 Routing and Resource Discovery

Since routing in centralized P2P systems is straightforward, we only focus on routing strategies in decentralized P2P systems and hybrid P2P systems. In particular, we have presented three basic routing strategies for decentralized structured P2P systems, decentralized unstructured P2P systems, and hybrid P2P systems.

- Since there is no control on the topology of the overlay network, unstructured P2P systems often employ routing techniques such as bread-first search (BFS) and depth-first search (DFS) for query processing. Moreover, to avoid flooding the network with query messages, each query is assigned a time-to-live (TTL) and a query should be deleted when its TTL is expired. Besides the basic routing strategies, heuristic algorithms such as random walkers, adaptive probabilistic search and bloom filter based search have also been proposed to improve the efficiency and effectiveness of query processing.
- Different from unstructured P2P systems, structured P2P systems employ fixed topologies to organize nodes and index data. As a result, routing in this type of systems depends on the overlay network topology. In general, there are three main categories of structured P2P systems: distributed hash table based systems, skip list based systems and tree based systems. Each has its own strengths and weaknesses. For example, distributed hash table based systems are often good in load balancing while systems in the remaining two categories deal well with range queries.

— Whether structured architecture or unstructured architecture is employed for servers in hybrid P2P systems, hybrid P2P systems are still more efficient than unstructured P2P systems in locating resources while having less constraints in the network topologies (even if structured architecture is used, only a small part of the system, servers, are required to follow the topology). The routing strategy in this type of architecture is actually a combination of client-server routing strategy and structured or unstructured routing strategies.

10.1.3 Data-Centric Applications

File sharing is the most common type of data sharing in P2P systems. Search on file sharing applications can be conducted at three granularity levels: search on file title, file description, and file content.

— Search on file title: routing techniques in the previous section are applied i.e., if the overlay network is an unstructured P2P system, bread-first search, depth-first search, and their variants can be employed while if the overlay network is a structured P2P system, the specific routing algorithm of the system is applied.
— Search on file description: can be done by two basic solutions. The first one is the straightforward solution that indexes every descriptive attribute and processes a query from any indexed attribute. The second one, on the other hand, considers each descriptive attribute as a dimension in a multi-dimensional space. In this solution, data are indexed and queries are processed in the same multi-dimensional space. To support multi-dimensional index in P2P systems, traditional multi-dimensional index structures used in centralized systems such as R-Tree and R^+-tree are employed. The difference, however, is that, when these tree structures are deployed in a P2P environment, it is necessary to avoid the bottleneck at the root node by mapping the peer to only leaf nodes of the tree structures and letting leaf nodes maintain information of internal nodes in the path from their position to the root for routing purpose.
— Search on file content: while file content can be represented as data in multi-dimensional space, it is necessary to map the data to a lower dimensional space to avoid a high cost in indexing and query processing. A simple solution for this purpose is to employ Space Filling Curves. However, since this simple solution is not efficient, an alternative solution is to rotate high-dimensional data to a series of low-dimensional data for indexing while queries are also rotated before processing. On the other hand, in mapping-based approach, high-dimensional data can be indexed based on its distance to a set of predefined points. In hashing-based approach, locality hash functions are used to index data. In special cases where sharing files are textual documents, besides the above general solution, information retrieval (IR) approaches can also be applied in P2P systems.

Besides file sharing applications, there exist structured data sharing applications such as relational databases or xml. In this type of application, the most important task is to deal with the heterogeneity of different data sources. Basically, there are four solutions to address this challenge.

- Using schema mediation to create maps between pairs of data sources. These maps are built by either mapping rules or mapping tables.
- Using information retrieval techniques to search similar annotations specified by users when they construct data sources. These matched annotations are used to map data sources.
- Using distributed hash table to hash similar data items to the same bucket. Queries are processed by looking items similar to the hash values of queries.
- Using distributed catalogs: terms are classified and similar terms are put in the same catalog. As a result, queries can be processed by searching similar catalogs.

10.1.4 Load Balancing and Replication

Since peers often have different resource capacities and data distribution is often skewed, load balancing plays an important role in P2P systems. To manage load balancing, it is necessary to determine when a node is overloaded or underloaded. There are three possible solutions to monitor peer loads.

- *Sampling*: periodically, a node samples the load of a number of nodes in the system from which it can determine if it has a heavy, light, or normal load compared to other nodes.
- *Histograms*: can be constructed and maintained by sampling loads of nodes or using gossiping algorithm to propagate node's load. As a result, at any point of time the approximate load information of nodes in the system can be retrieved from histograms.
- *A monitoring system*: can be built to maintain exact load of nodes in the system. Even though this method incurs a high cost in maintaining, it can provide a bound of load imbalance between any pair of nodes in the system.

Replication is orthogonal and complementary to load balancing. It is used to improve the performance of query processing and the availability of data in case of failure, to avoid bottleneck at nodes holding popular data, and to shorten data failure's recovery latency. Replication can be done at two granularity levels: file level (the whole file is replicated) and block level (only a part of a file is replicated). The biggest challenge in replication is how to keep replicas consistent with the original data. A simple solution is to refresh replicas after sometime. Otherwise, the system needs to maintain links between replicas and their original data for update purposes.

10.1.5 Programming Models

The past 10 years of peer-to-peer research have created the need for tools to design, create, and deploy such overlays faster and without reinventing the wheel whenever a new architecture is considered. While low-level network programming offers the highest flexibility and is already familiar to many distributed systems programmers, there are also a handful of tools now available to reduce the amount of programming that needs to be done to deploy a peer-to-peer network. As usual, the simplest are the most widely used: BOINC, a framework to deploy projects with high computational needs at the edges of the Internet, is by far the most used system. JXTA, a set of standards developed with the support of SUN Microsystems over the past 6–7 years is the next most popular system, and a set of implementations are available, for structured or unstructured overlays, for mobile devices or for different programming languages.

As the research community put more emphasis on structured peer-to-peer networks, some libraries have started to appear. While many proposals of such systems come with open-source libraries to develop applications on top of the newly proposed overlay, in this book we have described systems that allow the user to specify the structure of the overlay itself. Such systems are still in their infancy, mostly because there is little interest coming from the industry, but we see a potential development in the direction of structured *adaptable* overlays, as a consequence of a communication framework able to handle different structures in a unified way.

Finally, regardless of how one develops a peer-to-peer application, testing it realistically is a challenge in itself, because simulating multiple machines on only one is very hard, both for technical reasons (i.e., limited resources available on a machine), but, more importantly, for conceptual reasons (i.e., loss of realistic operating environment). PlanetLab is the largest distributed system that offers computing resources to participating academia and industry. Based on a fair-trade policy, it increases as more participants use it and it offers a realistic testing ground because the machines are physically located at different institutions across the world. Still, PlanetLab does require a cost of entrance to the system, even for academic institutions. Emulab, on the other hand, is completely free, but because all the machines are located at one site, the user faces the same challenge as that of using a single machine: making sure that the tests simulate accurately a distributed environment, with delays and interferences. The same problem occurs if one is a commercial entity and thus does not have access to Emulab and instead is using a commercial system such as the Elastic Computing Cloud of Amazon.com Inc.

10.1.6 Security Problems

Due to the openness and autonomous nature of nodes in a P2P systems, securing applications in a P2P environment is a big challenge. Common attacks and solutions to prevent them are presented as follows.

– To prevent *routing attacks* means to secure the message routing process so that a message sent from a nonmalicious node should reach the target nonmalicious node. This can be done by three techniques (1) secure assignment of node identifiers so that attackers cannot control the node identifier assignment; (2) secure the maintenance of routing tables that they do not contain many malicious nodes; and (3) secure message forwarding by sending messages to multiple and diverse routes.

- To prevent *storage and retrieval attacks* means to guarantee that data could always be stored in and retrieved from the system. This can be done by a replication mechanism that guarantees a document have at least $(m + k + 1)$ replicas if k peers can fail at the same time and there may be m malicious node. Thus, in any case, there is at least one active replica around.

- To prevent *denial of service (DoS) attacks* means to protect the availability of a node from overwhelming requests of malicious nodes. One solution is to provide each client a quota limit on service resources. As a result, the node is still able to serve other clients during the attack. The other solution is to detect DoS attacks at the time they are happening and to disconnect malicious nodes involving the attacks to recover the system.

- To avoid harmful or incorrect data returned from malicious nodes. A straightforward solution is to store and to retrieve data only on trusted nodes. Otherwise, it is necessary to provide a solution to test *data integrity and verification* means. The popular approach is to use hash functions to create identifiers or digests of data so that they can be used to verify the correctness of data later.

Besides attacks, other problems that may occur in P2P systems and their solutions are described as follows.

- For P2P systems whose sharing resources are computing resources, it is necessary to *verify integrity of computation*. The basic solution is to exploit redundancy i.e., to assign each computing task to multiple nodes and compare the returned results from them.

- *Free riding* is also a concern in a P2P system. To provide fairness to peers in the system, the basic solution is to record the contribution and consumption of peers. Depending on this statistics, the system determines the amount of resources a peer is allowed to use.

- While P2P systems are open to all users, it is important to maintain the *privacy* of data and the *anonymity* of users. On the one hand, the privacy of data is often achieved by some encryption techniques. On the other hand, the anonymity of users can be protected by setting secure channels for routing messages. Finally, to provide authentication and authorization of resources, techniques based on the X.509 public-key infrastructure can be used.

10.1.7 Trust Management

Trust is an important aspect of P2P systems. Since peers are anonymous, before every transaction, peers involved in the transaction often want to know if the partner can be trusted. Even though trust can be classified in two types: *trust in action* and *trust in recommendation*, people do not usually differentiate them. Actually, when a peer trusts another peer, it trusts both action and recommendation from that peer. In P2P systems, trust can be assigned values at different granularities: single value, binary values, multiple values, and continuous values, and is verified by two basic trust models as follows.

— *Credential based.* In this model, credentials are used to determine trust of a peer. If a peer has a credential satisfying specified policies, it is trustworthy. Otherwise, it cannot be trusted. A typical way for checking credential of a peer is based on the public/private key of that peer.
— *Reputation based.* The trust value of a peer is based on its reputation i.e. past actions. In this model, the trust value of a peer changes after each of its transactions. Furthermore, since the behavior of a peer may be influenced by the behaviors of others in the society it belongs to, some P2P systems combine both the individual reputation of a peer and the reputation of its society to derive the reputation of the peer.

Trust is generally managed by the same overlay network employed by the P2P system (since trust values are just special data). In particular, if the system uses centralized P2P architecture, trust values are stored at servers. If the system utilizes unstructured P2P architecture, trust values are maintained at every node and gossiping algorithm is used to distribute trust values. Finally, if the system builds on structured P2P architecture, peer identifiers are used as keys for inserting trust values to the system.

10.2 Potential Research Directions

The research on P2P is still at its infancy, and there are many research problems that are yet to be solved. We discuss some of them in this section.

10.2.1 Sharing Structured Databases

Even though there have been initial works to support structured data sharing in P2P systems, these works only focus on solutions for mapping heterogeneous data sources. Naturally, there are still many open problems.

— *Query optimization.* Since the execution order of operations in a query has an important effect on the performance of query processing i.e., a good execution sequence (query plan) allows a fast processing speed and low consumed bandwidth, while a bad execution sequence leads to a slow processing speed and high consumed bandwidth, it is important to find a near optimal execution sequence for a query. In a centralized DBMS, the basic approach to solve this task is to build an initial query plan for the query from data statistics. The challenge, however, is that it is not cost-effective to obtain accurate data statistics in P2P systems.

- *Complex queries.* Join query is just a type of query in structured data. Complex queries such as aggregate queries, top-K queries and skyline queries require a much more sophisticated query optimizer. The dynamism and autonomy of P2P systems further complicate the derivation of efficient query execution plan.
- Database transaction: besides queries, it is necessary to support data manipulation operations, which leads to the demand of supporting database transactions. While applications in centralized systems often require four basic ACID properties: atomic, consistent, isolated, and durable, applications in P2P systems may not require strict ACID properties to be enforced because the nature of P2P environment may make it hard to do this. In general, the context has to be taken into consideration during the design of the transaction management. Depending on the specific requests of applications, only some properties are required while others can be omitted. For example, updates due to migration of data for load balancing and synchronization updates will require the updates to commit and be lasting.

Furthermore, current solutions for mapping heterogeneous data sources can only work well in small-scale systems while P2P systems are often large. New solutions for this challenge, that can work in large-scale systems, are still needed.

10.2.2 Security

Security is an important aspect in P2P systems. Even though there have been several proposals to address security issues in P2P systems, it is still an ongoing research direction. In particular, the following security aspects need to be properly addressed.

- As discussed before, the most critical problem in file sharing P2P systems is the problem of bad sharing files that contain viruses, spyware, or illegal copyright files. Current solutions can only identify these files after they have been activated and caused harm to the users. We need a better solution that identifies and isolates bad files before they are activated. As the saying goes, prevention is better than rescue.
- Detecting and eliminating malicious peers: even though existing solutions can identify malicious peers after they join the system by checking their reputation, malicious peers can circumvent these solutions by leaving and rejoining the system frequently. Everytime these peers rejoin the system, they can change their identifier, and hence clear their bad reputation in the past. As a result, we need a new solution that is able to keep track of the reputation of a peer even if they change their identifier the system. In other words, the solution needs to recognize the behavior of malicious peers so that we can identify them as soon as they rejoin the system.

10.2.3 Data Stream Processing

Since there is a huge amount of data transferring amongst peers in P2P systems, data stream processing plays an important role in these systems. A straightforward application that needs stream data processing in a P2P system, is system monitoring. Challenges of stream processing in P2P systems fall in four main aspects as follows.

— Processing speed: even though the amount of data stream is huge, the processing speed still needs to be fast. Ideally, data should be processed on the fly without causing any latency.
— Computation cost: in P2P systems, the computation resources such as memory and cpu are often limited. As a result, it is necessary to have a low requirement on computation resources.
— Global statistics: while individual data streams can be processed at different nodes to generate local results, it is necessary to aggregate these local results to form a global result.
— Consumed network bandwidth: while local results are exchange to obtain a global result, it should not consume much network bandwidth. In many cases, the challenge of using network bandwidth is actually in how to put/assign operations to nodes efficiently.

10.2.4 Testbed and Benchmarks

Most of the reported work in the literature have employed simulation in their performance study. While simulation models can provide quick insights to performance of a scheme, they often rely on some assumptions that may not be realistic and they cannot adequately capture all parameters. Thus, it is necessary to develop a testbed and a set of benchmarks for P2P systems. In general, the testbed should satisfy the following properties.

— Simulated network properties: the testbed should be able to capture different properties of a real system. For example, the testbed should be able to simulate a system with different topologies, different churn rate, different failure rate, different resource capability, etc.
— Scalability: this property is an important property of a P2P system. As a result, it is necessary that the testbed has this property. However, it is important to note that the testbed should not require many resources to achieve this property. For example, it is infeasible if the testbed requires one million computers to simulate a one million node network.
— Statistics: the testbed should be able to provide statistics in different aspects of the system according to the benchmarks. In particular, a graphical display for statistics is desirable. Additionally, the statistics should be storable for subsequent references.

– Usability: the testbed should be easily used to deploy new P2P systems. Ideally, the testbed should provide a script language so that a new system can be described for deployment by using the language. Alternatively, the testbed can provide extendable API for implementing the new system.

10.3 Applications in Industry

Even though peer-to-peer technology has been adopted with enthusiasm by the personal users, it has been facing a staunch resistance from business users and it has been very difficult to find a way to monetize the networks generated by the P2P software.

The successful applications of peer-to-peer have involved using a hybrid technological approach. In most cases, the P2P technology is usually combined with more traditional centralized approaches. For example, in the case of Kontiki,[1] a P2P delivery management system, the service developed is partially using P2P and partially using centralized servers to distribute content. Similarly, Skype,[2] probably the most successful P2P application, uses the overlay to improve transfer rate, but also has a small set of servers that provide user account management services.

On the corporate side we will probably see the research being applied to enhance existing products, like McAfee's Rumor Technology for distributing antivirus updates [219], but it is most unlikely that a corporate client will rely 100% on a pure P2P solution. Even for SMEs, the best effort that is characteristic of peer-to-peer networks will prove to be a powerful deterrent that will not resist against centralized products that are also becoming more commoditized and, consequently, cheaper. Still, as the "Cloud" paradigm becomes more and more popular, the lessons learned from P2P technology will be useful to efficiently handle scalability issues in environments where the sheer size of the cloud and its required flexibility means that failures are a constant rather than an exceptional event. In particular, addressing data scalability issues will require significant attention, with potential solutions in distributed online aggregation techniques [338].

If we think about P2P uses in industry, we observe two driving forces that may appear to come from very different angles, but for which P2P is a common solution:

– First, a need to push data towards the end user, especially when there is lots of data, like in the case of multimedia or software distribution (video on demand, voice over IP, software updates, etc.)
– Second, a need to retain control over the entire data that the provider makes available, potentially temporarily, to a set of users. In this case, when there are several providers, or collaborators, then P2P technology is the only viable solution if there is no trusted external party.

---

[1]http://www.kontiki.com.

[2]http://www.skype.com.

While the first approach has been implemented with reasonable success, in this chapter, we will make the case for peer-to-peer as a solution for the second driving force. In fact, it is not hard to imagine a scenario where companies would benefit from sharing data with partners, and even competitors, but do not want to give access to their data centers. The idea here is to automate the transfer of information, by allowing each participating entity to specify what parts of its data it allows other to see, and what kind of data it needs from others. The ultimate goal is to make the peer-to-peer network transparent and let each partner have a global view of the data.

A perfect example for this kind of scenario is a Supply Chain Management application: there are potentially many partners (from manufacturer to retailer, maybe via governmental control institutions), large amounts of dynamic data, as items travel around the world.

10.3.1 Supply Chain Management Case Study

As enterprises are forced to cooperate across national boundaries, to specialize in what they do in-house and at the same time diversify their offer to the customers, they are driven to create stronger links and develop collaborations with other enterprises. In this scenario, they need help in managing their relationships with other entities, be they suppliers, customers or service providers. Companies must be able to have access to pertinent, updated information as soon as the provider of information makes it available.

In the particular scenario of a supply chain management (SCM) application, a strong demand for a particular item should trigger queries in the entire chain for parts that make that particular item and identify automatically potential bottlenecks. Waiting for a human operator to see the request, identify suppliers and send queries introduces delays that could otherwise be avoided.

Effective and timely sharing of critical data among consumers and suppliers is very important for SCM. Recently, renouncing monolithic applications, emphasizing global accessibility and scalability as well as the development of tools to facilitate repeatable deployments have been identified as key technology success factors.

A centralized solution may be envisaged, but few companies are willing to store their data, even if it was previously pruned of possibly sensitive information, on a machine outside their control. Even more, a centralized solution is hard to deploy and even harder to maintain when the number of clients grows. What should be done instead, is distribute the management costs by making each participant entity responsible for providing a reliable, yet relatively small, server that would act as a proxy between its internal data structure and the potential partners.

Existing solutions in the market use data centers to manage the shared information from all the participants in the supply chain. It has the advantage of reliability, but the maintenance cost is huge. However, in a context where every participant is strongly motivated to maintain its presence in the network, the reliability of the entire system will be a consequence of the reliability of the individual participating entities.

Fig. 10.1 Architecture of a
peer-to-peer SCM application

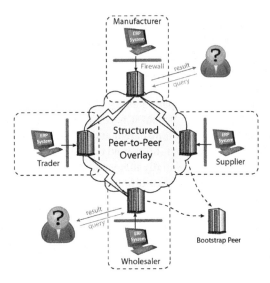

We envision an infrastructure for distributed information sharing among different parties based on Peer-to-Peer technology. Using distributed hash tables, the indexing mechanism is both efficient and scalable, but challenges arise due to the heterogeneous nature of the data as well as due to the potential security threats that are characteristic of peer-to-peer networks. We will address these shortly, but first let us consider why would we even want to use this approach.

The main advantage of a distributed solution would initially appear to be the cost: it is much cheaper to use off-the-shelf servers than to have a custom made super-computer. However, this argument does not stand its ground in front of the traditional view of peer-to-peer networks: unreliable, "best effort" approaches that target bargain seekers. The fact is that this view is wrong—there is nothing inherently unsafe in a peer-to-peer network, not more than it is in general in the Internet.

However, cost is still not the main decision factor. The true advantage of a distributed solution is the larger control that it gives to each participating entity. By not moving data around, but only publishing indexing information, each participant maintains full control over its data, who accesses it, when and at what cost. Such a participant can implement several layers of security and make available only part of its data, while keeping the rest behind a highly secured firewall.

Furthermore, if data is not moved around, the participants may dynamically join and depart from the network. When the participant leaves the network, its data should not be accessed any more. This introduces huge maintenance cost to the warehouse solution. Instead, we require a nimble, distributed, lightweight, and scalable data management system, as an alternative to the centralized data warehouse, for corporate network applications.

10.3.1.1 Potential Issues

The heterogeneous nature of the data present at different participating entities constitutes a considerable challenge to this approach of letting each participant manage its own repository.

First, there is the issue of different schemas: each participant will have its data in a more or less customized schema and there is a need to merge all these different schemas. While there is substantial and high quality work in the area of automatic schema merging in peer data management systems [149], in the case of an SCM application it seems more appropriate to have one entity define a global schema and then let each participant define a mapping from its own data to this new schema. Such an approach would prove to be more reliable than having each participant define mappings to any other participant (and more scalable). Using an intermediary approach (e.g., X has a mapping to Y, Y has a mapping to Z, consequently X has a mapping to Z) is not always feasible and, since each mapping makes certain, unknown, compromises, a long chain of intermediaries will lead to unpredictable results.

The global schema approach does not represent a significant diversion from the peer-to-peer idea. The server managing this global schema needs to be contacted infrequently (e.g., only upon initial connection to the network) and schema updates can be broadcast into the network since they are equally expected to be rare occurrences.

Apart from the issue of schema mapping, another problem that has to be addressed with respect to the heterogeneity of the data is that each entity, when storing data for its own use, makes a number of assumptions that it takes as given and consequently does not store them in the database. A very simple example of this are measure units or currencies (most enterprises will not store the currency explicitly, but assume they always work in one particular currency). Consequently, when data is put together, such assumptions would conflict, resulting in serious errors in the global database. What is needed here is a way to add these assumptions into the data. The COntext INterchange (COIN) strategy [135] is an approach to solving the problem of interoperability of semantically heterogeneous data sources through context mediation. The existing implementation of COIN uses its own notation and syntax for representing ontologies. More recently, an extension of the COIN strategy to the semantic web has been proposed [206] to solve context disparity and ontology interoperability problems in the emerging Semantic Web both at the ontology level and at the data level.

Another potential issue that might arise when talking about a peer-to-peer network for business purposes is that of *security*, *privacy*, and *confidentiality*. However, it is hard to argue why such a network would be inherently less secured than accessing a central server over the internet. After all, the TCP-IP stack of protocols also hops over unknown and potentially unreliable intermediary servers and the tunneling approach that is used there can equally well be used in peer-to-peer, when necessary.

To create credentials, the system would require again the presence of a trusted third party (again, not unlike current practices in the Internet), but even more, the access to the actual data would be managed by the individual data providers. While the trusted third party (i.e., the service provider) could define prespecified roles and access rights, the ultimate decision remains with the participating entities, since they have full control over their servers.

10.3.1.2 Queries

We have mentioned so far issues pertaining to the data: who publishes it, how, and where, as well as access control to this data. We can naturally ask ourselves what kind of queries would, or should, such a system be able to answer. The starting point of this line of though would be a traditional data warehouse. One of the reasons, if not the main reason for having a data warehouse is to provide business intelligence tools to harness the large amount of information and create reports and forecasts. While these may be desirable goals even for a distributed SCM application, it is hard to see how they can be achieved in a distributed context due to two reasons:

1. The data may be incomplete: since every entity decides what to make publicly available, not all data may be available. Making forecasts on incomplete data is obviously not recommended practice.
2. Even if we assume that all the data is available, the scale envisioned for this network (global, with hundreds or thousands of participating databases) would make most data mining techniques grind to a halt.

However, most queries in a SCM application's day to day use would be selection and aggregation queries. A lightweight solution, based on the indexing tools provided by the distributed hash table infrastructure, would suffice for such queries.

To sum up, the example of the supply chain management application is typical of potential uses for peer-to-peer concepts. The set of concepts and ideas that are characteristic of the P2P environment are useful, in more or less pure forms, wherever multiple entities participate as equals. However, a peer-to-peer framework is a disruptive technology, and the fact that multiple independent participants need to agree on a set of standards makes it even more difficult to adopt than any actual technical difficulty. Through this book, we aimed at presenting peer-to-peer for what it is, notably much more than a controversial file sharing technology. It is a complex area, with many challenges and many opportunities.

References

1. Emulab—total network testbed, http://www.emulab.com
2. Folding@home, http://folding.stanford.edu
3. Freenet, http://freenet.sourceforge.net
4. Furi, http://www.jps.net/williamw/furi
5. Gnewtella, http://sourceforge.net/projects/gnewtella
6. Gnotella, http://www.overnet-download.de/filesharing/gnotella.html
7. Gnutella, http://gnutella.wego.com
8. The Gnutella protocol specification v0.4, http://www.clip2.com
9. Icq, http://www.icq.com
10. JXTA Project Home Page, http://www.jxta.org
11. Magi, http://www.endeavors.com
12. Napster, http://www.napster.com
13. Napster protocol, http://david.weekly.org/code
14. Star craft, http://www.blizzard.com
15. The Network Simulator—ns-2, http://www.isi.edu/nsnam/ns/
16. Secure Hash Standard (SHS), National Institute of Standards and Technology, FIPS Publication, 180-1, April 1995
17. K. Aberer, P-Grid: a self-organizing access structure for P2P information systems, in *Proceedings of the 9th International Conference on Cooperative Information Systems (CoopIS)*, 2001
18. K. Aberer, P. Cudre-Mauroux, M. Hauswirth, The chatty web: emergent semantics through gossiping, in *Proceedings of the 12th World Wide Web Conference (WWW)*, 2003
19. K. Aberer, Z. Despotovic, Managing trust in a peer-2-peer information system, in *Proceedings of the 10th ACM International Conference on Information and Knowledge Management (CIKM)*, 2001
20. L.A. Adamic, R.M. Lukose, A.R. Puniyani, B.A. Huberman, Search in power-law networks. *Phys. Rev.* **64** (2001)
21. E. Adar, B.A. Huberman, Free riding on Gnutella. *First Monday* **5**(10) (2000)
22. D.A. Agarwal, O. Chevassut, M.R. Thompson, G. Tsudik, An integrated solution for secure group communication in wide-area networks, in *Proceedings of the 6th IEEE Symposium on Computers and Communications*, pp. 22–28, Hammamet, Tunisia, July 2001
23. R. Albert, H. Jeong, A. Barabasi, Error and attack tolerance in complex networks. *Nature* **406**, 378–382 (2000)
24. M. Altinel, M. Franklin, Efficient filtering of XML documents for selective dissemination, in *Proceedings of the 26th International Conference on Very Large Databases (VLDB)*, 2000
25. Amazon, http://www.amazon.com
26. Amazon Auctions, http://auctions.amazon.com

27. K.G. Anagnostakis, M.B. Greenwald, Exchange-based incentive mechanisms for peer-to-peer file sharing, in *Proceedings of the 24th International Conference on Distributed Computing Systems (ICDCS)*, pp. 524–533, Tokyo, Japan, March 2004

28. D. Anderson, SETI@home, in *Peer-to-Peer: Harnessing the Power of Disruptive Technologies* (O'Reilly & Associates, 2001), pp. 67–76

29. A. Andrzejak, Z. Xu, Scalable, efficient range queries for grid information services, in *Proceedings of the 2nd International Conference on Peer-To-Peer Computing*, pp. 33–40, 2002

30. M. Arenas, V. Kantere, A. Kementsietsidis, I. Kiringa, R. Miller, J. Mylopoulos, The Hyperion project: from data integration to data coordination. *SIGMOD Rec.* **32**(3) (2003)

31. J. Aspnes, G. Shah, Skip graphs, in *Proceedings of the 14th Annual ACM-SIAM Symposium on Discrete Algorithms (SODA)*, pp. 384–393, 2003

32. R. Axelrod, *The Evolution of Cooperation* (Basic Books, New York, 1984)

33. R.A. Baeza-Yates, B.A. Ribeiro-Neto, *Modern Information Retrieval* (ACM Press/Addison-Wesley, New York, 1999)

34. B. Bakos, L. Farkas, Nomadic sharing of media: proximity delivery of mass content within P2P social networks, in *Proceedings of IWUC*, 2006

35. H. Balakrishnan, M.F. Kaashoek, D. Karger, R. Morris, I. Stoica, Looking up data in P2P systems. *Commun. ACM* **46**(2), 43–48 (2003)

36. I. Balbin, K. Ramamohanarao, A generalization of the differential approach to recursive query emulation. *J. Log. Program.* **4**(3) (1987)

37. B. Barber, *Logic and Limits of Trust* (Rutgers University Press, New Jersey, 1983)

38. C. Batten, K. Barr, A. Saraf, S. Treptin, pStore: a secure peer-to-peer backup system. Technical Memo MIT-LCS-TM-632, MIT Laboratory for Computer Science, December 2001

39. M. Bawa, T. Condie, P. Ganesan, LSH forest: self-tuning indexes for similarity search, in *Proceedings of the 14th World Wide Web Conference (WWW)*, pp. 651–660, 2005

40. D. Bedell, Search for extraterrestrials or extra cash, in *The Dallas Morning News*, December 1999

41. M. Bender, S. Michel, C. Zimmer, G. Weikum, The MINERVA project: database selection in the Context of P2P search, in *Proceedings of the GI-Fachtagung fur Datenbanksysteme in Business, Technologie und Web (BTW)*, 2005

42. J.L. Bentley, Multidimensional binary search trees used for associative searching. *Commun. ACM* **18**(9), 509–517 (1975)

43. S. Berchtold, C. Bohm, H.-P. Kriegel, The Pyramid-technique: towards breaking the curse of dimensionality, in *Proceedings of the ACM SIGMOD International Conference on Management of Data*, pp. 142–153, 1998

44. S. Berchtold, D.A. Keim, H.-P. Kriegel, The X-tree: an index structure for high-dimensional data, in *Proceedings of the 22nd International Conference on Very Large Databases (VLDB)*, 1996

45. K. Berket, A. Essiari, A. Muratas, PKI-based security for peer-to-peer information sharing, in *Proceedings of the 4th IEEE International Conference on Peer-to-Peer Computing*, August 2004

46. P.A. Bernstein, F. Giunchiglia, A. Kementsietsidis, J. Mylopoulos, L. Serafini, I. Zaihrayeu, Data management for peer-to-peer computing: a vision, in *Proceedings of the 5th International Workshop on the Web and Databases (WebDB)*, 2002

47. M. Berry, Z. Drmac, E. Jessup, Matrices, vector spaces, and information retrieval. *SIAM Rev.* **41**(2), 335–362 (1999)

48. E. Bertino, E. Ferrari, A.C. Squicciarini, Trust-X: a peer-to-peer framework for trust establishment. *IEEE Trans. Knowl. Data Eng.* **7**, 827–842 (2004)

49. A.R. Bharambe, M. Agrawal, S. Seshan, Mercury: supporting scalable multi-attribute range queries, in *Proceedings of the ACM SIGCOMM Conference*, 2004

50. M. Blaze, J. Feigenbaum, J. Ioannidis, A. Keromytis, The KeyNote trust management system, version 2. RFC-2704. IETF, 1999

51. M. Blaze, J. Feigenbaum, Decentralized trust management, in *Proceedings of the IEEE Symposium on Security and Privacy (S&P)*, 1996

52. Blizzard, http://www.blizzard.com/, 2001
53. B.H. Bloom, Space/time trade-offs in hash coding with allowable errors. *Commun. ACM* **13**(7), 422–426 (1970)
54. S. Boag, D. Chamberlin, M.F. Fernandez, D. Florescu, J. Robie, J. Simeon, M. Stefanescu, XQuery 1.0: An XML query language. W3C working draft, April 2002
55. W.J. Bolosky, J.R. Douceur, D. Ely, M. Theimer, Feasibility of a serverless distributed file system deployed on an existing set of desktop pcs, in *Proceedings of the ACM SIGMETRICS International Conference on Measurement and Modeling of Computer Systems* (ACM, New York, 2000), pp. 34–43
56. A. Broder, M. Mitzenmacher, Network applications of bloom filters: a survey, in *Allerton*, 2002
57. S. Burleigh, V. Cerf, R. Durst, K. Fall, A. Hooke, K. Scott, H. Weiss, The interplanetary internet: a communications infrastructure for Mars exploration, in *Proceedings of the International Astronautical Congress*, 2002
58. J. Byers, J. Considine, M. Mitzenmacher, Simple load balancing for distributed hash tables, in *Proceedings of the 2nd International Workshop on Peer-to-Peer Systems (IPTPS)*, 2003
59. J.W. Byers, M. Luby, M. Mitzenmacher, A. Rege, A digital fountain approach to reliable distribution of bulk data, in *Proceedings of the ACM SIGCOMM Conference*, pp. 56–67, 1998
60. R. Caceres, F. Douglis, A. Feldmann, G. Glass, M. Rabinovich, Web proxy caching: the devil is in the details, in *Proceedings of the 2nd Workshop on Internet Server Performance (WISP)*, 1999
61. M. Cai, M. Frank, J. Chen, P. Szekely, MAAN: a multi-attribute addressable network for grid information services, in *Proceedings of the 2nd International Workshop on Peer-to-Peer Systems (IPTPS)*, 2003
62. D. Carney, U. Cetintemel, M. Cherniack, C. Convey, S. Lee, G. Seidman, M. Stonebraker, N. Tatbul, S. Zdonik, Monitoring streams: a new class of data management applications, in *Proceedings of the 28th International Conference on Very Large Databases (VLDB)*, 2002
63. D. Carroll, C. Rahmlow, T. Psiaki, G. Wojtaszczyk, Distributing science. http://boinc.berkeley.edu/trac/wiki/BoincPapers, 2005
64. M. Castro, P. Druschel, A. Ganesh, A. Rowstron, D.S. Wallach, Security for peer-to-peer routing overlays, in *Proceedings of the 5th USENIX Symposium on Operating Systems Design and Implementation (OSDI)*, Boston, Massachusetts, December 2002
65. J. Cates, Robust and efficient data management for a distributed hash table. Master's thesis, Massachusetts Institute of Technology, 2003
66. V. Cerf, S. Burleigh, A. Hooke, L. Torgerson, R. Durst, K. Scott, K. Fall, H. Weiss, Delay-tolerant network architecture. IETF RFC 4838, http://www.ietf.org/rfc/rfc4838.txt, April 2007
67. S. Ceri, G. Gottlob, L. Tanca, *Logic Programming and Databases*. Surveys in Computer Science (Springer, Berlin, 1990)
68. C. Chan, P. Felber, M. Garofalakis, R. Rastogi, Efficient filtering of XML documents with XPath expressions, in *Proceedings of the 18th IEEE International Conference on Data Engineering (ICDE)*, 2002
69. S. Chandrasekaran, O. Cooper, A. Deshpande, M.J. Franklin, J.M. Hellerstein, W. Hong, S. Krishnamurthy, S.R. Madden, V. Raman, F. Reiss, M.A. Shah, TelegraphCQ: continuous dataflow processing for an uncertain world, in *Proceedings of the 1st Conference on Innovative Data Systems Research (CIDR)*, 2003
70. D. Chaum, Untraceable electronic mail, return addresses, and digital pseudonyms. *Commun. ACM* **4**(2) (1982)
71. J. Chen, D.J. DeWitt, F. Tian, Y. Wang, NiagaraCQ: a scalable continuous query system for internet databases, in *Proceedings of the ACM SIGMOD International Conference on Management of Data*, 2000
72. Y. Chen, R.H. Katz, J. Kubiatowicz, Dynamic replica placement for scalable content delivery, in *Proceedings of the 1st International Workshop on Peer-to-Peer Systems (IPTPS)*, pp. 306–318, 2002

73. M. Cherniack, H. Balakrishnan, M. Balazinska, Scalable distributed stream processing, in *Proceedings of the 1st Conference on Innovative Data Systems Research (CIDR)*, 2003
74. S. Cheshire, M. Krochmal, DNS-Based Service Discovery. http://tools.ietf.org/html/draft-cheshire-dnsext-dns-sd
75. Y.-H. Chu, J. Feigenbaum, B. LaMacchia, P. Resnick, M. Strauss, REFEREE: trust management for web applications. *Comput. Netw. ISDN Syst.* **29**(8–13), 953–964 (1997)
76. B. Chun, D. Culler, T. Roscoe, A. Bavier, L. Peterson, M. Wawrzoniak, M. Bowman, Planetlab: an overlay testbed for broad-coverage services. *ACM SIGCOMM Comput. Commun. Rev.* **33**(3) (2003)
77. P. Ciaccia, M. Patella, P. Zezula, M-Tree: an efficient access method for similarity search in metric spaces, in *Proceedings of the 23rd International Conference on Very Large Databases (VLDB)*, pp. 426–435, 1997
78. I. Clark, O. Sandberg, B. Wiley, T. Hong, Freenet: a distributed anonymous information storage and retrieval system, in *Proceedings of the Workshop on Design Issues in Anonymity and Unobservability (DIAU)*, Berkeley, CA, 2000
79. I. Clarke, T.W. Hong, S.G. Miller, O. Sandberg, B. Wiley, Protecting free expression online with Freenet. *IEEE Internet Comput.* **6**(1), 40–49 (2002)
80. E. Cohen, S. Shenker, Replication strategies in unstructured peer-to-peer networks, in *Proceedings of the ACM SIGCOMM Conference*, pp. 177–190, 2002
81. T.E. Condie, S.D. Kamvar, H. Garcia-Molina, Adaptive peer-to-peer topologies, in *Proceedings of the 4th IEEE International Conference on Peer-to-Peer Computing*, August 2004
82. B. Cooper, M. Bawa, N. Daswani, H. Garcia-Molina, Protecting the pipe from malicious peers. Technical report, Computer Sciences Dept, Stanford University, 2002
83. F. Cornelli, E. Damiani, S.D.C. di Vimercati, S. Paraboschi, P. Samarati, Choosing reputable servents in a P2P network, in *Proceedings of the 11th World Wide Web Conference (WWW)*, 2002
84. L.P. Cox, C.D. Murray, B.D. Noble, Pastiche: making backup cheap and easy, in *Proceedings of the 5th USENIX Symposium on Operating Systems Design and Implementation (OSDI)*, Boston, MA, December 2002
85. L.P. Cox, B.D. Noble, Samsara: honor among thieves in peer-to-peer storage, in *Proceedings of the 19th ACM Symposium on Operating Systems Principles (SOSP)*, Bolton Landing, NY, October 2003
86. A. Crainiceanu, P. Linga, J. Gehrke, J. Shanmugasundaram, Querying peer-to-peer networks using P-trees, in *Proceedings of the 7th International Workshop on the Web and Databases (WebDB)*, pp. 25–30, 2004
87. A. Crainiceanu, P. Linga, A. Machanavajjhala, J. Gehrke, J. Shanmugasundaram, P-Ring: an efficient and robust P2P range index structure, in *Proceedings of the ACM SIGMOD International Conference on Management of Data*, 2007
88. A. Crespo, H. Garcia-Molina, Routing indices for peer-to-peer systems, in *Proceedings of the 22nd International Conference on Distributed Computing Systems (ICDCS)*, 2002
89. A. Crespo, H. Garcia-Molina, Routing indices for peer-to-peer systems, in *Proceedings of the 22nd International Conference on Distributed Computing Systems (ICDCS)*, 2002
90. A. Crespo, H. Garcia-Molina, Semantic overlay networks for P2P systems. Technical report, Computer Science Department, Stanford University, 2003
91. F. Cuenca-Acuna, T. Nguyen, Text-based content search and retrieval in ad hoc P2P communities. Technical Report DCS-TR-483, Rutgers University, 2002
92. F.M. Cuenca-Acuna, C. Peery, R.P. Martin, T.D. Nguyen, PlanetP: using gossiping to build content addressable peer-to-peer information sharing communities, in *Proceedings of the 12th IEEE International Symposium on High Performance Distributed Computing (HPDC)*, 2003
93. F. Dabek, M.F. Kaashoek, D. Karger, R. Morris, I. Stoica, Wide-area cooperative storage with CFS, in *Proceedings of the 18th ACM Symposium on Operating Systems Principles (SOSP)*, 2001

94. E. Damiani, D.C. di Vimercati, S. Paraboschi, P. Samarati, F. Violante, A reputation-based approach for choosing reliable resources in peer-to-peer networks, in *Proceedings of the 9th ACM Conference on Computer and Communications Security (CCS)*, 2002

95. N. Daswani, H. Garcia-Molina, Query-flood DoS attacks in Gnutella, in *Proceedings of the 9th ACM Conference on Computer and Communications Security (CCS)*, pp. 181–192, Washington, DC, 2002

96. A. Datta, M. Hauswirth, K. Aberer, Updates in highly unreliable, replicated peer-to-peer systems, in *Proceedings of the 23rd International Conference on Distributed Computing Systems (ICDCS)*, 2003

97. A. Datta, M. Hauswirth, R. John, R. Schmidt, K. Aberer, Range queries in tree-structured overlays, in *Proceedings of the 3rd International Workshop on Databases, Information Systems and Peer-to-Peer Computing (DBISP2P)*, 2005

98. I. Daubechies, *Ten Lectures on Wavelets* (Society for Industrial and Applied Mathematics, Philadelphia, 1992)

99. J. Dawei, X. Han, M. Lupu, B.C. Ooi, H.T. Vo, Q.H. Vu, S. Wu, BestPeer: a peer-to-peer based platform for corporate network applications in *Distributed Online Aggregation*, ed. by S. Wu, S. Jiang, B.C. Ooi, K.L. Tan. Proceedings of the International Conference on Very Large Data Bases, July 2008 (National University of Singapore, Singapore, 2009)

100. M. Dean, D. Connolly, F. van Harmelen, J. Hendler, I. Horrocks, D. McGuinness, P. Patel-Schneider, L. Stein, OWL web ontology language 1.0 reference, 2002

101. G. Decandia, D. Hastorun, M. Jampani, G. Kakulapati, A. Lakshman, A. Pilchin, S. Sivasubramanian, P. Vosshall, W. Vogels, Dynamo: Amazon's highly available key-value store, in *Proceedings of the 21st ACM Symposium on Operating Systems Principles (SOSP)*, pp. 205–220, 2007

102. S. Deerwester, S. Dumais, G. Furnas, R. Harshman, Indexing by latent semantic analysis. *J. Am. Soc. Inf. Sci.* **41**, 391–407 (1990)

103. M. Deutsch, Cooperation and trust: some theoretical notes, in *Nebraska Symposium on Motivation*, 1962

104. M. Deutsch, *The Resolution of Conflict* (Yale University Press, New Haven, 1973)

105. P. Devanbu, M. Gertz, C. Martel, S.G. Stubblebine, Authentic data publication over the internet. *J. Comput. Secur.* **11**(3), 291–314 (2003)

106. Y. Diao, P. Fischer, M. Franklin, R. To, YFilter: efficient and scalable filtering of XML documents, in *Proceedings of the 18th IEEE International Conference on Data Engineering (ICDE)*, 2002

107. P. Digital, Magic mirror backup, 2003

108. R. Dingledine, M. Freedman, D. Molnar, Free Haven, in *Peer-to-Peer: Harnessing the Power of Disruptive Technologies* (O'Reilly & Associates, 2001), pp. 159–187

109. S. Djilali, P2P-rpc: programming scientific applications on peer-to-peer systems with remote procedure call, in *Proceedings of the 3st International Symposium on Cluster Computing and the Grid (CCGRID)* (IEEE Computer Society, Washington, 2003), pp. 406–413

110. S. Djilali, T. Herault, O. Lodygensky, T. Morlier, G. Fedak, F. Cappello, RPC-V: toward fault-tolerant rpc for internet connected desktop grids with volatile nodes, in *Proceedings of the ACM/IEEE conference on Supercomputing (SC)* (IEEE Computer Society, Washington, 2004), p. 39

111. J.R. Douceur, The Sybil attack, in *Proceedings of the 1st International Workshop on Peer-to-Peer Systems (IPTPS)*, pp. 251–260, Cambridge, MA, 2002

112. C. Doulkeridis, A. Vlachou, Y. Kotidis, M. Vazirgiannis, Peer-to-peer similarity search in metric spaces, in *Proceedings of the 33rd International Conference on Very Large Databases (VLDB)*, 2007

113. B. Dragovic, B. Kotsovinos, S. Hand, P.R. Pietzuch, Xenotrust: event-based distributed trust management, in *Proceedings of the 2nd International Workshop on Trust and Privacy in Digital Business (TrustBus)*, 2003

114. P. Druschel, A. Rowstron, PAST: a large-scale, persistent peer-to-peer storage utility, in *Proceedings of the 8th Workshop on Hot Topics in Operating Systems (HotOS)* (IEEE Computer Society Press, Los Alamitos, 2001), pp. 75–80

115. W. Du, J. Jia, M. Mangal, M. Murugesan, Uncheatable grid computing, in *Proceedings of the 24th International Conference on Distributed Computing Systems (ICDCS)*, pp. 4–11, Tokyo, Japan, March 2004

116. eBay, http://www.ebay.com

117. H. Evans, P. Dickman, Peer-to-peer programming with Teaq, in *Proceedings of the Workshop on Web Engineering and Peer-to-Peer Computing*, pp. 289–294, 2002

118. J. Feigenbaum, C. Papadimitriou, R. Sami, S. Shenker, A BGP-based mechanism for lowest-cost routing, in *Proceedings of the 21st ACM Symposium on Principles of Distributed Computing (PODC)*, pp. 173–182, 2002

119. J. Feigenbaum, C. Papadimitriou, S. Shenker, Sharing the cost of multicast transmissions. *J. Comput. Syst. Sci.* **63**, 21–41 (2001)

120. M. Feldman, K. Lai, J. Chuang, I. Stoica, Quantifying disincentives in peer-to-peer networks, in *Proceedings of the 1st Workshop on Economics of Peer-to-Peer Systems (P2PEcon)*, Berkeley, CA, June 2003

121. I. Foster, A. Iamnitchi, On death, taxes, and the convergence of peer-to-peer and grid computing, in *Proceedings of the 2nd International Workshop on Peer-to-Peer Systems (IPTPS)*, Berkeley, CA, USA, 2003

122. I. Foster, C. Kesselman (eds.), *The Grid: Blueprint for a New Computing Infrastructure* (Morgan Kaufmann, San Mateo, 1998)

123. M.J. Freedman, R. Morris, Tarzan: a peer-to-peer anonymizing network layer, in *Proceedings of the 9th ACM Conference on Computer and Communications Security (CCS)* (ACM, Washington, 2002), pp. 193–206

124. D. Gambetta, *Trust* (Blackwell, Oxford, 1990)

125. P. Ganesan, M. Bawa, H. Garcia-Molina, Online balancing of range-partitioned data with applications to peer-to-peer systems, in *Proceedings of the 30th International Conference on Very Large Databases (VLDB)*, 2004

126. P. Ganesan, K. Gummadi, H. Garcia-Molina, Canon in G major: designing DHTs with hierarchical structure, in *Proceedings of the 24th International Conference on Distributed Computing Systems (ICDCS)*, pp. 263–272, 2004

127. L. Garber, Denial-of-service attacks rip the internet. *Computer* **33**(4), 12–17 (2000)

128. L. Ge, J. Luo, Y. Xu, Developing and managing trust in peer-to-peer systems, in *Proceedings of the 17th International Conference on Database and Expert Systems Applications (DEXA)*, 2006

129. B. Gedik, L. Liu, PeerCQ: a decentralized and self-configuring peer-to-peer information monitoring system, in *Proceedings of the 23rd International Conference on Distributed Computing Systems (ICDCS)*, 2003

130. Genome@home, http://genomeathome.stanford.edu/

131. A. Ghodsi, L.O. Alima, S. Haridi, Symmetric replication for structured peer-to-peer systems, in *Proceedings of the 3rd International Workshop on Databases, Information Systems and Peer-to-Peer Computing (DBISP2P)*, 2005

132. G. Giakkoupis, V. Hadzilacos, A scheme for load balancing in heterogenous distributed hash tables, in *Proceedings of the 24th ACM Symposium on Principles of Distributed Computing (PODC)*, 2005

133. Gnutella, http://www.gnutella.com

134. P.B. Godfrey, I. Stoica, Heterogeneity and load balance in distributed hash tables, in *Proceedings of 24th Annual Joint Conference of the IEEE Computer and Communications Societies (INFOCOM)*, 2005

135. C.H. Goh, S. Bressan, S. Madnick, M. Siegel, Context interchange: new features and formalisms for the intelligent integration of information. *ACM Trans. Inf. Syst.* **17**(3), 270–293 (1999)

136. Google. Google web toolkit. http://code.google.com/webtoolkit/

137. T.J. Green, G. Miklau, M. Onizuka, D. Suciu, Processing XML streams with deterministic automata, in *Proceedings of ICDT'2003*, 2003

138. S. Gribble, A. Halevy, Z. Ives, M. Rodrig, D. Suciu, What can databases do for peer-to-peer, in *Proceedings of the 4th International Workshop on the Web and Databases (WebDB)*, 2001

139. Groove, http://www.groove.net

140. S. Guha, N. Daswani, R. Jain, An experimental study of the Skype peer-to-peer VoIP system, in *Proceedings of the 5th International Workshop on Peer-to-Peer Systems (IPTPS)*, 2006

141. A. Gupta, D. Agrawal, A.E. Abbadi, Approximate range selection queries in peer-to-peer systems, in *Proceedings of the 1st Conference on Innovative Data Systems Research (CIDR)*, 2003

142. A.K. Gupta, A.Y. Halevy, D. Suciu, View selection for stream processing, in *Proceedings of the 5th International Workshop on the Web and Databases (WebDB)*, 2002

143. A.K. Gupta, D. Suciu, Stream processing of XPath queries with predicates, in *Proceedings of the ACM SIGMOD International Conference on Management of Data*, 2003

144. A.K. Gupta, D. Suciu, A.Y. Halevy, The view selection problem for XML content based routing, in *Proceedings of the 22nd ACM Symposium on Principles of Database Systems (PODS)*, 2003

145. A. Guttman, R-trees: a dynamic index structure for spatial searching, in *Proceedings of the ACM SIGMOD International Conference on Management of Data*, pp. 47–57, 1984

146. A. Halevy, O. Etzioni, A. Doan, Z. Ives, J. Madhavan, L. McDowell, I. Tatarinov, Crossing the structure chasm, in *Proceedings of the 1st Conference on Innovative Data Systems Research (CIDR)*, 2003

147. A. Halevy, Z. Ives, P. Monk, I. Tatarinov, Piazza: data management infrastructure for semantic web applications, in *Proceedings of the 12th World Wide Web Conference (WWW)*, 2003

148. A. Halevy, Z. Ives, P. Mork, I. Tatarinov, Piazza: data management infrastructure for semantic web applications, in *Proceedings of the 12th World Wide Web Conference (WWW)*, 2003

149. A. Halevy, Z. Ives, D. Suciu, I. Tatarinov, Schema mediation in peer data management systems, in *Proceedings of the 19th IEEE International Conference on Data Engineering (ICDE)*, 2003

150. S. Hand, T. Harris, E. Kotsovinos, I. Pratt, Controlling the XenoServer open platform, in *Proceedings of the 6th IEEE Conference on Open Architectures and Network Programming (OpenArch)*, 2003

151. E.N. Hanson, C. Carnes, L. Huang, M. Konyala, L. Noronha, S. Parthasarathy, J.B. Park, A. Vernon, Scalable trigger processing, in *Proceedings of the 15th IEEE International Conference on Data Engineering (ICDE)*, 1999

152. G. Hardin, The tragedy of the commons. *Science* **162**, 1243–1248 (1968)

153. M. Harren, J.M. Hellerstein, R. Huebsch, B.T. Loo, S. Shenker, I. Stoica, Complex queries in DHT-based peer-to-peer networks, in *Proceedings of the 1st International Workshop on Peer-to-Peer Systems (IPTPS)*, 2002

154. N.J.A. Harvey, M.B. Jones, S. Sarioiu, M. Theimer, A. Wolman, SkipNet: a scalable overlay network with practical locality properties, in *Proceedings of the USENIX Symposium on Internet Technologies and Systems (USITS)*, 2003

155. Free Haven, http://www.freehaven.net/

156. K. Hinrichs, J. Nievergelt, The grid file: a data structure designed to support proximity queries on spatial objects, in *Proceedings of the 9th International Workshop on Graph-Theoretic Concepts in Computer Science (WG)*, 1983

157. HiveCache, Swarmbackup: a peer-to-peer backup system, 2003

158. R. Housley, W. Ford, W. Polk, D. Solo, Internet x.509 public key infrastructure certificate and crl profile, in *RFC 2459*, 1999

159. R. Huebsch, J.M. Hellerstein, N. Lanham, B.T. Loo, S. Shenker, I. Stoica, Querying the internet with PIER, in *Proceedings of the 29th International Conference on Very Large Databases (VLDB)*, 2003

160. P. Indyk, R. Motwani, Approximate nearest neighbor—towards removing the curse of dimensionality, in *Proceedings of the 30th Annual ACM Symposium on the Theory of Computing (STOC)*, 1998

161. M. Ingram, Online music-swap firm napster forms strategic alliance with media giant bertlesmann. http://www.wsws.org/articles/2000/nov2000/nap-n04.shtml, November 2000

162. International Telegraph and Telephone Consultative Committee (CCITT). *The Directory—Authentication Framework, Recommendation X. 509*. 1993 update

163. S. Iyer, A. Rowstron, P. Drusche, SQUIRREL: a decentralized, peer-to-peer web cache, in *Proceedings of the 21st ACM Symposium on Principles of Distributed Computing (PODC)*, 2002

164. Jabber, http://www.jabber.org/

165. H.V. Jagadish, B.C. Ooi, K.-L. Tan, C. Yu, R. Zhang, iDistance: an adaptive B^+-tree based indexing method for nearest neighbor search. *ACM Trans. Database Syst.* **30**(2), 364–397 (2005)

166. H.V. Jagadish, B.C. Ooi, Q.H. Vu, BATON: a balanced tree structure for peer-to-peer networks, in *Proceedings of the 31st International Conference on Very Large Databases (VLDB)*, pp. 661–672, 2005

167. H.V. Jagadish, B.C. Ooi, Q.H. Vu, R. Zhang, A. Zhou, VBI-tree: a peer-to-peer framework for supporting multi-dimensional indexing schemes, in *Proceedings of the 22nd IEEE International Conference on Data Engineering (ICDE)*, 2006

168. Joost. Joost P2P tv. http://www.joost.com/

169. P. Kalnis, W.S. Ng, B.C. Ooi, D. Papadias, K.-L. Tan, An adaptive peer-to-peer network for distributed caching of OLAP results, in *Proceedings of the ACM SIGMOD International Conference on Management of Data*, 2002

170. V. Kalogeraki, D. Gunopulos, D. Zeinalipour-yazti, A local search mechanism for peer-to-peer networks, in *Proceedings of the 11th ACM International Conference on Information and Knowledge Management (CIKM)*, 2002

171. S. Kamvar, M. Schlosser, H. Garcia-Molina, Eigenrep: reputation management in P2P networks, in *Proceedings of the 12th World Wide Web Conference (WWW)*, 2003

172. G. Kan, Gnutella, in *Peer-to-Peer: Harnessing the Power of Disruptive Technologies* (O'Reilly & Associates, 2001), pp. 94–122

173. D. Karger, F. Kaashoek, I. Stoica, R. Morris, H. Balakrishnan, Chord: a scalable peer-to-peer lookup service for internet applications, in *Proceedings of the ACM SIGCOMM Conference*, pp. 149–160, 2001

174. D. Karger, M. Ruhl, Simple efficient load balancing algorithms for peer-to-peer systems, in *Proceedings of the 3rd International Workshop on Peer-to-Peer Systems (IPTPS)*, 2004

175. D.R. Karger, M.F. Kaashoek, Koorde: a simple degree-optimal distributed hash table, in *Proceedings of the 2nd International Workshop on Peer-to-Peer Systems (IPTPS)*, 2003

176. T. Katchaounov, V. Josifovski, T. Risch, Scalable view expansion in a peer mediator system, in *Proceedings of the 8th International Conference on Database Systems for Advanced Applications (DASFAA)*, 2003

177. D. Kato, GISP: global information sharing protocol—a distributed index for peer-to-peer systems, in *Proceedings of 2nd IEEE International Conference on Peer-to-Peer Computing*, 2002

178. A. Kementsietsidis, M. Arenas, Data sharing through query translation in autonomous sources, in *Proceedings of the 30th International Conference on Very Large Databases (VLDB)*, 2004

179. A. Kementsietsidis, M. Arenas, R.J. Miller, Managing data mappings in the Hyperion project, in *Proceeding of the 19th IEEE International Conference on Data Engineering (ICDE)*, 2003

180. A. Kementsietsidis, M. Arenas, R.J. Miller, Mapping data in peer-to-peer systems: semantics and algorithmic issues, in *Proceedings of the ACM SIGMOD International Conference on Management of Data*, 2003

181. A. Kementsietsidis, M. Arenas, R.J. Miller, Mapping data in peer-to-peer systems: semantics and algorithmic issues, in *Proceedings of the ACM SIGMOD International Conference on Management of Data*, 2003

182. K. Kenthapadi, G.S. Manku, Decentralized algorithms using both local and random probes for P2P load balancing, in *Proceedings of the ACM Symposium on Parallel Algorithms and Architectures (SPAA)*, 2004

183. P. Keyani, B. Larson, M. Senthil, Peer pressure: Distributed recovery from attacks in peer-to-peer systems. *Lect. Notes Comput. Sci.* **2376**, 306–320 (2002)

184. C. Killian, J.W. Anderson, R. Braud, R. Jhala, A. Vahdat, Mace: language support for building distributed systems, in *Proceedings of PLDI Conference*, 2007
185. R.A. Kowalski, The early years of logic programming. *Commun. ACM* **31**(1), 38–43 (1988)
186. J. Kubiatowicz, D. Bindel, Y. Chen, P. Eaton, D. Geels, R. Gummadi, S. Rhea, H. Weatherspoon, W. Weimer, C. Wells, B. Zhao, Oceanstore: an architecture for global-scale persistent storage, in *Proceedings of the 9th International Conference on Architectural Support for Programming Languages and Operating Systems (ASPLOS)* (ACM, New York, 2000), pp. 190–201
187. V. Kumar, Trust and security in peer-to-peer system, in *Proceedings of the 17th International Conference on Database and Expert Systems Applications (DEXA)*, pp. 703–707, 2006
188. M. Landers, H. Zhang, K.-L. Tan, PeerStore: better performance by relaxing in peer-to-peer backup, in *Proceedings of the 4th IEEE International Conference on Peer-to-Peer Computing*, pp. 72–79, August 2004
189. A. Langley, Freenet, in *Peer-to-Peer: Harnessing the Power of Disruptive Technologies* (O'Reilly & Associates, 2001), pp. 123–132
190. J. Lee, H. Lee, S. Kang, S. Choe, J. Song, CISS: an efficient object clustering framework for DHT-based peer-to-peer applications, in *Proceedings of the 2nd International Workshop on Databases, Information Systems and Peer-to-Peer Computing (DBISP2P)*, pp. 215–229, 2004
191. S. Lee, R. Sherwood, B. Bhattacharjee, Cooperative peer groups in nice, in *Proceedings of 22nd Annual Joint Conference of the IEEE Computer and Communications Societies (INFO-COM)*, 2003
192. M. Li, W.-C. Lee, A. Sivasubramaniam, DPTree: a balanced tree based indexing framework for peer-to-peer systems, in *Proceedings of the 14th International Conference on Network Protocols (ICNP)*, 2006
193. X. Li, J. Wu, Searching techniques in peer-to-peer networks, in *Handbook of Theoretical and Algorithmic Aspects of Ad Hoc, Sensor and Peer-to-Peer Network*, pp. 613–642. Averbach, 2006
194. C.Y. Liau, W.S. Ng, Y. Shu, K.-L. Tan, S. Bressan, Efficient range queries and fast lookup services for scalable P2P networks, in *Proceedings of the 2nd International Workshop on Databases, Information Systems and Peer-to-Peer Computing (DBISP2P)*, pp. 78–92, 2004
195. M. Lillibridge, S. Elnikety, A. Birrel, M. Burrows, M. Isard, A cooperative internet backup scheme, in *Proceedings of the USENIX Annual Technical Conference*, pp. 29–41, 2003
196. B. Ling, Z. Lu, W.S. Ng, B.C. Ooi, K.-L. Tan, A. Zhou, A content-based resource location mechanism in PeerIS, in *Proceedings of the 3rd International Conference on Web Information Systems Engineering (WISE)*, pp. 279–290, 2002
197. L. Liu, C. Pu, W. Tang, Continual queries for internet scale event-driven information delivery. *IEEE Trans. Knowl. Data Eng., Special Issue on Web Technology* (1999)
198. B.T. Loo, The design and implementation of declarative networks. PhD thesis, University of California at Berkeley, 2006
199. B.T. Loo, R. Huebsch, I. Stoica, J. Hellerstein, The case for a hybrid P2P search infrastructure, in *Proceedings of the 3rd International Workshop on Peer-to-Peer Systems (IPTPS)*, 2004
200. Sharman Networks Ltd. Kazaa media desktop. http://www.kazaa.com, 2001
201. J. Lu, J. Callan, Content-based retrieval in hybrid peer-to-peer networks, in *Proceedings of the 12th ACM International Conference on Information and Knowledge Management (CIKM)*, pp. 199–206, 2003
202. J. Lu, J. Callan, Federated search of text-based digital libraries in hierarchical peer-to-peer networks, in *Proceedings of the 27th European Conference on Information Retrieval (ECIR)*, pp. 52–66, 2005
203. S. Ludwig, J. Beda, P. Saint-Andre, R. McQueen, S. Egan, J. Hildebrand, Jingle: XMPP extension protocol 0166. http://xmpp.org/extensions/xep-0166.html
204. N. Luhmann, *Trust and Power* (Wiley, Chichester, 1979)

205. M. Lupu, J. Li, B.C. Ooi, S. Shi, Clustering wavelets to speed-up data dissemination in structured P2P MANETs, in *Proceeding of the 23rd IEEE International Conference on Data Engineering (ICDE)*, 2007

206. M. Lupu, S. Madnick, Implementing the COntext INterchange (COIN) approach through use of semantic web tools, in *LNCS*, vol. 5005 (Springer, Berlin, 2008), pp. 77–98

207. M. Lupu, B.C. Ooi, Y.C. Tay, Paths to stardom: calibrating the potential of a peer-based data management system, in *Proceedings of the ACM SIGMOD International Conference on Management of Data*, 2008

208. M. Lupu, B. Yu, HiWaRPP—hierarchical wavelet-based retrieval on peer-to-peer network, in *Proceedings of the 22nd IEEE International Conference on Data Engineering (ICDE)*, p. 133, 2006

209. T. Luu, F. Klemm, I. Podnar, M. Rajman, K. Aberer, Alvis peers: a scalable full-text peer-to-peer retrieval engine, in *Proceedings of P2PIR*, pp. 41–48, 2006

210. Q. Lv, P. Cao, E. Cohen, K. Li, S. Shenker, Search and replication in unstructured peer-to-peer networks, in *Proceedings of the 16th ACM International Conference on Supercomputing (ICS)*, pp. 84–95, 2002

211. S. Madden, M. Shah, J.M. Hellerstein, V. Raman, Continuously adaptive continuous queries over streams, in *Proceedings of the ACM SIGMOD International Conference on Management of Data*, 2002

212. J. Madhavan, A. Halevy, Composing mappings among data sources, in *Proceedings of the 29th International Conference on Very Large Databases (VLDB)*, 2003

213. D. Malkhi, M. Naor, D. Ratajczak, Viceroy: a scalable and dynamic emulation of the butterfly, in *Proceedings of the 21st ACM Symposium on Principles of Distributed Computing (PODC)*, 2002

214. U. Manber, Finding similar files in a large file system, in *Proceedings of the USENIX Winter 1994 Technical Conference*, pp. 1–10, 17–21, San Fransisco, CA, USA, 1994

215. G.S. Manku, Balanced binary trees for ID management and load balance in distributed hash tables, in *Proceedings of the 23rd ACM Symposium on Principles of Distributed Computing (PODC)*, 2004

216. S. Marsh, Formalising trust as a computational concept. PhD thesis, University of Stirling, Stirling, 1994

217. E. Martinian, Distributed Internet Backup System (DIBS), 2003

218. P. Maymounkov, D. Mazieres, Kademlia: a peer-to-peer information system based on the xor metric, in *Proceedings of the 1st International Workshop on Peer-to-Peer Systems (IPTPS)*, March 2002

219. McAfee, McAfee rumor technology. http://www.mcafeeasap.com/intl/EN/content/virusscan_asap/rumor.asp

220. R.C. Merkle, A certified digital signature, in *Proceedings of the 9th International Cryptology Conference (CRYPTO)*, pp. 218–238, Santa Barbara, CA, August 1989

221. Microsoft, Peer name resolution protocol (PNRP) version 4.0 specification. http://msdn.microsoft.com/en-us/library/cc239047.aspx, 2008

222. J. Miller, Jabber: conversational technologies, in *Peer-to-Peer: Harnessing the Power of Disruptive Technologies* (O'Reilly & Associates, 2001), pp. 77–88

223. M. Mitzenmacher, The power of two choices in randomized load balancing. *IEEE Trans. Parallel Distrib. Syst.* **12**(10), 1094–1104 (2001)

224. A.T. Mizrak, Y. Cheng, V. Kumar, S. Savage, Structured superpeers: leveraging heterogeneity to provide constant-time lookup, in *Proceedings of the 3rd IEEE Workshop on Internet Applications (WIAPP)*, 2003

225. A. Mondal, Y. Lifu, M. Kitsuregawa, P2PR-Tree: an R-tree-based spatial index for peer-to-peer environments, in *Proceedings of the EDBT Workshop on P2P and Databases (P2PDB)*, 2004

226. Napster filesharing system, shutdown as of March 2001. http://www.napster.com, 2000

227. R.M. Needham, Denial-of-service: an example. *Commun. ACM* **37**(11), 42–46 (1994)

228. W. Nejdl, W. Siberski, M. Sintek, Design issues and challenges for rdf- and schema-based peer-to-peer systems. *SIGMOD Rec.* **32**(3), 41–46 (2003)

229. W. Nejdl, B. Wolf, C. Qu, S. Decker, M. Sintek, A. Naeve, M. Nilsson, M. Palmer, T. Risch, Edutella: a P2P networking infrastructure based on rdf, in *Proceedings of the 11th World Wide Web Conference (WWW)*, 2002

230. Net-Z, http://www.proksim.com/

231. P.G. Neumann, Inside risks: denial-of-service attacks. *Commun. ACM* **43**(4), 136–136 (2000)

232. C.H. Ng, K.C. Sia, Peer clustering and firework query model, in *Proceedings of the 11th World Wide Web Conference (WWW)*, 2002

233. W.S. Ng, B.C. Ooi, Y.F. Shu, K.-L. Tan, W.H. Tok, Efficient distributed CQ processing using peers, in *Proceedings of the 12th World Wide Web Conference (WWW)*, 2003

234. W.S. Ng, B.C. Ooi, K.L. Tan, BestPeer: a self-configurable peer-to-peer system, in *Proceedings of the 18th IEEE International Conference on Data Engineering (ICDE)*, p. 272, San Jose, CA, April 2002

235. W.S. Ng, B.C. Ooi, K.-L. Tan, A. Zhou, PeerDB: a P2P-based system for distributed data sharing, in *Proceedings of the 19th IEEE International Conference on Data Engineering (ICDE)* (IEEE Press, New York, 2003)

236. W.S. Ng, W.H. Tok, B.C. Ooi, K.-L. Tan, A. Zhou, Efficient pervasive continuous query processing using peers. Technical report, Department of Computer Science, National University of Singapore, 2002

237. T.-W. Ngan, D. Wallach, P. Druschel, Enforcing fair sharing of peer-to-peer resources, in *Proceedings of the 2nd International Workshop on Peer-to-Peer Systems (IPTPS)*, Berkeley, CA, USA, 2003

238. NICE, http://www.cs.umd.edu/projects/nice/

239. M. Nottingham, Caching tutorial for web authors and webmasters. http://www.mnot.net/cache_docs/, 2003

240. D. Novak, P. Zezula, M-Chord: a scalable distributed similarity search structure, in *Proceedings of the 1st International Conference on Scalable Information Systems (INFOSCALE)*, 2006

241. M.A. Nowak, K. Sigmund, Evolution of indirect reciprocity by image scoring. *Nature* **393**, 573–577 (1998)

242. OceanStore, http://oceanstore.cs.berkeley.edu/

243. C. O'Donnell, V. Vaikuntanathan, Information leak in the chord lookup protocol, in *Proceedings of the 4th IEEE International Conference on Peer-to-Peer Computing*, August 2004

244. L. Oliveira, L. Lopes, F. Silva, P3: parallel peer to peer an internet parallel programming environment, in *Proceedings of the Workshop on Web Engineering and Peer-to-Peer Computing*, pp. 274–288, 2002

245. B.C. Ooi, K.-L. Tan, C. Yu, S. Bressan, indexing the edges—a simple and yet efficient approach to high-dimensional indexing, in *Proceedings of the 19th ACM Symposium on Principles of Database Systems (PODS)*, pp. 166–174, 2000

246. Openext, http://www.openext.com/

247. A. Oram (ed.), Peer-to-Peer: Harnessing the Power of Disruptive Technologies (O'Reilly & Associates, 2001)

248. A. Oram, Gnutella and Freenet represent true technological innovation. http://www.openp2p.com/pub/a/208, 2003

249. J. Ott, D. Kutscher, Applying DTN to mobile internet access: an experiment with HTTP. Technical Report tr-tzi-050701, Helsinki University of Technology, Networking Laboratory, 2005

250. H. Pang, K.-L. Tan, Authenticating query results in edge computing, in *Proceedings of the 20th IEEE Conference on Data Engineering (ICDE)* (IEEE Press, New York, 2004), pp. 572–583

251. X. Pang, B. Catania, K.-L. Tan, Securing your data in agent-based P2P systems, in *Proceedings of the 8th International Conference on Database Systems for Advanced Applications (DASFAA)*, 2003

252. V. Papadimos, D. Maier, Mutant query plans. *Inf. Softw. Technol.* **44**(4), 197–206 (2002)

253. V. Papadimos, D. Maier, K. Tufte, Distributed query processing and catalogs for peer-to-peer systems, in *Proceedings of the 1st Conference on Innovative Data Systems Research (CIDR)*, 2003

254. M. Papazoglou, *Web Services: Principles and Technology* (Addison-Wesley Longman, Reading, 2007)

255. A. Pfitzmann, M. Köhntopp, Anonymity, unobservability, and pseudonymity: a proposal for terminology. http://www.koehntopp.de/marit/pub/anon/Anon_Terminology_IHW.pdf, 2001

256. M. Pitkanen, J. Ott, Enabling opportunistic storage for mobile DTNs. in *Pervasive and Mobile Computing*, 2008

257. C. Plaxton, R. Rajaraman, A. Richa, Accessing nearby copies of replicated objects in a distributed environment, in *Proceedings of the ACM Symposium on Parallel Algorithms and Architectures (SPAA)*, pp. 311–320, 1997

258. C.G. Plaxton, R. Rajaraman, A.W. Richa, Accessing nearby copies of replicated objects in a distributed environment, in *Proceedings of the ACM Symposium on Parallel Algorithms and Architectures (SPAA)*, pp. 311–320, 1997

259. V. Pless, *Introduction to the Theory of Error-Correcting Codes*, 3rd edn. (Wiley, New York, 1998)

260. W. Pugh, Skip lists: a probabilistic alternative to balanced trees. *Commun. ACM* **33**(6), 668–676 (1990)

261. J. Pujol, R. Sanguesa, Extracting reputation in multi agent systems by means of social network topology, in *Proceedings of the 1st International Joint Conference on Autonomous Agents and Multi-Agent Systems (AAMAS)*, 2002

262. C. Qu, W. Nejdl, M. Kriesell, Cayley DHTs—a group theoretic framework for analyzing DHTs based on Cayley graphs, in *Proceedings of the 2nd International Symposium on Parallel and Distributed Processing and Applications (ISPA)*, 2004

263. V. Ramasubramanian, E.G. Sirer, Beehive: exploiting power law query distributions for O(1) lookup performance in peer to peer overlays, in *Proceedings of the 1st USENIX Symposium on Networked Systems Design and Implementation (NSDI)*, pp. 331–342, 2004

264. A. Rao, K. Lakshminarayanan, S. Surana, R. Karp, I. Stoica, Load balancing in structured P2P systems, in *Proceedings of the 2nd International Workshop on Peer-to-Peer Systems (IPTPS)*, 2003

265. D. Ratajczak, J.M. Hellerstein, Deconstructing DHTs. Technical Report IRB-TR-04-042, Intel Research Berkeley, November 2003

266. S. Ratnasamy, P. Francis, M. Handley, R. Karp, S. Shenker, A scalable content-addressable network, in *Proceedings of the ACM SIGCOMM Conference*, pp. 161–172, 2001

267. D. Reed, I. Pratt, P. Menage, S. Early, N. Stratford, Xenoservers: accounted execution of untrusted code, in *Proceedings of the 7th Workshop on Hot Topics in Operating Systems (HotOS)*, 1999

268. M.E. Renada, J. Callan, The robustness of content-based search in hierarchical peer to peer networks, in *Proceedings of the 13th ACM International Conference on Information and Knowledge Management (CIKM)*, pp. 562–570, 2004

269. P. Reynolds, A. Vahdat, Efficient peer-to-peer keyword searching, in *Proceedings of the International Conference on Middleware*, pp. 21–40, 2003

270. S.C. Rhea, J. Kubiatowicz, Probabilistic location and routing, in *Proceedings of the 21st Annual Joint Conference of the IEEE Computer and Communications Societies (INFOCOM)*, 2002

271. R.L. Rivest, RFC 1321: the MD5 message-digest algorithm, in *Internet Activities Board*, April 1992

272. A. Rodriguez, C. Killian, S. Bhat, D. Kostic, A. Vahdat, MACEDON: methodology for automatically creating, evaluating and designing overlay networks, in *Proceedings of NSDI Symposium*, 2004

273. P. Rodriguez-Gianolli, A. Kementsietsidis, M. Garzetti, I. Kiringa, L. Jiang, M. Masud, R.J. Miller, J. Mylopoulos, Data sharing in the Hyperion peer database system, in *Proceedings of the 31st International Conference on Very Large Databases (VLDB)*, 2005

274. M. Roussopoulos, M. Baker, CUP: Controlled update propagation in peer-to-peer networks, in *Proceedings of the 2003 USENIX Annual Technical Conference*, 2003

275. A. Rowstron, P. Druschel, Pastry: scalable, distributed object location and routing for large-scale peer-to-peer systems, in *Proceedings of the 18th IFIP/ACM International Conference of Distributed Systems Platforms (Middleware)*, pp. 329–350, 2001

276. A. Rowstron, P. Druschel, Storage management and caching in PAST: a large-scale, persistent peer-to-peer storage utility, in *Proceedings of the 18th ACM Symposium on Operating Systems Principles (SOSP)*, pp. 188–201, Banff, Canada, October 2001

277. J. Sabater, C. Sierra, Regret: a reputation model for gregarious societies, in *Proceedings of the 4th Workshop on Deception, Fraud and Trust in Agetn Societies*, 2001

278. H. Sagan, *Space-Filling Curves* (Springer, Berlin, 1994)

279. O.D. Sahin, F. Emekci, D. Agrawal, A.E. Abbadi, Content-based similarity search over peer-to-peer systems, in *Proceedings of the 2nd International Workshop On Databases, Information Systems and Peer-to-Peer Computing (DBISP2P)*, pp. 61–78, 2004

280. O.D. Sahin, A. Gulbeden, F. Emekci, D. Agrawal, A. El Abbadi, PRISM: indexing multidimensional data in P2P networks using reference vectors, in *Proceedings of the 13th annual ACM International Conference on Multimedia*, pp. 946–955, 2005

281. O.D. Sahin, A. Gupta, D. Agrawal, A. El Abbadi, A peer-to-peer framework for caching range queries, in *Proceedings of the 20th IEEE International Conference on Data Engineering (ICDE)*, 2004

282. P. Saint-Andre, Serverless messaging: XMPP extension protocol 0174. http://xmpp.org/extensions/xep-0174.html

283. G. Salton, A. Wong, C.S. Yang, A vector space model for automatic indexing. *Commun. ACM* **18**(11), 613–620 (1975)

284. S. Saroiu, P.K. Gummadi, S.D. Gribble, A measurement study of peer-to-peer file sharing systems, in *Proceedings of the 9th Multimedia Computing and Networking (MMCN)*, 2002

285. M. Schlosser, M. Sintek, S. Decker, W. Nejdl, A scalable and ontology-based P2P infrastructure for semantic web services, in *Proceedings of 2nd IEEE International Conference on Peer-to-Peer Computing*, 2002

286. M.T. Schlosser, M. Sintek, S. Decker, W. Nejdl, HyperCuP—hypercubes, ontologies, and efficient search on peer-to-peer networks, in *Proceedings of the International Workshop on Agents and Peer-to-Peer Computing (AP2PC)*, pp. 112–124, 2002

287. C. Schmidt, M. Parashar, Flexible information discovery in decentralized distributed systems, in *Proceedings of the 12th International Symposium on High Performance Distributed Computing (HPDC)*, 2003

288. SETI@home, http://setiathome.ssl.berkeley.edu/

289. Shareaza, http://www.shareaza.com/

290. H. Shen, Y. Shu, B. Yu, Efficient semantic-based content search in P2P network. *IEEE Trans. Knowl. Data Eng.* **16**(7), 813–826 (2004)

291. C. Shirky, Listening to Napster, in *Peer-to-Peer: Harnessing the Power of Disruptive Technologies*. (O'Reilly & Associates, 2001)

292. C. Shirky, What is P2P... and what isn't. http://www.openp2p.com/pub/a/p2p/2000/11/24/shirky1-whatisp2p.html

293. Y. Shu, K.-L. Tan, A. Zhou, Adapting the content native space for load balanced, in *Proceedings of the 2nd International Workshop On Databases, Information Systems and Peer-to-Peer Computing (DBISP2P)*, pp. 122–135, 2004

294. K. Shudo, Y. Tanaka, S. Sekiguchi, Overlay weaver: an overlay construction toolkit. Comput. Commun. **31**(2) (2008)

295. A. Singla, C. Rohrs, Ultrapeers: another step towards Gnutella scalability. http://groups.yahoo.com/group/the_gdf/files/Proposals/Working%20Proposals/Ultrapeer/, 2002

296. E. Sit, J. Cates, R. Cox, A DHT-based backup system, in *Proceedings of the 1st IRIS Student Workshop*, 2003

297. E. Sit, A. Haeberlen, F. Dabek, B.-G. Chun, H. Weatherspoon, R. Morris, M.F. Kaashoek, J. Kubiatowicz, Proactive replication, for data durability, in *Proceedings of the 3rd International Workshop on Peer-to-Peer Systems (IPTPS)*, 2006

298. E. Sit, R. Morris, Security considerations for peer-to-peer distributed hash tables, in *Proceedings of the 1st International Workshop on Peer-to-Peer Systems (IPTPS)*, pp. 261–269, Cambridge, MA, 2002

299. M. Slee, A. Agarwal, M. Kwiatkowski, Thrift: scalable cross-language services implementation. http://developers.facebook.com/thrift/, 2007

300. A.C. Snoeren, K. Conley, D.K. Gifford, Mesh-based content routing using XML, in *Proceedings of the 18th ACM Symposium on Operating Systems Principles (SOSP)*, 2001

301. K. Sripanidkulchai, B. Maggs, H. Zhang, Efficient content location using interest-based locality in peer-to-peer systems, in *Proceedings of the 22nd Annual Joint Conference of the IEEE Computer and Communications Societies (INFOCOM)*, 2003

302. M. Srivatsa, L. Xiong, L. Liu, Trustguard: countering vulnerabilities in reputation management for decentralized overlay networks, in *Proceedings of the 14th World Wide Web Conference (WWW)*, 2005

303. N. Stakhanova, S. Basu, J. Wang, O. Stakhanov, Trust framework for P2P networks using peer-profile based anamoly technique, in *Proceedings of the 25th International Conference on Distributed Computing Systems (ICDCS)*, 2005

304. W.R. Stevens, *UNIX Network Programming* (Prentice-Hall, New York, 1998)

305. J. Stribling, I.G. Councill, J. Li, M.F. Kaashoek, D.R. Karger, R. Morris, S. Shenker, OverCite: a cooperative digital research library, in *Proceedings of the 4th International Workshop on Peer-to-Peer Systems (IPTPS)*, pp. 69–79, 2005

306. T. Suel, C. Mathur, J. Wu, J. Zhang, A. Delis, M. Kharrazi, X. Long, K. Shanmugasundaram, ODISSEA: a peer-to-peer architecture for scalable web search and information retrieval, in *Proceedings of the 6th International Workshop on the Web and Databases (WebDB)*, 2003

307. Q. Sun, H. Garcia-Molina, SLIC: a selfish link-based incentive mechanism for unstructured peer-to-peer networks, in *Proceedings of the 24th International Conference on Distributed Computing Systems (ICDCS)*, pp. 506–515, Tokyo, Japan, March 2004

308. G. Suryanarayana, R.N. Taylor, A survey of trust management and resource discovery technologies in peer-to-peer applications. Technical report, UC Irvine, July 2004

309. A.S. Tanenbaum, *Modern Operating Systems* (Prentice-Hall, Upper Saddle River, 2001)

310. C. Tang, S. Dwarkadas, Hybrid global-local indexing for efficient peer-to-peer information retrieval, in *Proceedings of the 1st USENIX Symposium on Networked Systems Design and Implementation (NSDI)*, pp. 211–224, 2004

311. C. Tang, Z. Xu, S. Dwarkadas, Peer-to-peer information retrieval using self-organizing semantic overlay networks, in *Proceedings of the ACM SIGCOMM Conference*, pp. 175–186, 2003

312. C. Tang, Z. Xu, M. Mahalingam, pSearch: information retrieval in structured overlays, in *Proceedings of the 1st Workshop on Hot Topics in Networks (HotNets)*, 2002

313. I. Tatarinov, A. Halevy, Efficient query reformulation in peer-data management systems, in *Proceedings of the ACM SIGMOD International Conference on Management of Data*, 2004

314. The TLS Protocol Version 1.0. IETF RFC 2246. http://www.ietf.org/rfc/rfc2246.txt

315. M.R. Thompson, A. Essiari, S. Mudumbai, Certificate-based authorization policy in a PKI environment. *ACM Trans. Inf. Syst. Secur.* **6**(4), 566–588 (2003)

316. W.H. Tok, S. Bressan, Efficient and adaptive processing of multiple continuous queries, in *Proceedings of the 8th International Conference on Extending Database Technology (EDBT)*, 2002

317. B. Traversat, M. Abdelaziz, E. Pouyoul, Project jxta: a loosely-consistent dht rendezvous walker, 2003

318. P. Triantafillow, C. Xiruhaki, M. Koubarakis, N. Ntarmos, Towards high performance peer-to-peer content and resource sharing systems, in *Proceedings of the 1st Conference on Innovative Data Systems Research (CIDR)*, 2003

319. A. Tridgell, Efficient algorithms for sorting and synchronization. PhD thesis, Australian National University, 1999

320. C. Tryfonopoulos, S. Idreos, M. Koubarakis, LibraRing: an architecture for distributed digital libraries based on DHTs, in *Proceedings of the 9th European Conference on Research and Advanced Technology for Digital Libraries (ECDL)*, pp. 25–36, 2005

321. D. Tsoumakos, N. Roussopoulos, Adaptive probabilistic search in peer-to-peer networks, in *Proceedings of the 2nd International Workshop on Peer-to-Peer Systems (IPTPS)*, 2003

322. VeriSign, Addressing the effective enterprise communication challenge. White paper, October 2007

323. A. Vlachou, C. Doulkeridis, Y. Kotidis, M. Vazirgiannis, SKYPEER: efficient subspace skyline computation over distributed data, in *Proceedings of the 23rd IEEE International Conference on Data Engineering (ICDE)*, 2007

324. Q.H. Vu, B.C. Ooi, D. Papadias, A.K.H. Tung, A graph method for keyword-based selection of the top-K databases, in *Proceedings of the ACM SIGMOD International Conference on Management of Data*, 2008

325. W3C, Simple object access protocol recommendation (second edition). http://www.w3.org/TR/soap/, April 2007

326. M. Waldman, L. Cranor, A. Rubin, Publius, in *Peer-to-Peer: Harnessing the Power of Disruptive Technologies* (O'Reilly & Associates, 2001), pp. 145–158

327. D. Wallach, A survey on peer-to-peer security issues, in *Proceedings of the International Symposium on Software Security*, Tokyo, Japan, November 2002

328. J. Wang, A survey of web caching schemes for the internet. *ACM Comput. Commun. Rev.* **25**(9), 36–46 (1999)

329. S. Wang, B.C. Ooi, A.K.H. Tung, L. Xu, Efficient skyline query processing on peer-to-peer networks, in *Proceedings of the 23rd IEEE International Conference on Data Engineering (ICDE)*, 2007

330. X. Wang, W.S. Ng, B.C. Ooi, K.-L. Tan, A. Zhou, BuddyWeb: a P2P-based collaborative web caching system, in *Proceedings of the Web Engineering and Peer-to-Peer Computing, Networking Workshops*, pp. 247–251, Pisa, Italy, 2002

331. Y. Wang, V. Viradharajan, Trust^2: developing trust in peer-to-peer environments, in *Proceedings of the IEEE International Conference on Services Computing (SCC)*, pp. 24–31, 2005

332. Y. Wang, V. Viradharajan, Dynamictrust: the trust development in peer-to-peer environments, in *Proceedings of the IEEE International Conference on Sensor Networks, Ubiquitous, and Trustworthy Computing (SUTC)*, pp. 302–305, 2006

333. H. Weatherspoon, J. Kubiatowicz, Erasure coding vs. replication: a quantitative comparison, in *Proceedings of the 1st International Workshop on Peer-to-Peer Systems (IPTPS)*, March 2002

334. H. Weatherspoon, J. Kubiatowicz, Naming and integrity: self-verifying data in peer-to-peer systems, in *Proceedings of the International Workshop on Future Directions in Distributed Computing (FuDiCo)*, pp. 142–147, 2003

335. A. Wierzbicki, N. Leibowitz, M. Ripeanu, R. Wozniak, Cache replacement policies revisited: the case of P2P traffic, in *Proceedings of the 4th International Workshop on Global and Peer-to-Peer Computing (GP2P)*, 2004

336. S.K.M. Wong, W. Ziarko, V.V. Raghavan, P.C.N. Wong, On modeling of information retrieval concepts in vector spaces. *ACM Trans. Database Syst.* **12**(3), 299–321 (1987)

337. P. Wu, C. Zhang, Y. Feng, B.Y. Zhao, D. Agrawal, A.E. Abbadi, Parallelizing skyline queries for scalable distribution, in *Proceedings of the 10th International Conference on Extending Database Technology (EDBT)*, pp. 112–130, 2006

338. S. Wu, S. Jiang, B.C. Ooi, K.L. Tan, Distributed online aggregation, in *Proceedings of the International Conference on Very Large Data Bases*, 2009

339. S. Wu, J. Li, B.C. Ooi, K.-L. Tan, Just-in-time query retrieval over partially indexed data on structured P2P overlays, in *Proceedings of the ACM SIGMOD International Conference on Management of Data*, 2008

340. L. Xiong, L. Liu, Peertrust: supporting reputation-based trust for peer-to-peer electronic communities. *IEEE Trans. Knowl. Data Eng.* **7**, 843–857 (2004)

341. B. Yang, H. Garcia-Molina, Comparing hybrid peer-to-peer systems, in *Proceedings of the 27th International Conference on Very Large Data Bases (VLDB)*, 2001

342. B. Yang, H. Garcia-Molina, Efficient search in peer-to-peer networks, in *Proceedings of the 21st International Conference on Distributed Computing Systems (ICDCS)*, 2001

343. B. Yang, H. Garcia-Molina, Improving search in peer-to-peer networks, in *Proceedings of the 22nd International Conference on Distributed Computing Systems (ICDCS)*, 2002

344. B. Yang, H. Garcia-Molina, Designing a super-peer network, in *Proceedings of the 19th IEEE International Conference on Data Engineering (ICDE)*, 2003

345. P.N. Yianilos, Data structures and algorithms for nearest neighbor search in general metric spaces, in *Proceedings of the 4th Annual ACM-SIAM Symposium on Discrete Algorithms (SODA)*, 1993

346. B. Yu, G. Li, K. Sollins, A.K.H. Tung, Effective keyword-based selection of relational databases, in *Proceedings of the ACM SIGMOD International Conference on Management of Data*, 2007

347. M.J. Yuan, Mobile P2P messaging. http://www.ibm.com/developerworks/wireless/library/wi-p2pmsg/, December 2002

348. C. Zhang, A. Krishnamurthy, R.Y. Wang, SkipIndex: towards a scalable peer-to-peer index service for high dimensional data. Technical Report TR-703-04, Princeton University, 2004

349. B.Y. Zhao, J.D. Kubiatowicz, A.D. Joseph, Tapestry: an infrastructure for fault-tolerant wide-area location and routing. Technical Report UCB/CSD-01-1141, Computer Science Division, University of California, Berkeley, Berkeley, CA, 2001

350. R. Zhou, K. Hwang, Powertrust: a robust and scalable reputation system for trusted peer-to-peer computing. *IEEE Trans. Parallel Distrib. Syst.* **29**(8–13), 953–964 (2006)

351. S. Zhou, Z. Zhang, W. Qian, A. Zhou, SIPPER: selecting informative peers in structured P2P environment for content-based retrieval, in *Proceedings of the 22nd IEEE International Conference on Data Engineering (ICDE)*, p. 161, 2006

352. P. Zimmermann, *PGP User's Guide* (MIT Press, Cambridge, 1994)

Index

Q.H. Vu et al., *Peer-to-Peer Computing*,
DOI 10.1007/978-3-642-03514-2, © Springer-Verlag Berlin Heidelberg 2010